100 + Top Tips

For

Effective Leadership

Written by Charles Marshall, Mike Nelson, Ian Munro

Copyright 2017

Published by Ian S Munro

1

Licence and Copyright Notes

Front and rear cover design - by Deborah Wood

Printed in the United Kingdom by Printondemand-worldwide.com

A CPI catalogue record for this book is available from the British Library.

ISBN: 978-0-9934658-6-4

The publisher has taken every precaution to ensure that the information contained in this book is accurate and complete.

With thanks to

Healthskills Limited

Healthskills is a leading provider of 'Leadership, Learning and Organisational Development' programmes and a range of related services.

Their programmes are delivered across all levels of organisations and they receive constant accolades from those who participate in their programmes.

They operate under the Healthskills name in the public sector and under their Organisation Health name in the private sector.

The authors first made contact as associates of this company and had this not happened this book would never have been written.

For that reason the authors are delighted to be associated and wish Healthskills continued good health!

http://healthskills.co.uk

BOOKS IN THIS SERIES

BLUE BOOKS FOR PERSONAL DEVELOPMENT

100 + TOP TIPS FOR JOB SEEKERS
ISBN 978-095700-853-3

100 + TOP TIPS FOR DEVELOPING YOUR CAREER
ISBN 978-095700-858-8

100 + TOP TIPS FOR EFFECIVE LEADERSHIP
ISBN 978-0-9934658-6-4

RED BOOKS FOR IMPROVING YOUR ORGANISATION – SMALL AND LARGE

100 + TOP TIPS FOR SETTING UP AND RUNNING AN ONLINE BUSINESS
ISBN 978-099346-580-2

100 + TOP TIPS FOR EFFECTIVE SALES MANAGEMENT
ISBN 978-095700-859-5

100 + TOP TIPS FOR EFFECTIVELY USING ONLINE SOCIAL MEDIA
ISBN 978-099346-582-6

100 + TOP TIPS FOR SETTING UP YOUR OWN BUSINESS
ISBN 978-099346-584-0

Books can be purchased in Paperback or eBook format by visiting www.100toptips.com

Introduction

Broadly speaking there are two groups of leader. One group is generally in full time employment and come from organisations of various size in the private, public and voluntary sectors where leaders play a key part in organisation growth and development.

Another group sometimes find themselves in a Leadership role more by accident than design and then begin to wonder "I am a leader, what exactly is a leader?" This group could be in full time employment or play a leading part on a voluntary basis to a charity or local organisation or even be running a sports team.

In our work in Coaching and Leadership Development, leaders in both groups tell us they would like to have a book that gives guidance about how leadership works and also give tips to help them become more effective leaders

We have written this book to meet that demand. Our book is written in a straightforward, snappy style. We explain how to become an effective leader, stripping away some of the fanciful ideas about what a leader is or is not. We also aim to explain how Leadership works and how to avoid some of the pitfalls associated with poor leadership.

On that basis you are likely to be one of three types of people

1. Newly promoted leader and looking for ways to cope with your new leadership role
2. An experienced leader looking for further development but in a convenient and practical way.
3. An employee, looking to have a greater impact on your organisation, but struggling to find a suitable platform on which to build your case.

Contents

Licence and Copyright Notes 2

With thanks to 3

BOOKS IN THIS SERIES 5

Introduction 6

Chapter 1   Top 10 tips for Effective Leadership 8

Chapter 2   Top 10 tips for leading the learning
                 organisation 14

Chapter 3   Top 10 Tips for developing effective
                 communication 24

Chapter 4   Top 10 tips for developing leadership
                 strength 33

Chapter 5   Top 10 tips for developing leadership
                 character 41

Chapter 6   Top 10 tips for developing team leadership
                 52

Chapter 7   Top 10 tips for leading self 62

Chapter 8   Top 10 tips for leadership   dilemmas . 77

Chapter 9   Top 10 tips for leadership strategy 85

Chapter 10   Top 10 tips for Leadership Intelligence
                 94

Chapter 11   Top 10 tips for Documenting Progress and
                 Tools to help you on the way 102

Summary   127

About the Authors 128

Some of the other books we mention 129

Chapter 1

Top 10 tips for Effective Leadership

This book covers a wide range of topics. To help you understand chapter content, this chapter lists the top tips in each chapter.

Chapter 2 - Top 10 tips for leading the learning organisation - Mike Nelson

1. The learning organisation
2. Learning to learn
3. Methodology
4. Reflection
5. Self-Directed learning
6. Creating a learning environment
7. Coaching for Performance
8. Review
9. Qualifications
10. Applying and Sustaining Learning

Chapter 3 - Top 10 Tips for developing effective communication – Ian Munro

1. Be sure about what it is you need to communicate
2. Develop Clarity in the content
3. Be assertive
4. Focus on "Two Way" communication
5. Build rapport
6. Be empathetic
7. Check Understanding
8. Select the right methodology
9. Use technology wisely
10. Role model the behaviours you want to instil.

Chapter 4 - Top 10 tips for developing leadership strength – Mike Nelson

1. Attribution
2. Personal renewal
3. De-clutter
4. Sustainability
5. Ambiguity
6. Time Management
7. Personal Vision
8. Focus
9. Stress and pressure
10. Motivation

Chapter 5 - Top 10 tips for developing leadership character – Charles Marshall

1. Strive to be authentic in your dealings with others
2. Be creative – throw away the blueprint
3. Understand and demonstrate integrity
4. Develop Gravitas in your interactions with others
5. Intuition – developing far sighted insight
6. He who hesitates is lost
7. A positive state of mind
8. Choosing our Attitude – do we play from a zero, or play from a ten
9. Humility
10. Honesty

Chapter 6 - Top 10 tips for developing team leadership – Charles Marshall

1. Establish Trust within the team
2. Encourage strong challenge round the table
3. Drive for commitment
4. Develop a culture of joint accountability
5. Agree clear outcomes

6. Achieve a sense of balance
7. Create a climate of motivation
8. Be aware of inputs - begin with the end in mind.
9. Establish clear processes for the team
10. Measure Outputs and make the results transparent

Chapter 7 - Top 10 tips for leading self – Charles Marshall

1. Align your behaviour to your values.
2. Maintain a positive mind-set and play from a ten.
3. Develop a high level of self-awareness
4. Develop strategies for self management
5. Social awareness - understand and develop empathy
6. Inner Dialogue and self talk
7. More about values and behaviours
8. Reflection
9. Personal Development
10. Develop Strength and Resilience

Chapter 8 - Top 10 tips for leadership dilemmas – Charles Marshall

- Dilemma one - to control or let go?
- Dilemma two – Idealism versus self-interest, fear or misplaced loyalty
- Dilemma three – Detachment versus close relationships
- Dilemma four – Humility versus decisiveness
- Dilemma five – Actions versus empty words
- Dilemma Six – Rigid planning or opportunism
- Dilemma Seven – Collaborative or evidence based
- Dilemma Eight – Hard or Soft wiring
- Dilemma Nine – Manager or transformer
- Dilemma Ten – Strict rules or discretionary flexibility

Chapter 9 - Top 10 tips for leadership strategy – Mike Nelson

1. Analysis
2. Strategy
3. Planning
4. Vision
5. Performance
6. Evaluation
7. Dashboard
8. Data Gathering
9. Balanced Scorecard
10. Delivery

Chapter 10 - Top 10 tips for Leadership Intelligence – Ian Munro

1. Recognising the three types of Intelligence
2. Intelligence Quotient - IQ
3. Emotional Quotient - EQ
4. Social Intelligence - SI
5. What are the implications from 2,3,4 above
6. Developing an understanding of Leadership Intelligence in your team
7. Using Leadership Intelligence with leaders who directly report to you
8. Using Leadership Intelligence in Matrix structures
9. Upward leadership
10. Summarising your next steps

Chapter 11 - Top 10 tips for measuring and documenting your progress and Tools to help you on the way – Ian Munro

1. Core leadership objectives

2. Monthly/Quarterly Action Plans
3. The 5 dysfunctions of a team – Chapter 6
4. The Leadership Challenge
5. Learning Styles – Chapter 7
6. SWOT and PESTILE Analysis – Chapter9
7. The Kirkpatrick Evaluation Model – Chapter 2
8. Impact of Stress on Performance – Chapter 4
9. Johari Window – Chapter 5
10. Putting Things First – Chapter 4

Chapter 2

Top 10 tips for leading the learning organisation

By

Mike Nelson

The "Learning Organisation" is a term that has been in use for a number of years and as ever with this type of broad terminology it is often interpreted in many different ways in different organisations.

This chapter aims to set out the essence of what we mean by a Learning Organisation and what would be some key elements that would go to make this a reality in your organisation.

1   The learning organisation

- Take a look round your organisation... what do you see in the way that learning is conducted. Anything from the provision of basic training courses to the way that individuals and teams learn from experience and apply that learning for the benefit of themselves and the organisation will tell you the extent to which your organisation has the ability to use learning as an effective part of your business strategy.
- Learning is a strategic action and as such should be built into all activities; to be effective the learning strategy should have measurable objectives and it should be clear how learning in the organisation will contribute to current and future organisational success.
- As a leader be prepared to role-model learning... if you learn then you set a strong example for others to follow.

2 Learning to learn

- There is a concept of learned helplessness where individuals or whole cultures do not develop the habit of learning and tend to rely on others for the answers... as a leader this habit/cycle needs to be broken and the first step is to stop answering all the questions that come your way. Instead reverse the question back, encourage individuals to seek to find an answer themselves before they ask.
- Learning is not always easy – it can be challenging to review mistakes and change behaviour – especially when it makes us uncomfortable. As a leader encourage this discomfort and get yourself and others used to learning from experience.
- Make positive steps to dissociate learning with what we all did at school.... Adults learn not only from the classroom but from coaching and from live experiences. Use the ratio of 70:20:10 in your organisation. This describes adult learning as being effective when it comes from a mixture of Reviewing Experience (70%), Coaching/Mentoring (20%) and Off-the-Job (10%).

3 Methodology

- Humans learn in a variety of ways.... Honey & Mumford described 4 basic learning styles – that of Activist, Reflector, Pragmatist & Theorist. How do you learn best? Once you know this you can tailor how you take learning on board and make it stick.
- The same applies to your organisation so a variety of learning methodologies should be considered to meet varying styles. Also how to fit learning into

busy schedules in lean organisations.
Workshops (short and long), seminars, forums, books, magazines, internet, Apps, workbooks, secondments, job-swaps, sabbaticals.

- Ensure that this all fits into your Performance review systems... do performance reviews agenda time for learning and reflection to ensure that you and your teams stretch and grow for the future.

4 Reflection

- Gosh! A whole tip on reflection – "I'll need to think about that!"
- I once heard a very confident leader describe themselves as being very experienced – 30 years' experience in the same function. A colleague of mine immediately asked... "Is that 30 years' experience or is it one year repeated thirty times?"
- Find the time and space to observe and reflect. Develop a set of reflective questions.... As a 'starter for ten' – What has gone well and why, what could have been done differently and why, what have I learned, what have we learned? How can we apply this learning to future scenarios?

5 Self-Directed learning

- Encourage a culture of self-directed learning in yourself and others. By this we mean that the individual holds full accountability for their own learning and development and its outcomes. This can be supported in turn by the organisation and other colleagues and line managers.

- Self-directed learning occurs when the individual is motivated within themselves to learn... they have a strategy/goal/plan for their development and their development has real meaning for them – this includes you as a leader.
- Encourage risk-taking... in yourself and in others... this doesn't mean thoughtless/reckless behaviour but encouraging calculated risk will challenge the self-directed learner to rise to the challenge of a task, be motivated to learn and is more likely to develop new learning rather than the same solutions always applied.

6   Creating a learning environment

- Reading through the tips so far in this section you will either already know or are realising that effective learning takes effort, time and space. What steps have you/will you take in your organisation to create the environment in which this can take place?
- One of the biggest inhibitors to learning is how you and your organisation deals with mistakes.... Treat mistakes as opportunities to learn and not for immediate punishment. Clearly repetition of the same error or negligent behaviour do not qualify but leaders who work on the principle of no-blame learning can greatly benefit from the openness and honesty this approach to learning can take.
- Build at least one learning objective into yours and your team's KRA/KPI list.

7   Coaching for Performance

- Coaching is both a mind-set and a skill. Done well it is a powerful learning tool; done badly it can be the opposite. Coaching is not teaching nor is it counselling – they have their place but have different methodologies. Do you have the mind-set of a coach – if not think about how you develop this? Like other tips in this section you can greatly influence the amount of this valuable activity by your role-modelling as a coach.
- Good coaches do all of the following: listen carefully, ask questions, give quality feedback, challenge, encourage and allow the 'coachee' to own the problem/challenge and the outcome. Ask a colleague to observe you coaching someone and give you feedback to develop your skills.
- Create an environment of trust... often a problem presented to a coach covers a more fundamental issue – developing high rapport and trust with others will enable you to coach them properly by both you as the coach and them as an individual getting to the root cause of a performance issue.

8   Review

- Build a habit of reviewing into your work. For example – at the end of any meeting ask how effective was the meeting, what was good about the meeting and what could be better? How could the meeting be more effective next time?
- Encourage your team to be self-critical of their work – both the good and the less good.

- Develop a habit of advance review – e.g. How can we make this the best project ever? What will success look like? What have we learned from past work that will help us be better in this work?

9 Qualifications

- Used appropriately, qualifications can greatly enhance the learning process in your organisation.
- Provide qualifications that are relevant to individual's current and/or future roles. A mixture of in-house accreditations and external qualifications should be considered. Don't allow qualifications just for their own sake….
- Sending all of your middle/senior management on MBAs might look good but will it give the individuals and the organisation a return on the investment of cost, time and endeavour?
- When you or your team achieve a qualification – celebrate it. This will not have been achieved without considerable effort and it is worth recognising the achievement for the benefit of motivation and application to the job.

10 Applying and Sustaining Learning

- Learning has to be applied for it to stick so making the learning relevant to the individual and the organisation as outlined above is essential to give both the application and sustainability for the future.

- Evaluation is key... Kirkpatrick described the evaluation of learning as a series of levels (from completing 'happy sheets' at the end of a course through to organisational impact of a learning strategy). At the very least review learning and application to the individual and their role some distance out from the learning event or programme. Ask questions like – what did you learn? How did you apply this learning? What has been the impact on you, your job and the organisation as a result? *See Top Tip 7 in Chapter 11*

- Finally, never forget that as humans we are learning from the moment we are born (indeed some now say even before we are born!). It is counter intuitive to inhibit human growth and development so encourage learning, application and sustainability throughout your organisation... role model it yourself and others will follow you.

YOUR NOTES FROM CHAPTER 2

Chapter 3

Top 10 Tips for developing effective communication

By

Ian Munro

Effective leaders use effective communication. Poor communication leads to ambiguity, a lack of clarity and purpose. This chapter is about developing the skills required to communicate effectively and engage others in a shared purpose and ambition.

1   Be sure about what it is you need to communicate

- Take some time to prepare what you need to communicate. The complexity of the message will determine the approach you need to take.
- Tailor the message to the recipients; ensure that you are pitching the communication at the right level to the right people.
- Having completed the communication, check understanding with some specific questions, the answers will enable you to assess how well the communication has been received.
- Use open questions starting with who, what, where, when, why and how which means they have to answer.

2   Develop Clarity in the content

- If you are communicating verbally try to ensure that you have conveyed the message in a clear and concise way. Preparation will enhance this process and it is helpful to leave spaces rather than fill them with "Ums and Aaahs".
- If the communication is in writing, particularly via email ensure that you read it back to yourself before sending. Are you sure you have the right tone and clarity you were looking for, could any of your words be misconstrued?

25

- Check your content and delivery for jargon. Even if you are communicating with someone in the same kind of environment, it is often embarrassing for people to ask for clarification about things they think they should know, so save them the discomfort.

3   Be assertive

- Be conscious of the difference between assertion and aggression but try to ensure you communicate assertively. Strong leadership requires assertion - people respond positively to assertion but aggression can lead to all kinds of problems further down the line.
- Non - assertive communication can create problems as it conveys signs of weakness and uncertainty. Even when the message is difficult or contentious it is still important to maintain an assertive stance.
- Assertion requires a high level of self - awareness and a strong set of values, in respect of oneself and those with whom you are communicating. Assertive behaviour always respects the values of others as well as your own, aggressive behaviour rarely does.

4   Focus on "Two Way" communication

- Communication is contextual – decide on the urgency, intensity, importance of the message and communicate accordingly. The meaning of communication is the response you get so you need to listen.

- Make sure that you listen and not just hear. Active listening requires skill and concentration. Acknowledge what you hear and respond in an appropriate way.
- People respond better to people who are interested rather than interesting, so ask open questions, qualify points and build the conversation rather than follow a linear argument.

5   Build rapport

- Active listening is one way to build rapport so demonstrate as many aspects as possible to demonstrate you are connecting with the person or persons in communication.
- Use positive body language to emphasise the message. There will be a range of situations and messages underpinning each communication, so it is important that these are reflected in the way you put the message across.
    - 7% of Communication is the Words we use
    - 55% is represented by our Physiology i.e. Body Language
    - 38% comes from our Voice and Tonality

- Avoid being manipulative, rapport is a natural process and can be undermined when falsely represented.

6   Be empathetic

- Rapport can be enhanced greatly by the use of empathy, understanding the position of others is critical in the process of effective communication

- Be certain of the boundaries between sympathy and empathy, they are not the same, empathy can be a very powerful tool even when conveying bad news or in difficult conversations.
- Being empathetic can also enable you to anticipate possible objections or obstacles as it enables you to see things from an alternative point of view, and build a credible case for your own standpoint.

7   Check Understanding

- How many times have you walked away from a discussion, only to find later down the line that what comes back is different than what you thought had been agreed?
- Make sure when you conclude matters that you have heard back from others, their interpretation of the communication. It may be time consuming but it can save hours going forward.
- Build in techniques which will help to avoid frustration, as this can be an exhausting process. It is even more important to control this and avoid it coming out in your behaviour. There may be occasions however, when it might be very helpful to express your frustration, depending on the circumstances.

8   Select the right methodology

- Different circumstances will dictate different methods of communication and each situation will be fairly unique. This is often a judgement call but an important one.

- There will be times when face to face ommunication is important, but again, this can depend on the situation.

- With a team, it is not always helpful to gather them together, as the message may be better conveyed one to one in the first instance.
- Written communication can often be an efficient way to convey information, face to face may be better if there is an emotive aspect to the message, telephone may be a staging post between the two.

9   Use technology wisely

- Leading on from methodology is the question of how best to use technology in communication, given the plethora of opportunities and the range of situations you are likely to encounter.
- From a leadership point of view, we are generally focussing on people and specifically those people under your stewardship. This tends to focus on the more personal form of communication best represented by face to face contact, telecommunication (including Skype and FaceTime) and e mail.
- The most effective approach is generally a good mix of all technologies as people respond in a variety of different ways. Bearing in mind that people are essentially responsive to auditory, visual and kinaesthetic (experiential) stimuli in differing degrees, it makes sense to incorporate a mix of communication options when choosing the approach, to ensure you have covered all the bases.

10   Role model the behaviours you want to instil.

- There is a tendency for followers to emulate the behaviours of their leaders, they want to belong and they want to be recognised. It makes sense therefore for the leader to demonstrate what they want to see in their people.
- There is a lot of evidence to support the premise that your immediate leader at work has more impact on you as an employee than any other person or thing in the work environment, it stands to reason therefore that this puts a huge responsibility on anyone in a leadership position.
- Finally, people notice everything – so be authentic and credible in your communication. It is essential that there is alignment between what you say and what you do.

YOUR NOTES FROM CHAPTER 3

Chapter 4

Top 10 tips for developing leadership strength

By

Mike Nelson

In an increasingly complex and hyper-connected world, the ability to be resilient is becoming an essential quality in order to lead with thoughtful, considered behaviours and actions. This chapter is about looking at ways in which you can manage pressure, keep motivated and use other techniques to ensure you do not get overwhelmed by the forces and changes going on in the environment around you and your organisation

1   Attribution

- How do you currently attribute your successes or failures? Ensure you internalise why things succeed and are constructively critical when they don't succeed.
- Challenge your level of optimism vs. pessimism. There is a famous quote "*If you think you can or think you can't – you are right".*
- Ensure a sense of optimism within your team... celebrate successes, praise achievements.

2   Personal Renewal

- Take some time out of your schedule to reflect on your work/life balance and other factors that influence your health and well-being. What is working well at the moment and how can you do more/reinforce this? What is working less well and what can you do to change this?
- Get a buddy/coach/mentor... it is useful to have someone to challenge you with the way things are, the way you want them to be and how you can change this.

- Go on a retreat... take some real time out to take stock and renew life, priorities, work goals, strategy.

3   De-clutter

- Clear your diary and your desk. Ensure that you and your team's working environment is not bogged down in trivial items which get in the way of working towards your goals.
- Clear your mind. What is distracting you from getting on with the job in hand? Learn and practise Mindfulness or similar techniques to allow you to keep clear headed.
- Restrict who can put things in your diary... who is in control of your diary? Ensure that only appropriate things get in there and don't let the diary re-fill with meetings that are not essential.

4   Sustainability

- Ensure you have an overall purpose, vision and strategy. These must all be connected and congruent. If you are leading a part of a larger organisation ensure the above is also properly aligned with the wider organisational strategy.
- What is happening in the world around you... your clients/customers, competitors, environment, politics, law. Ensure that your current tactics are properly taking into account changing factors in the world around you.
- Review, review, review....Often we are too busy to take stock and review progress but it has been said that the time you most need a review is the time when you think you don't have time to review.

Create the habit of reviewing progress and instil this in your team as well. What is working well and less well? What needs to be done to improve? What are you learning along the way you can apply another time?

5 Ambiguity

- Be clear with your team that there is ambiguity in the current project. Encourage them to try things out and readjust if they don't work out the first time, keep making and recording progress, however small.
- Seek clarity wherever you can. What is known and unknown and how will you deal with the unknown elements.
- Sometimes a job is good enough and you can prevent perfectionism taking over from getting the job done. Let your team know when things are good enough.

6 Time Management

- Review all of your tasks in the course of a business cycle. Categorise using the framework of Important, Not important versus Urgent, Not urgent. Take a step back and review as if you were reviewing someone else's schedule.
- What are you doing that you shouldn't be doing – either delegated or not done at all?
- Plan for meetings in advance and allow time for review of output afterwards. Shorten meetings to make them more focussed and less prone to drift in the agenda.

- Ensure meetings are chaired and ensure a discipline of keeping to the agreed outcomes. Finally review attendees – are the right people in the room to get the job done.
- Harness new technology to get work done more efficiently, meeting on Skype or Hangouts, learn how to use this effectively and ensure all of your team get appropriate training and the tools to work in this way.
  See Top Tip 10 in Chapter 11

7   Personal Vision

- Develop a personal vision for yourself... what do you want in work? In life? What would this look like/feel like when you have achieved this vision? What will it give you when you have realised your vision?
- What can you do to work towards your vision, what steps do you need to take and how will you take them. Build these steps into your learning and development plan.
- Market your vision... tell yourself, tell others. Develop your "30-second" elevator pitch about yourself. Keep rehearsing this until it becomes strong in your own mind.

8   Focus

- How do you currently focus your attention on the job in hand, what techniques do you use that help you focus and what distracts you from getting done what you need to get done. How can you deal with the distractions?

- Different tasks require different mental activity; checking a report for spelling and grammar is quite different from a creative session to design a new process or campaign. Think about what enables you to perform these different types of task and how best to create the right environment for the particular job in hand.
- Prioritisation is an essential tool in keeping focused, the tasks that need your best attention should be planned into your best time of day/week.

9   Stress & pressure

- Recognise that all of us are affected in different ways by the impact of the environment around us, and that stress is our body's response to the pressures around us and the pressure we place upon ourselves to achieve. Make a list of your top three stress causing items. How are you currently reacting to them and what could you change to reduce the impact of this upon you?
- In a period of high stress, practise the art of taking fewer, deeper breaths... relax your muscles and slowly count down from ten.
- "Man is not disturbed by things, but the views he takes of them". With this quote in mind review how your thinking is reacting to stresses in the environment around you. We often fear the worst and it is useful to catch ourselves making assumptions about how bad things will be. Challenge your internal assumptions and think about how you could get more information to change the way you are thinking about the current situation.

See Top Tip 8 in Chapter 11

10   Motivation

- Motivating forces can come from the outside world and from within. The most sustainable motivators are those internal ones we decide for ourselves and which connect with our values and purpose in life and work.
- Set good goals. It is essential to have clear, unambiguous and measurable goals. Break the goals down from the big measurable items into things you can actually do to make progress toward your goals. Review goals on a regular basis. Find the motivation by recognising what delivery of these goals will give you; what will it feel like when you have completed them.
- If there is a job which you are finding difficult to get yourself motivated, carry out a 'Force Field Analysis'. Identify/list those things which are inhibiting factors and things which are driving forces. Reflect on this; how can you minimise the inhibitors and strengthen the drivers?

YOUR NOTES FROM CHAPTER 4

Chapter 5

Top 10 tips for developing leadership character

By

Charles Marshall

In his widely acclaimed book, the 7 habits of Highly Effective People, Stephen Covey describes management as "Doing things right" and leadership as "Doing the right thing". This chapter explores how values and principles are critical to developing a leadership style which is both credible and influential.

1   Strive to be authentic in your dealings with others

- Authenticity is often expressed by phrases such as "it does what is says on the tin" or "you get what you see". Like all key leadership attributes it reflects underlying values and beliefs. Most people respond best to the truth and authenticity is all about how well you reflect the truth.

- It often presents itself as consistency, as an authentic approach should not vary with the conditions. Authentic leaders are true to their values rather than responding to the conditions around them.

- Authentic leaders also display reliability and can be depended upon to provide clarity and an assertive view on the reality of the situation. When weaker leaders may fudge the issue and try to soften the blow, authentic leaders will grasp the reality of what they are dealing with and not shy away from difficult conversations.

2   Be creative – throw away the blueprint.

- It is often said that in today's environment, managers provide previously developed solutions to recurrent problems whereas leaders are involved with "wicked problems" to which there are no obvious solutions.
- If this is the case, then leaders need to be creative, comfortable with risk and adopt an innovative approach to everything they encounter. Finding new directions and original strategies is one of their core skills. Whilst they may have to use good delegation to enable others to develop technical solutions, they need to be the driving force behind the process.
- A need to question and challenge the status quo lies behind the creativity. Good leaders are rarely satisfied with the obvious and are never happy with mediocrity. A drive for excellence and originality is essential.

3   Understand and demonstrate integrity

- Integrity is best described when we examine the inextricable link which exists between a person's values and their behaviour. A leader's words and their actions must be aligned. So many toxic issues within organisations have arisen from situations where leaders have paid lip service to a set of values, only to behave in a completely different way.

- There are too many examples where people at the head of organisations subscribe to values such as empowerment, enablement, distributed power, but yet preside over a system which either tolerates or worse still encourages bullying, harassment in a culture which is restrictive, over managed and draconian in nature.
- Leaders who demonstrate integrity develop organisational cultures which are supportive, empowering and exciting to be part of. Instead of organisations driven by fear they develop an environment which is demanding because of the speed at which it operates. They expect a lot of their people but provide a culture in which they can grow and flourish.

4 Develop Gravitas in your interactions with others

- It could be argued that gravitas is best described by its opposite, in that leaders who fail to make the grade are often described as "lightweight". Gravitas is largely about impact and strength of character but is underpinned by a number of key behaviours.
- Clear, assertive communication is the hallmark of a leader with gravitas; good eye contact and positive body language are always there in support. Competence, backed by good knowledge, a clear grounding in reality and well developed interpersonal skills all play a key part in developing this attribute.
- Although the title suggests a fairly serious approach, this is really about appropriateness and it is important to remember that a sense of humour is never lost when developing relationships.

- A leader with gravitas is listened to, noticed and respected. They are influential without being pompous and overbearing, it is also worth noting that along with many of these key leadership characteristics, it is often very transparent when they are fake (see authentic – above).

5   Intuition – developing far sighted insight

- There is no substitute for experience, however, there is a difference between individuals with 15 years' experience and those with 1 years' experience 15 time over. It is too easy to assume that being around for a while equals wisdom and insight. So personal development must figure somewhere in the equation. A thirst for improvement and a willingness to learn is perhaps the first essential building block to building intuition.
- Coupled with this approach must also be a willingness and opportunity to reflect. Busy lives build pressure and can often get in the way of good quality reflection, yet without reflection it is more or less impossible to develop the kind of intuition required to be a really effective leader. This will without doubt require effort, either by allocating time or resources. Coaching is an ideal way of developing a more reflective approach if self-discipline is not enough on its own; as a good coach will force you to reflect and what is perhaps more important – take action.
- There are many factors which can block intuition; arrogance, fear, pressure, panic or simply lacking the self-awareness to spot the bigger picture.

- A wide range of tools can be used to aid this process - Myers Briggs Personality Inventory (MBTI), Firo B, 360 degree Leadership Practices Inventory (as developed by Kouzes and Posner) to name but a few.
- Valuable insight can be gained into hidden sides of the Johari Window, but it might be wise to consider using a trained facilitator or coach to take you through this process.
  See Top Tip 9 in Chapter 11

6   He who hesitates is lost

- There is some validity in the argument that any decision is better than no decision, but there must some caveats to this.
- Competence must be present in order to undertake any decision linked with leadership. Whilst good leadership does not always require a detailed technical knowledge of the area concerned, it is essential to seek guidance from those team members who possess that knowledge before an informed decision can be made. The best leaders take responsibility for making decisions but are inclusive in their approach, this not only enhances the quality of the decision but also the buy in from the rest of the team.
- This in itself leads to credibility, which is another key factor in decision making. Leadership requires followership and without sufficient credibility it unlikely that people will accept decisions at face value, if they do, it may be begrudgingly, making action and change difficult to sustain.

- Related to these critical factors is also judgement. This can feed off a number of contributors – insight, experience, competence; all play a part in developing a good sense of judgement. So we can perhaps modify the initial statement in so much as decisions based on competence, credibility and good judgement, are always better than no decisions. Making the right decision every time, however, may be placing too much faith in human nature, but if the correct elements are engaged every time, it will significantly reduce the risks.

7   A positive state of mind.

- This has been around some time now and a good number of people have written extensively in support of the impact of a positive mental attitude. Again, this requires a caveat in that positivity is OK but it is important that the leader is also well grounded. – It could be said that there is nothing as dangerous as a motivated idiot! So what are the safeguards required to get the most out of positivity?
    - o Question your limiting beliefs
    - o Develop strength and energy
    - o Have a clear vision and an ability to inspire those around you.
    - o Develop resilience
    - o Surround yourself with positive people and shut our negativity

8   Choosing our Attitude – do we play from a zero, or play from a ten

- There is a micro and macro aspect to attitude which both play a significant role in the leadership process. On the smaller scale, attitude can vary from day to day, or even hour to hour, depending on a range of circumstances. Let's start with the premise that we all have a range of "how we feel" at any one time – best represented by a 10 - being us at our best, and 0 being our worst. Faced with adverse situations and difficulties which inevitably crop up during the course of a day, it's easy to drift towards a zero and forget that we do actually have a choice in this.

- Being conscious of this and making a rational choice about how we react to situations is the key to the process, it's a simple choice – would I prefer to be hostage to negative emotions or can I turn this into something positive which will get me a better outcome in the future.

- Whichever choices we make on a regular basis consequently affects our overall long term attitude to life, and there is no doubt that life can be richer and more fulfilling if we practice and successfully play from a ten on a regular basis.

9   Humility

- We have established that leaders need to be decisive, leaders need to be confident and leaders need to be assertive, however, if this leads to arrogance and an over bearing approach it is clear that things have gone too far.

- Humility and vulnerability in leaders is one of the top three qualities identified as critical from extensive surveys and 360 degree assessments. So how do we demonstrate humility as a leader? Here are some suggestions.
- Listening to others and giving due consideration to opinions other than your own before making decisions.
- Accepting that we do not always know the answer and working through strengths possessed by other team members.
- Continually searching for knowledge and seeking improvement.
- Showing respect for others and recognising their credibility.
- Operating at the same level as the people you are dealing with and ignoring artificial boundaries determined by rank or office.
- Humility is not weakness, it is the basis of relationship building and that in turn is the fuel of good leadership.

10   Honesty

- It is hard to imagine a successful leader who is dishonest. It may sometimes take a while to "uncover" dishonesty but in 99 % of cases this kind of leader is eventually found out.
- Honesty is a wider concept however than simply not telling lies. It is more about authenticity, credibility, and above all trustworthiness. In order to develop trust in a team or indeed an organisation, leaders have to be trustworthy and develop a culture of trust around them.

- This in turn builds an organisation founded on principles and values and one where the culture physically reflects those values in terms of "the way we do things around here."
- In a way, the organisation has to be "honest" and credible, transparent in the way it operates and exemplary in the way it treats its people. That all starts with a strong leader who models the way and strives continually to develop people in the same mould.

YOUR NOTES FROM CHAPTER 5

Chapter 6

Top 10 tips for developing team leadership

By

Charles Marshall

In his book on team development, Patrick Lencioni describes the 5 dysfunctions of team which prevents them moving forward.
See Top Tip 3 in Chapter 11

This chapter focuses on those 5 areas from a slightly different perspective with the addition of a number of other "required steps" to achieve effectiveness in team leadership.

1   Establish Trust within the team

- For a team to function effectively, there needs to be a significant amount of trust between its members. Lack of trust can lead to a whole range of unhealthy behaviours which will undermine the overall performance of the team. Individuals protect themselves from blame by developing a "Teflon" skin - in other words, nothing sticks to them. Being vulnerable and willing to accept responsibility for things which go wrong is a necessary component of a trusting team.
- Lack of trust is therefore often reflected by a culture of blame, where an individual's success is often achieved at the expense of another team member's failure. There is a lack of openness between team members and mutual support, recognition, and an awareness of well-being is lacking.
- Interventions which encourage greater awareness of individual members, the value of diversity within the team and a recognition of different styles would be a recommended course of action.

2   Encourage strong challenge round the table

- When trust is lacking within a team, there is often a reluctance to contribute strongly to issues which the team are struggling to overcome. Conflict often exists but in its most unhealthy form of political manoeuvring, back stabbing and undermining each other's progress.
- What is required is a level of passion around the team concerning the key issues and a willingness to debate these openly. Of course, this will lead to challenge and conflict but this is healthy and to be encouraged. Team members need to be confident enough to represent their own views and opinions and to be assured that they will not be attacked as a result.
- Direct effort needs to go into identifying these areas of conflict and to create a climate whereby they can be addressed openly. The leader in these situations is crucial and must be prepared to withstand the discomfort created by these situations.

3   Drive for commitment

- The challenge and conflict created by the above process is critical in achieving commitment. Gaining 100% agreement is unlikely, but team members need to know that their views have been aired and listened to. A team leader's role here is to gain an agreement to disagree and moving things along towards a clear outcome.

- The clarity of this outcome is crucial as the alternative is lip service which runs the risk of creating ambiguity further down the chain as different team members will take different conclusions away from the meeting.
- All teams have a wide range of issues to handle, but there is usually one overarching objective which trumps the rest. Finding that and agreeing a clear course of action is where the team leader needs to focus the team and only move on when the whole team is satisfied that they have found a real way forward.

4   Develop a culture of joint accountability

- Having reached consensus on the major objective, there will inevitably be a number of actions which each team member will need to achieve in order to make it happen. The responsibility for this sits both with the individual and the team as a whole. In other words, if we have trust within the team, missing an objective should not result in a witch hunt and victimisation but a recognition that the whole team bears some responsibility for the failure and is in a position potentially to help find a solution.
- This approach drives up performance and promotes a problem solving approach within the team rather than recrimination and an acceptance of mediocrity.
- Again, tackling this requires a lot of trust and a lot of openness about what each individual brings to the team and what lets them down.

- There are a number of ways of generating this kind of feedback but it needs to be handled in a safe way and in a way that individuals can accept as a genuine part of their development.

5   Agree clear outcomes

- Having agreed on where the focus of the team should be, this needs to be pursued relentlessly. A team needs a reason to exist and needs to see what contribution it is making. Performance should therefore be reviewed on a regular basis and the leader should be transparent in the way this performance is measured.
- It is critical that this effort is not side tracked and confused by secondary objectives and the moving of goal posts. Clearly we live in the real world and few things are constant, but where possible, the focus should stay on results around the issue that the team has identified as its priority.
- This is designed to prevent team leaders and team members pursuing objectives which are based more on ego and status than on the reason they are in post.

6   Achieve a sense of balance

- Teams by their very nature are diverse and there is a real need to recognise the value of this diversity in the makeup of a team. There are a wide range of tools available to both measure and develop this diversity or simply to check that as a leader, you are on the right track.

- Personality tests such as MBTI and Insights provide specific profile for each individual and allow the leader to see where the balance lies or whether there is a predominance of one or two personalities within the team.
- Team assessments such as Belbin measure the roles which individuals tend to adopt when they are in a team situation and again allow the leader to view the team as a whole and assess the spread of the different roles. These are not literal roles as defined by job description but more about the approach each person takes and the contribution that can make to the team.
- Other useful intervention can be undertaken which look at different approaches to conflict by individual team members, problem solving processes and how people form interpersonal relationships.

7   Create a climate of motivation

- There is some strength in the argument that people motivate themselves and as leaders, our role is to create the kind of climate whereby that can take place.
- Expect the best in others by setting high standards and be on the lookout to catch people doing things right. It is important to be creative and avoid being stuck in the same kind of recognition loop.

- Link performance and rewards and ensure that you make sure they know what is expected, rewarding exceptional performance and not mediocrity.
- Provide constant feedback, both positive and negative as people are concerned about the reality of where they stand, platitudes are unproductive.

8 Be aware of inputs - begin with the end in mind.

- When developing the team it is critical to ensure that this aligns to the environment in which the team is operating, different strengths may be required in different situations and an environmental assessment should be undertaken as the team is put together
- There also needs to be absolute clarity around the task in hand. What are the requirements of the team and the expectations placed upon them, is there a clear idea of what success should look like.
- Composition relating back to the different functions and roles within the team, again this needs to be carefully matched to environment and task.

9   Establish clear processes for the team

- Well defined processes enable teams to operate effectively, however it is important to strike a balance between essential bureaucracy and unnecessary control mechanisms. The main thing is that teams are clear about their objectives and that there are enough systems in place by which performance against those objectives can be measured.
- It is also important to provide sufficient opportunity for team members to participate in the creation of

those objectives and measurements as buy in to those concepts will inevitably improve compliance and recognition.

- Building in time to reflect on performance is also important as there is a tendency to rush from one objective to another as priorities change and as goal posts move, the credibility of any objective based system can be severely undermined.
- How decisions are made and how those are communicated needs careful thought. One of the key roles for any team is problem solving and basing quality decisions on the back of that process. Providing time and structure for this to take place is an important requirement of any team leader.

10   Measure Outputs and make the results transparent.

- There is a need to continually be aware of outcomes. Inputs into how a team needs to perform tend to proliferate, but there also needs to be a strong focus on outcomes. Targets should be geared towards this rather than activity and an emphasis on the quality of those outcomes needs to be built in.
- Cost effectiveness is normally a major section of any balanced scorecard, but often gets confused with simply "cost". What needs to be stressed is the value or effectiveness of any expenditure, only that

way can it be truly evaluated as a measure of performance.

- Stress levels and turnover within the team are clear indicators of internal health and often reflect the style in which some of the above outcome measures are applied.

- There are a whole range of interventions mentioned earlier in this chapter which are designed to ensure that stress does not always result from an environment of high performance, there may be pressure, but that should not be allowed to tip over into stress.

YOUR NOTES FROM CHAPTER 6

Chapter 7

Top 10 tips for leading self

By

Charles Marshall

Leadership can be a lonely place. Making decisions which can be unpopular, having difficult conversations with people as they develop, encouraging others in times of adversity can all put a huge strain on leaders. First and foremost, they need to be able to get themselves in the right place. This chapter offers insight into some of the thought processes and inner dialogue which can encourage effective personal leadership.

1   Align your behaviour to your values.

- One of the common criticisms of poor leaders is that they say one thing and do another. In order to guard against this it is important that leaders have developed enough self- awareness to be conscious of their own values and beliefs.
- These values and beliefs drive our behaviour unconsciously and it is only by recognition of who, and what we are that we become aware of their power. This has a critical role to play in understanding diversity and avoiding defensive behaviour when our opinions are threatened. Each of us has our own set of beliefs and values and these manifest themselves in our individual behavioural differences.
- We may often be required to act against our instincts but it becomes uncomfortable when we try and act against our values. Leaders need to position themselves clearly so that this compromise is not required.

2   Maintain a positive mind-set and play from a ten.

- The values and beliefs we hold can dictate our overall mind set. If we hold on to beliefs which limit us (usually beginning with – "I can't") then this will trigger behaviours which are negative and pessimistic. Leadership is a privilege not a right, and as such we owe it to ourselves and our teams, to approach it with a positive state of mind.
- Starting with the self -awareness of the above tip, we need to challenge these limiting beliefs as they spring to mind. They are often unfounded and unsubstantiated and as such we need to continually challenge them. As with any other practice, this eventually becomes second nature and the number of doubts we have creeping into our minds will diminish.
- It is also critical that we accept our own role in outcomes we achieve or don't achieve. Given any event, interaction or occurrence, it is often our own response which dictates the outcome. Being mindful of this, puts us more in control and prevents us being a hostage to fortune. This has powerful effects on stress reduction and increasing assertiveness – as leaders this is a critical survival skill.

3   Develop a high level of self-awareness

- Goleman's book on emotional intelligence maps out 4 key areas –

  Self -awareness, self -management, social awareness and social skills, we now need to examine each of these in more detail.

Self -awareness has already been referred to as an essential skill but still raises the question of how. There a many self- assessment processes and methodologies available, but the mainstays are:

- **Myers Briggs Type Inventory or MBTI**. This develops awareness of our own personality type and that of others with whom we work. It encourages awareness and diversity as we develop an understanding of the fact that ours is not the only way
  - **Insights** – is based on MBTI but takes the model further making it more accessible and relevant to modern working life
  - **Firo B** – examines our interpersonal approaches via inclusion, control and openness, giving ourselves insight into how we approach interpersonal situations.
  - **HBDI** – a colour coded reflection of our thinking styles looking at the 4 parameters of creativity / social / Strategic and structure.
  - **Learning styles** – providing insight into how we learn best via the 4 learning styles – pragmatic, theoretical, reflective and active.
  - There are many more but these standards provide a really useful starting point for developing self- awareness.
    See Top Tip 5 in Chapter 11

True self awareness however goes much further than simply "categorising" our personality as it hinges around being aware of our mood and our thoughts about that mood.

This can either engulf us and create a feeling of helplessness or create a sense of resignation where we accept the "feeling" and shun the fact that we can actually change it.

4   Develop strategies for self management

- Self management in this context, is all about accepting the fact that we are actually capable of being in control of these moods, feelings and attitudes and by building on the concept of self awareness become aware of the way we react to the things which affect us on a day to basis. Leaders, by nature of their role are often in positions of organisational exposure, and consequently it is essential that they are adept at this level of self management. Recognising negative emotions and exercising control over them is the key to self management.

- Anger is a commonly experienced negative emotion. It is often subject to a chain of re-enforcing influences which create a "boiling point". Each event, feeds the last and what might have been ignored under normal circumstances becomes more significant in this heightened state. In reality, there are thoughts driving the anger which are often irrational and need to be challenged. The sooner these triggers can be challenged during the anger cycle, the less likely the anger will be to escalate. In addition, physical activity such as exercise in combination with the mental "challenge" of the thought process has been found to be highly effective in controlling the anger.

- Anxiety and worry are also common negative emotions and are also fuelled by irrational thought and are cyclical in nature. They tend to be impervious to reason and lock the individual into a single inflexible view of the source of anxiety.

- Consequently, helpful advice such as "don't worry" or "just forget about it" is futile. Self awareness is again, the starting point and a recognition of what triggers the anxiety the first step. Early challenge of these triggers and a sense of perspective is essential by contemplating a range of equally plausible points to keep the worrying factor at bay.

- The concept of mindfulness is a current hot topic and can play a big part in managing a range of negative emotions. Whilst there is a whole science sitting behind the concept, this text is about tips and finding an accessible route into some of these more complex concepts. A good starting point is to consider the amount of "noise" which we are assaulted with on a day to day basis, emails, texts, Twitter, Facebook, LinkedIn to name but 5. Finding space in the day to escape if only for 20 minutes to allow the noise to evaporate can be very powerful. Being aware of your surroundings but letting thoughts escape and clearing the mind can be incredibly refreshing.

5   Social awareness - understand and develop empathy

- Leadership is essentially the business of relationships. By and large we are required to lead people, and connecting with people is a necessary step in creating a sustainable group of followers.

- Again, the roots of empathy begin with self awareness, a knowledge of your own emotions is a good training ground for recognising the same thing in others.
- People rarely, however, talk openly about their emotions and the requirement of empathy is that we are sufficiently skilled to recognise these via a series of non-verbal cues - tone of voice, gestures, facial expression and body language. Being able to interpret this non-verbal language, and respond appropriately is the key to building rapport.
- Being aware of our own non-verbal language is similarly important as we need to be aware of the kind of emotional signals we are sending. In the context of self management it all combines to create the picture of a credible leader. Someone who conveys control and stability and also someone who responds appropriately to emotions in others.
- Social skills are therefore an essential range of behaviours which support the development of rapport and relationships within the context of leadership. Goleman describes 4 major skills which are underpinned by the kind of rapport building ability described above.
  - o Organising groups - the ability to network and influence within and beyond one's immediate sphere of responsibility.
  - o Negotiating solutions - finding win / win solutions and preventing conflicts and stalemates.
  - o Personal connections - creating good relationships in a range of different circles and bringing together people in the most productive alignments.

o Social analysis - an awareness of other people's feelings and emotions and external relationships. Reading situations accurately and being able to make the most appropriate interventions.

6   Inner Dialogue and Self Talk.

- This process has been referred to several times in the above sections and underpins a great deal of what self leadership is all about. Breaking down the process by which self talk occurs provides a useful insight into how this can be best managed.
- The overwhelming volume of information coming at us at any one time means that we have to prioritise and attend to the things we feel are most important. In order to do this effectively we have to "filter" information using psychological filters -
  - o *Deletions* - we only notice things which are important to us, as when buying a new car, we tend to see more cars of the same make on the road when making a decision, the rest get "deleted".
  - o *Distortions* - Our preferences and prejudices force us to see events in a different light to people with different preferences and prejudices.
  - o *Generalisations* - used as a shortcut to put people and situations into categories based on previous experiences.
- The above filters are developed over time based on our experiences, values and beliefs and can differ significantly between us all. They create an inner dialogue when confronted with situations and influence our behaviour.

69

- Being aware of this inner dialogue and being able to challenge it when it results in unproductive outcomes is the key to successful self talk.
- A positive mind set with a "can do" attitude is more appropriate for leaders than a defeatist approach and being in control of that self talk helps to put the individual back in charge.

7   More about values and behaviours

- The above section firmly establishes the relationship between values, beliefs and behaviours. Further examination of values is now required to consolidate this understanding.
- As we develop as leaders, there are a plethora of training opportunities which focus on "leadership behaviours". How to be more assertive, decisive, strategic, influential and so on. The focus on behaviours however, is misplaced. It may create a range of techniques and skills which are technically useful, but it fails to get to the real nub of the issue.
- If, on the other hand, we can recognise the values and beliefs which drive our behaviour and start to evaluate and change them, this brings about lasting change and a fundamental paradigm shift which is need for leaders to be credible and confident in their own ability.
- The starting point therefore for this is to ask ourselves a series of questions.
  - *What are the core values which drive us as individuals and to what extent are they being honoured by the environment in which we work?*

> o   *How successful are we in creating positive outcomes as leaders and what role do our values play in creating those outcomes?*
> o   *Are our values aligned with our behaviours - do we do what we say we are going to do?*
> o   *What kind of attitudes are our values creating on a daily basis, are we happy in what we do and confident that our values as leaders are intact?*

8   Reflection

- The preceding tips provide a range of techniques which all come together under one heading - Reflection. One of the most fundamental skills required of a leader and one which is most often overlooked. We have provided a whole chapter of reflective approaches which if used regularly, can drive the self-development required to become a truly effective leader. However, they all need time and space, and modern leaders often complain that the pressure on them is too great to be able to afford such a luxury.

- We would argue that without that time and space, effective leadership will always be a step away, as you become more and more embroiled in the operational day to day crises which every organisation creates.

- Discipline yourself to create time for reflection. It does not require great swathes of time, often a couple of minutes following a conversation or a meeting and a few relevant questions.
  - o   *What kind of outcome did I achieve and how could it have been improved?*

71

- o *How did my actions contribute to that outcome?*
- o *What could I have done better?*
- o *Did I stick to my values or was there compromise?*
- In time, reflection becomes a habit, but like most things it requires practice and repetition, as the skill develops the time needed to do it reduces and the insights reached become more profound.

9   Personal Development

It is a common cliché that learning never stops but for effective leaders it is part of their DNA. The reflective process is a fundamental skill required of successful leaders but a more complete picture is needed for all round development.

- Seek an appraisal. A credible appraisal from an immediate manager or director should be a regular occurrence. This should happen formally on an annual or bi annual basis, but also informally on an ongoing basis via one to one sessions as required. Leaders also need to be mindful of their obligation to others to provide this as part of their ongoing development.
- Get a coach. Appraisal from our boss is one thing, but challenge from an impartial, qualified coach is a highly effective way to develop the kind of insight required as a leader. This can be expensive but compared to other forms of professional development can be good value for money. Choose your coach carefully and ensure that they are compliant with professional coaching standards and ethics.

- Seek 360 degree feedback. Acquiring feedback from above, below and across can provide useful insight as to how you are perceived as a leaders from all angles. This can provide a helpful platform for further development and can also provide a useful starting point for any coaching you might undertake. There are a number of different 360 degree tools available, some specifically focused on leadership.

10   Develop Strength and Resilience

Moments of crisis and extreme circumstances can sometimes bring out strengths and qualities in people they never imagined possible. Personal leadership however, is different in that it requires that strength and tenacity to be present continually, day to day, month to month and year to year. Just when one project or task is successfully completed, it is time to start a new one, as one obstacle is overcome, another one arises in the distance.

- It is perhaps a truism to say that leadership will never be easy and as such, may well not be for everyone. Just as athletes are required to maintain a high level of physical fitness, leaders must also maintain high levels of psychological fitness, sustained by practising some of the tips outlined in this chapter.
- Maintain high levels of physical energy and stamina. Just as behaviours become the outward manifestation of beliefs and attitudes, being

physically fit and active can have a positive effect on our psychology.

- It is almost impossible to feel depressed when exercising so it makes sense to wind up the physical element of our day to day activities to generate resilient energy.
- Stay positive, play from a 10 and provide sufficient defence to ward off the effects of negative attitudes. We are constantly surrounded by "mood hoovers". They are people who suck all the positive energy out of you with their negative approach to life.
  Make sure you spend most time with positivity and people who want to succeed. One of the pitfalls of leadership is the time demanded of us to take care of problems, we need to counterbalance this by spending time with success and achievement.
- Be swift and impactful in dealing with problems and issues. Operate the "one minute manager" principle and ensure that every minute of your time is spent on issues which are important for success.
- Prioritise and manage your time effectively, the more time you spend dealing with issues that are important rather than urgent, the more you will avoid the stress and anxiety which accompany crisis management.

YOUR NOTES FROM CHAPTER 7

Chapter 8

Top 10 tips for leadership dilemmas

By

Charles Marshall

Experience suggests that there is no ready- made solution for leadership. Kouzes and Posner define leadership as *"the art of mobilising others to want to struggle for shared aspirations"*

This in itself suggests that there is a non-scientific, intuitive side to leadership, not to mention a degree of hardship and uncertainty. Leaders need to be decisive, but in that process face a series of conflicting choices which are far from black and white, but getting the balance right in these situations is critical. This chapter focuses on some of those choices or dilemmas and attempts to provide an overview of some of the critical steps in making those choices.

Dilemma one - to control or let go?

- The art of letting go, through effective empowerment is well recognised as a key leadership skill. However, we have to recognise the need for good monitoring systems and controls to instil confidence and assurance.
- The first dilemma therefore presents the challenge as to how to achieve the right balance.
- There are issues around clear lines of accountability, recognition of potential, good delegation and enhanced interpersonal skills but there is no exact formula for success other than experience and recognition of best practice.

Dilemma two – Idealism versus self-interest, fear or misplaced loyalty

- There has been clear evidence, particularly in health and medicine that misplaced loyalty and/or self-interest has prevented people from doing "the right thing".

- This in turn has put patients at risk and sustained a culture of bullying and repression – clearly wrong.
- At what stage is it right to intervene, to "whistle blow", and what price should we put on loyalty to existing leaders in the name of effective team functionality?
- It is only when we examine the boundaries that such dilemmas become apparent – it is easy to talk about extreme cases but where does the line actually lie?

Dilemma three – Detachment versus close relationships

- Successful leaders tend on the whole to be popular, well liked or at least respected.
- However, we all know the dangers of getting too close to the team, conspiring and blurring the boundaries between empathy and sympathy.
- Detachment is essential if "the difficult conversation" is ever to be had, not to mention the ambiguity which can ensue if false harmony is followed by draconian management. Finding the right balance is clearly critical to effective leadership, but where is the manual? Again, we probably rely on experience and mentoring to guide us through.

Dilemma four – Humility versus decisiveness

- Not knowing the answer and being willing to admit it, is regarded as a sign of strong leadership, and we all know that there is nothing more dangerous in leadership than a motivated idiot (to which anyone who watches The Apprentice will attest).

- However, being able and willing to make decisions, both popular and unpopular is clearly an essential part of leadership.
- When people get the balance right, it is fairly easy to spot, but describing the skill is less straightforward and I doubt there are many "serious" leaders who have not lost sleep over this particular dilemma.

Dilemma five – Actions versus empty words

- We all want to be able to re-assure our teams and organisations that we are "on the case" – they also need to know that we are representing their best interests and fighting their corner.
- I fear however, that many of us are guilty as leaders of using the famous statement – "leave it with me" and then ducking the issue when the time comes.
- There are a number of issues which sit beneath this involving assertiveness, proactivity, and judgment but none of them can effectively be "prescribed" making clear instruction and effective training very elusive.

Dilemma Six – Rigid planning or opportunism

- Strategic planning is a well-documented requirement of any senior management group. The ability to map out a strategy and then have the courage to stick to that strategy is often a solid anchor for successful companies.
- Markets however, don't always behave to plan and in today's high speed, technical environment there

is a need to be flexible enough to respond to immediate opportunities.
- The dilemma therefore is clear, how long should you stick to a plan in the hope that it will eventually win through or how soon should you have the courage to ditch the original paradigm and consider a more "in the moment" alternative.

Dilemma Seven – Collaborative or evidence based

- This is really about decision making. It is a contradiction in styles.
- Can a decision reached in isolation, through careful consideration of existing research be of better quality than one reached by a process of collaboration with real people sat around a table?
- The collaborative approach has clear attractions, but it is important to recognise the fact that people sat around a table often have conflicting values and opinions and reaching an objective agreement through this process can be extremely hazardous.
- A balanced approach is appealing using both approaches, but there still has to be an emphasis or bias in reaching the final decision.

Dilemma Eight – Hard or Soft wiring.

- The battle between logic and feelings - a central theme in Myers Briggs model of personality - recognised by them as a critical part of how we make decisions.

Do we consider how decisions impact on people and their circumstances or even society or do we simply look at the bottom line, the factual benefits and the hard outcomes which can be accurately measured.

81

- From opposite ends of the spectrum, it is hard to make sense and accommodate what seems to be an incomprehensible approach from the other side of the divide.
- What is absolutely essential, is to develop an awareness that there is more than one approach here and to become aware of the underpinning factors in both approaches. This is of course, the value of instruments like MBTI and the insight they provide.

Dilemma Nine – Manager or transformer

- It is tempting to open the debate on leadership versus management but that is not really the dilemma here. The key question is whether leaders exist to create successful organisations which run well, have good governance and maintain a solid balance sheet, or do they exist to continually change and transform the organisations approach to its environment, never happy with standing still and encouraging a creative approach to strategy.
- The answer is obvious, but woe betide the leader who neglects the fundamentals as the two should work in harmony.
- The dilemma is where to commit the time resource as each side of the equation potentially absorbs resource from the other.
- Experience would suggest that successful leaders spend the majority of their time focusing on strategy and change but having the right systems in place to keep their finger on the pulse of the business.

Dilemma Ten – Strict rules or discretionary flexibility

- Organisations need systems and systems need rules. But when systems and rules outweigh common sense and translate opportunities into unacceptable risks then there is something wrong with the balance.
- The leader's job is to make those critical decisions as to when the rules should be overridden for the good of the organisation. Situations like this often lead to permanent change for the better without which stagnation would be the outcome.
- The risk is anarchy when discretionary flexibility is the norm throughout the entire organisation, so there needs to be a degree of control and a number of processes which can be applied to critically appraise existing norms and rules without retribution.

YOUR NOTES FROM CHAPTER 8

Chapter 9

Top 10 tips for leadership strategy

By

Mike Nelson

Strategy: at its simplest a high-level plan, designed to drive your organisation towards a new vision or goal. This chapter aims to set out some of the key elements required in setting and executing an effective strategy.

1   Analysis

- Fundamental to reviewing or setting strategy is gathering data about your own organisation and (usually) about the external world (competitors, marketplace, economy etc.). You may employ one or a variety of methods and your own team or external analysts to do this. Vitally you need to satisfy yourself that the data is as accurate and reliable as it can be. Have you also cast the net wide enough to ensure you have all the data you need in order to develop your strategy on a solid foundation.
- There are a variety of analytical methods from using a simple collation service from an online service (such as 'Survey Monkey') through to paying an external consultancy (of varying size/weight/cost) to do this analysis on your behalf. In-house, often used are methodologies such as SWOT analysis (for the 'here and now') or PESTLE (for an eye on the future).
  See Top Tip 6 in Chapter 11

- What will you use as a benchmark to evaluate the current status of your organisation? You may already have a dashboard1 which provides a reliable benchmark or you may need to develop one. It may be time to review benchmarks such as 'Who is the best in the marketplace or environment in which we operate?" or "What would be a real stretch for us?"

2   Strategy

- The very word strategy is probably one of the most widely interpreted also misunderstood words in the entire management/leadership lexicon. For the purposes of this book we set out that a Strategy is a high-level plan, designed to deliver an outcome and/or vision. It will usually be set out over a number of years (typically 3-5 although this duration has been decreasing recently as the instability of the business and global environment can sometimes render strategies impotent overnight).
- Any strategy is effectively powerless unless it is:
  - Aimed at achieving an outcome and or vision
  - Is aligned with the purpose of your organisation
  - Is supportive of organisational values and beliefs

  In other words the strategy must be there to deliver what you desire as an organisation – output, growth, purpose, vision etc.
- The strategy must be clear and unambiguous. It is often too wordy or confused. The best strategies are clear, simple with defined milestones. The overall strategy must be able to be understood or explained to every member of the organisation so they can see the part they play in delivering it.

3   Planning

- The Strategic Plan is the translation of the overall strategy into a set of clearly defined steps that can actually be delivered. It may be most useful to initially break down your strategy into a series of milestones, measurable targets that will make clear progress towards you strategy as each one is delivered.

Each milestone can then have objectives (Specific, Measurable, Achievable, Relevant & Time-constrained or S.M.A.R.T. for short).

- Once you have determined milestones and objectives develop them into a timeline. Look at the flow, what needs to be delivered before what, what is dependent on what so that the timeline ensures the objectives are delivered in the most effective way without duplication of effort and without missing out key stages.
- Execute the plan, review as you go, ensure the deliverables are moving you towards the milestones (if not then do something to get you back on track).

4   Vision

- "You can't discover new lands until you lose sight of the shore." This simple yet powerful quote aims to get to the heart of a true vision for your business. A vision is a descriptive statement of what the future will look like... for your business, your customers, your team. The vision should be simple and anyone in your organisation should be able to see how their work effort will contribute towards that overall goal.
- The best vision statements will inspire and motivate you and your team to want to move towards them. Whilst not an impossible dream the vision should be stretching and not something that can be achieved next week... it will indeed be the foundation of why your business exists – what are you trying to achieve.
- Simplicity is key, too many Vision statements are in fact 'Mission' statements.

- Often quoted, one of the most simple yet effective Vision statements was that of NASA in the 1960's – everyone in the organisation was there to "Put a Man on the Moon" - even the cleaners in NASA knew this and understood how important their part was in achieving this vision.

5   Performance

- Performance of course lies at the heart of delivering the necessary plans, milestones and eventually the strategy which will achieve your vision. On a daily basis it is the things that you and your team will do that will achieve the objectives. Be ruthless in only doing those things that will achieve agreed objectives – the section on time management will help with this – chapter 4 paragraph 6.
- Ensure you create the right environment for you and your team to deliver effective performance. Ensuring your team are motived to perform and avoiding a slave-galley leadership style make sure that your team have the necessary resources, training and support to be effective.
- Measure performance regularly – in the most empowered organisations the individual is accountable for their own performance and can report back in regular reviews progress made and what is getting in their way. It has been said that the true aim of a leader is to remove obstacles to their team's success.

6   Evaluation

- Evaluation is key to fine tuning your plans as they unfold.

- It will help you keep on track and to get a handle on how well you are progressing to your objectives, milestones and ultimately your strategy.
- Evaluate on a regular, rolling basis. As you collect evaluation data always ask the question: What can we learn from this? The question applies equally well to those things that are going well and making progress as well as to those things which are proving to be a barrier. Failure to evaluate can be one of the biggest contributors to failed strategies. Remember it is often at the time when you don't believe you should stop and evaluate is probably the time you most need to do it.
- Act on the evaluation as the lessons become clear from the evaluation then do something about them (once you can see a clear trend or reasons for not being on track).

7   Dashboard

- A so called Dashboard is simply a way of showing clear progress toward your objectives. Just like a car dashboard or an aeroplane instrument readout the dashboard should show the critical measures that will ensure you are always up to date with progress. A good dashboard can often be useful on display in the organisation (or subject to regular circulation) so that all employees can get an idea of how progress is being achieved.
- Ensure your dashboard is accurate – it will simply fail to help if it is out of date or is populated with inaccurate information.
- You may wish to develop two dashboards – one for the whole workforce which shows clear and simple indicators of progress and one for your leadership team where some of the more sensitive (financial

perhaps) measures can be seen by those who have that level of responsibly in your organisation.

8   Data Gathering

- Lead by walking about... you can have all the spreadsheets and other data sources in the world but the best leaders regularly walk about their organisation. Talk to employees, customers, stakeholders as an enquiry. Don't react (unless of course you see something downright dangerous or in need of immediate attention). Bring back your observations – what do they tell you about what is really going on in your organisation in terms of the culture, motivation and effort to delivery your strategy and vision. If things are wrong how will you tackle these to get the delivery back on track?

- Surveys are useful and can be easy to implement to get a wide sample of opinions from employees and/or customers. There are some excellent websites (such as Survey Monkey) where it is relatively easy to set up and conduct a survey within your organisation.

- As you gather data and start to form conclusions, ask yourself: "What is this REALLY telling me?" Symptoms are one thing but the root cause can be something else entirely so before you apply course corrections do the best you can to establish that it will fix the real, underlying problem.

9   Balanced Scorecard

- A balanced scorecard is a method of refining your dashboard to ensure you are really measuring the right things in your organisation. It can link to your internal dashboard and is a very useful tool in the periodic reviews of strategy.

- A good scorecard will have the balance of hard and soft measures and look at both internal and external viewpoints. Essential is to have customer or stakeholder measures.

- Don't forget to ensure that the scorecard is linked to the delivery of strategy, vision and purpose of your organisation.

10   Delivery

- There is a story attributed to the CEO of Clarks Shoes. Anyone entering his office with an idea had to answer the question "Does it sell shoes?" The idea being to challenge spurious activity, procrastination and anything else trying to throw delivery off track.
- Deliver some yourself- let your team/employees see you making some of the effort yourself. It doesn't have to take up much of your working month but leaders who visibly demonstrate their ability to get their sleeves rolled up and contribute can make a real difference to the internal motivation in their organisation.
- Share achievements–relentlessly. After talk in previous sections of evaluation and course correction, do make sure you share and celebrate progress and achievements. Never cease to do this is it provides a lot of positive drive and energy as well as creating a belief in the organisation that you can achieve even the seemingly impossible.

YOUR NOTES FROM CHAPTER 9

Chapter 10

Top 10 tips for Leadership Intelligence

By

Ian Munro

An awareness about the various types of intelligence and how they interact is essential for any leader, as you will find out in this chapter. Academics wax lyrical on this topic as I found when researching this content. I have tried to save the reader from the purist theories and present a more pragmatic hands-on description of what is for all readers an important understanding.

1   Recognising the three types of Intelligence

- Intelligence Quotient – IQ – the traditional test many of us took at school.
- Emotional Intelligence – EQ – been on the scene since Daniel Golman penned the term in a book in 1995.
- Social Intelligence – SI - Increasingly the theorists believed there to be a gap in IQ and EQ in areas such as understanding social situations, relationships etc.

2   IQ

- This is the traditional way of measuring intelligence and it has been generally accepted as a measurement of individual intelligence.
- Generally a higher number of IQ was determined as identifying someone who would make a good leader as they made good decisions and would therefore lead an organisation to success.
- Business leaders and business schools recognised that there were other factors too which led to the eventual emergence of EQ.

3   EQ

- In 1995 Daniel Golman wrote his book "Emotional Intelligence "and so a new term and area of intelligence was created.
- The main components are; self-awareness, self-regulation, motivation, empathy and social skill
- You can see that from a perspective of using the traditional IQ this brought a whole new range of factors into play into what made for a successful leader.
- The wider understanding and debate about what made for a great leader was further added to in 2002 with the emergence of Social Intelligence.

4   SI

- Whilst Social skills is seen as a part of EQ, it was more on the periphery and in reality SI plays a major part in leadership.
- The water gets slightly muddy here as some call this Social Intelligence and others talk about "CQ" – Character Quotient.
- CQ and SI are to me entwined. David Town – a US facilitator and coach of leadership and management principles states that CQ represents the strength of your character.
- Others believe that SI was always there but not recognised for the major part it plays in leadership.

5   What are the implications from 2, 3, and 4 above?

- Recent research on the approach by leading organisations shows that their top talent assessment programmes cover all three mentioned above – by inference to be seen as part of the top talent team, you need to have a good understanding of all three.
- Those of us who are leaders – including my co-authors in this book – have always accepted that leaders are a blend of not just cognitive intelligence (IQ), but a wider range of people and functional skills, competencies and personal qualities.
- Others have written that IQ is innate and cannot be increased (Ronald Riggio). However both emotional and social intelligence skills can be developed, implying there might be some development and assessment work needed by all current leaders.

6   Developing an understanding of Leadership Intelligence in your team

- It is an accepted feature that the behaviours and style of good leaders are often copied by others.
- The skills, competencies and personal qualities that make for a good leader requires a level of self-awareness that leaders do not always understand.
- Leaders should be self-aware and also prepared to communicate why they are good leaders to their team members.
- Part of the role of a leader is to develop others which is made more difficult if the leader is not adequately self-aware.

7   Using Leadership Intelligence with leaders who directly report to you

- As mentioned above, many leaders have teams of leaders reporting to them. It is not enough for the leader to just lead. They should see part of their responsibility is to help other leaders develop into better leaders.
- This means developing or adopting assessment methods that crystallise other leaders in the three key assessment areas IQ, EQ and SI.
- Ownership of these tools may rest with the Talent Management Team within the Human Resources department in larger organisations. It would be expected that they would help in assessment areas.
- Smaller organisations still need to develop leaders and help from third party assessment organisations may be needed to ensure the longer term development of future leaders.

8   Using Leadership Intelligence in Matrix structures

- Matrix organisations are a fact of life in almost every large organisation.
- As a leader you are likely to have others reporting to you by a dotted line and how do these people in turn become effective leaders?
- Most of the organisations we work with who face this situation rely on the outputs, style and approach of their leaders to lead by example.

- A number of our clients face real challenges in the matrix where performance can reduce because of leadership challenges/focus elsewhere.
- This is where the real leader emerges where by example they can raise the standards. However it often takes a decision at a higher level to have an across the board development programme for better leaders. Given the sheer number of matrix operations in organisations today there is a real need to see emerging leader programmes.

9   Upward leadership

- There is a natural tendency to see leaders either operating within peer groups, in teams or a matrix.
- All of these are at two levels – peers and those less senior - but the successful leader has to lead upwards too. This can be the most challenging because the leader in this situation is unlikely to be the most senior.
- Successful upwards relationships is a necessary step for anyone at any level in an organisation's structure, but leaders in particular have this as a prime area of responsibility.
- Given the example in 8 above of the risks to matrix based organisation of not developing leaders because of how the matrix works shows how essential it is for leaders to upwardly lead as well as manage.

10   Summarising your next steps

- Leaders may need to quantify how they measure up in the three main headings; IQ, EQ, SI.

- Whilst there will be little they can do under IQ there are lots of self-awareness issues they can consider under the other 2.
- Looking at your role and the organisation identify what development work could you be doing as leader under the areas of; those at a higher level that you, peer groups, those at a lower level.
- Develop an assessment model to track these steps against target achievement dates.

  See Top Tips 1 and 2 in Chapter 11

YOUR NOTES FROM CHAPTER 10

Chapter 11

Top 10 tips for Documenting Progress and Tools to help you on the way

By

Ian Munro

A challenge that comes with leadership is "how do you document and control the process?"

In our Coaching and Leadership Development work, many leaders have challenges because they do not have a process to help them manage key leadership areas – or they have one that they do not use!

Having process allows you to bring some black and white evidence about how you are - or are not progressing.

As practitioners and leaders, we use the straight forward tools and models below to help keep us on track. Some of these tools were created for and by a number of the leaders we have coached over the years. Some which are excellent are the work of other authors.

Where these tools feature in a specific chapter you will see that chapter number shown below. Where no chapter is shown that topic is raised several times in the book

1   **Core leadership objectives – Chapter 10**

2   **Monthly/Quarterly Action Plans – Chapter 10**

3   **The 5 dysfunctions of a team – Chapter 6**

4   **The Leadership Challenge**

5   **Learning Styles – Chapter 7**

6   **SWOT and PESTILE Analysis – Chapter9**

7   **The Kirkpatrick Evaluation Model – Chapter 2**

8   **Impact of Stress on Performance – Chapter 4**

9   **Johari Window – Chapter 5**

10   **Putting First Things First – Chapter 4**

1   Core Leadership Objectives:

Your leadership strategy is probably in place but is undocumented.

If you have not set yourself some core leadership objectives, you run the risk of being a rudderless ship responding to the demands and needs of others. By setting some core objectives you will feel much more focussed as you progress. You will also gain satisfaction from achieving your objectives from time to time.

Here are some of the topics based on this books chapters you may need to address and a selection of objectives. It is important though that you see this process as getting control of YOUR leadership.

Topics	Objectives
Leading a Learning Organisation	What are my perceived challenges?
Developing Effective Communication	Putting structure and behaviours in place
Developing Resilience	What are my learning tasks
Developing Leadership characteristics	Identify my strength and weaknesses here
Team Leadership	Listing key requirements
Leading self	Steps needed to lead self
Leadership Dilemmas	Identify any that apply to me
Strategy	Creating my strategic plans
Leadership Intelligence	Plan to gather information
Documenting your progress	Set up and update monthly

Based on these ideas, complete your Core Leadership Objectives.

No:	Objective	Review date
1		
2		
3		
4		
5		
6		
7		
8		
9		
10		

Note: If you go to www.100toptips.com and register as a user, you can freely download a blank of this form

2   Monthly/Quarterly Action Plans

This tool allows you to create either monthly or quarterly
Action Plans
The aim is that in each period you progress up to six of
your Key Objectives.

This does that mean that you will completely achieve the
objective, certainly you should see advancement by the
end of the monthly or quarterly period.

Having set the objectives you now set the tasks you will
work on to advance the objective. The document provides
space for four tasks, you might only have one or even six
– it is up to you.

You are now set up and as the month or quarter advances,
you will begin to see outcomes which should be recorded.

At the end of the period you may wish to add some notes
and then the cycle starts again for the next period.

In this next period you might wish to continue to work on
specific objectives or replace them with other ones from
your objectives list.

QUARTERLY ACTION PLAN

Quarter ___ /Year ___

List your key objectives for the current quarter, followed by the tasks for each objective. As the quarter progresses complete the outcome box. Start the process again at the following quarter.

OBJECTIVE	TASKS FOR QUARTER	OUTCOME	NOTES
1.	1.1 1.2 1.3 1.4	1.1 1.2 1.3 1.4	
2	2.1 2.2 2.3 2.4	2.1 2.2 2.3 2.4	
3	3.1 3.2 3.3 3.4	3.1 3.2 3.3 3.4	
4	4.1 4.2 4.3 4.4	4.1 4.2 4.3 4.4	
5	5.1 5.2 5.3 5.4	5.1 5.2 5.3 5.4	
6	6.1 6.2 6.3 6.4	6.1 6.2 6.3 6.4	

© Transformational Coaches Limited 2013 onwards

Note: If you go to www.100toptips.com and register as a user, you can freely download a blank of this form

3   The 5 dysfunctions of a team.

In chapter 6 we described the profile of a successful team – in his book *"The 5 Dysfunctions of teams"*, Patrick Lencioni outlines 5 key elements which often de-rail effective teams –

1. **Absence of trust** – trust and vulnerability needs to exist in a team to enable them to move forward. When defensiveness and invulnerability persist, team members will spend more time watching their back than focussing on the key issues.

2. **Fear of conflict and challenge** – when trust is missing within teams they will be cautious and as such will tend to avoid situations where they will enter free, unrestricted debate around key issues. False harmony will persist and they will rarely get around the table to tackle the difficult issues.

3. **Lack of commitment** – even when teams disagree over key issues, they will at some stage need to focus and move on. If this stage has not been successfully achieved, they will never reach the stage where they are clear about their priorities and ambiguity will arise within their organisations.

4. **Avoidance of accountability** – Once a team is clearly committed to its primary objective, a climate must exist, where they are willing to be held accountable to each other for the achievement of that objective. In this way teams develop a self - propelled momentum, and don't need to rely on a leader constantly pressing them for performance.

5. **Inattention to results** – Teams which achieve success in the 4 stages outlined above, are very likely to set aside their individual agendas and focus on what is best for the team. They do not give in to the temptation of ego driven status and internal politics.

ACTIONS FROM THE ABOVE

Action	Date achieved
Reading the book	
Assessing my own team	
Team development action plan	
Key objectives set for team	
Mid- term outcomes	

4   The Leadership Challenge

Throughout the book we refer many times to personal development in the context of leadership, together with the need for self-awareness and self-development.

In their series of books based on their original text "The Leadership Challenge" Jim Kouzes and Barry Posner describe 5 key practices of exemplary leaders. Around these practices they have developed a 360 degree Leadership Practice Inventory which provides a useful tool with which aspiring leaders can assess their own leadership capability, and receive feedback on the same from colleagues, managers and reports.

The Five practices are as follows:

Model The Way – Leaders need to find their voice by clarifying their personal values, they then need to align their actions with these values and demonstrate authenticity.

Inspire a Shared Vision – It is important for leaders to provide a clear vision of how they see the future, and enlist others in that vision by establishing shared aspirations.

Challenge the Process – Good leaders rarely accept the status quo. They search for new opportunities via innovation, experimentation and calculated risk. They learn from their mistakes.

Enable Others to Act – Leadership is about collaboration and building trust. Strong leaders develop strength in others by sharing power and discretion.

Encourage the Heart – It is crucial for leaders to spend time recognising the contribution of others by showing appreciation for excellence and outstanding performance. This creates a spirit of community and success which goes on to foster even greater success.

Action	Date achieved
Reading the book	
Taking the 360 LPI	
Setting a personal development plan	
Administering the 360 for others in the organisation.	
Mid- term outcomes	

5   Learning Styles

Various references are made by us in the Top Tips to Honey and Mumford's "Learning Styles"(featured in chapter 7 for example).

In his work on learning styles, Peter Honey describes a combination of 4 essential components which we all use to a greater or lesser extent when we learn and develop.

He has also developed a comprehensive questionnaire which enables individuals to assess their preferred learning style, make appropriate development plans for learning in a way which will benefit them most. It also provides insight into the learning styles of others enabling employers to agree effective learning and development plans for their staff.

The learning styles are described thus:

Activists – like to take action. They are enthusiastic and welcome challenge. They are less interested in the past or the broader context, living very much in the here and now. They think on their feet and learn best by participating, having fun and trying new things.

Reflectors – think about things in detail before they act. They are thoughtful, good listeners and tend to take a low profile. They listen, observe, evaluate and learn best when given time to consider, assimilate and prepare.

Theorists – like to see how things fit into an overall pattern, they are logical, objective and take a sequential approach to solving problems.

They like concepts and models and learn best by having the opportunity to ask questions, having clear objectives and a structured plan.

Pragmatists – like to see how things work in reality. They enjoy experimentation, new ideas and are very down to earth and practical. They like to see the relevance of their work and the practical application of their learning. They learn best when there is ample opportunity to practice and experiment. They love tips and techniques and how learning will benefit immediate performance.

Action	Date achieved
Assessed my own learning style	
Drawn up a personal learning and development plan	
Assessed my teams members learning styles	
Drawn up an L and D plan for the team	
Mid- term outcomes	

6   SWOT AND PESTLE ANALYSIS

SWOT ANALYSIS

Swot analysis is such an everyday tool that we need not go into too much detail here. However for readers who need some clarity it is a four box matrix used to analyse the today situation of a brand, service or organisation as shown below;

Strength	Weakness
Opportunity	Threat

It is used to often clarify choice and options and provides a discussion point with teams at all levels

PESTLE ANALYSIS

Many organisations around the world use Pestle Analysis as a tool to assess current products and/or services. This is an in depth analysis that considers all aspects under the headings below from the current situation to projections years ahead.

It brings an awareness of getting strategy and planning right in the first place closely followed by market trends and risk analysis. Sometimes a point has been reached in the products/services performance where a major review is necessary. This is one of the tools used by the biggest and the best organisations:

- Political

- Economic

- Social

- Technological

- Legal

- Ecological (or Environmental)

Given the importance of strategy in your leadership role, we suggest that you take either a product or service from your existing work and conduct a PESTLE analysis.

7   Kirkpatrick Evaluation Model

In chapter 2 we had a look at Evaluation as part of the learning process. It must be said that effective evaluation of learning can be considered something of a Holy Grail sought after as part of the learning strategy in an organisation but often is not or carried through to the conclusion. Millions of pounds are invested in learning but what is the return? Remember at this juncture not just to include the input costs of development solutions (course design, materials, tutor, venues, software, handouts etc.) but there is also a considerable cost in the time that employees spend in this type of activity – each hour spent could be regarded as 'unproductive' unless of course you can justify the return on the total investment.

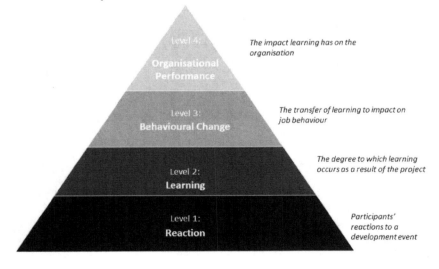

Kirkpatrick Evaluation Model

Very often a programme (especially away day types of delivery) is accompanied by the inevitable "Happy Sheet" which is to be filled in before the delegates depart. Often as much focus is placed upon the quality of the food and drink on offer and the 'trainer' getting rated on a 1-10 scale or similar. Space for comments are included but even with some qualitative evaluation how often is this collated into something meaningful. Finally, on the day evaluation fails to consider any reflection or application of learning on the job after the event so missed the real value (and therefore ROI).

The Kirkpatrick evaluation model provides a framework to evaluate learning interventions at a variety of levels from participant's reactions to a development event (i.e. 'Happy Sheets') through the impact of the learning on the individual, how they have applied that to their role and ultimately the impact of the learning intervention of organisational performance. The following table sets out how you might do this:

Kirkpatrick Level	Suggested Activity
Level 1 - Reaction	Use a method of capturing the reactions of the delegates during the intervention. A 'scribble pad' during a programme day, or short notes sections or 'tests' in e-learning. Questions such as "What's worked well in this training?" "What could be improved?" As a link into Level 2 asking "What will you do differently because of this training?" or "How will you apply this learning?" will start a reflection process that can be captured sometime

	after the learning intervention.
Level 2 - Learning	Often best captured at a short interval after the intervention. Telephone survey, email forms or surveys (such as 'Survey Monkey') are different methods. Questions such as "What have you learned?" How are you now working differently?" What further questions do you have?" are all aimed at getting the individual to think about what they have learned and how they are applying it as well as providing data for you as Leader to see what learning had taken place.
Level 3 – Behavioural Change	Telephone surveys or focus groups are probably better here because of the interaction in asking individuals how they have changed because of the intervention. "What are they now doing differently?" "How are they applying the learning?" are typical questions you can ask.
Level 4 – Organisational Performance	This is where you truly evaluate the ROI. It must be linked to why the training was planned in the first place – what were you looking to achieve by doing this. Use all the data

	collected as a result of evaluating at levels 1-3. Ask line managers what has changed, how is the work area different, how well have the initial aims of the intervention been met.

8   The Impact of Stress on Performance

The impact of stress on performance

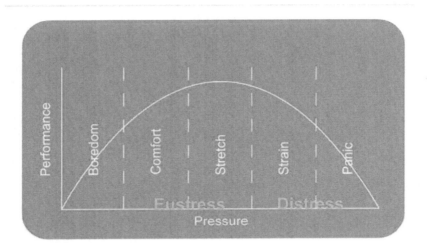

In Chapter 4 we looked at how being resilient can improve your effectiveness as a leader. One of the fundamental parts to this is to look at how we are all affected by pressure of varying levels. The chart shows in general terms how increasing levels of pressure to perform or get things done can at first improve our performance before we reach a zenith following which performance tends to fall away as the increasing pressure causes 'Distress' rather than having 'Good stress' and whilst not shown on the chart there comes an increasing risk of mental burnout or even break down.

Make a list of all the things that are putting pressure on you now.

How are you currently dealing with these (if indeed you are at all?)

What could you do differently? For example, how are you thinking about this pressure point? Is it as bad as you really think it is? Could you delegate, break it down into smaller steps or simply not do it at all (what would happen if you don't do this)?

How well are you looking after yourself – there is much evidence to suggest that eating more healthily, drinking less and keeping fit all help to make you more resistant to the effects of Adrenaline and Cortisone – the two hormones most closely involved with our body's response to pressure.

Talk to someone – coach, mentor, trusted advisor, spouse, friend – if the latter ask them not to try to 'fix' the problem but to listen and ask you some questions to help clear your thinking.

9 JOHARI WINDOW

Chapter 5 covers the requirement for successful leaders to possess "Leadership Character". This is an abstract concept which, with difficulty needs some definition. A large part of this concept relates to the need for better self-awareness and a willingness to pursue personal development.

One tool which has been used extensively for this purpose is the Johari window. Developed at UCLA by (Harry) Ingham and (Joe) Luft this is a 4 quadrant model which describes various areas of awareness within our psychology.

Johari Window

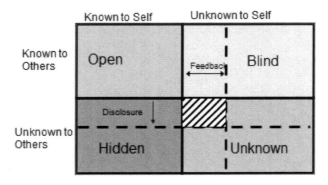

Source Luft and Ingham (1955)

The Open Quadrant relates to that part of our psychology which is known to ourselves and to others around us, it is the transparent element which we are happy to share.

The Blind Quadrant relates to that part of us which is known by others but not to ourselves, it is the naive part of our psychology which can often disadvantage us as we are acting unawares of the reactions and interpretations of others. The purpose behind the model is to encourage willingness to seek feedback and appraisal in order to strengthen and improve this area, thus enhancing our self-awareness.

The Hidden Quadrant describes the part of us which we wish to keep hidden from others. Whilst there will always be a part of us which remains secret, the construct of the model encourages us to develop deeper and more meaningful relationships by sharing and disclosure. When developed at the same time as the blind quadrant, this is seen to reflect a more assertive and rounded character, essential to successful leadership.

The Unknown Quadrant represents that part of us which is unknown to us and others – possibly inherited characteristics which are naturally part of our personality from our genetics and upbringing. Whilst this can be affected positively by feedback, development in this area is a much bigger challenge than the other 3 quadrants. Questionnaires are widely available to facilitate some of these processes seeking both positive and negative feedback from close colleagues and associates.

See exercise on next page.

Action	Date achieved
Researching the model further	
Use of questionnaire to gain feedback – 5 colleagues.	
Personal development action plan	
Key objectives from questionnaire	
Mid- term outcomes	

10 PUTTING FIRST THINGS FIRST

In 1992, Stephen Covey's book – The 7 Habits of Highly Effective People, created a significant shift in many of the paradigms which had dominated leadership theory for many years. There are many aspects of his work which could be related to the top tips we have outlined in this book, however, our emphasis in Chapter 4 on the current roll of stress and anxiety in leadership is particularly pertinent.

Covey outlined a 4 quadrant model which attempted to enable us to focus on issues which truly impacted on our roles as leaders, and not the usual "white noise" which surrounds our modern day roles.

Model of Prioritisation

	Urgent	Not Urgent
Important		
Not Important		

Covey, (1992)

Coveys stresses the fact that most of us spend our time being deflected into the "Urgent / Important" quadrant.

This causes us to be reactive, pressured and ineffective as we spend our time firefighting.

He encourages strong leaders to push back against this, particularly if the urgency is determined by the agendas of others and focus more on the "Non urgent / important" quadrant which is where the transformational shifts in leadership tend to occur. This area is all about planning, strategy, vision and self-development. He argues that the current high pressure environment in which we operate, encourages too much Q1 activity and far too little Q2. Quadrant 3 activity is highlighted as the place to begin, cutting out activity which is seen by organisations as "urgent" but are of little importance in the great scheme of things. For those of us with management experience, it does not take much imagination to recognise these tasks. Covey encourages us to review our regular activities in all the roles we undertake and categorise them in the context of the model. This then enables us to carry out an objective audit of our activities and start making a shift towards Q2 where the real quality resides.

Action	Date achieved
Researching the model further	
Carrying out a 4 quadrant audit	
Identifying unnecessary time consuming behaviours.	
Developing a personal action plan	
Mid- term outcomes	

Summary

We hope that you will have found this book of real benefit.

As stated in the Introduction we have tried to make this a clear guide about how to become an effective leader in plain English with pragmatic tips.

Feedback from readers helps us to further fine tune our material, so please keep the emails coming.

Our best wishes to you all.

Charles **Mike** **Ian**

Please email us your comments to:

leadership@100toptips.com

About the Authors

Mike Nelson is an organisation consultant with specific expertise in leadership development. With 10 years in UK Healthcare followed by 15 years in a national UK retailer Mike has consistently put his leadership expertise into practice. Mike is now in his 12th Year as an independent Organisational Consultant.

Charles Marshall has put his leadership expertise to practice in management roles in the commercial Pharmaceutical sector and the NHS. With over twenty years' track record as a senior business manager and director, leadership development has played a key role in his ongoing work. He has run leadership development programmes at all levels in organisations

Ian Munro has worked at board level for over 20 years as an operating and main board director, as a non-executive director and as a consultant, coach and mentor. He works in the private and public sectors. An ongoing feature of his work is improving leadership performance across all levels in organisations. Today he continues to hold several directorships

****

Some of the other books we mention

7 Habits of Highly Effective People – Steven Covey – Simon & Shuster 1992

Myers-Briggs Foundation – MBTI

Firo B Shutz W.C. and Firo A 3 Dimensional Theory of Interpersonal Behaviour

Leadership Practices Inventory – B Posner & Kouzes – Pfeiffer 2003

Johari Window – A Graphic Model of Interpersonal Awareness- Luft & Ingham – UCLA

The 5 Dysfunctions of a Team – Patrick Lencioni – Jossey/Bass – 2002

Putting Learning Styles to work – Alan Mumford – Action Learning at work – Gower - 1997

Emotional Intelligence – D Goleman – Bloomsbury - 1996

Insights Discovery System

Belbin.M – Management Teams – Heinmann – 1981

The one minute Manager – Blanchard & Johnson – Fontana/Collins – 1983

THIS FINAL PAGE IS FOR YOUR LAST NOTES!

Here is a final tip. If you lend this book to someone, put their name and the date you lent it on this page. This may improve your chances of getting it back!

The Insiders'
to UK Medical
Schools 2005/2006

The Alternative Prospectus compiled by the BMA Medical Students Committee

Edited by

**Joanna Burgess,
Sally Girgis and
Karen Hebert**

Published by Blackwell Publishing Ltd
Blackwell Publishing, Inc., 350 Main Street, Malden, Massachusetts 02148–5020, USA
Blackwell Publishing Ltd, 9600 Garsington Road, Oxford OX4 2DQ, UK
Blackwell Publishing Asia Pty Ltd, 550 Swanston Street, Carlton, Victoria 3053, Australia

First published 1998
Second edition 1999
Third edition 2000
Fourth edition 2001
Fifth edition 2002
Second impression 2002
Sixth edition 2003
Seventh edition 2004
Eighth edition 2005
Reprinted 2006 (twice)

Catalogue records for this title are available from the British Library and the Library of Congress

ISBN-13: 978-1-405131-04-9
ISBN-10: 1-405131-04-7

A catalogue record for this title is available from the British Library

Set in 9/11 pt Helvetica Light by Sparks, Oxford – www.sparks.co.uk
Printed and bound in Great Britain by TJ International Ltd, Padstow, Cornwall

Commissioning Editor: Mary Banks
Development Editor: Veronica Pock
Production Controller: Debbie Wyer

Cartoons © Clive Featherstone
For further information on Blackwell Publishing, visit our website:
http://www.blackwellpublishing.com

Contents

Foreword   vii

Preface   ix

Acknowledgements
and contributors   xi

Meet Mikey and Michelle   xiii

Part 1: Insiders' information   1

    1.   Is medicine for you?   3
    2.   Life as a medical student   6
    3.   Applying to medical school   19
    4.   Graduate and premedical courses   30
    5.   Funding your way through   35
    6.   Life beyond graduation …   43

Part 2: The A–Z of UK medical schools   49

How to use Part 2

    Aberdeen   53
    Bart's and The London   61
    Belfast   70
    Birmingham   77
    Brighton and Sussex Medical School   85
    Bristol   95
    Cambridge   102
    Derby   113
    Dundee   119
    East Anglia   128
    Edinburgh   138

Glasgow	145
Guy's, King's and St Thomas'	152
Hull York Medical School	160
Imperial College London	168
Leeds	176
Leicester	183
Liverpool	191
Manchester, Keele and Preston	198
Newcastle and Durham (Queen's Campus, Stockton)	210
Nottingham	221
Oxford	228
Peninsula	237
Royal Free and University College London	245
St Andrews	254
St George's	261
Sheffield	269
Southampton	277
Wales College of Medicine	283
Warwick	290
Appendices	297
Mikey & Michelle's quick compare table	298
Glossary	301
Further information	304

Joanna Burgess is in her fourth year of medicine at the University of Leicester. She is known to have an extensive shoe collection, attributing any exam success to her exceptionally high heeled pointy ones!

Sally Girgis is Secretary of the Medical Students Committee at the British Medical Association. She is an Australian living in London.

Karen Hebert is a fourth-year medical student at the University of Bristol. Having lived in South Africa until the age of seventeen, her friends still tease her about the way she says 'black.'

Foreword

'A doctor's mission should not just be about preventing death but also improving quality of life. That's why you treat a disease, you win, you lose. You treat a person, I guarantee you – you win, no matter what the outcome.'

Patch Adams

As well as representing medical students in the UK I am a third-year student at UEA Medical School in Norwich. As you read this foreword, think of me travelling home from my GP placement in Kesgrave feeling absolutely exhausted. I am trying to put myself in your shoes as you consider your future within medicine, and I know how nervous, determined and excited you must be as you think about your potential career as a doctor.

Medicine can offer you so much opportunity. Today in clinical practice I met a young girl who had a hole in one of the chambers of her heart. This intelligent 4-year-old secretly pointed to her heart and winked at me to ensure that my poor knowledge of anatomy was not made apparent to my teachers and colleagues. The same day I met an elderly lady with an overactive thyroid and a gentleman who had developed Parkinson's, a condition in which the brain has a deficiency of dopamine. Medicine is a vocation that will offer you fresh challenges every day, and 40 years down the line you will still be challenged by the job you undertake. What other profession will equip you with the skills to work in any continent on the planet? What other vocation will give you the skills to impact lives of people in such a huge way? What other job gives you the opportunity to laugh and cry with patients and their families?

Life at medical school also offers you many extracurricular opportunities: sport, politics, religion, parties, and a chance to really challenge and develop your personal beliefs. You should of course spend time deeply enthralled in your medical books during your degree, but do drag yourself away every so often to harass people to join the bone marrow register, fight for students from poorer socio-economic backgrounds, get involved in the university orchestra or even argue with your philosophy flatmates till 3 AM about the meaning of life and love.

A degree in medicine will equip you to be more than a practising doctor: it will equip you with skills that can be applied to journalism, teaching or management and, at some point in your career, you are likely to call upon these life skills to effect change, whether in the local community or at a national level.

This is the second opportunity I have had to write the foreword for this book and I must encourage you to read it thoroughly. Karen, Sally and Jo have worked extremely hard to contact national representatives and admissions offices, and put together pertinent information about medical schools in the UK. Use this book to get the students' perspective of their own medical schools. The information gathered highlights the great, the bad and the interesting features of each UK medical school. If you are still pondering over which schools offer the teaching methods, extracurricular activities or night life that is most suited to you, this book may make the decision much easier.

Gaining access to medical school is perhaps one of the most challenging things you will do, however, it is a worthwhile and stimulating career that offers so many great prospects. On behalf of the British Medical Association and the Medical Students Committee may I wish you the very best of luck with your application.

Leigh Bissett
Chair
BMA Medical Students Committee

Preface

'To study the phenomenon of disease without books is to sail an uncharted sea, while to study books without patients is not to go to sea at all.'

Sir William Osler

'You never really understand a man until you consider things from his point of view.'

Harper Lee

Different types of people will apply to medical school. There are those that are pushed into doing so by their families, teachers or schools. There are those that do so because they don't know what else to study; and those that do so because they think that medicine will bring them status, influence and money. Then of course there are the majority of students who apply because they truly feel a pull to become a doctor. Many of us have spent many years – if not most of our lives – aspiring to become a doctor, and so applying to medical school is the defining moment in our careers and lives.

Medical school isn't easy. You will be studying full time for at least 4 years, you will be expected to work out of hours and travel a fair amount. You will be given heavy workloads, and put under a lot of pressure as well as financial burden. As a doctor you will be stressed and tired, working long hours, still having to sit numerous exams, and trying to do your best for patients. From the moment you step into medical school you will always be competing with your colleagues. For this reason it is essential that you are absolutely certain that you want to be a doctor – really think about it and be sure the decision is your own.

It is now well recognised that medicine is not merely the ability to diagnose and prescribe; the 'art' of medicine is at the heart of the diversity of the profession. Look inside any hospital or medical school and the vast spectrum of individuals will be apparent. The heart of the medical profession however is in its ability to unite around a common passion – the patient. It is wonderful, both as a student and a doctor, to feel you are making a real difference in being a part of people's lives for that short time. When they don't need you any more it is a good feeling – in a positive way!

Most doctors agree that medicine is still largely a vocation. Thankfully there is now a modern age of medicine which means that as doctors we will be working more humane hours and be able to enjoy our families, other interests and simply a full life outside of medicine. However medicine is not easy and all of us will have difficult phases – and it is then that our true vocation keeps us motivated.

You are applying at a time when medical student places are maximal and there is a wide selection of medical schools to choose from. The medical schools differ vastly – in terms of class size, location, teaching methods, curriculum, patient contact, research and travel opportunities, and more. You also need to consider your own personality, individuality and other interests and make sure that the university and city that you apply to will suit you. Through this book we hope to equip you with the knowledge that you need to make informed decisions about medical schools. We feel that this book is invaluable – it is written by current medical students, which means you truly are getting an 'insider's guide.'

You will be spending many years at medical school. In addition, the majority of students will remain in the area of their medical school to work as a doctor – even if only for a number of years. So this decision is important – take your time, read our book, read the prospectuses, go to open days – make sure you choose the right medical school for you!

Choose wisely, good luck with your studies, have fun, enjoy life and medicine and most importantly always remain true to yourself.

With best wishes for the future,

Joanna Burgess, Sally Girgis and Karen Hebert

Acknowledgements and contributors

We would like to thank all the many individuals and institutions that have provided the information and views contained in this book. It would not have been possible without their help. We would also like to thank the numerous BMA and BMJ staff that have contributed at various stages in the preparation of this book. Their support and efforts on our behalf have been invaluable and are very much appreciated. In particular we would like to extend our warmest thanks to Paul Gadsby (admissions office liaison), who has worked tirelessly on the book despite very busy schedules.

The need for an *Insiders' Guide* and the vision for its production were first dreamt up many years ago by members of the medical students committee who have long since graduated and are busy working as doctors. Each edition has built upon the hard work and ideas of the editions that have preceded it and to these past pioneers and editors we are extremely grateful. Finally we would like to thank all the members of the BMA's Medical Students Committee, both past and present, who have contributed to the *Insiders' Guide*. We believe it is a fantastic resource and we hope it will continue to go from strength to strength in the years to come.

If you have any suggestions for ways in which the *Insiders' Guide* could be improved we would very much like to hear them. Please email: students@bma.org.uk.

Past editors:
Alex Almourdaris, Simon Calvert, Jennie Ciechan, Deborah Cohen, Lizz Corps, Chris Ferguson, Kristian Mears, Richard Partridge, Kinesh Patel, Philip Smith, Jill Spencer and Ian Urmston

Specialist area contributors to the 2005/2006 edition:
Beverley Almeida, Dan Gibbons, Ian Harwood, Jane Margetts, Parampal Tung and Paul Sutton

Student contributors in the 2005/2006 edition:
Jennifer Affleck, Zubir Ahmed, Ian Anderson, Laura Armstrong, Mohammed Atcha, Harnaik Bajwa, Lucy-Jane Davis, Fiona Beaumont, David Burke, Matthew Carey, Tim Cooksely, Adam Cox, Steven Cull, Andy Currie, David Dean, Mary Docherty, Rick Gosh, Rhydian Harris, Mhairi Hepburn, Janice Jenkinson, Steve Kinnear, Sarah Khan, Craig Knott, Liv Knutzen, Kathryn Lang, Kirsty Lloyd, Alexander Hamilton, David McConnell, Dave Miranda, Shirley Moore, Jerry Raju, Alastair Richards, Emily Rigby, Imran Sajid, Francis Sansbury, Jessie Sohal, Robert Stellman, Abul Siddiky, Phillip Spreadborough, Sabrina Talukdar, Krishna Vakharia, Johann Malawana, Kitty Mohan, David Utting, James Watson, Rebecca Wells, Deborah White, Chris Wincup, Edward Yates

Cartoons created by:
Clive Featherstone

Editorial assistance:
Paul Gadsby and Claire Martin

With apologies to any contributors we may accidentally have missed out

Joanna's personal acknowledgements:
To my family and friends for their love and support over the years, without which I would not be following my dream. Also to Christina, Tim, Becky and Christine for their patience and help amidst my chaos! My thanks go to you all.

Karen's personal acknowledgements:
To my mother, who is my true rock and who has enabled me to attain my dreams … and to Andy, for his love. I love you both very much.

Meet Mikey and Michelle

Hi, we're Mikey and Michelle.

We're here to give you the inside information on life as a medical student and a career in medicine. To help guide you through the information in this book, it is split into two parts:

Part 1 contains insiders' information designed to help you decide whether medicine is the right choice for you, how to choose the right medical school, how to apply, and information on other important considerations such as managing your finances and dealing with hurdles.

Part 2 gives valuable information and views about every medical school in the UK written by students at that medical school. Each medical school entry has been divided for ease into three categories: Education, Welfare, and Sports and Social. Students have also provided insight into the 'great' and 'bad' things about each school.

To make flicking through easier, the following symbols will appear throughout the book:

 Education

 Welfare

 Sports and social

 Great things about the medical school

 Bad things about the medical school

Now, it won't surprise you that student life differs radically from one university to the next. What may surprise you is that each medical school offers a course which is to some extent unique. Medics, more than anyone else, can give you the low-down on the distinguishing features you may want to consider. However, it is best to also make use of the other resources available, such as the university prospectuses and open day visits.

REMEMBER:

☑ Read the medical school/university prospectus.
☑ Read the alternative prospectus.
☑ Visit the medical school (some have open days) and the town or city.
☑ Talk to students studying at the medical school.
☑ Visit the medical school website.

GOOD LUCK!

A book like this could never claim to be totally objective or definitive about all the differences and similarities, or strengths and weaknesses between the medical schools. Every effort has been made to ensure that the opinions of the medical students who contributed to the book are based on factual information. Take the opinions offered here into account and we strongly recommend this book alongside other material you will have collected (for prospectuses or the opinions of others) as you draw up your shortlist of where to apply.

Part 1
Insiders' information

Is medicine for you?

'Some patients, though conscious that their condition is perilous, recover their health simply through their contentment with the goodness of the physician.'

Hippocrates (460–400 BC)

Ask the average student why they are applying to study medicine and they'll probably tell you it's because they enjoy science and want to help people. Probe a little deeper and they may mention ideas such as money, and the fact that they are expected to get good A-level grades. Medicine may even command a certain amount of kudos and possibly sex appeal!

Although trends may be changing, doctors have traditionally been held in high regard by the general public, which many students find an appealing prospect. Indeed a 2002 MORI public opinion poll reported that doctors were the most trusted profession. However, with this respect comes responsibility and pressure: one only has to read a small selection of newspapers to see that doctors are a major focus of media attention and public interest, and not all of the resulting coverage is favourable or fair.

Knowing that you are under constant scrutiny, and not always from people who understand clinical medicine, adds to the demands of the job. As a doctor you will be faced with difficult decisions involving ethical and clinical dilemmas, and these situations can be very stressful. There are also many unpleasant tasks, like breaking bad news or dealing with abusive patients or relatives and at times you will be frustrated at the lack of resources and time available to you. Curing patients is fulfilling and exciting – it happens regularly in some specialties – but there will be many patients whom you cannot cure, many symptoms that cannot be controlled, and many 'worried well' who cannot be persuaded that they are not in fact ill.

The number of people applying to study medicine continues to rise. This is partly due to the expansion of the number of medical schools and medical school places in the last few years and partly due to the increasing availability of places for applicants from nontraditional routes and for graduates on

3

fast-track courses. However, despite the increasing number of places, there is still a shortage of doctors in the UK, which means there are more than enough jobs to go round.

Salaries for junior doctors have increased significantly over the last few years and are set to continue rising. Indeed some junior doctors can be paid an annual salary of around £34,000 before tax. It must be remembered that the workload can be very demanding and salaries reflect the working pattern, intensity of work and the antisocial nature of the post. As you become more senior in your chosen field, pay improves, often with the scope for private income. Yet if your only aim in medicine is to make endless amounts of money, to prance around in a white coat looking like a star from a television drama, or to prove how able you are to pass exams, forget it. There are many easier ways to make money and the work is only occasionally glamorous. Application and dedication to patient care and learning are far more important attributes and a doctor's focus must be on a desire to serve. It is also worth bearing in mind that graduates from other shorter courses may be in a job and earning more money than you will be when you qualify, when you still have two more years of unpaid study left to go.

To follow particular career directions in medicine you will need to study hard and to sit a number of postgraduate exams after qualifying. It is vital that you continue your medical education if you are to keep your skills and knowledge up to date. Even as a fully qualified GP or a consultant you will be required to regularly prove your expertise and grasp of current developments to keep your licence to practise medicine. It's a long haul, and requires a commitment and devotion that far exceed any financial rewards. Whilst many of your friends in other professions will be able to relax at the end of a working day, you may finish a long shift only to have to begin your study for the evening, and young doctors frequently spend their weekends working. Whatever combination of reasons has made you consider medicine, remember it is a vocation. Those who enter medical school with a strong commitment to work hard, to learn, and to serve patients to their best ability are the people most likely to find life as a doctor richly rewarding and stimulating.

The medical profession is increasingly diverse, with ethnic minorities comprising 30% of the intake to medical school and women approximately 60%. It would be untrue to say that racial and sexual discrimination does not occur in medical schools or the health service, but the BMA, the Department of Health and all medical schools all actively promote equal opportunities.

Many gay, lesbian and bisexual applicants are unsure whether their sexuality may affect their future career. Although some within the profession may hold unsympathetic views, they are a decreasing minority. Be reassured that gay, lesbian and bisexual doctors are found at all grades, across all specialties. Although many are happy to be open with colleagues about their sexuality, others still prefer to keep their personal lives private.

The Human Rights Act, which came into effect in 2001, offers greater protection to people who are not treated equally and the General Medical Council states that all applicants who have the potential to meet the learning outcomes set by the GMC should be considered without prejudice. The law and the intentions of professional bodies are laudable, but tackling the issue of diversity with respect to age, disability, ethnic origin, gender and sexual orientation is challenging. However, as the medical student population becomes increasingly diverse it is much easier for mature students and students with dependants, disabilities and ill health to study medicine than in the past. In addition the government has committed policy and money to schemes aimed at widening participation in medicine and the health care professions. In 2004 the final parts of the Disability Discrimination Act came into force, which should ensure that disabled applicants have a fairer chance when applying to study medicine.

Nonetheless students with particular needs should consider their choice of medical school carefully and advice is contained in later sections of this book to help guide you.

Don't be surprised if you have any doubts about studying medicine. Many potential medics will also be flirting with the idea of pharmacy, law, veterinary science and other courses. Speak to some doctors – your own GP might be a start – and, if you can, arrange some work experience at your local hospital. Entering medicine is not a decision to be taken lightly or for the wrong reasons and first-hand experience in a medical environment is the best way of determining whether you are actually suited to a career as a doctor before entering medical school.

Finally, the choice to study medicine should be your own. It will be you who needs to find the force of character to spend endless nights before exams revising. It will be you who needs to find the capacity to carry on studying for up to three years after the rest of your school friends have graduated and begun earning. Ultimately, the choices you make now will determine the rest of your working life. If you feel others are making these choices for you, now is the time to muster the courage and face up to those who put pressure on you. However if you are truly 'being called' to medicine then you will find no better career option for you.

2

Life as a medical student

'Medical education is not completed at the medical school, it is only begun.'

William H. Welch (1850–1934)

'How unfair! Only one health, and so many diseases.'

Victor Schlichter, attributed by his son Dr. Andres J. Schlichter,
Children´s Hospital, Buenos Aires, Argentina.

How am I going to be taught?

In the past, there was a view that medical students spent their first couple of years cramming a vast amount of knowledge without ever seeing a patient, and then emerged brainwashed, unable to think and unable to communicate.

If this ever was the case, it is now certainly a thing of the past. Recommendations in the General Medical Council (GMC) report called *Tomorrow's Doctors* encouraged medical schools to reduce the emphasis on learning factual information and concentrate much more on developing the skills and attitudes needed to become a doctor. The foundations of factual knowledge established at medical school would then be built on whilst practising as a doctor. The report also recommended the introduction of special study modules (SSMs) to give students the chance to undertake projects of their own choosing. Alongside this, the GMC encouraged schools to adopt a more 'problem-based' learning approach to teaching, where facts are taught within a framework of real-life clinical scenarios.

Developing research skills and encouraging intellectual curiosity and enthusiasm for learning are now as important as knowledge. The emphasis is placed very firmly on producing graduates who will be life-long learners. The majority of medical schools have already changed their curricula so that older courses (in which science and clinical practice were taught separately) have given way to more 'integrated' curricula. In other words, instead of learning subjects separately – for example anatomy, biochemistry, and physiology ('subject-based teaching') – students are more likely to learn about respiration, reproduction, diet, and metabolism in a more 'system-based' approach.

Mikey's view: A day in the life of a preclinical student

Just another Tuesday. My alarm clock indicates I have precisely 13 minutes to make the bed-to-medschool journey. Suffering from the throes of a fantastic hangover (courtesy of the Medics' Pub Crawl), I head with the feeling of impending doom towards the dissection room. I try all the usual methods of sobering up but realize that it is probably a lost cause. We start by reviewing the very systems we were abusing the night before – the liver and the gastrointestinal tract (GI) system. Unfortunately the air conditioning system seems to be on the blink as I am quite sure that the smell from the cadaver really isn't meant to be quite so horrendous. Despite feeling distinctly nauseous all morning I seem to be ravenous by the time our coffee break arrives and treat myself to a bacon sandwich.

Unfortunately the bacon sandwich takes longer than anticipated to arrive and so I arrive a good 10 minutes late for my 3-hour lecture block consisting of physiology of the liver, followed by pathology of the GI system. I arrive at the back of the lecture theatre only to realize that the only spare seats are at the front! Clutching my bottle of water I try to slip in unnoticed but fail miserably.

The only thing that seems to be keeping me awake is the excitement that our Professor in physiology might beat his own personal best for the number of times he says 'schematic' in a 50-minute lecture! Shortly after the peak of my excitement I feel a nudge in the shoulder. I knew I wasn't going to make it all the way through without falling asleep, but at least I don't snore! It's now 2 hours in and I think I'm about ready to be turned. One can't be too careful, as pressure sores are a very real occupational hazard! The final lecture comes to an early climax (no pun intended) due to a technical hitch, so we all leave merrily.

Lunch has to take a back burner today (now very thankful for that bacon sandwich), as next up is a communication skills assessment. This involves me taking a history from one of my female friends who is pretending to be a 76-year-old man with erectile dysfunction! How am I supposed to keep a straight face when it's all being recorded on video camera?

Still another 2 hours to go, but one of them is with my favourite lecturer in the skills lab. We're learning the basics of urinalysis, and how the presence of certain molecules in the urine indicates certain diseases.

(Continued)

(*Continued*)

The final session of the day is a physiology practical. I get to dilate my housemate's pupils and he gets to do the same back to me. Almost forgot my hangover for a while there!

It always amazes me how the end of the day makes me feel so much more energetic. We start planning the night ahead on our walk home. Feeling very self-righteous I decide that I will be sensible and stay in, as I have a hospital visit tomorrow and must be in for 8.30 AM. Hospital visits are a real highlight, and one of the few opportunities us preclinical students get to play doctors and nurses. I get home, dust down the stethoscope and start rereading my notes. After some revision I feel I've definitely earned some time to myself. Rugby being my game, I head down to the pitch for a rather intense training session. Our team's doing really well this year, and there's an important tournament on the horizon. It's late when I get back, so a big group of us order takeaway and stay up for hours talking shop. I am sure I had to be up for something in the morning but can't quite remember what.

My alarm goes. It's 7.30 AM, I'm running late and I appear to have slept in a pizza box. Damn my lack of will power! This hospital visit is going to be a real struggle ...

In most schools, students will have some regular contact with clinicians and patients from the outset. The early years still have less clinical content and more lecture and laboratory teaching, but the traditional preclinical/clinical divide is dying. An important effect of these changes is that students need to be much more responsible for their own studies, so self-motivation and self-discipline is essential. Clinical skills laboratories have been introduced in most schools so that students can practise procedures and take exams on dummies and this helps to build confidence before going on the wards and carrying out the same examinations on patients. The balance between lectures, problem-based learning, SSMs and clinical exposure will vary between schools and is worth considering carefully in order to help you choose the medical school which best suits your preferred style of learning. You need to decide what type of learner you are – some people prefer more structured timetables and so prefer the lecture-based curricula; others prefer more independence and flexibility and are likely to enjoy problem-based learning more.

Clinical work takes place in local teaching hospitals and district general hospitals (DGHs), which can be many miles away from the medical school. These 'attachments' take you out of town, but getting away from the big city hospitals often provides the opportunity to be more involved in a team, gain more hands-on experience and ultimately to learn more. Most schools provide free accommodation within the hospitals if commuting is not practical. Some schools will even allow overseas attachments in addition to the elective. Due to the increasing number of students studying medicine most universities have to send their students further afield for a longer period of time. It is important that you fully understand the implications of this, as it is almost certain that you will be spending significant time away from your main university address.

But I'm squeamish!

As you would imagine, there is a fair amount of blood and gore in medicine at various stages (for example physiology practicals, postmortems, dissection, and taking blood). Many students become used to this remarkably quickly. For others, it may take longer. It may surprise you to know that some doctors are still squeamish after many years of practice. If you are very concerned about how you might react, try to arrange some appropriate work experience at your local hospital.

I've heard it's really hard work!

Now that the emphasis is placed more on learning appropriate skills and attitudes, rather than cramming vast amounts of facts, the ability to be able to list off reams of detailed biochemistry or pathology is less important. Nonetheless there are still exams and the amount that a medical student is expected to know on graduation is still considerable. More importantly, the amount that you learn during your time at medical school will have a direct impact on your ability to perform as a new doctor, and the thought that the well-being of patients will shortly be in your hands is an incredible motivation to work hard.

Medicine remains a very demanding course and friends studying for other degrees may have as many hours timetabled per week as you will have in one day. Attendance at lectures and practicals can last from 9 AM until 5 PM every day, and regular evening and weekend study is essential. During the clinical years the hours spent in hospital are frequently much longer and additional time is still needed for personal study and revision. There is no doubt that if you want an easy option at university, medicine is not the right subject for you.

Michelle's view: A day in the life of a clinical student

The day starts with the rather unwelcome sound of the alarm clock at the ungodly hour of 6.30 AM. It's still pitch black outside. After showering, dressing, making my lunch and managing only half of my measly slice of toast, I'm already running late. I jump into the car at 8.10 AM only to end up in a traffic jam! Typical!

After the 20-mile journey which has taken 45 minutes, I manage to make it to the outpatients department where the urology clinic starts at 9 AM. Actually, I'm 'on take' today which means

(*Continued*)

(*Continued*)

I need to help receive the emergency patients into hospital. However normally nothing really happens until after lunch when the GPs have had a chance to send some patients in. So, since I'm at the clinic before the surgeon and the junior doctors, I start to clerk all the new patients. Interestingly one has a hydrocoele (a collection of fluid in the scrotum) which is a condition I have never seen before. At 11.30 AM I have to leave as radiology teaching is about to start.

Together with my fellow students, we await the arrival of the consultant. Twenty minutes after the session was due to begin, a message is sent to say that our teaching has been cancelled as the consultant is too busy with an ultrasound list to teach us this morning. It is a nuisance as the clinic I had been at was really interesting but cancelled teaching is something we have to accept as part of the course

It's midday and at the surgical admission unit things are quiet except for one patient who needs a cannula inserted (a cannula is a needle through which to give medication and fluid). As I'm the only person who has turned up to the unit in the last 4 hours, the nurses jump on me as though I'm their oasis of hope and ask me to do it. My blood pressure's rising as I've been put on the spot and can't really say no – but it's a good chance to practise my clinical skills. I have to look in three different places for a vein that I can use, as there doesn't seem to be a decent one (they're not the greatest I've ever seen). However I finally decide on the best. Confidence is definitely not oozing from me and I'm half expecting the vein to disappear but despite shaking, I manage to get it in. I am filled with pride and really feel quite useful for a change!

The on-call registrar arrives on the ward, so I let him know the cannula is in and find out there is an emergency appendicectomy about to take place. As a result I rush to eat my sandwiches whilst walking to theatres; it's 2.15 PM and I'm hungry. Having changed into scrubs, the surgeon asks me to 'scrub up' and assist. He lets me hold things out of the way and cut a few stitches and he talks me through the anatomy.

After completing the operation in 5 hours (it was complicated), a vascular surgeon informs me that there is a patient who is coming in with an abdominal aortic aneurysm which is suspected to be leaking. An aortic aneurysm is when the main artery in the body is dangerously dilated. As he is currently on the CT scanner having images to identify any problems, I head towards the Radiology department again. However there is hoard of people running in that direction too and when I arrive I find that the patient has had a cardiac arrest. As medical students, we're advised to observe such situations if we can before we qualify for 'learning purposes'. However I feel awkward standing in the corner watching the patient being resuscitated. A nurse spots me and asks me to count how long they've been resuscitating for. Although for once I'm being useful, the mêlée in front of me is a distraction. I don't want to be seen as a gawking 'spectator'. This isn't *ER* or *Casualty* – this is a real person dying in front of me. After 20 minutes, the patient is pronounced dead. People gradually exit one by one and I'm left not quite knowing what to do. Eventually I say a prayer for the patient and wonder if I'll still be doing the same thing when I've been to many more crash calls as a Junior House Officer.

The Senior House Officer comes over – 'Is that the first person you've seen die?' 'Yes', I say still trying to take the situation in. 'If you need to talk about what you've just witnessed, then I'm happy to listen'. 'Thanks, but I'll be okay.' At 9.00 PM (time flies) – I make the decision to leave for home, recounting the events of the day. I'm exhausted and feel quite drained. After walking what seems like 20 miles through the hospital back to the car, driving home in the dark is not fun – I've barely seen the light today!

It's been a very busy day and I've been running on only some toast and a sandwich. Time for food! But before bed, preparation of some material must be done for a presentation tomorrow to one of the consultants. Sleep finally calls to me, at midnight, but I must be up early again for the post-take ward round…

In recent years, many medical schools have placed a greater emphasis on continuous assessment and a number have rearranged final exams so that they are taken over a longer period rather than all at once. Many students have found this to be a sensible development which has reduced a lot of the episodic pressure. Some, however, argue that this has only spread the pressure throughout the year; the increased number of exams can lead to exam fatigue and at schools with more traditional courses, 'finals' are still dreaded.

Is it fun?

Despite all these pressures, medical students have no trouble being sporty and sociable. In fact, we often excel at both. There is a wide mixture of students at every medical school and every group will contain a range of public school and state school, working class and middle class, medical family and nonmedical family backgrounds. You will be able to pursue your noncourse interests as well as your studies. 'Work hard and play hard' is the maxim that unites medical students and the medical profession has an enviable community spirit – a 'we're all in it together' attitude. Year groups vary in size but are often large (200+). Nonetheless, because everyone is doing the same course, you get to know your colleagues very quickly and very well. The downside of this is that medical students sometimes have a reputation for not mixing with students on other courses. It is also why we have the enviable reputation for the best social life! The common shared purpose amongst those studying medicine results in a closeness, which is one of the best aspects of life as a medical student.

Getting the balance right…

Maintaining a healthy balance between academic and extra-curricular activities whilst at medical school is very important. One of the greatest benefits of university life is in enabling students to develop as people as well as train as doctors. A healthy interest in sport, music, theatre, or even in just spending time relaxing with friends will be important to your development as a well-balanced person, in addition to influencing your success as a doctor. Medicine is a demanding course and learning how to manage a healthy work-to-life balance early on will enable you to maintain it through the pressures of life as a doctor and increase your ability to cope with stress.

If you find that you have no time at all for socializing or pursuing a hobby, then something is wrong. Either you are working too hard and need to relax, possibly with the help of a stress counsellor, or you are living and/or studying in an inefficient way and would benefit from some coaching on organisation

and study techniques. This is available at most universities in addition to a range of written resources including *How to Study Medicine* produced by the BMA. The importance of developing a well-balanced life during medical school can not be overemphasised. Doctors are particularly vulnerable to stress-related conditions, depression, divorce and alcohol abuse, and developing good practices as a student will help safeguard your health and happiness in the future.

It is also important to note that with the seemingly endless range of opportunities available at university and the active social life, it is easy to become involved in too much and find yourself pulled in too many directions. This situation can prove equally stressful and may cause academic difficulties. Most medical schools provide formative exams during the early terms, which should help you to gauge your academic progress. Use these as the excellent tool they are to check that you have an appropriate balance between study and play, and adjust your activities as necessary.

Finally, it is worth bearing in mind that at the end of your time at medical school you will be applying for House Officer positions alongside a great number of other medical students with almost identical qualifications. Whilst there are enough jobs for everyone, if you have your heart set on a particular job, is helpful to have something that makes your curriculum vitae stand out from the crowd.

Can I combine medicine with pursuing another degree subject?

You can interrupt most courses to study for an extra 'intercalated' degree, which is normally a medical science degree (BSc, BMedSci) undertaken during an extra year (or two) of study. This is particularly worthwhile if you are considering a career in research or academic medicine. Intercalated degrees are commonly taken after the second or third year, and entry policies vary between schools. They are compulsory in some, actively encouraged in others, and some allow students to intercalate by invitation only. In some schools where it is voluntary, as many as 50% of each year group intercalate at some stage in their studies. The main consideration to extending an already long course to complete an intercalated degree is the issue of financing an extra twelve months. At some schools tuition fees for the intercalated degree year are paid for, but you will still need to finance your living costs for an extra year. There are a number of significant bursaries available for intercalating students both via the university and via external bodies and it is definitely worth finding out about these.

Is it possible to travel abroad for any part of the course?

When people say the world is your oyster, there is really no other profession that this applies to more aptly. Medicine truly is your passport to the world and doctors are trusted and welcomed in every corner, culture and society. Medical schools have embraced this fact for many years now, and have incorporated a period within the medical curriculum dedicated to the students' own self-directed learning, termed an **elective**. The elective is usually over a period of between 8 and 12 weeks depending on which medical school you attend. To many students this means the chance to study overseas for a prolonged period. The elective is viewed as one of the major highlights of the undergraduate curriculum. Not only is it a fantastic learning experience but it is also a chance to escape the NHS and see part of the world you have never seen before. Medicine is practised in diverse environments and settings, many of which are very different from the health care system students will eventually enter. The elective allows the opportunity to experience how different health care systems contrast to our own. This may be the ultrasophisticated and technologically advanced system that exists in the USA or the humble resource-stricken system that exists in much of the developing world. Many students choose to place themselves in the latter environment because they are likely to gain a level of hands-on experience unavailable in more developed and regulated health services.

The timing of the elective varies between medical schools, but usually takes place during the clinical years so that students have a broad base of clinical knowledge before embarking on the elective period to maximize learning. All schools encourage the elective period to be used primarily as an invaluable learning resource and not just a holiday, although a holiday certainly can be incorporated. A number of schools require either clinical or academic research to be undertaken as part of the elective. Students decide to go on a particular elective depending on their interests and what they intend to achieve. For example, the adventurous may choose trauma in Johannesburg, whilst a student keen for a more relaxed experience may prefer to spend their elective in the Seychelles. With enough time and motivation, the opportunities are endless. For example, previous students have benefited from electives with NASA in the USA, the flying doctors in Australia and the mountain rescuers in Nepal.

You do not have to go abroad for your elective and many students choose instead to organize an equally rewarding experience in the UK: perhaps delving into medical politics, carrying out a project at an academic or pharmaceutical research centre, or working with the team doctor at a football club. The elective really is what you make it. Generally, students organize their own elective with the assistance of the medical school, reports from previous students and relevant elective literature. There really is no limit to what you can get out of your elective if you are prepared to put the effort in to organizing it.

It can be expensive, depending on what you choose to do; however, there are numerous grants and prizes available which allocate money especially to help fund medical student electives, so if you are well organized it is often possible to obtain considerable financial support. Generally it is easier to obtain sponsorship and grants if your elective incorporates research.

Whatever you choose to do as part of your elective, the memories and experience you will gain will be something you will never forget throughout your future career as a doctor.

In addition to electives, a few medical schools allow students to take one or more special study modules (shorter periods designed to allow students to study an area of particular interest) abroad. Furthermore a small number of universities allow medical students to take part in exchange programmes with other European nations for part of the course, and even to study a foreign language. This is called Erasmus and the ability to undertake these at each medical school is outlined in the second half of the book. If these opportunities interest you then it is important to read the information for each medical school carefully as practices vary considerably and medical schools facilitating such opportunities are currently in the minority.

Is it wise to study medicine with a chronic illness or disability?

The Disability Discrimination Act 1995 requires universities and medical schools to take into account the needs of disabled students. They must provide statements about the facilities available for such students, which should include details such as access, the specialist equipment and counselling available, admission arrangements, and complaints and appeals procedures for disabled students. The Act applies in Northern Ireland with exceptions.

Medical school is tough. It is tough for everyone – even those who are 100% healthy. It places pressures on students academically, financially and emotionally. The decision to study medicine should not be taken lightly or without prior knowledge of those facts, particularly if you are chronically unwell or have a disability to contend with in addition to studying, and even more so if your health status fluctuates. This all sounds very daunting and may make you wonder whether you should even consider doing medicine. Believe it or not, you are probably the best-equipped individuals to tackle this vocational subject. The challenges and obstacles that you have faced are the same ones that the patients you will eventually serve experience. Your deeper understanding of illness is something that – although unfortunate – is invaluable to you and the profession. You really do know what it is like at both ends of the bed!

Medical schools are endeavouring to widen access to all potential students whatever their circumstance and all medical schools are obliged to provide some form of pastoral care and support. However the approach of the different medical schools to students with health problems and disabilities varies, as does the quality of the pastoral support available. Unfortunately, the 'caring profession' isn't always as caring to its own. It is well worth considering these factors carefully when choosing which medical schools to apply to. This is explained in more detail in Chapter 3.

Because of the many demanding aspects to medical work, any disability that might impede clinical capability needs to be considered carefully. Depending on the disability or health problem, medical schools may require the applicant to have a skills assessment to ensure that they are fit to perform the tasks involved in becoming a doctor. This will focus on what the student can do, rather than what they cannot do. Medical school faculties and occupational health services may be able to offer skills assessment and Deans of medical schools should be able to offer further information and advice. Students may be eligible for financial help, such as the disabled students' allowance. Following a publication by its Disabled Doctors Working Party titled *Meeting the Needs of Doctors with Disabilities*, the BMA launched a service for disabled medical students and doctors. This aims to provide information about aids, facilities, equipment, and financial help. It also puts disabled medical students and doctors in touch with each other. Further information may be obtained from the Medical Education Department of the BMA (see Further Information chapter).

Despite the efforts of good medical faculties and the best intentions of the majority of students within a year, it is very easy to feel isolated when you are struggling with health problems. In order to reduce the impact of this on both your studies and your health, it is helpful to:

* accept your limitations – the most important rule;
* keep the relevant people informed at all times, particularly when you feel there may be a problem around the corner – medical faculties are able to help and to take circumstances into consideration if they know in advance;
* don't be afraid to ask for help – you are only human;
* always remember your health is the most important thing. You don't want to end up next to the patients you are treating.

Medicine should be for everyone so do not be put off. The old mentality of 'if it's too hot, get out of the kitchen' is gradually fading. As more people with illnesses and disabilities enter the profession, this attitude will hopefully disappear completely.

What about studying medicine as a mature student?

Over recent years there has been a dramatic increase in the number of applications from both graduate and mature students wanting to study medicine. Much of this has resulted from the introduction of 4-year fast track medical degrees for students who meet certain criteria, but even mature and graduate applications to traditional 5- and 6-year courses have increased. Previous experience and maturity are becoming increasingly valued and medical schools often view mature students as reliable and likely to 'stay the course'. These applicants have often achieved another degree or worked in professions allied to medicine, such as nursing, and many argue that these students have spent more time assessing whether they really want to be a doctor before taking the plunge into medicine.

In 2003 some 20% of applicants to medicine were over the age of 21. In some undergraduate medical courses as many as 15% of students are mature students, and the staff are used to dealing with their different needs. However in other schools older students are a rarity. Indeed, until recently there were a significant number of medical schools that would not even accept applications from those aged over 25, 30 or 40. Despite current government initiatives against ageism, some medical schools continue to overtly dissuade applications from those who do not fit rigid age categories. The BMA continues to oppose age limits in UK medical education and the success of both mature and graduate students means that more and more schools are welcoming applications from mature students.

Depending on their academic background, mature students may be eligible to join one of the fast-track graduate courses whereas others may have to complete a **premedical** year. In these cases it is essential that applicants contact the admissions department of the medical schools to find out if there are specific entrance requirements. Graduate entry programmes (GEP) and premedical courses are discussed in more detail in Chapter 4.

A large proportion of mature students will be self-funding if they have previously completed undergraduate degrees, and consequently are likely to incur higher levels of debt than their younger colleagues. However, finances should not put you off applying to medical school if you are motivated and have a true desire to study medicine and become a doctor.

Before applying, it is worth listing honestly the pros and cons of returning to or continuing education for at least another 4 years. This is not a useless exercise as you can be sure that those interviewing you will want to be very sure of your motives and future plans. The BMA's graduate and mature students' group has identified specific issues that cause additional concern for those who are planning to change their lifestyle to study medicine. As a mature applicant there are additional factors to consider.

- *Finance*. Can you afford it? What about your fees?
- *Partners and family matters*. What will this mean for them and for your relationship(s)?
- *Children, childcare and future pregnancies*. How will you fit them in?
- *Lifestyle changes* (such as loss of regular income, working unsociable hours). How will you cope if you are expected to live in a shared student flat?
- *Work/study mix*. Due to the demands of the course, most students are not able to work enough part-time hours to fund their courses.
- *Attitudinal challenges*. Both your own and from teachers and fellow students.

When considering applying to medicine as a mature or graduate student it is important to realise that attitudes towards and the support systems in place to help with the needs of mature students varies across UK medical schools. The majority of mature students thoroughly enjoy their time at medical school, but you must take responsibility for maximizing your chances of satisfaction by choosing the medical schools you apply to carefully.

Do many students manage to study medicine and care for dependants?

As if studying for one of the longest degrees, arguably involving some of the most mind-numbing memory work was not enough, some students like to liven things up a bit by choosing to start their studies with a ready-made family of their own in tow. Others add the challenge of a pregnancy or two, to the otherwise all-too-quiet time we have as medical students.

In fact medical students have always done this. It's just that with more mature students these days, and greater choices for women in the workplace, it has become talked about, and rightly so. Scan the website of any of the university medical schools in the UK for their maternity policy for students and you'll be hard-pressed to find one. The sad fact is that when you approach your tutor to say:

- you need to take time off because your child has chicken pox;
- your child-care has fallen through and you'll be late for lectures;
- you want 6 months off because you're pregnant,

you are not likely to get the sort of treatment you would get if you were at work. For example we are aware of a case of a student whose daughter died but whose university tried to give her a fail mark for missing the OSCE she should have sat rather than being at her daughter's bedside in the paediatric intensive care. Another university offered such scant support to one pregnant student that she felt forced to leave and transferred to another medical school.

Nevertheless there are success stories. An increasing number of students manage to give birth and pick up on their studies by timing matters rather well to fit in with holiday periods (especially in the preclinical years when the holidays are longer). Others take a full year out and slot back in to the next year. Indeed, some think having a baby as a student is the best way to do it. After all it's not going to be any easier when you are a stressed out junior doctor, or when you're 15 years older and a consultant.

As more and more students with children or other dependants enter medicine, the provision of support and understanding will improve in the same way that flexible working patterns for doctors have had to radically improve as a result of the large number of both male and female practitioners who have demanded a better work-to-life balance. In the meantime enjoy your family *and* your time as a student. Remember many people are already doing just that. And the more students that do it, the more we can one day look forward to persuading universities to offer flexible degrees in the same way as there are flexible working arrangements.

Studying as an international student?

Medical students come from all over the world to study in the United Kingdom, with the majority coming

from former Commonwealth nations in East Asia, South Asia, the Middle-East and Africa. Students come from a wide variety of backgrounds and experiences, and find it to be a great opportunity to meet people and learn about cultures that they would never be able to in their own country.

Coming to the UK can be an overwhelming experience, as things can be quite unlike what you are accustomed to at home. From the type of food and entertainment, to the cultural values and way of life, you may find it very different from what you are used to; this can be a good thing. Britain is a very multicultural society, and it is generally easy to fit in and feel comfortable with your surroundings. It also means that you are likely to find at least one restaurant that serves a dish from your country, as there is more to British food than fish and chips!

It is generally a good idea to live on campus for the first year, so you can get to know other students at your university and make new friends. It also gives you time to adapt to the British culture and way of life, before you move out into the 'real world'. Some universities allow international students to live on campus for up to 2 years. When students do move out, they tend to share accommodation with friends and colleagues they have met during their first year, which is the norm in the UK.

If you can get over the weather and the funny accents, the United Kingdom is an excellent place to undertake your undergraduate training. Most people involved in your training are keen to teach, the nurses and staff are helpful and the patients are very friendly and willing for medical students to practise their clinical skills on them; all in the name of learning.

3

Applying to medical school

'Medicine, the only profession that labours incessantly to destroy the reason for its existence.'

Sir James Bryce (1838–1922)

Choosing the right medical schools

Entrance requirements

Most medical schools require students to get A or B grades (mainly As) in at least three full A-level subjects (discounting general studies) or five Scottish Highers. Many schools also require the Scottish Certificate of Sixth Year Studies from applicants educated in Scotland. The entry requirements have gone up, and have remained high despite a downward trend in applicants (which has recently reversed). The average requirement is now AAB (AAABB). Chemistry is usually a compulsory requirement because the principles of chemistry are the key to understanding medical biochemistry, and it would be difficult to teach to the required standard during the course. Surprisingly, many schools don't insist on biology, although many medics have it as one of their A-levels. In most schools medical teaching covers elementary biology, and there may be supplementary classes for nonbiologists during the first year.

Traditionally, the other subjects studied at A-level are sciences or mathematics, but many medical schools now acknowledge that students who pursue other subjects at school are not disadvantaged when they begin studying medicine and that a broad range of knowledge, and enthusiasm for the subjects studied can be beneficial. Some schools accept applications from students taking chemistry, another science subject and an arts A-level. However it is essential to check with each school before you make your final choices: don't rely upon what others have chosen before if your choices are an atypical combination. Where possible, the *key facts* box in the following chapters reflects each medical school's requirements.

Health status

In addition to academic qualifications, you will also have to fulfil certain health-related entry requirements. Individual schools will outline their requirements in the prospectus and will inform you of the process in more detail if your application is successful. In general you will need immunity against rubella and tuberculosis if you don't already have it. A majority of schools used to require you to prove your hepatitis B status before admission, but the situation is changing. In the future, occupational health checks will be conducted after admission to medical school.

Work experience

Work experience is a fantastic way to gain exposure to medicine and can be incredibly enjoyable and rewarding. It is also a good opportunity to test whether life as a health care professional is the right choice for you.

Although not a stated prerequisite for entry to medical school some exposure to the health care setting is regarded by many schools as evidence that you are seriously interested in a medical career. It is helpful therefore if your personal statement shows that you have tried to understand what a medical career will entail. You don't need to shadow a doctor for a few days – it is accepted this is difficult enough given the busy nature of doctors' lives, but even harder if you do not know any doctors to contact. There are many opportunities to undertake work experience in caring-type roles and working as a nursing auxiliary or as a volunteer within hospitals will enable you to experience the broader health care environment. It will also give you invaluable perspective as to the role of other health professionals in the overall system. Think laterally about the range of opportunities open to you including contacting current medical students to ask what they did.

If you do contact a doctor for work experience, remember to adhere to patient confidentiality rules and observe your own limitations. It is particularly important that you do not agree to do anything for which you are not qualified, or that you would not want someone of equivalent experience to do to you or a member of your family. The BMA has produced a set of work experience guidelines available on the BMA website and the Department of Health also provides guidance for NHS managers to which you can refer.

Several universities offer opportunities to participate in summer schools or medical student shadowing schemes to give tasters of medical student life, use the contact details later in the book to find out what is available. Universities local to you may have specific programmes for those attending local schools, and remember to apply early!

Open days and further information

It is very important that you find out as much as possible about the medical schools that you are considering applying to. In Part 2 of this book we give you admission information and views and opinions for you to consider. Only by visiting the school and reading the prospectus and any alternative guides will you be able to assess the atmosphere and whether you will enjoy studying there. Remember, no one knows what life at medical school is like better than those already there. Don't be afraid to approach current medical students: we are generally a friendly bunch and would be more than happy to chat over a coffee about any aspect of medical school life.

Open days will help you decide whether you would prefer a medical school that is part of a larger university, on a campus or spread across a town, in a big city or near the countryside, and where you'd like to live should you accept a place there. It will also allow you to talk to the medics who are already there. Starting university can be a daunting experience, but if you know what to expect then you will be much more at ease. If you can't afford the cost of travelling, get a group together and ask if your school or college will sponsor a minibus or take a coach to an open day. Many open days take place in the summer after students have had their exams and before applications are due. It is better to go early, before students go on vacation, although there are clinical students milling around all year. Well-organised open days have a welcoming team to escort visitors from the station, and organise events, talks, tours, displays, and demonstrations. However, organisation varies greatly from school to school.

Some medical schools run intensive open days during which you may sample lectures and some operate 'summer schools' – extended periods of experience of life as a medical student, with opportunities to work alongside students and others interested in applying to medicine. There are courses run commercially, giving application advice as well as an insight into life as a medical student. These can be expensive but may be a good way of helping you decide whether medicine is the right choice for you. Your careers tutor might be able to help you find out about these courses and open days.

If you can't attend an open day there are a number of people you could write to. The Student Union can deal with enquiries and may have promotional material to send you. The Medical Faculty office should also be able to supply you with the name of the president of the Medical Society, the student group responsible for representing medics and organising sports and social events, so you can contact the students directly. BMA student representatives are always happy to answer questions, and they may be contacted through the medical school or via the BMA Medical Students Committee (see Further information section).

Applicants with disabilities

As medicine is a vocational course, medical schools do not tend to accept students unless they are confident that the applicant has the potential to meet the requirements of the preregistration house officer year. This year is based on a series of learning outcomes, details of which can be obtained from the General Medical Council. Where an applicant has a disability or chronic health problem which may impact on their study, good admission practice suggests that medical schools should first assess an applicant without reference to their illness or disability. If the school is happy to offer that student a place but feels that clarification of the health challenge is necessary, the applicant should undergo an occupational health assessment to determine whether they would be physically and mentally capable of meeting the learning outcomes of the preregistration year.

Although the attitude of most medical schools is changing, and some have in place very positive practices, it can still be difficult for a student with a significant disability to gain a place at medical school. When considering which medical schools to apply to, it is very important to speak to the medical faculties prior to applying in order to gain an impression of their attitudes. The good medical schools will have past or present students with health problems or disabilities that they can put you in touch with, and the medical faculty personnel will be encouraging and keen to help. It can also be very helpful to try and arrange a meeting with either the Dean or the Admissions Officer prior to applying.

There are a number of organizations which may be of assistance to you; in particular, SKILL, the National Bureau for Students with Disabilities (see Further information section). Details of support for people who feel that they are being treated unfairly can be found in the Further information section of this book.

Mature applicants

Do your research! Much will be gained from making contact with the admissions tutors at those medical schools that you are interested in applying to. The attitude of the admissions staff and the tone of the welcome you receive can provide clues as to the possible reactions to your application. Do not forget that as a mature applicant, you are entitled to send 'supporting material' to the admissions teams in addition to your UCAS form – do not just limit this to a CV. Discuss with the school the form that this should take. Determine what will make your case most effective. You can use letters of support, details of relevant courses, work experiences, etc. The newer medical schools have been reported to be much more welcoming to those who have had a career elsewhere or who do not fit the typical school-leaver applicant's profile. Some older establishments, however, are also keen to recruit more mature students. Contact the schools directly. Read the prospectuses carefully.

Above all, be sure that this is what you want to do. At interview, be prepared to be grilled as to the reasons why you want to change your life at this point in time. Remember, nothing sounds as good or as convincing as the truth!

Applicants with dependants

Before selecting where to apply, talk to the universities on your short list. Find out:

- whether it has any medical students with dependants that you can talk to;
- its policy on maternity leave for students;
- whether childcare is provided, and whether it is subsidised for students;
- whether there is specific support available for mature students or students with dependants;
- whether there any special hardship grants for students with dependants.

Apply to universities that are encouraging and positive towards you. The admissions tutor's response to your initial enquiries will speak volumes about the University's potential attitude towards you in the future. Remember, mature women students with young children are more likely than any other group to abandon their course and it doesn't take many brain cells to work out why.

International applicants

The first step for a prospective international student considering studying in Britain is to determine the cost of education in its entirety (including tuition fees, equipment, books and living expenses), as this can be very high. The next step is to find out if your country of origin offers any loans, scholarships or grants to study abroad, as some governments do offer financial relief for their citizens to experience medical training in another country. It is also worth finding out if the university you are considering offers any scholarships to international students. The best way to find this out is to contact the university directly and ask. British Embassies or High Commissions and your own country's education authorities may also be able to advise you on grants and scholarships.

After reading the university prospectus, it is a good idea to contact the school and clarify and verify any information as the situation can change, and may influence your decision to attend a particular school. The British Council will have information about UK universities and medical schools. It will also be able to guide you on whether your qualifications are recognised in the UK. If you are not studying UK-examined A-levels, then contact the admissions office at the medical school to check whether your subject choices and qualifications are acceptable. There are growing links between overseas medical schools and UK schools, and you may be able to do some of your studies in the UK even if you don't get a full-time place on the course. If you are applying to medical schools in other countries you might want to enquire about this.

Applicants from outside the UK must also apply via UCAS and should follow the instructions in the *UCAS Handbook*. You can get copies of the UCAS information from British Council offices or by writing to UCAS. Many schools and colleges will order supplies for you.

Gap years

Many sixth-form students defer entry to university for 12 months. Gap years are looked on favourably by most colleges and universities. The majority, however, expect you to use the time profitably by working and/or travelling. It is important that you check the medical school's attitude before you apply if you intend to defer entry. Time out between school and university is not just for those who have the money for a 'round the world' air ticket: a well-planned gap year will give you time to think about how to get through university and let you assess what you want to get out of the next 5 or more years. Time spent well will boost your confidence and broaden your experience. This can have a very positive effect on your performance. Student debt is increasing all the time. You could try to save some money and be in better financial shape for your eventual university career. A gap year may also be used to gain some more work experience in health care, although there is no need to overdo it.

Note: A minority of colleges at Oxford and Cambridge don't approve of gap years. It is best to check the attitude of the individual college(s) you are thinking of applying to.

The application process

The UCAS form

Medical schools only accept applications made through the Universities and Colleges Admissions Service (UCAS). Read through the *UCAS Handbook* and follow the advice closely. Make several drafts of your UCAS form before finalising your application. Your careers tutor at school or college will be able to help you fill in the form. If you do not have a careers tutor try to find someone else to read through a draft version for you before you write it up – perhaps a family friend or your work experience supervisor. When you do write it up, remember to make it accurate and legible.

The most important part of the form is the personal statement. This is your chance to stand out from the crowd and make the admissions tutors want to interview you. What you write will go a long way towards determining how many medical schools offer you an interview or a place. The comments below apply equally to electronic and paper applications.

You can expect – not surprisingly – that the medical school will want to know why you want to study medicine and, as there is so much competition, you must seize this opportunity to demonstrate your commitment to joining the profession. For example, you may want to try to describe what drives you to pursue a career in medicine. Medical schools will want to be sure that you know what you are getting yourself into and so it is very important to demonstrate how you have gone about trying to understand what a medical career will entail. However, don't take too much space to do this, as it will be at the expense of other important information. The challenge is to do this effectively with supporting evidence of a well-balanced character, for example, a hospital portering job or regularly visiting a local old people's home along with captaining the school netball team or editing the school magazine. These examples will prove to them that you are a good candidate and that you are well rounded in your interests.

It should be clear from the information supplied by your school or college whether you have the potential to get the grades, so the personal statement must show you as a potential asset to the medical school and, later, the medical profession. They will be looking for:

- signs of good interpersonal skills;
- evidence of a social life;
- details of your interests/hobbies;
- any notable achievements.

You could mention:

- sports achievements;

- academic prizes;
- organisational or supervisory positions of responsibility;
- voluntary work, part-time work or work experience;
- musical or travel interests;
- projects you have particularly enjoyed or unusual hobbies.

If you are deferring entry for a year you should explain how you are going to use your time.

There is no need to explain your choice of A-levels/Highers unless you have something interesting to say about them, for example: 'I am studying computing as an A-level as I think it may lie at the heart of medicine in the future'. Don't be afraid of making bold comments as long as you can justify them. They also offer signposts for interviewers that can be prepared for before an interview (see interview section below).

If you are called for an interview the panel will question you on the contents of this section, so don't lie or exaggerate your interests or achievements. Remember, you may be asked to talk about any of the things you mention, so be truthful – it will probably show very quickly if you have embellished too much!

Admissions staff read hundreds of UCAS forms, and if yours stands out then you will have a better chance of being called for interview. The admissions tutor will want to know that you are prepared for what a career in medicine entails, and that you have realistic expectations, so by the time you post your application form you should have done your research and thinking.

You can use this book to help you decide which schools to apply to, but don't put an overt preference in the application. Another medical school may dismiss your application if they think that you will turn down their offer, and if you change your mind or your first choice medical school do not offer you a place, you will have limited your options. Also, think carefully about how your statement will appear to an admissions tutor reading it in his or her office. If you express a passionate interest in premiership football an admissions tutor at Peninsula might think you would not enjoy being miles from any of the top clubs and not offer you an interview. Equally, an application to a Scottish medical school might appear eminently sensible from a student interested in ceilidh dancing.

When to apply

Apply as early as possible, but do not rush your application form. Importantly, remember to submit it well before the appropriate deadlines bearing in mind that applications to certain universities may be earlier than others – such as Cambridge and Oxford. The UCAS guide and website give you all the details. You can submit your application electronically. You may receive replies from medical schools virtually as soon as you apply or you may be kept waiting until the last week that offers can be made. Either way do not read too much in to it. Some schools may make a conditional offer on your application alone, whereas others will conduct many rounds of interviews before they make offers or rejections. You may think you have been forgotten – this is very unlikely, but it does happen. If you are in doubt, and the deadline is approaching, contact the admissions office. You can arrange for UCAS to acknowledge receipt of your form, and you will be given an application number so you can check progress if you feel it is taking too long. Admissions offices will be very busy during this time, but a telephone call may put your mind at ease even if they can't give you a decision on your application.

The interview

If you are called to an interview, make sure you have done your homework thoroughly. The key to a good interview is excellent preparation and lots of practice. Prepare draft answers to the questions you are likely to be asked. Do not learn these by heart, as you will sound rehearsed, but by thinking ideas through before the interview you will be prepared for possible pitfalls and have thought about the most important information you want to include. Practice interviews with anyone who is willing to spare ten minutes. Ask them to suggest ways of improving your answers or style. This will help you to be more relaxed when it comes to the real thing.

Interviewers will be looking at your UCAS form for inspiration. They will probably be interested in what is special and unusual (but not weird) about you: they would be fascinated to find out what drove you to do a llama herding course in South America during your gap year – tell them! Reread your personal statement and anticipate the kinds of questions you might be asked. This is where your personal statement and your interview should mesh. Place signposts in your personal statement that interviewers can pick up on and question you about. Remember, they may be interviewing forty people in one day, and you can make it easier for them by doing this. You should also keep up to date with medical news stories and developments, as these may be the subject of some questioning.

Dress smartly and arrive in good time. If you are going to be shown around the medical school, remember that this is an opportunity to ask current students any questions you might have. Don't feel obliged to ask any questions in the interview, and don't ask questions which are already answered in the prospectus. In some ways an interview is a chance for the medical school to assess the potential it has recognised in your application form. It is not an academic test. Treat it as an opportunity to show that you are serious about your career choice, and that you will be a future asset to the profession.

If you do not think that the interviewers are asking you the questions which will allow you to shine, it is possible to use an answer to one question to lead on to the subject that you would like to talk about. For example, if they have not asked you about your sporting activities then you can reply to a question about why you have applied to their university to talk about the excellent sporting opportunities available and how that would suit you well in your endeavours as a County Junior Athlete. Whilst it is not a good idea to start rambling off on a complete tangent, a skilful interviewee can heavily influence the direction of the interview.

Most importantly, enjoy your interview. It is an opportunity for the panel to get a feel for the sort of person you are. Be polite and respectful, but yourself. If you don't agree with something then say so, as long as you can justify your disagreement logically and concisely. Although it is difficult to predict the exact questions you will be asked a number that reoccur time and time again include:

- Why do you want to be a doctor? Why a doctor and not a nurse?
- If you are so fascinated by the human body, why don't you do biology or physiology instead?
- Why do you want to come to this medical school?
- What can you offer the medical school?
- What are the most important characteristics of a doctor? What makes a good doctor?
- Do you know about the medical career structure?
- Do you know what sort of doctor you would like to be?
- What is the one thing you would like to change about the health service?
- Please give me three of your strengths and three of your weaknesses? (Be careful when selecting your weaknesses – you do not want to be so honest that it counts against you. An example would be 'I'm prone to being too much of a perfectionist at times. I think that I will have to work on this during my time at medical school so that I can manage the demands of being a doctor without getting too frustrated at the lack of time to do everything quite as well as I would like'.)
- Can you describe a situation when you worked in a team?
- Can you describe a time when you have had to make a difficult decision? What is the hardest decision you've ever had to make?
- Questions that try to elicit whether you can think from a doctor's *and* a patient's perspective.
- You may be given an ethical situation that you have to go through. (Here interviewers may be looking for characteristics such as teamwork, or dealing with uncertainty.)
- You may be asked to talk about a life-changing event.

What if I don't get in?

The number of applicants to study medicine dropped more than 3% in 2000 to 9291, but increased to 11,030 in 2002. In spite of this and the increased number of places, medical schools in the UK are still vastly oversubscribed. There are often 10 applicants for each place, and only a small fraction of them will make it to interview, selected on the basis of their UCAS forms and references; even fewer will get a place. Oxford and Cambridge have fewer applicants per place, which might mean that, although the academic requirements are high, you stand a slightly greater chance of at least being called to interview. However, not getting a place to read medicine is simply a reflection of the pressure on places and not a great indictment of your character and abilities. Even if you maximize your chances of being selected for interview, you may still be unsuccessful in your application.

You need to know what to do next. First, think long and hard! Do you still want to study medicine? Medical schools try to select people who will make good doctors and who have the right ability and motivations for studying medicine, but even so some students choose to leave midcourse and others fail exams. The interview panel has a responsibility to make the right decision for the medical school, and you have a responsibility to yourself and your potential future patients to make sure you are making the correct choice. Examine your reasons for wanting to study medicine. If in doubt, or if you have felt pushed in the direction of medicine, it might be better to look at different courses or careers.

If you still want to study medicine, then start by asking yourself why you weren't successful in your application. Did you get an interview? If you did, your school might be able to get some feedback from the medical school. This is unlikely to be in depth, but might give you some useful information. Discuss the prospect of your chances with teachers. Reflecting on your disappointment at this stage may prove difficult, but it is in your interests to be honest and realistic. Think about the possibility of following another course, whether in a related field – for example physiology, pharmacy, physiotherapy, biochemistry – or something totally unrelated. Most universities offer places on degree courses through 'clearing'. If your grades are good then many other courses will be open to you. It is possible to reapply to read medicine, but some schools will only consider a second application if you applied there first time round. If you do reapply, your A-level results should be at least as good as the estimates that your school originally made. There are some schools that will consider candidates who are resitting but others do not. Save your own time and energies by asking your preferred schools if they would accept an application from you. This could prevent you from wasting future UCAS choices. It is only advisable to resit exams if you are sure about getting A grades the second time around or if there were extenuating circumstances, such as bereavement or serious illness, in the months preceding your A-levels first time around.

There are a growing number of places available for graduates to read medicine, which means that you could do a degree and see after graduation whether you still want to become a doctor. Some students start university studying a parallel course, such as physiology and then apply to switch to medicine at the end of the first or second year when the university has had a chance to measure their potential and character. These students would still have to start medicine from the first year though, and this method of entry is very rare and should not be relied on. Graduates usually follow the full undergraduate medical course unless they can be exempted from part of it because of the nature of their first degree (for example, biochemistry or dentistry). Graduates with a purely arts background at A-level or degree could try to take a medical foundation year (premed year) before the medical course proper. This is not available at all institutions. Many schools don't normally consider applicants over 30 years of age. Graduate entry, however, is one of the ways into a career as a doctor. The BMA, and many other interested parties, have recognised the desirability of graduate entry and, as more places are being reserved for graduates, it is sensible to consider this route as an option.

I have accepted a place at medical school – what next?

You are undoubtedly both nervous and excited about starting at medical school. Most students are extremely eager to get started and throw themselves into student life. Having been there already there were a few pointers we thought might come in handy.

- Don't buy textbooks until you start the course. Freshers tend to buy an armful of books which they hardly use and could easily have borrowed from the library. Wait a while and make selective purchases.
- Make sure you read and are happy with everything you sign. Many medical schools will require you to sign a student contract. Most of these are reasonable and follow the GMC's requirements. However it is important to understand what you are signing and do ask a tutor for explanations and advice if you feel unhappy or unsure about the content. If you are a member of the BMA, you can also contact your local office.
- Get involved with the medic social scene. As a fresher it may seem daunting but these people will be your colleagues for the next 5 years at least and it is amazing how many friendships stem from the very first week at medical school. Most medical schools will organise a specific medics freshers' event and this is often well attended by the more senior medical students. Get to know

them – their advice will be invaluable later on. It may seem cheesy but medics can provide a real family away from home and this support will prove essential.

- Come to medical school armed with some decent passport photos. You will be surprised at how many people want a photo of you!
- Make the most of the free offers available at freshers' events. Organisations like the BMA offer free membership to first-year medical students and can provide invaluable support and benefits to you throughout the course, and when you become a doctor.
- Don't feel pressured to drink or take drugs – standing up for your opinion from the start will make things an awful lot easier in the long run.

4

Graduate and premedical courses

'The work of the doctor will, in the future, be ever more that of an educator, and ever less that of a man who treats ailments.'

Lord Horder

'If you want something done right, you have to do it yourself. This especially includes your health care.'

Dr. Andrew Saul

Not everyone knows from an early age that medicine is the career for them. Many students gain A-levels or even degrees before deciding to pursue a career in medicine. This section gives course information for these students interested in fast-track courses, along with details of application procedures. Of course, this is not the only option for graduate students – many apply to the standard courses which last around 5 years.

Graduate entry programmes (GEP)

Nowadays more and more entrants to medical school have already completed an undergraduate degree and may be eligible to undertake a 4-year fast-track graduate entry programme (GEP). In fact, many of the government's planned new places are being reserved for graduates as schools develop graduate-only courses. Medical schools view graduates as reliable and likely to 'stay the course'. These mature students have done something else with their lives – often another degree – before taking the plunge into medicine and, it can be argued, have spent more time assessing whether they really want to be a doctor. In some schools as many as 15% of students are graduate entrants, and the staff are used to dealing with their different needs.

The number of graduate entry programmes available has increased dramatically over the past few years. These courses vary in their entry requirements so it is worth investigating thoroughly. Most universities' requirements include, at least a 2:1 degree in a science-based or health-related subject. However, many also take students from any discipline. In addition, the majority of schools require applicants to undertake an entrance exam, the results of which are used to offer interviews. Details on the graduate entry programmes offered by universities can be seen in the table below. However, students are encouraged to contact the relevant universities for more information.

University	Places	Course details
Birmingham	40	• 4-year medical course open to graduates of life science subjects with minimum 2:1in first degree; sound knowledge of chemistry • students are taught in a separate stream for the first 2 years, before joining the specialty clinical rotations of years 4 and 5 of the 5-year MBChB degree
Bristol	19	• 4-year medical course requiring at least a 2:1 BSc with biomedical science in first degree
Cambridge	20	• 4-year medical course open to graduates of **any** discipline • all candidates are required to take the Medical and Veterinary Admissions Test (MVAT), after application and before interview
Derby	91	• 4-year medical course open to graduates of **any** discipline who have obtained or are predicted to obtain, a minimum of Bachelors (Honours) degree classified 2:2 or better • applicants have to complete the GAMSAT test (this tests knowledge, reasoning skills and communication across a range of disciplines); a structured interview for a place on the course is offered to those who achieve the highest marks
GKT	40	• 4-year medical course open to graduates of **any** discipline with at least a 2:1 in their first degree • suitable candidates for the course take a written aptitude test; interviews offered on the basis of the application form and the aptitude test results
Leicester	40	• 4-year medical course open to graduates with at least a 2:1 degree in health sciences
Liverpool	40	• 4-year medical course open to graduates with at least a 2:1 in biomedical and health sciences and from approved social care professions • the programme covers the first 2 years of the 5-year course in one academic year (expanded by an extra 10 weeks)

(*Continued*)

(*Continued*)

University	Places	Course details
Newcastle	95	• 4-year medical course open to graduates of **any** discipline • offers to graduates will be conditional on at least a 2:1 or a 2:2 degree combined with a PhD • applications from those whose prior professional experience matriculates them for entry are welcomed • candidates interviewed for the accelerated programme are likely to be required to sit an admissions test, the results of which will form part of the overall selection process
Oxford	30	• 4-year graduate entry course for biological science graduates • a special 2-year transition course is taught at the hospital site, with college-based tutorials, leading to the final 2 years of the standard clinical course • applicants must complete a Biomedical Admissions Test
Southampton	40	• 4-year medical course open to graduates of **any** discipline with at least a 2:1 in their first degree • there is no entrance examination or interview
St Bart's	40	• 4-year medical course open to graduates with at least a 2:1 degree in a science or health-related studies degree • those who meet the criteria are allocated a random number and a computer generates a random list of numbers; the first 140 of these sit the Personal Qualities Assessment (PQA) test • those who perform satisfactorily in the PQA will be invited to attend an interview – offers are made to those who score best at interview • priority for 14 places is given to applicants from the Biomedical Sciences, Materials Science and Engineering courses at Queen Mary, University of London
St George's	70	• 4-year medical course open to graduates in **any** discipline • they must have or be predicted at least a 2:2 degree in any discipline • applicants have to complete the GAMSAT test; those who perform well in the test are offered an interview
Swansea	30	• 4-year medical course open to graduates of **any** discipline with at least a 2:1 in their first degree • applicants have to complete the GAMSAT test; those who perform well in the test are offered an interview
Warwick	164	• 4-year degree open to biological science graduates with at least a 2:1 in their first degree • core subjects are cell biology, molecular biology, genetics and biochemistry • applicants sit MSAT and complete a supplementary application form

Most self-funding students and many graduate entrants will incur higher levels of debt than their younger colleagues. However, finances should not put you off applying to medical school if you have a true desire to become a doctor. Students on approved 4-year graduate entry courses are eligible for an NHS bursary from year 2 of studies onwards. Although many schools do not normally consider applicants over 30 years of age, some graduate programmes have no upper age limit. However, it must be noted that competition for places on these programmes are high, and the number of spaces available is relatively small.

Premedical courses

While most medical degrees last 5 or 6 years some schools offer a premedical year. This year, which is intended as a foundation year in basic sciences, gives students with good nonscience A-level grades (and some nonscience graduates, if there is not an appropriate graduate entry programme) a way into the medicine degree course.

There are significant variations in the way these courses are taught and organised, and the exact nature of the premedical course varies from school to school. At some schools, students who complete the year successfully can apply to join the medical degree course, whereas at others there is automatic transfer to the first year of the 5-year course.

Premedical courses may be taught within the medical faculty or in other university departments. Exemptions from parts of the course may be offered if that subject has already been studied to a sufficient level, and some schools offer a choice of subject studied. In addition, certain schools also specify that particular science subjects are needed at GCSE/Standard Grade level.

Medical schools offering premedical courses are listed below, along with some course details. However, students are encouraged to contact the relevant universities for more information.

University	Places	Course details
Belfast	5	• course for students with more broadly based qualifications than A-levels, e.g. Scottish Highers or Irish Leaving Certificate • students attend first-year courses in chemistry, physics and biological science
Bristol	10	• students who have not studied science at A-level are admitted into a 'preliminary year' where they can acquire the necessary science background before commencing the 5-year programme • the premedical year is spent studying the equivalent of A-levels in chemistry, biology and physics • premedical students study alongside predental students
Cardiff	12	• the premedical course is restricted to applicants who cannot meet the programme requirements for direct entry to the 5-year programme • it is a modular programme and studies centre on the chemical and biological sciences, or other subjects selected according to the student's prior qualifications

(*Continued*)

(*Continued*)

University	Places	Course details
Dundee	Up to 14	• the course is designed to meet a demand, and if this demand is not apparent, it is not important if the number of students in the premedical year is very small • the year is provided for applicants with good passes in nonscience subjects and is not available for applicants whose passes in science subjects do not meet requirements for first year • premed students join with first-year BSc courses in chemistry, biology and physics
Edinburgh	No set number	• the premedical year is an extra year of study for applicants who do not have the subject entrance requirements for the 5-year programme • it consists of selected courses from the first year of the Biological Sciences course • successful students continue on to the 5-year course
GKT	40	• the premedical year is an extra year of study for applicants who do not have the subject entrance requirements for the 5-year programme, but achieve the academic requirements • applicants with qualifications not considered for the 5-year programme may also apply • the course covers biology, chemistry, physics, and maths • students study alongside those taking BSc degrees
Manchester	18–20	• the Premedical/Predental Programme occupies a single year and is designed for students who do not have the required science qualifications for direct entry into 5-year programme but have achieved good grades, in mainly arts subjects, or in the case of mature students, have a good arts degree • students learn fundamentals of biology, physics, and chemistry in an environment which has a relevance to clinical medicine; this is achieved with problem-based learning cases, theatre events, and skills sessions • entry to the next year of the medical course is automatic on satisfactory completion of this year
Newcastle	10–15	• the premedical year is open only to applicants without a science background • students study a combination of chemistry, biological sciences, and medical data handling
Sheffield	15	• the premedical science foundation course is a modified 'Access to Science' course which has been tailored to give students with a nonscientific background the necessary basic scientific knowledge to undertake the medical course • the course is designed to prepare students for the first part of the medical course, and is studied at Barnsley College • visits are made to the medical physics, clinical chemistry and anaesthetic departments of a local hospital • students also gain basic scientific knowledge through studying biology, chemistry and physics

5

Funding your way through

'The physician should not treat the disease but the patient who is suffering from it.'

Maimonides

What to expect

Money is an issue close to most students' hearts, and medical students are no exception. Government reforms of the higher education funding system, such as the introduction of tuition fees and the abolition of maintenance grants in 1998, have meant that the issue of debt is one that is affecting many more students than in previous years.

A recent BMA report (*Annual Survey of Medical Students' Finances 2003/2004*) found that the average total debt among final-year students was over £17,000. More than 30% of final-year medical students had debts in excess of £20,000. Although this may seem quite daunting you shouldn't let it put you off studying medicine. Yes, you are likely to be in more debt after graduation than someone who takes a 3-year degree course, but this is balanced by excellent future career prospects and good job security. Medical student intake reflects all sectors of society. If you are not supported by wealthy or generous parents **you won't be alone** in being in debt and it won't be forever. There are currently more jobs than there are doctors in the UK, and this trend looks set to continue for some time, so unemployment after graduation is not really an issue. Most medical graduates pay off their debt within 5 years of graduation, which helps to explain why bank managers tend to be very welcoming to medics!

Medicine, depending on where you choose to study it, can take you between 4 years and 6 years, so you will have to consider how you will support yourself for that time. The first 2 years are often the least financially demanding, as a great proportion of your year will be holidays. For many, this allows living at home for half the year and saving some costs; also, you will have plenty of time to earn cash in the holidays, if you want or need to. It gets a little trickier in your clinical years (when you spend more time in hospital): a total annual holiday of 6 weeks is considered good! During this time you'll have to pay for rent and food for the whole year, and it becomes difficult to find paid work when you have only 6 weeks off. Some students get part-time jobs during term time, although it is not always easy to fit this in. There are many kinds of expenses involved in studying medicine, and debt is likely to stare you in the face earlier than you might anticipate. Medicine is different from almost any degree course and there are several additional expenses: for example, there will be many expensive books to buy – you could spend at least £150 per year – and medical equipment, such as stethoscopes, can cost around £60. As always however, the advice remains that you should shop around where possible as there are good deals out there! You will also need some smart clothing once you're in hospitals regularly. This is to make you look and feel like part of the medical profession, and to help you gain the trust of your patients.

The financial issue of the moment is the introduction of '**top-up tuition fees**', which will mean that from 2006, tuition fees could be as much as £3000 per year of study. Student bodies and the BMA are opposed to their introduction, as they may discourage people from attending university because they simply cannot afford it. The BMA's Medical Students Committee (MSC) is campaigning to minimize their impact and is in ongoing discussions with the Department of Health. More information is available on the BMA website but changes are not likely to come into force until 2006. Please contact individual universities and see what financial assistance would be available to you from all sources to find out what the exact situation will be when you commence studies.

The obvious question is 'How will I pay for all this?' The first port of call for many people will be parents, guardians, or family, who may be able to give you something towards the cost of studying. If they are generous the problem is solved, but if not (which applies to most of us) then there are government loans, bank loans, overdrafts, and many other ways to fund yourself through university.

The type of funding you receive depends on a couple of factors: where you live in the UK and whether you have a previous degree. Funding arrangements for Scottish and graduate students will be discussed later in the chapter. The situation is changing and devolved nations may have different funding issues from England in the years to come.

The year 2002 saw the introduction of the NHS bursary, which means funding arrangements are different depending on which year of the course you are in, but this will be explained in the following sections.

Costs associated with studying medicine

Tuition fees

Since October 1998, students have been required to contribute towards the cost of their education. For 2003/2004 the maximum home students had to pay was £1125 per year. With inflation, this figure is likely to be £1150 in 2005–06. If your family income is below a certain level (£21,475 pa) you will not be expected to pay tuition fees at all. The full amount will only be payable if your parents' residual income is in excess of £31,973. Tuition fees make up a proportion of the cost of your tuition, the rest of which is made up by your Local Education Authority (LEA) in the form of mandatory and discretionary awards.

The BMA's MSC persuaded the government that special consideration needed to be given to medical students because of the length and expense of the course, and the Department of Health agreed to pay tuition fees for medical students from their fifth year of study onwards. This also applies to students doing premedical or intercalated years. This means that you will only pay tuition fees for the first 4 years of your course. For students on graduate entry programmes, the arrangements are more generous meaning that tuition fees are paid from the second year of study onwards. See that section for more information

Living costs

It is likely that paying for basic living costs will form the largest part of any debt you accumulate throughout your degree. Money for accommodation, food, transport, books, and beer will come from parental contributions, maintenance loans and, invariably, banks. The amount of maintenance loan you will be entitled to will depend on where you study and what year you are in. Loans are administered by the Student Loans Company: 25% of the loan is means tested and will depend largely upon your parents' income. The maximum loan available in 2004/2005 for students outside London was £4095 and for those in London was £5050 with smaller amounts being available to students living at home. Student loan repayments will be paid in instalments after graduation, once your income is over £15000 per year. For medics, repayments will begin during your first house officer job, which will generally be in the April after finals. There is extra money available for courses that last longer than 30 weeks.

In response to campaigns by the MSC, the Department of Health has agreed to provide means-tested nonrepayable NHS bursaries for medical students from year 5 onwards, which students will be able to apply for in addition to student loans. Students taking premedical and/or intercalated years will also be able to apply for this from year 5 onwards.

Travelling expenses

Most of the teaching on medical courses takes place on clinical attachments in hospitals and GP surgeries. These can be quite a distance from your main medical school base, meaning that travelling expenses can be considerable. Some medical schools offer travel expenses reimbursement, but this is by no means universal; the best way to find out is to contact the medical schools that you are thinking of applying to. It is expected that most students will fund travel expenses out of maintenance loans, although some may be claimed back from your LEA. The rules currently state that you can claim back travelling expenses incurred in attending clinical placements, although the first £265 must be borne by you. The amount you receive will be means tested. You should contact your local LEA to find out the arrangements for claiming expenses, and keep receipts and a record of journeys made to help your claim. If you have access to the NHS bursary you may be able to claim some of your travel expenses back.

Boosting your funds

High-street bank

In addition to the maintenance loan, a bank overdraft is likely to be required. Surviving at medical school makes this an almost essential part of your finances. Most banks and building societies offer students special terms on bank accounts. These normally include interest-free overdrafts. Keeping your bank manager happy by not exceeding the agreed overdraft limit is good practice, and also helps you avoid penalty charges and punishing interest rates. If you want to extend your overdraft, go and discuss it with the manager face to face. The bank wants your custom because you will have a good job at the end of your university career, and they are experienced at helping students out with money problems. Banks are more likely to be generous and sympathetic with students who keep them informed than those who constantly surprise them. If you need more cash than an overdraft gives you, then you may need a loan. Look around to make sure you have accessed all other sources of funding before you take out a loan, for example hardship funds and charitable funds (see below). Banks can be willing to accept begging letters and IOUs from medics, and many have specially tailored loans of up to £20,000 for medical students.

Remember, however, the debt you incur will have to be paid back regardless. Do not be blasé – heaven forbid that through illness, failure, or other unpredictable circumstances you do not qualify and are unable to repay your debts. Such instances are rare, but it would be irresponsible for us to overlook these possibilities. Make sure you fully understand the terms of the loan and shop around for the best deal. Don't just go to the bank you have an account with – it won't necessarily offer you the best deal.

Charities

There are literally hundreds of educational trust funds and charities in the UK, many of which support medical students. They tend to be open to mature and graduate students rather than school leavers, but it may be worth trying to find some funding from these sources. General directories of charitable trusts are available in the reference section of most public libraries and some are listed in the Further information section of this book. Spending time searching through the lists and applying for grants may be to your advantage. Many small trusts have bizarre criteria for offering awards, and you may be surprised to find that by meeting the unusual requirements you can get help towards your expenses.

Access funds, hardship funds and hardship loans

Universities receive money from the government to help students in the poorest financial shape. Applications for the money are processed locally and policies on how these funds are distributed vary widely from school to school. It is important to be aware that this money is available.

Higher education grant

In 2005 the government introduced a grant to higher education students, worth up to £1000 a year. The amount received depends on your income (if you are over the age of independence) or the income of your family. If this was under £15,200 students are entitled to the full amount of the grant. If income is between £15,201 and £21,185, students receive a partial grant. Those with income over £21,185 are not entitled to any grant. More information can be found from the Department of Education and Skills.

Work

For the majority of medical undergraduates, working during vacations in the early part of the course is a necessity. As well as casual work in bars and restaurants, many students work as healthcare assistants and medical secretaries. Work can usually be arranged through the teaching hospital or other local hospitals. The experience of working in a hospital environment in a role other than as a medical practitioner can be very valuable. As the course progresses, however, the holidays get shorter as term time extends and periods of elective study intervene, and it then becomes more difficult to find employment for these shorter periods. You might consider taking a part-time job during term. The medical course is undoubtedly challenging and demands a lot of your time in studying, no matter how gifted you are. Because of this, some medical schools discourage students from working during term. They cannot actually prevent you from doing so, but be warned that they may take a dim view. Check out the school's attitude with the medics on open days. Do not let a job get in the way of studies.

Some medical students sign up to one of the Armed Forces medical cadet schemes. A 'salary' is paid to cadets for 2–3 years. In return for this support during undergraduate training, cadets serve as an officer with, for example, the Royal Army Medical Corps, for a minimum period of duty (normally 6 years after full qualification). The income cadets receive is very generous compared to other students' incomes, but the quid pro quo is the 6-year short service commission. You will continue to practise as a doctor, but the Ministry of Defence will require you to support military initiatives anywhere in the world. Working as a doctor in the Armed Forces can be very rewarding and challenging. It is the advice of the authors of this guide that students who embark on medical cadetships should be committed to a career in the Services after graduation, and not simply addressing the funding of their course. The Forces recruit during the early years of the medical degree course and offer familiarisation visits for interested students. Contact details for each Service are given in the Further information section at the end of the book.

Elective funding

Students who organise themselves well in advance can often get enough funding to pay for some (if not all) of the cost of their elective. You should have a wonderful time wherever you go, but it is so much nicer if you know you haven't paid for it all yourself. Depending on where you want to go and what you will be studying, there are numerous grants, research awards, sponsorships, and bursaries available (the BMA holds a list of organisations that you can apply to for funds). Some will be open for all UK students to apply for, and other funds will be distributed locally. Most awards and grants are given in exchange for some sort of project report or research work.

Graduate students

Tuition fees

Fees for graduate students or self-funding students on standard courses will vary from institution to institution (see later). Some charge the standard £1150 per year, whereas others charge more for the preclinical stage of the course and more again for the clinical stage, so it is important to bear this in mind before applying and check with each medical school. Graduates who have received support from public funds for their first degree are not entitled to receive any mandatory or discretionary funding from their LEA and would therefore be liable to pay the full cost of tuition throughout the course. The MSC has been calling on medical schools to limit the amount of fees payable by graduates to the standard £1150, but there is no guarantee of success. In response to campaigns by the MSC, the government has introduced concessions for graduate medical students on the 4-year accelerated degree courses being held at Cambridge, St George's, and Leicester/Warwick. Tuition fees are paid by the Department of Health in years 2, 3, and 4 of the course and fees are payable by the students in year 1 only. The MSC is trying to persuade government to extend this scheme to graduate entrants on any medical degree course.

Scottish students studying on an accelerated course in the UK do not receive NHS tuition fee and bursary support in years 2–4, and are treated as though they were graduate students on a standard course, that is, means-tested maintenance loans and tuition fees.

Living costs

Graduate medical students are entitled to apply to the Student Loans Company for help with their living costs. The maximum loan available in 2003/2004 for students outside London was £4,095 and for those in London it was £5050 – 25% of the loan is means tested and will depend largely upon your personal/spousal income. These figures are revised annually. Graduates on accelerated courses can apply for funding to the NHS bursary scheme in years 2, 3, and 4 of the course. Under-25s are subject to a parental means test if they apply for a bursary, and this limits its availability. The MSC is pressing for this criterion to be relaxed. Graduates on standard courses will be able to apply to the NHS bursary from year 5 onwards.

Scottish students

Arrangements for Scottish students vary according to whether they are studying in Scotland or elsewhere in the UK. The student awards agency for Scotland (SAAS) is the body that deals with student support in Scotland (see Further information section).

Tuition fees

Students studying at Scottish universities will not have to make a contribution to tuition fees. The Scottish Executive has set up a graduate endowment scheme whereby graduates will contribute a sum of £2154 after they have left university (2004/2005 entrant figures). The funds raised will be used to support future students. Repayment of the endowment begins after you start earning more than £15,000 pa (in your preregistration house officer year). The 'St Andrew's anomaly', where the preclinical students go on to do clinical studies elsewhere (usually Manchester), and therefore which funding scheme they fit into, is yet to be settled. At the time of writing the Scottish Executive was also considering introducing medical tuition fees.

Living costs

The living support package you will receive differs according to whether you are classed as a young or a mature student. The Scottish Executive has introduced non-repayable maintenance grants of up to £2050 per year for students from families on low incomes and mature students with children. Maintenance loans from the Student Loans Company are also available.

Scottish students studying elsewhere in the UK

The funding for students studying outside Scotland is quite similar to that of other UK students. Your entitlement to tuition fee support is parental income assessed (up to £1100 for 2002/2003). Where there is a contribution to be deducted from the tuition fee support, the SAAS will pay the remainder.

Living costs support comes from student loans, which are the same as in the rest of the UK. There is an additional 'Young Students Outside Scotland Bursary' which is available for students from families with an income below £18,400. Mature students may apply for additional grants towards the cost of childcare. By 2006, Scottish students studying outside Scotland will have to pay the same 'top-up fees' as other students at that institution.

Support in the fifth year and beyond

All Scottish students, regardless of their place of study, can claim an income-assessed NHS bursary and free tuition. You will also have access to a non-income-assessed student loan, repayable once your income has reached a set level, currently around £10,000 pa.

Welsh students

The current financial arrangements for Welsh students are the same as for their English counterparts, that is, fixed-rate tuition fee and student loans. You may have access to an assembly learning grant of £1500 per annum providing you have an assessed income of less than £15,720 pa. Following the Rees Report, the Welsh assembly announced that top-up fees would not be introduced for Welsh higher education institutions. If you are a Welsh student studying outside Wales though, you will be subject to the tuition fee of your host university. You can however apply for a means-tested maintenance grant of up to £2700, through the Welsh assembly, regardless of your place of study.

Northern Irish students

Although funding issues may in future be altered depending on the impact of the Northern Ireland Assembly, at the time of writing, fees and funding remain the same as for English students. The BMA website will show updates as and when they occur.

The final balance...

Irrespective of your personal circumstances, studying medicine means undertaking a serious financial commitment. In common with many other students you will have to face up to some debt and financial worries. By accepting this reality and planning before you start how your tuition fees, parents' contribution, bank overdraft, student loan and bank loans will fit together over the years, you will come to terms with it better. You can find information about funding in our Further information section. Make sure your acquaintance with debt is on your own terms. Do not avoid dealing with tough money questions and do not adopt a head-in-the-sand approach to your finances. If you anticipate difficulties during the course, take advice from the Students' Union welfare services, the university and your bank.

Don't leave it too late to take action – there are very few miracle workers, and the people who are there to help are more likely to be helpful if they are given time. This talk of poverty and debt is depressing, but remember these two things.

- Debt is now a fact of life for students, and the vast majority survive and free themselves from it!
- Medical students are better placed than most to pay off their debts at the end of the day, with excellent employment prospects and job security.

6

Life beyond graduation ...

'The education of the doctor which goes on after he has his degree is, after all, the most important part of his education.'

John Shaw Billings (1838–1913)

The early years

Graduating or qualifying from medical school does not in itself, allow you to practise medicine: first you must register with the GMC. Initially, registration with the Council is only provisional, but you can call yourself Doctor. To register fully, newly qualified doctors are required to complete 12 months of paid work and achieve defined competencies as a house officer. This has traditionally consisted of a 6-month post in medicine and a 6-month post in surgery. However, from August 2005 hospital trusts, in partnership with the postgraduate deanery, will offer 2-year foundation programme posts which consist of units in medicine, surgery, then further units in other specialties such as paediatrics, general practice, accident and emergency or psychiatry, within which core competencies will be attained.

The ability to tailor your future career during your early working life should increase when reforms to junior doctor training are rolled out in August 2005. The push to modernize medical careers will introduce an integrated 2-year programme after graduation called the **foundation programme** and shorter training times to full specialization as a GP or a consultant. Details of the foundation programme are still being finalized but a key aim is to ensure better supervision, clear educational and training outcomes, and career mentoring and advice in the first 2 years of working.

Regardless of these changes all house officer posts must be approved by the GMC for the experience to count towards full registration. At the end of your first year of working you can demonstrate that the minimum competencies have been achieved you can apply for full GMC registration. Free hospital accommodation is provided for your job because the GMC believes that the right type of experience is only gained if you are resident, so don't worry if your jobs are in parts of the country you didn't choose: there will be accommodation provided. More information about the PRHO year can be found in the BMA document *First House Job*.

Applying for your first job

Most areas operate some sort of matching scheme in the final (or penultimate) year, which is normally co-ordinated by the postgraduate deanery in conjunction with your medical school. At the time of writing two or three postgraduate deaneries are piloting regional matching schemes and a matching scheme has covered all of Scotland for some time. A house officer job-matching scheme does what it suggests – it matches prospective house officers to house officer posts. Some schemes are open to medics from any UK medical school, and some are open only to the university's own students. Some only cover the posts in the university teaching hospitals, and some cover all the hospitals in the region. Normally, the school that sends students to a hospital for clinical experience will supply the same hospital with its new house officers, but some schemes include posts that are many miles away. If you are clear that you want to work in a particular part of the country, it might be worth finding out about the matching scheme.

The advantage of matching schemes is that some of the work needed to find a job is done for you and you will be placed only in university-approved jobs. The downside is that some schemes give you little notice of where your first house job will be or leave you feeling alienated from the process. Some medical schools produce too few graduates to fill all the regional posts and some produce too many, but for the foreseeable future medics have good prospects of getting work. If you cannot get a house job in the particular town or city you would like to work in, don't worry. During the training years you can apply for jobs elsewhere in the country (and abroad). Hospitals in Australasia, for example, recruit UK doctors for short-term posts.

The BMA also provides an interactive house jobs guide for members on its website. The guide has information from hospital trusts as well as from junior doctors actually working in the trust. Having a look at this guide when you reach years 4 and 5 of medical school may prove helpful.

As arrangements may change by the time you graduate, you should take an active role in considering where you would like to live after graduation and what type of post you would like to do well before you reach your final year at medical school.

Life as the house dog

The year as a house surgeon and physician is often the toughest in a medical career. There is much to do and learn, and sometimes providing a service to patients and your employer is at the cost of your continuing education. Current reforms aim to redress this balance and ensure that a core set of doctoring skills, as well as improved education are gained by all house officers in the future. Be under no illusions that you are at the bottom of the medical hierarchy. Demands from your patients, your colleagues, and your bosses can be overpowering. Hours of work are long (50 + per week), however changes to European law that come into effect in 2005 mean that the situation is improving. Working intensively at night or weekends (on call) can be exhausting. Further information about the working arrangements for junior doctors can be found on the BMA website.

As a house officer you will be responsible for taking histories from new patients, organising tests, following up consultants' instructions, and helping at outpatient clinics and with theatre sessions. However, there are controls and ways of reducing the strains upon you. There will probably be times when you are fed up and may want to quit medicine. Some do, but the vast majority stay on. You will become more confident, more able to cope, and the work will eventually become more interesting (and challenging).

Beyond the house officer year

From 2005, after you have completed your first year as a house officer and have received registration from the GMC you can begin to have more lengthy exposure to the career path you want. This has traditionally been in senior house officer posts through basic specialist training and, later, in specialist or GP registrar posts. If you have a strong idea about what specialty you want to practise in or you know you want to become a GP, then you can begin to take the appropriate path in the second year of the **foundation programme** and continue through the new **training grades**. Don't worry if you don't know which branch of medicine you want to be in now or even, for that matter, during the first few years after graduation. Many junior doctors don't decide on their final career until well into their postgraduate training and a core element of government reform is to ensure that career advice is more readily available. The three main areas of practice are general practice, hospital medicine and surgery. The BMA is working with government on ensuring that changes to junior doctor training and structures to specialization do not disadvantage future generations of doctors and dovetail with existing professional outcomes.

A career in general practice

General practice is changing significantly, both as a result of changes to training pathways and because of the new contract negotiated for GPs between the BMA and Government. Many GPs will continue to be self-employed doctors who provide general medical services to patients for a Primary Care Trust although there is also the ability to work as a paid employee in the same way as consultants are employed by Hospital Trusts. GPs usually work in small, relatively autonomous business partnerships with other GPs. The most common route to becoming a principal is to do three years' training as a GP registrar. This is divided into 2 years of hospital posts (in specialties such as general medicine, general surgery, A&E, obstetrics, geriatrics or psychiatry) and 1 year working as a 'trainee' in general practice. Most doctors training to enter general practice follow vocational training schemes in which the particular posts they will rotate through are preplanned from the outset. By the time the most recent entrants to medical school graduate, it is anticipated that a greater percentage of GPs will be employees rather than independent contractors.

A career in hospital medicine or surgery

In order to become a hospital consultant, junior doctors normally rotate through 2 or 3 years of SHO jobs in medical or surgical specialties. After this, and once their choice of specialty is clear, they spend between 4 and 5 years studying in registrar posts. There are specialist registrar 'rotations' which allow a doctor to prearrange 3 or 4 years of training in different hospital posts. When this training is completed satisfactorily, a Certificate of Completion of Specialist Training (CCST) is issued and the doctor can apply for consultant posts.

Similar to GPs, the future training paths and conditions of service for hospital doctors are also undergoing change. The BMA has agreed a new contract for consultants and there is discussion of a Certificate of Specialist Training (CST) that could be awarded for shorter periods of time served in the training grades. The BMA is opposed to the introduction a CST and continues to discuss alternative options with government.

Other career paths

General practice and hospital posts provide the greatest number of jobs for doctors in the health service, but there are many other career paths. Many doctors work in public health medicine, as medical academics, as researchers for pharmaceutical companies, for the Armed Forces, and in private medicine. A great strength of practising as a doctor is the range of experience you can find in work. Flexible training is becoming more common and part-time posts are numerous. Many doctors have more than one string to their bow and it is not uncommon, for example, for a doctor to mix private work or part-time work with their main NHS job. Putting together a portfolio career as a doctor is possible. A consultant might add some medical journalism and legal work in courts as an expert witness to their weekly duties as a hospital specialist; a director of public health might do voluntary medical work with a charity; or a GP might work part time with a local rugby club. The following diagram shows a simplified path of career options in medicine for doctors in the UK.

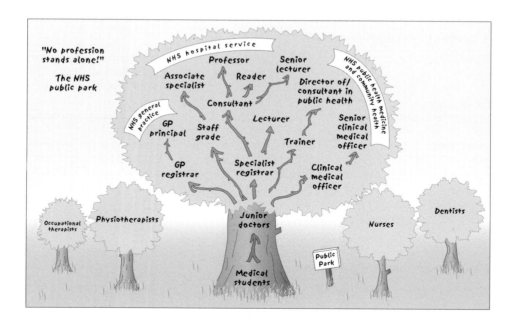

There are many options open to those seeking a career in medicine. The medical career structure is outlined in the tree diagram and gives an indication of the huge variety of choices available.

Continuing medical education

Don't think that studying is over once you have graduate from medical school! The GMC's view is that undergraduate medical education is just the first step toward lifelong learning. It means that doctors must continue to study to some extent throughout their working lives and are expected to keep their skills and knowledge up to date to remain registered as a doctor. The GMC has introduced a system of formal reassessment for all doctors on its register – *revalidation*. Many skills and much knowledge will be acquired 'on the job', but most career paths require some formal qualifications and exams will have to be passed to retain registration with the GMC. From autumn 2005 the **Postgraduate Medical Education and Training Board** will be responsible for continuing medical education, and will oversee the standards required for all specialties that will enable you get on in your career. This may include passing Royal College exams either as a minimum requirement for membership or to supplement the minimum standards required. Both the introduction of revalidation and establishment of the Postgraduate Medical Education Board will allow transparency in ongoing educational requirements across the entire profession.

Part 2
The A–Z of UK medical schools

How to use Part 2

Numerous factors influence which medical schools suit you most and which ones you may decide to apply to. In this chapter, we have summarised a number of important areas we think you should take into consideration before making a decision. Each medical school chapter in the following section has been deliberately divided into three sections (Education, Welfare, Sports and Social) to make it easier for you to compare different schools. A snapshot of key information for all schools can also be found at Mikey and Michelle's quick compare table on page 299.

Education

Although all students need to reach the same standard outlined by the GMC by the time they graduate, courses at different medical schools can vary considerably in the way this is achieved. More often than not the courses on offer are subject to change, and many of us at medical school are on different courses from those outlined in the original prospectus. Don't, whatever you do, get bogged down in the details of individual courses. You'll just get confused. However, it may be worthwhile considering the following areas.

Teaching

There are two broad teaching methods, either of which may be used on their own in some schools or combined to offer a mix of the two. 'Traditional' teaching relies heavily on lectures and practicals, with a large portion of the week devoted to didactic teaching where students are in lecture theatres for long periods.

Problem-based learning (PBL) is the more recent approach, and usually has fewer timetabled commitments. Commonly, students work in small groups and discuss patient case studies, from which they form study agendas for the coming week. Students then work through their own study objectives, which are supplemented with laboratory sessions such as pathology and anatomy in the preclinical years, and maybe attendance at outpatient clinics in the clinical years. With the PBL approach, it is essential that students, and their groups sustain a significant amount of self-motivation.

The structure of courses also varies considerably. Some medical schools maintain the traditional preclinical/clinical divide with core science subjects, such as anatomy, biochemistry, pharmacology and pathology taught in the early years and speciality based clinical subjects such as obstetrics and gynaecology, paediatrics and surgery taught in the later years. Other medical schools choose a system-based approach and combine both core sciences and clinical experience in all years. Between these two extremes there is all number of shades of grey and it is worth developing an idea of which style you feel you would enjoy the most.

Anatomy teaching has also seen many changes in recent years, and in some medical schools the dissection of cadavers by students has been replaced, partly or fully, with demonstration sections (or prosections) dissected by staff before class. This is often less gruesome and does not necessitate students 'getting their hands wet'. However, some students prefer the 'hands on' approach both in and out of dissection.

Assessment

The type of assessment varies significantly between schools. Commonly used methods include multiple choice question papers (sometimes negatively marked), essay papers, short answer questions, computer examinations, literature review papers, case studies and papers which require candidates to match questions to answers…as well as many more. Some schools have final exams in the penultimate year and others have finals at the end of the last year. Increasingly a number of schools are choosing to place a greater amount of emphasis on continuous assessment, which reduces the impact of finals at the end of the course.

When choosing which medical schools to apply for, decide whether you would prefer exams and assessments spread out during the years and the course, or whether you would prefer to take cumulative exams once everything has had a chance to fit into place. Either way, you still have to learn it all!

Intercalated degrees

This is where medical students can obtain a Bachelor of Science (BSc), Batchelor of Art (BA) or Batchelor of Medical Science (BMedSci) degree for undertaking an extra year of study (although some can be done within the 'normal' 5-year course), once they have completed at least two years of their medical training. These degrees can be undertaken in a variety of subjects related to medicine and provide an opportunity for students to pursue further study in an area they are interested in. Medical schools in the UK take a variety of approaches to intercalated degrees. In some (although this approach is gradually disappearing) the extra degree is open only to the academic high-flyers, some offer courses to almost any medical student, and at others it is compulsory. If you anticipate being interested in some extra in-depth research leading to a qualification, or if you think you might like to follow an academic or teaching career, then think about this before you apply. Many medical schools also allow students to study for the extra degree within other faculties of the university or at other institutions.

Special study modules (SSM) and electives

Schools devote markedly different portions of the course to studying areas of special interest (SSMs) and to overseas work placements (electives). Although there is an accepted minimum provision, it is worth considering this when choosing your medical school. Some medical schools will allow 2- to 4-week SSMs in diverse medical subjects such as history of medicine, medicine and art, and modern languages, and certain schools allow students to take one or more SSMs abroad in addition to their elective period. The vast majority of UK medical schools offer students an opportunity to spend a longer part of the course (around 2 months), known as the elective, anywhere in the world to experience medicine in a foreign health care setting. The exact nature of these placements varies slightly between schools. However, wherever you choose to study, these placements are seen as one of the highlights of medical school life.

Welfare

Student support

Pastoral support systems should be in place at all universities and all students should be allocated a personal tutor or 'Director of Studies'. However standards of support tend to vary markedly and it is well worth asking existing medical students about the provision and success of such schemes when attending the open days. Some universities will provide support through the medical faculty as well as via the main campus, and a friendly, approachable and understanding medical faculty can make a considerable difference to a student's experience at university – especially if it is necessary for the student to manage ill-health or dependants in addition to their medical studies. Most schools have in-house counselling and advice services.

At many universities freshers are allocated students from later years to be a 'mummy' or a 'daddy' – or one of each – during their first few weeks at medical school. Such schemes can be very beneficial, helping new students to settle in and providing them with support and guidance during their early years. Many students remain in touch with their 'academic families' well beyond graduation.

Accommodation

The accommodation the university provides and where it is located will have an important effect on your experience of university: remember you will spend a large portion of your time there and so you want to be happy. Important questions to ask include:

- Is accommodation provided for the first year?
- Are meals provided or is the residence self-catering?
- Is it just for medics or for a range of students?
- Is the accommodation mixed?
- Is the accommodation on campus, and if not, how far away is it?
- How expensive is the accommodation for the first and subsequent years?

Placements

Most schools will send you away from the main university hospital base for some modules. The distances involved can vary significantly. Are you the type who enjoys travelling and seeing different parts of the country or would you rather stay nearer to the medical school and spend less on travel? These are important questions to consider when applying to medical schools that have a larger number of 'peripheral' hospitals. Each chapter lists examples of the distance from campus of hospital placements and journey time to give you an indication of what to expect.

Sports and social

Most universities organise social weekends and freshers' weeks before the start of freshers' term, and this is a great way of making friends early on. The comfort of walking into the bar on the first evening of term and recognising a friendly face from such a weekend relieves some of the initial anxiety of leaving home and making new friends.

All medical schools offer medics' sports teams. Only students studying medicine will be able to represent these clubs. As almost all medical schools are now part of larger universities you will also be able to play for the university side. However, you tend to find that most medics pride themselves on playing for the medics. The camaraderie and social life are unrivalled and a constant envy of nonmedics. However, this has also led to accusations of 'cliquishness'. The only limit on the number of teams you can join is the amount of time you are willing to devote. Most students wonder how medics can study during the day, train in the evenings and play matches week in and week out: the answer is that you develop good time management skills. However, it is important to get the balance right. One beauty of medics' sports is that all skill levels are catered for, and as you progress in your medical career you may find you take on more responsibility for your club, from organising the mundane such as kit, to the extravagant, such as tours of Europe!

Other than sports teams, most medical schools have choirs, drama clubs and even organise annual medic shows and comedy reviews. Furthermore, most schools have medical societies that organise social events and you can also get involved with events organised by the Medical Students International Network (MedSIN), for example, Sexpression (students running sex education initiatives in their local area), or Marrow (a student-led initiative which aims to recruit volunteers to the bone marrow register) as well as others. There is something for everyone! Again, in addition to the medical school clubs, there is a wealth of university social and hobby clubs and students are always welcome to start new ones.

Top tip: Do get involved, try something new, excel at something old, but most importantly, ENJOY IT!

Aberdeen

Key facts	Undergraduate
Course length	5 years
Total number of medical undergraduates	949
Applicants in 2005	1900
Interviews given in 2005	1250
Places available in 2005	162 Home 13 OS
Places available in 2006	162 Home 13 OS
Open days 2006	29 August
Entrance requirements	AAB
Mandatory subjects	2 science or maths
Male:female ratio	1:1.3
Is an exam included in the selection process? If yes, what form does this exam take?	No UKCAT in 2007
Qualification gained	MBChB

Fascinating fact: Marischal College, home to the dissecting room, is the second largest granite building in the world.

The grey colour and cold temperature of the 'granite city' bear no relation to the warm and friendly atmosphere and busy social life that is Aberdeen. The oldest medical school in the English-speaking world hasn't grown as much as most UK medical schools, with relatively small year sizes – generally about 175 – allowing you to get to know most of your class. The medical school is on the same site (at Foresterhill) as the main teaching hospitals (20–25 minutes' walk from the main University campus, and a similar distance from the city centre), so you can go straight from lectures to wards.

Education

The scoring system used in selecting students for interview and at interview are described on the prospective students website (referenced at the end of this chapter), which also includes a lot of other useful information about the application process, as well as about studying medicine and student life in Aberdeen. Offers are made based upon combined academic, UCAS form and interview scores.

Aberdeen is involved in the Scottish pilot study of psychometric testing, but participation is voluntary and separate from the admissions process.

Teaching

The 5 years are split into four phases: fundamentals of medical science; principles of clinical medicine; specialist clinical practice; and professional practice. A core syllabus focusing on integrated systems is counterbalanced with special study modules (SSMs). Students must complete each phase before passing on to the next. The course is predominantly lecture-based in the first 3 years, with some tutorial-based learning sessions. However, there is a large amount of excellent small group teaching during the clinical years; in fact, there is so much you sometimes feel you are being dragged away from the patients! Some of the course is taught through self-study packages.

Student views and problems can be formally voiced at Staff–Student Liaison Committee (SSLC) meetings. Student representatives sit on both the year group SSLCs and the over-arching MBChB SSLC. A senior student is also elected to sit on a number of other university and medical school committees.

Aberdeen received a very high rating in the last Scottish Higher Education Funding Council Teaching Quality assessment. Students experience many different learning environments, such as general practice, specialist hospital wards, lecture theatres, tutorial groups and the Clinical Skills Centre. Anatomy is taught via study of prosections, models and radiographic images. Computer-assisted learning (CAL) is integrated within each phase of medical training, supplementing the compulsory ward teaching and tutorials.

Assessment

Assessment is both in-course, though much of this is formative, and exam based (written and clinical), with vivas for pass-fail candidates in summative assessments. Should you fail a degree assessment, there are three more chances to pass by way of two vivas and a further written exam. Students are supported and encouraged should this occur.

Intercalated degrees

About 30–40 students each year choose to do an intercalated degree (BSc in Medical Sciences) at the end of year 3. In order to choose this option you must have passed all exams in year 2 and year 3 at the first sitting.

The BSc course starts, unusually, in April and runs until the March of the following year. The first 2 months are spent following a core syllabus, presented as lectures and small group tutorials, after which there are a number of summer exams. On returning from the summer break in September, students undertake an individual research project which is to be completed and written up for the following March. These projects are generally chosen from a list and give the opportunity for students to work in a range of different research settings.

Projects are virtually all carried out in Aberdeen, as the unusual timing of the BSc does not allow students to join intercalated courses at other UK medical schools (which normally run from September to September). A very small number of students have carried out projects abroad or at other institutions in the UK, but little help is offered for those who wish to do this.

Some financial awards are available to help with the cost of taking on an extra year at university, generally based on either your academic grades or project topic.

Should you chose to do an intercalated BSc, advantages include learning to work confidently as part of a team, organising your own work schedule, and the possibility of having your work published. Some also feel an extra year gives you the edge by allowing you the time to mature before the hard work of year 4 begins.

Special study modules and electives

All of the four phases of the course include special study modules. Special study modules and electives prior to final year are chosen from lists of prescribed topics under different themes (e.g. population-based disease) and generally require the writing of a report and preparation of a presentation in a group of about 8 students. You may well not get your first choice of topic and there is little flexibility to pursue your own interests.

The final phase SSM is nonmedical, offering the opportunity to study subjects such as Spanish, history of medicine, music or sign language. During the final phase, students also have a 7-week elective period which can be spent abroad, almost anywhere in the world. Unlike other medical schools, this includes a short research project, which contributes towards your final degree. It is not a holiday!

Erasmus

Overseas travel opportunities are during the final year elective and, for a limited number, the nonmedical SSM.

Facilities

Library The medical school has its own library on the Foresterhill site. Opening hours are good (9 AM–10 PM Monday to Thursday; 9 AM–8 PM Friday; 9 AM–10 PM Saturday; 1 PM–10 PM Sunday). Texts and journals are plentiful, as is access to Medline. Photocopying and printing cost approximately 5p/sheet.

Computers There are many computers available, with free internet and email. There are CAL packages for a variety of subjects, as well as exam-style online self-assessment questions. Many lecture presentations are available on the internet. There is 24-hour access to computer laboratories on the university campus and at the medical school.

Clinical skills The joint University of Aberdeen, Robert Gordon University and NHS Clinical Skills

Centre on the Foresterhill site is equipped with models to practise almost every procedure you can think of, plus all the standard clinical equipment. It is used for teaching clinical skills and procedures to all medical students, qualified doctors, and other health care students and staff, with timetabled access and 'drop-in' sessions. Skills teaching includes examination skills, use of equipment, communication skills (interviewing simulated patients), and many practical procedures, e.g. IV access, suturing, catheterisation, defibrillation, etc. A 'Harvey' cardiology patient simulator is now used to teach all students from year 2 onwards.

Welfare

Student support

Support for medical students is led by the clerk to the degrees in medicine, who co-ordinates the *regent* (personal tutor) scheme. Each student is paired up with a regent when they enter medical school and is required to meet with them at least twice in year 1 and once in subsequent years; as with all relationships, regent–regentee relationships vary from excellent to totally dysfunctional! Students can change their regent at any stage.

All the general university support services, such as the counselling service and the chaplain, are also available to medical students. The Students Association also provide welfare services. However, medical students may find the service difficult to access because of the geographical distance between the medical school and the main university campus.

Accommodation

The university has recently sold off a number of its halls and flats, although much of this accommodation has been bought by private companies and is still available to students. First-year students are guaranteed a place in university accommodation. Most people move into private accommodation after their first year and seem to have no problem finding somewhere within walking distance of the Foresterhill hospitals to live.

Placements

Most of your first year will be spent at Marischal College in the centre of Aberdeen, with a small amount of time spent at the main university campus and at Foresterhill (this has changed recently and is likely to change again, however.) The vast majority of years 2 and 3 will be spent at the medical school on the Foresterhill site, with contact with patients through placements on wards, usually two mornings per week. The aim of these attachments is to develop skills and confidence in clinical examination and history taking.

Years 4 and 5 are spent almost entirely on clinical rotations through all the specialties and general practice. During year 4, you will have to spend at least 10 weeks on attachment in Inverness and most people will spend part of their final year in Inverness, Elgin, Fort William or Stornoway. Moreover, GP attachments in years 4 and 5 are available throughout Scotland, from Wick to West Fife. Free accommodation is provided, as is travel at the beginning and end of the attachments.

Some students will always prefer to remain in Aberdeen, but the peripheral attachments are generally popular and it is not uncommon for students to deliberately choose to spend all or almost all of their final year away from Aberdeen. There is some element of choice in when and where you do most of these attachments, although, of course, not everyone's preferences can be met. One of the distinctive features of the Aberdeen course is the opportunity to have exposure to such a geographically varied range of working environments and many students feel they benefit from this.

Location of clinical placement/ name of hospital	Distance away from medical school (miles)	Difficulty getting there on public transport*
Elgin	65	
Inverness	105	
Fort William	157	
Stornoway	174 (as the crow flies!)	
GP attachments	All over Scotland	depending on distance

* : walking/cycling distance; : use public transport; : need own car or lift; : get up early – tricky to get to!

Sports and social

City life

Aberdeen is a small but busy city. With two universities, there is a large student population and accompanying vibrant nightlife. The city centre is compact and lively, with most pubs/clubs within 10 minutes' walk of each other and 20 minutes' walk from most student halls. There is a good selection of bars, pubs, theatres and cinemas, from mainstream to alternative. Nights out need not cost you an arm and a leg, with many venues having free entry, especially before midnight.

Just a short journey from the buzzing centre is the beach, with roller coasters, an ice-rink, and a cinema. A few miles north of this traditional promenade, it is possible to wander through the sand dunes of Balmedie beach, the perfect location for a summer BBQ, but you will need a car to get you there. In the other direction are the mountains and the outdoors: excellent for walking, climbing, winter and water sports. The northerly location means the climate can be very cold and, although there are good road, rail, and air links, Aberdeen is a considerable distance away from the rest of the UK.

University life

As the medical school is isolated from other parts of the university, medics need to make a bit of an effort to meet nonmedical students, but the first year is normally spent in halls and this gives students an opportunity to meet others outside medicine. The city centre union building closed for good in 2004, as it was not being used enough by students, mainly owing to competition from city centre bars' student-targeted promotions and theme nights.

University societies are numerous and healthy, however, covering a wide range of interests: sporting, dramatic, photography, musical, outdoor, university Armed Forces units (army, navy, and RAF), intellectual, malt whisky appreciation, etc. MedSoc holds functions every 2–3 weeks including the very popular annual ball, and has a few societies of its own, and the annual medical revue is well supported and popular.

Sports life

MedSoc has its own rugby, football, and hockey teams, which compete against the other Scottish medical schools. MedSoc members can join an exclusive gym in town for a discounted fee of £120 per year. University clubs offer a variety of sports from gliding, underwater hockey, archery and ultimate Frisbee, to the regulars such as rugby, hockey, and football. Members of all levels are given a warm welcome. There are no specific medical school facilities, but the university offers an inexpensive gym, pool, and tennis facilities, among others.

> **Top tip:** Buy a *Spree* book (£22 from most Aberdeen charities) – vouchers for buy-one-get-one-free in restaurants, takeaways, at the football, golf courses and swimming pool, plus discounts in shops and day passes for health clubs, amongst other things. The vouchers last a year, and £4 from your £22 goes to the charity you got your book from. Seems expensive for a little book, but saves you a fortune added up through the year.

Great things about Aberdeen

- Friendly small school, with teaching hospital and medical school buildings within a single site.
- Excellent clinical skills teaching and early clinical experience in year 2.
- Main exams are done by the end of year 4 – so you have got most of the knowledge and can concentrate on putting it into practice in year 5.
- Range of enthusiastic societies run by students for students – for example, MedSoc (of course!), the Wilderness Medical Society, the Ogston (surgical) Society and Aberdeen Medical Group, which discusses ethical issues.
- Excellent student social life, with civilised licensing laws (late opening).
- Easy access to the great outdoors (beach and mountains a very short distance away; skiing 45 minutes away; sailing locally).

Bad things about Aberdeen

- No dedicated medic social centre on site.
- Geographically isolated from the rest of the university, which means the majority of your student friends are medics. This is not helped by the different timings of exams and holidays.
- You cannot organise your own SSMs until your final year.
- The intercalated BSc year runs from April to March, so it is very difficult for students to do a BSc at other universities, where BSc programmes usually begin in September.
- It is a long way from most centres of population in the UK, so travelling times and costs can be a pain.
- OK, it can be cold – but isn't everywhere in the UK sometimes!

Further information

School of Medicine Office (Admissions)
Polwarth Building
Foresterhill
Aberdeen AB25 2ZD
Tel: 01224 553 015
Fax: 01224 554 761
Email: medicine@abdn.ac.uk
Web: http://www.abdn.ac.uk/medicine/prospective.shtml

Additional application information	
Average A-level requirements	• AAB
Average Scottish Higher requirements	• AAAAB
Make-up of interview panel	• Two selectors
Months in which interviews are held	• November–March
Proportion of overseas students	• 9.8%
Proportion of mature students	• 18.4%
Proportion of graduate students	• 8.9%
Faculty's view of students taking a gap year	• Acceptable
Proportion of students taking intercalated degrees	• 14.9%
Possibility of direct entrance to clinical phase	• No
Fees for overseas students	• £10,968 pa in years 1 and 2 • £20,484 pa in years 3, 4 and 5
Fees for graduates	• £2700 pending approval by the Scottish Executive
Ability to transfer to other medical schools If so, under what circumstances	• Transfer is possible but uncommon and constrained by the differing structure of medical courses. Previous students have transferred for family and personal reasons
Assistance for elective funding	• Limited funds are available locally and depend on your elective project proposal. There is a good notice board advising about external elective funding opportunities
Assistance for travel to attachments	• A bus is run to and from Inverness at the start and end of the year 4 attachments. Apart from this, one return journey to any attachment will be refunded. Travel to GP attachments commutable on a daily basis from Aberdeen is refunded less £2.50 per day
Access and hardship funds	• Access bursaries are awarded by the University across all areas of study. Limited hardship funds are awarded by the School once a year (in March) and the School recommends students for awards from other organisations
Weekly rent	• £45–£60 if sharing private accommodation
Pint of lager	• £2.10
Cinema	• £3.50
Nightclub	• £2 – though variable

Bart's and The London

Key facts	Undergraduate	Graduate
Course length	5 years	4 years
Total number of medical undergraduates	1809	46
Applicants in 2005	2500	950
Interviews given in 2005	900	150
Places available in 2005	277	46
Places available in 2006	277	46
Open days 2006	3 in July	April, May and June
Entrance requirements	AAB	2:1 science degree
Mandatory subjects	Chemistry and biology	–
Male:female ratio	1:1	1:2
Is an exam included in the selection process? If yes, what form does this exam take?	No UKCAT	Yes MSAT. UKCAT in 2007
Qualification gained	MBBS	MBBS

Fascinating fact: David Burckett St Laurent, a current final year student at Bart's and The London, became the youngest ever person to walk to the North Pole in 2003 to raise money for charity.

Bart's and The London was formed from the merger of St Bartholomew's Hospital Medical College and The London Hospital Medical College. It is centred in London's East End, one of the capital city's most exciting areas. Home to a large number of ethnic groups, this area is a fascinating place to study medicine as a result of the varied needs of its communities.

St Bartholomew's is the oldest hospital in the world and is a centre of excellence for many specialist disciplines. The London Hospital Medical College was the first medical school in England and is the site of our new medical school building. A new 1000 unit student village at the Mile End campus has also just opened.

The school strives to be progressive, and the 2004 intake will be the sixth year who will study the new 1999 curriculum, which has problem-based learning at its core and a greater emphasis on the integration of clinical and preclinical elements of medical training. We have just seen the first cohort of the students studying under the new curriculum qualify with remarkable results.

The combined school of Bart's and The London is part of Queen Mary College, University of London. We were the first school to complete the merger process in London, so all of the difficulties of merger are now a distant memory; we have grown into one of the most innovative and forward-thinking schools in the UK.

Education

Selectors are looking for candidates with the core qualities that a doctor or dentist must possess: good communication and listening skills; ability to work in a team; respect for colleagues; integrity; and ability to recognise his/her limitations, as well as those of others. Applicants should be able to demonstrate both a real understanding of what a career in medicine involves and their suitability for a caring profession. They must have an understanding of science, but the wider their knowledge and interests, the better.

A new curriculum started in 1999 and is centred on the technique of problem-based learning (PBL). This new approach involves a reduced number of lectures, and students are encouraged to find their own answers to clinical problems using textbooks, journals, and the internet, as well as practical experience. All students follow the same core course, and are then able to broaden their knowledge in areas of particular interest during special study modules (SSMs). The traditional preclinical/clinical divide is now less distinct, as the new course integrates basic medical, human, and clinical sciences from day 1 until graduation. Bart's and The London students are placed with both GPs and hospitals during the first 2 years.

Teaching

In the first 2 years of the course teaching is systems based, concentrating on 'Systems in Health' for year 1 and 'Systems in Disease' for year 2. There is a mixed approach, including lectures, PBL and workshop sessions, and all aspects of the body system, such as the cardiovascular system, are considered as an integrated whole. For the final 3 years, teaching is hospital based, with a continued emphasis on self-directed learning. Courses in communication skills (using actors and videotaping) and ethics run throughout the 5 years. Dissection is no longer part of the core course, and anatomy is taught using computer-aided learning programs, anatomical models, and already dissected specimens. Those who wish to dissect may do this as an SSM. St Bartholomew's, The Royal London, The London Chest and Homerton Hospital are the home sites for clinical teaching, although as with all of the great teaching hospitals in London there are a large number of other hospitals where students have an opportunity to get an experience of different types of medicine. These extend right out to Southend and Harlow.

The system of teaching at Bart's and The London is very responsive to student opinion. A lot of time and effort is spent by both staff and students in fine-tuning the course resulting in a course that both the staff and the students are very proud of.

Assessment

Summer exams are set for years 1–4 of the course, and with the new curriculum, 'big bang' final examinations are a thing of the past. Assessment is continuous, with credit being given for performance in both tutorials and examinations. The great importance that has been placed on student feedback and responsiveness to student opinion has resulted in huge strides being made in assessment, examples of this success include the fact that Bart's and The London can be one of few if not the only school in the country where the dreaded MCQ-style questions have been phased out of the assessment programme. At the end of year 5 students are assessed on their 'competence to practise' as a PRHO and must pass an integrated paper and clinical exams.

Intercalated degrees

Both BSc and BMedSci courses are offered. Popular courses include experimental pathology and bachelor of medical science (BMedSci), but some students have studied anthropology, psychology, and even German, although this kind of choice is rare. One of the newest and most popular courses currently is a BSc in sports medicine. Students can choose to stay at QMUL or go to another college for this year. If studying within QMUL all fees for the BSc year are currently paid by sponsors, additional funding is also available due to the school's extensive links with the City of London. Allocation of intercalated degrees is done on a competitive basis, but all courses offered within the school will involve research-based projects and not just library-based projects.

Special study modules and electives

There is a wide variety of SSMs available, including clinical, research, complementary medicine, and journalism. Students are encouraged to consider organising SSMs in subjects they find of interest if they do not find exactly what they want within the diverse selection available. It is also possible for some students to spend 3-month attachments at partner institutions in Europe. The elective lasts 2–3 months, during year 5 of the course. There are existing arrangements with institutions in other countries in Europe, and several student-led exchange programmes with institutions all around the world, which can make for a more easily organised trip. Students can, and have gone almost anywhere as long as they can find themselves a supervisor.

There are several opportunities with the course for foreign travel. Any of the SSMs, of which there are two every year, can be used as an opportunity to study abroad. Most students use one of the 4-week SSMs in the final year to study abroad, as well as the 6-week elective that is also in the final year.

Erasmus

Bart's and The London has a long history of exchanging students within the Erasmus programme with the world-famous Karolinska institute in Stockholm. Other regular exchanges occur with the Lund as well as several other institutions.

Facilities

Library There are three large libraries, one at each site. The two hospital libraries have wonderful architecture, history, and atmosphere. QMUL is large and can occasionally be noisy during the daytime. Availability of books can be variable. Libraries are open 9 AM–9 PM on weekdays, 9 AM–4 PM on Saturdays. The QMUL library is also open on Sundays. There are also two large pathology museums at the hospitals. Unfortunately, in light of the events at Alder Hey Hospital, access to these is now severely restricted.

Computers The school is well equipped on all three sites. All computing facilities and functions are available and regularly updated. Computers are increasingly used for teaching and are available during library hours and from 10 AM to 8 PM at weekends. There is also 24-hour internet access on the QMUL campus during the week. The computer rooms at the medical schools are also open late. All rooms in student halls have also now been fitted with computer access making internet access far easier.

Clinical skills The clinical skills centre at Bart's, which was one of the first in the country, is for use by both medical and nursing students. The clinical skills centre is available to everyone in the school. First-year students learn clinical skills in an adapted ward at Mile End Hospital.

Welfare

Student support

On the first day of college, freshers are assigned a senior student to act as their 'parent' and guide them through the first few weeks and beyond. 'Parents' introduce their 'children' to their friends, take them out to dinner, and offer advice on all issues, from simple things such as work to more complicated matters such as their love life. This makes for a lot of integration between students from different years. All students are allocated their own academic tutor; for personal and other problems they have use of a pastoral pool of sympathetic doctors and senior lecturers. The Medical and Dental Students' Association elects a student as welfare officer, as does QMUL Students' Union. Counselling is available within 24 hours at QMUL with a dedicated and independent advice and counselling service. Those with mental health problems can be seen in confidence by a consultant at another teaching hospital in a reciprocal arrangement with the school.

Accommodation

Students at Bart's and The London can spend 2–3 years of their studies in college accommodation. New first-year students choose whether they wish to live in Queen Mary College or University of London (intercollegiate) accommodation, and whether they wish to be catered for or to cook for themselves. Most first-year students live in either Dawson Hall, which is an old Bart's residence, or Floyer House at The Royal London. The new Mile End student village project provides new but rather expensive accommodation very close to lectures; places will be provided for all first-year students.

Dawson Hall is a very modern facility, the main attraction of which was its beautifully set location near St Paul's in the centre of London. It is very hard to get into as a first-year student and so early applications are essential. It allows students to self-cater, as does Floyer House which has recently been refurbished and is close to the Union. There have been questions of the safety of this residence set within Whitechapel. In central London, students from all colleges of the University of London live together in intercollegiate halls. These are also a 30-minute tube ride away from college. With all residences students should check whether or not rent is payable during holidays. As with all halls of residence in London the cost is relatively high. London generally is an expensive place to study and live although there is a lot of development going on.

Most senior students live in the East End in shared houses. Almost everyone lives within walking distance of The Royal London and QM sites. Property is slightly cheaper in east London than in other parts of the capital. The Griffin Community Trust provides cheap (approximately £60 per week including bills), luxurious housing in a very special development incorporating housing for the elderly, a community centre, and flats for clinical students. Student residents spend an hour or two a week with their elderly neighbours and play bingo, watch videos, or just chat. Both students and elders say how much they gain from the experience.

The important thing to remember is that Bart's and The London has a lot of relatively cheap, affordable housing very close. Therefore when it's time to move out of halls you are able to move to a location very close to college without having to spend too much time or money on travel.

Placements

The medicine course is based at three sites: Bart's, The London, and QMUL, which are all within 3 miles of each other in the City and East End of London. They are easily accessible by tube, bicycle, and bus. The medical sciences department at QMUL in Mile End is where the first 2 years are based currently although this should change in the coming year with the building of a new medical school in Whitechapel. This site has good facilities, including the Students' Union shop, computer laboratories, and the ever popular 'E1' nightclub. The final 3 years are spent in hospitals. Many of the district general hospitals used are in or close to the East End and accessible by bus or tube. Several are close enough to cycle to.

Students can expect to be sent to attachments outside the main teaching hospitals. Placements are in district general and other associated hospitals (accommodation is provided free). Destinations include Southend-on-Sea, Chelmsford and Harlow. GP attachments and SSMs can be arranged country-wide and worldwide.

Location of clinical placement/ name of hospital	Distance away from medical school (miles)	Difficulty getting there on public transport*
Bart's	2.4	
The Royal London	0	

(Continued)

(*Continued*)

Homerton	4.7	
Whipps Cross	6.8	
Newham	5.1	

* : walking/cycling distance; : use public transport; : need own car or lift; : get up early – tricky to get to!

Please note that there are a number of other hospitals at which you may be placed, all of which are within 50 miles of the main campus.

Sports and social

University life

The Medical and Dental Students' Association is thriving and provides social and sporting opportunities as well as welfare services for all. The two medical student bars at Bart's and The London hold regular discos and theme nights. Wednesdays (after sports matches) and Fridays are the big nights for going out. The summer ball at Bart's is popular, and there are smaller balls for freshers' week, Rag week, and at Christmas.

Rag week is one of the prides of the college with medical and dental students raking in over £150,000 last year from street collections, marathon running, and a fashion show, ranking us as one of the most successful Rags in the country and the biggest in London by far (we love beating Georges!). A large TV screen in the bar regularly shows the main sports events. Freshers' fortnight is equally popular, and a massive effort is made to welcome new students to the college, with a rerun in the new year, – freshers revisited – to cement the reputation of Bart's and The London as one of the most socially active schools in the country. A reputation the students work hard to maintain.

There are over 30 clubs and societies run by the Bart's and The London Students' Association, which offer students the chance to develop new interests, meet people, play sport, and have a good time. Among the most active societies are: the Drama Society, which stages productions every term, including the infamous Christmas show, and goes to the Edinburgh Festival; the Asian Society, which organise the famous international fashion show that celebrates diversity of culture within the school, and annually raises many thousands for charity; the music society, which includes the choir, orchestra, brass groups, and several bands. QMUL has more clubs and societies if there are not enough at the medical school, or if you have a particular interest not catered for.

Student social life revolves around the Association/Union buildings at both Bart's and The London. The Medical Student President is head of the Medical and Dental Students' Association and takes a sabbatical year from his or her studies, solely to represent and protect the interests of the medical and dental student community. The refurbished Association building at the London and the bar at Bart's are for use by medics, dentists, and their guests. In The London Association building there is a café-bar and bookshop. The official Association magazine, *M.A.D.*, comes out at least twice a term and reports on social, sporting, and other events. A large Students' Union is also available at QMUL Mile End campus.

Sports life

The Bart's and The London Students' Association clubs cater for nearly all sporting interests and welcome beginners. There is an off-site sports ground and swimming pools at both Bart's and The London Hospital. There are also gyms at Bart's, QMUL College, and squash courts at QMUL, as well as tennis and badminton courts. Bart's and The London have an enthusiastic rowing club based on the River Lea. Hockey, water polo, women's football, and rugby have had success in recent years. The cricket club is legendary, with strong first and second teams which win titles most years.

> **Top tip:** That old tip that you should not buy your books when you first get to college is completely true. The only exception is the world-famous Kumar and Clark's *Clinical Medicine*. Since both the editors are from Bart's and The London, and most of the chapters are written by your future lecturers, purchasing this is a guaranteed way that you will have all the information you will need for the first 3 years. This is the only book you need to have for the courses in years 1 and 2, so do not bother buying anything else.

Great things about Bart's and The London

- A brand new course, innovative curriculum and teaching, as well as enthusiastic and approachable staff.
- All students and visitors agree that we are a very friendly community with a close-knit atmosphere. Students tend to have friends from all years, rather than just their own.
- Reasonable rents for shared houses, considering that we are in the centre of London, and everyone lives close to everyone else.
- There are good year-round events, and the Union bar opens with regular late licences.
- Diverse area, with a wide range of things to do and cultures to experience. The East End is very trendy, with new bars and restaurants opening all the time. The *Evening Standard* recently nominated Tower Hamlets as London's sexiest borough!

Bad things about Bart's and The London

- Local areas – we are surrounded by very deprived communities, and although this means good clinical experience and pathology subject matter, it can be a bit depressing and at times it is necessary to be wary, as students have been assaulted.
- Travelling – some travelling between sites is required, and the rush hour lasts for hours, although congestion charging has meant very fast bus links.
- Little interaction with nonmedical and dental students in the past resulted in some rivalry between the medics and QMUL students, although most of these issues have been fully worked out now.
- London is such a massive place that it can take you some time to feel at ease with its vastness.
- Expense – living and studying in London is more expensive than elsewhere. This is the biggest drawback to studying at Bart's and The London, and London generally.

Further information

Admissions Office
Bart's and The London,
Queen Mary's School of Medicine and Dentistry, University of London
Turner Street
London E1 2AD
Tel: 020 7377 7611
Fax: 020 7377 7612
Email: medicaladmissions@qmul.ac.uk
Web: http://www.smd.qmul.ac.uk

Additional application information	
Average A-level requirements	• AAB
Average Scottish Higher requirements	• BB/AAA (Advanced Highers/Further Highers)
Graduate entry	• 2:1 science degree
Make-up of interview panel	• Undergraduate: three (one clinical, one non-clinical and one student) • Graduate: 6 station OSCE plus one clinical, one non-clinical and one student
Months in which interviews are held	• November–March (undergraduate) March–April (graduate)
Proportion of overseas students	• 8%
Proportion of mature students	• 30%
Proportion of graduate students	• 20%
Faculty's view of students taking a gap year	• Encouraged if constructive plans
Proportion of students taking intercalated degrees	• 6%
Possibility of direct entrance to clinical phase	• Yes – limited circumstances
Fees for overseas students	• £13,640 (years 1 and 2) £22,330 (years 3, 4 and 5)
Fees for graduates	• £3000 pa

Ability to transfer to other medical schools. If so, under what circumstances	• Students can transfer out to do intercalated degrees. However this is limited, owing to financial issues and so is only permitted where there is a very good reason – such as the course not being available within the college, or competitive places are offered to the top 10–15 students. Students may also transfer out for personal extenuating circumstances, and counselling is available for this prior to such a major decision being taken
Assistance for elective funding	• There are several elective bursaries available, although amounts are variable. The school also provides a list of potential external sponsors that have close links to Bart's and The London. Significant elective sponsorship is possible but is very much dependent on an individual's effort to gain it
Assistance for travel to attachments	• There are travel subsidies available to all students of the college. Records must be kept of expenses and claimed back from your LEA with supporting documentation from the School
Access and hardship funds	• There is financial assistance for students generally, but also specific hardship funds for medical and dental students. These are usually from trust funds left by alumni of St Bartholomew's or The London Hospital. The amounts of money are significant and the financial support easily accessible
Weekly rent	• £75–£85 per week for accommodation within walking distance of central campus and teaching hospital
Pint of lager	• £1.10 at the Student Association during happy hour, which is much longer than an hour!
Cinema	• £3.50 with a NUS card at Genesis in Mile End. • £4 with a NUS card at the much nicer UGC Multiplex in Canary Wharf, which is only slightly further
Nightclub	• Many nightclubs in London; prices vary

Belfast

Key facts	Undergraduate
Course length	5 years (Premedical: 6 years)
Total number of medical undergraduates	1036
Applicants in 2005	650
Interviews given in 2005	54
Places available in 2005	262
Places available in 2006	262
Open days 2006	tbc
Entrance requirements	AAA plus A at AS-level
Mandatory subjects	Chemistry to A-level and Biology at AS level
Male:female ratio	45:65
Is an exam included in the selection process? If yes, what form does this exam take?	Possible aptitude test
Qualification gained	MBBChBAO

Fascinating fact: The Belfast Medical Students' Association is the oldest and largest student society at Queen's

Queen's University of Belfast provides a relaxed and informal integrated medical course. Ninety per cent of the students come from Ireland (both north and south), and a strong emphasis is placed on social life and enjoyment. The school also sits in a perfect position to access Belfast's nightlife, arguably the best in the UK. Queen's is the only medical school where it is not illegal to enjoy a good night's craic!! Discussions are taking place to increase the size of the medical school, with more undergraduate places. However, as yet there have been no plans to implement a graduate accelerated course.

Education

Students with four to five A*s plus four A grades at GCSE received conditional offers in 2004, overall grades required were three As at A-level plus an A grade at AS level. Chemistry and one other science at A-level, and biology at A-level or AS level were prerequisites. There is no compulsory interview; however, a small proportion of applicants will be called for interview. An aptitude test for medicine may also be implemented in the future. Further information or selection criteria are available in the prospectus or on request from the admissions office.

A 6-year course (including premed year) is required for Irish Leaving Certificate students, needing four A1s and two Bs, and an A grade at Junior Certificate. Chemistry is compulsory.

Graduates with a minimum of three Bs or better at A-level who have obtained at least a 2:1 honours degree would be interviewed for entry into the 5-year medical course.

A traditional preclinical/clinical divide is less evident on the new course, and teaching combines a problem-based approach with more traditional lectures from the first year. Clinical skills are taught from year 1 in hospitals, in general practice, and in a clinical skills centre. Each year is divided into two semesters, and the trend is for year groups to be divided into smaller groups for teaching. In years 1 and 2 students learn the basic science of medicine with an integrated systems approach. The sociological and psychological aspects of medical practice are emphasised and special study modules are taken. In year 3 the systems are taught again, but with an emphasis on mechanisms of disease. More time is spent in hospital attachments at this stage, and year 4 students spend all their time on the wards in hospital attachments or in general practice. The final year is a consolidation process with no new subjects.

Teaching

Teaching in years 1 and 2 consists of lectures, tutorials, laboratory practicals and meeting patients, both on the wards and in general practice. There is a mixture of demonstration, dissection, and prosection for teaching, and animal tissue is used in physiology. During years 1 and 2 only half a day a week is spent on the wards. In year 3 blocks of specialty-based integrated teaching are supplemented by pathology lectures and tutorials. Teaching is very much self-directed, with the clinical aspects being taught on the wards. Years 4 and 5 are completely ward based. Computers and clinical skills are used for training throughout the course. Ward group sizes in teaching hospitals tend to vary, but efforts are made to keep the numbers as small as possible to benefit both the patients and the students. The friendliness of the staff and their willingness to teach varies from ward to ward. Most, however, are willing to help, in true Northern Ireland fashion.

Assessment

Years 1 and 2 have specific exams at the end of each semester with an overall recap exam at the end of year 2. Year 3 is examined through coursework throughout the year and end of semester/attachment clinical exams. There is a pathology written exam, covering two semesters, at the end of the year. In year 4 exams are at the end of each 8-week block. Resit examinations start in the second week of August and last for a week or two. Most try to give exams their best so as to maximise the holiday period. Procedure cards need to be completed as part of musculoskeletal and A&E medicine, ophthalmology, anaesthetics, fractures, and obstetrics and gynaecology. Final examinations take place in two parts. The written examinations take place between January and February of the final year, and the clinical examinations are held at the end of April of the final year, although there is a possibility that this will change. During the summer between fourth and final year the overseas elective and clinical project is carried out, and during the final year refresher clinical placements and a clinical apprenticeship are completed.

Intercalated degrees

Between 5% and 10% of students take a BSc during their course, usually after years 2 or 3. Science degrees are available in anatomy, biochemistry, physiology, microbiology, therapeutics and pharmacology, and molecular biology. It is possible to study degree subjects that are not available at Queen's by making arrangements with another institution. Approval for this, however, has to be sought from the Dean. If there is competition for places, previous results in the respective subject will determine entry. Students from Northern Ireland may be eligible for Local Education Authority (LEA) or bursary funding for the year.

Special study modules and electives

During the summer vacation between years 3 and 4 students have the option to arrange elective placements for a period of 4–6 weeks at a hospital in the UK. This is optional and the student takes responsibility for organisation. In the final year students are encouraged to spend their elective period overseas. Students must also carry out a 4-week clinical project, either overseas or at Queen's, followed by the production of a project report of between 6000 and 8000 words.

Erasmus

QUB is attempting to expand its Erasmus programme at present and is currently canvassing students for their opinions or interests. Opportunities already exist for students who wish to study at medical schools in Switzerland, Spain, Germany or Norway. Almost all students will use the overseas elective as an opportunity to see new shores and spread their horizons.

Facilities

Library There are two main medical libraries, the largest in the Royal Victoria Hospital (RVH) and a smaller one in the Belfast City Hospital (BCH). They both have online catalogues, with access to networked journals, Medline, and other databases. They close at 9.30 PM on weekdays and 12.30 PM on Saturdays. Study space is available at the Belfast City Hospital and at the Medical Biology Centre (MBC) outside the library opening hours. The MBC houses an anatomy study room with access to a library of microscope slides and computerised anatomical guides. Each peripheral attachment has some library provision although this varies from hospital to hospital and medical students are more than welcome to use the libraries and facilities of the wider QUB campus. All library books are catalogued in a computerised searchable database.

Computers The RVH and the MBC each have computer facilities available for medical students. When the IT suites and other libraries of QUB are taken into account computer provision is usually more then adequate, although just before an essay deadline or exam session things can tend to clog up. All computers are fully networked although certain applications for medicine can only be accessed from the MBC or RVH

Clinical skills The Clinical Skills Education Centre (CSEC) provides teaching on practical medicine and affords students a chance to do some 'hands-on' learning. Through a mix of simulated patients (often drama students doing some method acting or other arts students from QUB needing extra beer money!), life-like models and tuition from practising clinicians, students are taught various clinical skills which are later assessed in the CSEC at end of semester examinations. Students have the opportunity to practice clinical skills at the CSEC and also on their clinical attachments.

Welfare

Student support

Each medical student is allocated to a consultant, known as their 'faculty tutor', whose role is to help with any problems. Staff in the faculty office are friendly and approachable, as is the current dean. The Students' Union also has a counselling service and provides access to academic and financial advice. Rails, ramps, and lifts are available in many areas for disabled access. A recent minding scheme has been started (called MAFIA) whereby each student is allocated a 'godfather' who looks after the personal aspects of student life. As a fourth and final year student, you are now required to arrange a mentor, preferably a doctor from one of your clinical attachments, to watch over your clinical progress and act as a reference for your first foundation programme job.

Accommodation

Every student who comes from outside the Belfast area can apply to university halls of residence for accommodation during term time. The rooms tend to be warm and comfortable, with good food (if catered) but thin walls. Catered rooms cost between £56 sharing and £67 single per week and self-catering rooms £41–£70 per week, inclusive of heat and light. They are about half a mile from the university, but can mean a trek if an early lecture has been scheduled for the RVH. Private accommodation is available closer to faculty although there can be no guarantees as to price or quality. Generally a room in a private house will cost between £150 and £200 per month with the average rent being £170. The Lisburn Road area of Belfast is extremely popular with medical students as it is close to the MBC, the BCH and the RVH.

Placements

In years 1 and 2 most of the teaching takes place on campus in the MBC and the BCH, with some clinical and family attachment programmes spread throughout the greater Belfast area. The MBC and the BCH are about a 15–20-minute walk from the halls of residence. Other lectures and clinical work take place at the RVH, a 35–40-minute walk from the halls. However, a free bus runs from the BCH to the RVH every 15 minutes. From year 3 onwards students receive teaching in the RVH, and clinical attachments may be throughout the Province.

The RVH recently underwent renovation, the result of which is a brand new hospital, with great teaching facilities. In addition, hospitals and GP practices outside central Belfast are used from year 3 onwards. Hospital accommodation is free, and there is an allowance for peripheral GP attachments, with the furthest one might travel being about 80 miles from Belfast. This means spending part of the week in a peripheral hospital for a portion of the academic year – which can make a change from Belfast but can also seriously affect extra-curricular activities.

Location of clinical placement/ name of hospital	Distance away from medical school (miles)	Difficulty getting there on public transport*
Belfast City Hospital	0	🚶
Royal Victoria Hospital	1	🚶
Musgrave Park Hospital	2	🚶
The Ulster Hospital	5–6	🚗
Altnagelvin	72	💡

* 🚶 : walking/cycling distance; : use public transport; 🚗 : need own car or lift; 💡 : get up early – tricky to get to!

Sports and social 🏆

City life

Belfast is a lively, welcoming city with much to offer visitors. The student area is only a mile away from the city centre but surprisingly self-contained – many students only rarely venture out of the mainly student Malone and Stranmillis areas to Belfast's more upmarket city centre. All tastes are catered for in Belfast through a wide range of pubs, cafes and clubs, with the Students' Union hosting one of the biggest club nights in Ireland on a weekly basis. Those with a more cultural orientation will find themselves amply provided for by the range of drama, music and art available to students. The Queen's Film Theatre is an award-winning art-house cinema located within the University campus.

Although you may have your hands full coping with what Belfast has to offer, it is easy to travel further afield. Dublin is just over 2 hours away by train, and it is a must to visit the Giant's Causeway, the Mourne Mountains and the Fermanagh Lakes, all of which are within 1½ hours of Belfast.

University life

Student life in Belfast is largely centred around the Student Union building, a few other student venues and the physical education centre. For medical students the Belfast Medical Students' Association (BMSA) runs a very active and fun programme of social events, providing medicine with a social cohesion that is the envy of every other faculty. Every year the BMSA runs a freshers' three-legged pub crawl, a mystery tour, a fancy dress party, the annual faculty ball, a staff–student dinner, and regular discos which are attended by all years. The fourth year runs its own annual revue – tasteless but entertaining – and a medical charity called SWOT, which raises money by organising blood pressure clinics, street collections, a fashion show (with local TV celebrities), and pub quizzes. Queen's also has an active MedSIN group. The Students' Union has three bars and runs regular discos, balls, and concerts. Like most universities, there is likely to be a society for whatever you want to do.

Sports life

There are many sports clubs at Queen's, most of which compete in the Province's leagues. Near the university there are playing fields, tennis courts, and a boat club. The Queen's Physical Education Centre has everything you need to keep fit. It is beside the university, well equipped, and costs 70 pence to get in if you are a student.

Top tip: Take part on the Catwalk as a fourth year in the SWOT fashion show (one of the biggest in Northern Ireland), it is a great way to spring-board your MMC (Medical-Modelling Career!)

Great things about Queen's

- An updated curriculum so that students gain clinical experience from year 1 with small group teaching.
- Queen's has an international reputation for trauma care, cardiology, and ophthalmology.
- Belfast is compact as a capital city but has everything you need.
- The social life – fortnightly events are organised by the Belfast Medical Students' Association (BMSA) so inter-year relations are good.
- Relaxed and informal atmosphere.

Bad things about Queen's

- The weather – there is no danger of students blowing their allowance on suntan lotion.
- The weekends tend to be quiet. Many students go home at the weekend, particularly in the first year.
- The siting of the main medical library means that at night students can only get to it by car.
- The ready availability of the 'Ulster Fry' pushes your waistband.
- The high number of students on some attachments.

Further information

Admissions Officer
The Queen's University of Belfast
University Road
Belfast BT7 1NN
Tel: 02890 975 081
Fax: 02890 975 137
Email: admissions@qub.ac.uk
Web: http://www.qub.ac.uk

Dean's Office
Tel: 02890 972 186
Fax: 02890 330 571

Faculty site is http://www.qub.ac.uk/fmhs/
General QUB site is http://www.qub.ac.uk

Additional application information	
Average A-level requirements	• AAA at A level plus A at AS-level
Average Scottish Higher requirements	• AAAAA (including chemistry and biology)
Make-up of interview panel	• Four – admissions selector plus two members of academic staff and one administrator
Months in which interviews are held	• February and March
Proportion of overseas students	• 5%
Proportion of mature students	• Not known
Proportion of graduate students	• 6%
Faculty's view of students taking a gap year	• Acceptable
Proportion of students taking intercalated degrees	• 7%
Possibility of direct entrance to clinical phase	• No
Fees for overseas students	• £10,500 pa (years 1 and 2) and £19,800 pa (years 3, 4 and 5)
Fees for graduates	• 3000 pa
Ability to transfer to other medical schools	• None
Assistance for elective funding	• Yes! Plenty of different scholarships/ grants
Assistance for travel to attachments	• Can apply for reimbursement
Access and hardship funds	• Yes, means-tested yearly
Weekly rent	• From around £37
Pint of lager	• From £2
Cinema	• £1.80 at the Queen's Film Theatre
Nightclub	• £2–£10

Birmingham

Key facts	Undergraduate	Graduate
Course length	5 years	4 years
Total number of medical undergraduates	1800	120
Applicants in 2005	2700	650
Interviews given in 2005	900	90
Places available in 2006	370	40
Places available in 2006	370	40
Open days 2006	23 June and 15–16 September	23 June and 15–16 September
Entrance requirements	AAB (340–360 points)	2:1 (minimum)
Mandatory subjects	A-level chemistry and another science	Chemistry A-level
Male:female ratio	30:70	33:67
Is an exam included in the selection process? If yes, what form does this exam take?	Yes UKCAT	Yes UKCAT
Qualification gained	MBChB	

Fascinating fact: In 1978 Birmingham medical school was the last place in the world to have an outbreak of smallpox, where the labs were blamed for the death of Janet Parker, an anatomy photographer. The professor who had been careless with his lab work that led to the death then slit his own throat after an investigation was called for by the government. A little morbid – but a valuable piece of history that is too often pushed under the carpet by the medical school!

Birmingham medical school is on the north-west edge of the main University of Birmingham campus, just a few miles from the city centre. We are a large provincial medical school, with a huge diversity of students. We have a well-established modern course, with clinical experience introduced within the first few weeks of study. The admissions tutors strongly believe that doctors should be well-rounded individuals and not just dedicated bookworms, and this is reflected in the mix of students and the lively social scene at the medical school, from sport, drama, and politics to partying. From the first week as freshers, students at Birmingham can expect to work hard and play hard until their final-year dinner, held the week before graduation.

Education

The selection criteria that the medical school uses are available on the university web pages and at open days. Particular attention is paid to nonacademic interests, extra-curricular activities, and the personal statement and reference. The method of selecting students for both the graduate-entry 4-year course and the standard 5-year course is essentially the same. However for the graduate entry course, students are required to have a first class life science degree and a minimum grade C in A-Level chemistry. Currently at Birmingham there are no tests in the admission procedure, however the use of an objective test is under 'active consideration' for the graduate entry course only.

The first 2 years follow a systems-based approach, with regular patient contact in general practice beginning within a few weeks of starting the course. Full-time hospital teaching commences in year 3 in both medicine and surgery. Pathology and epidemiology are also taught during this year. Years 4 and 5 involve rotation through specialties such as paediatrics, oncology and orthopaedics, in addition to senior medicine and surgery. Throughout the degree there is an emphasis on the social aspect of medicine, which is well received by students. In particular Birmingham is one of the few, if not only, medical school to offer all three SSMs in Christian, Jewish and Islamic medical ethics – promoting and supporting diversity is something Birmingham is very proud of! Students on the graduate entry course will study the basic sciences in their first year. In their second year they will study a course similar to the standard year 3, and will be fully integrated with the rest of the medics for years 3 and 4.

Teaching

Preclinical teaching involves lectures and follow-up tutorials incorporating problem-based learning exercises. There is no dissection at Birmingham, but we have excellent plastinated models to work with in a specially designed laboratory. Histology teaching is all done by video and accompanied by colour course booklets – there is no straining down microscopes for Birmingham medics! Hospital teaching combines bedside teaching, observation, small group teaching sessions and participation in clinics and procedures.

Assessment

Modules are examined after Christmas and in the summer term by multiple choice question papers (MCQs) and short- and long-answer papers, and an anatomy viva examination in year 2. Some in-course assessment is a feature of most modules. Students are expected to pass every module in order to proceed to the next year. You will also have to pass a practical exam in basic life support during your first year. Viva examinations are no longer a feature of assessment in borderline pass candidates, and instead students can compensate losing up to 5% providing that all other modules have been adequately passed. Clinical subjects are examined by MCQ papers and objective structured clinical examinations (OSCEs).

Intercalated degrees

An increasing number of students at Birmingham are choosing to intercalate, typically after years 2, 3 or 4. This can be in the biological sciences, such as physiology, pharmacology, neuroscience, or pathology, and involves a laboratory-based research project (and a chance to publish!). Alternatively, you can do a medicine in society intercalation, such as public health, health care ethics and law, behavioural science, or history of medicine. History of medicine is particularly popular and we have an internationally renowned unit based in the medical school. The health care, ethics and law course is often oversubscribed each year, because of the well-respected and hard-working department of tutors that work on ethics. The medical school encourages students at the end of year 2 to apply for an intercalation in biological sciences and at the end of year 3 to apply for an integrated health science, and priority each year will be given to the students in these year groups. Applications for biological sciences from year 4 students are discouraged. For all intercalated degrees students must have demonstrated satisfactory academic progress in all subjects. A number of students each year opt to leave Birmingham for a year and pursue an intercalated degree at another medical school – this is allowed after permission has been sought. There is much information on intercalated degrees on the medical school website.

Special study modules and electives

Eight SSMs are completed during the course. There is a choice of many topics, with new ones starting all the time. In the clinical years, these become more clinically orientated, self-directed and are conducted outside the medical school. Electives are taken at the end of year 4, with an opportunity to travel anywhere in the world, normally lasting 2 months.

Erasmus

Through the Erasmus and other schemes, the medical school is developing a series of exchange programmes with medical schools in France, Germany, and the Czech Republic. The medical school is currently in discussions with other universities about the possibility of expanding these exchanges. The opportunity therefore exists for some medical students from Birmingham to go to these universities as part of this exchange, to undertake elective studies or clinical placements.

Facilities

Library The library is conveniently situated within the medical school and has an extensive range of medical textbooks and journals. It has plenty of quiet study areas and computer facilities with access to Medline, the internet, and library catalogues. It also has extensive photocopying facilities. During term time it is open from 8.45 AM to 9 PM Monday–Thursday, until 7 PM on Fridays, and from 10 AM–6 PM at weekends.

Computers The computer cluster is well equipped, and open 24 hours a day, 7 days a week all year round. There is a mixture of Apple Macs and iMacs (about 100) on the east side, and about 100 PCs on the west side. You are automatically credited with free laser print credits, and you can get free top-ups on your credits once you have run out. Every computer is online and allows full access to computer-assisted learning (CAL) packages that supplement the course. There are excellent, state-of-the-art computer facilities in the Learning Centre, located on the main university campus, however printing here costs 5 pence per A4 sheet. Computer facilities are also available in general practices, teaching hospitals, and all of the district general hospitals (DGH) that host student teaching.

Welfare 🏠

Student support

Students are placed into families, with three to four students from each year group. Each 'family' has two tutors that they can approach with problems, and the families meet throughout the year. However, the welfare system provided is far from perfect, with tutors being recruited from distant hospitals and some tutors not getting in contact with their students on a regular basis, leaving many students with little or no support. The medical school recognises the problem, particularly because of the large intake of students, and is continually attempting improvements to the welfare system. There is an effective student-run curriculum and welfare committee that is respected by staff.

Accommodation

Accepting a conditional offer from Birmingham guarantees a place in university hall/flats, providing you do not already reside in the Birmingham area. All university accommodation is within 2–3 miles of the campus and most are within walking distance. The Vale is a complex of several halls and flats and has the greatest overall capacity. The style of accommodation ranges from large traditional halls to flats with *en suite* bathrooms. All halls have good security and excellent committees and social events. All halls have resident student mentors who are older students in residence that provide welfare support to any student in need. The student mentor scheme is well received and allows students to have adequate information on welfare and support services within and outside of the university, and it adds to the security of living in halls. There is an excess of private rented accommodation available at reasonable prices in Selly Oak, a centre for students and just minutes away from campus. Selly Park, Harborne, and even Edgbaston (which is, in parts, very posh) are also very popular – and still reasonably priced.

Placements

Situated in the suburb of Edgbaston, the university is just a couple of miles from the city centre. The medical school (which adjoins the Queen Elizabeth teaching hospital) is found at the west end of a refreshingly spacious and green campus. It has benefited from the recent refurbishment and upgrading of lecture theatres, tutorial rooms, computer facilities, and student common rooms. There are four large teaching hospitals in the city of Birmingham, as well as specialist hospitals and numerous district general hospitals. Medics at Birmingham will have very few long-term attachments outside the West Midlands, and the majority of placements are within commuting distance of student accommodation. Don't be fooled by the relatively short mileage between the medical school and hospitals – the 12 miles to Heartlands can take anywhere between 15 and 45 minutes plus.

During years 1–4, groups of four students attend a general practice once every fortnight. This offers a valuable early introduction to patient contact and clinical skills. The family attachment scheme is another community-based project that takes place in year 2. From year 3 onwards, students attend hospital placements full time for most of the year, with occasional teaching sessions in the medical school.

Location of clinical placement/name of hospital	Distance away from medical school (miles)	Difficulty getting there on public transport*
Queen Elizabeth Hospital	1	🚶
Heartlands Hospital	12	🚗
City Hospital	12	🚶
Good Hope Hospital	15	🚗
Wolverhampton Hospital	20	💡

* 🚶: walking/cycling distance; 🚌: use public transport; 🚗: need own car or lift; 💡: get up early – tricky to get to!

Sports and social

City life

Birmingham is a cosmopolitan city. All the big-name stores and designer shops can be found in the city centre, most of them in the new Bullring complex – a Mecca for those who list 'shopping' as one of their hobbies. The city has a vast selection of restaurants, serving everything from Alaska cod to zabaglione, plus all the curry you could ever wish for. Birmingham boasts a vibrant nightlife, ranging from the quintessential student night to jazz clubs and trendy bars. There are plenty of theatres, and the national indoor arena, NEC and Symphony Hall regularly play host to major international acts and are literally on our doorstep! The city and surrounding area are well served by public transport. There is in fact a train station just next to the medical school that connects to Birmingham New Street station, and from there to just about anywhere. Birmingham International Airport is also accessible directly by train. More rural locations, such as the Malverns, Stratford upon Avon, and the Black Country, are all easily reached.

University life

Not only is medicine the largest faculty in the university, but related courses such as medical science and physiotherapy are based in the medical school. Dentistry and nursing students are also based in and around the medical school. There is considerable social integration between all these students and between different year groups. An enthusiastic medical society and final-year dinner committee ensure there is always something happening. As the medical school is located on campus, medics can easily retain involvement in university activities and social events and thus experience the best of both worlds.

The medical society organises the renowned freshers' week, regular pub crawls, wine tasting, curry quizzes, theatre trips, ski trips, and a post-exam annual camping extravaganza to the Gower. An equally strong society in Birmingham is MedSIN, which gives students the opportunity to participate in helping the local community through action projects, and also gives students the chance to participate in national conferences and projects abroad. The MedSIN projects in Birmingham are very popular and give students an appealing alternative to the usual binge-drinking related activities. Calendar events held in the medical school include the musical, a very funny comedy revue, and the glamorous final-year fashion show. Many events are held in city centre venues, which are easily accessible by public transport and cheap for a taxi home. The medical school magazine, QMM, was revived a few years ago and affords an opportunity to put pen to paper, and there is an active surgical society for those people who think they might be budding surgeons. The University of Birmingham Guild of Students (BUGS) houses the usual complement of bars, clubs, and pool tables, as well as a society for every imaginable interest, from Rag committees to cocktail parties!

Sports life

The university has an excellent reputation for sport. The athletics union runs an impressive range of different sporting clubs. The medics also run large clubs for hockey, rugby, football, netball, cricket, tennis, and basketball. Medics' rugby, hockey, and netball teams have all been national medical school champions in recent years. The clubs are friendly and well supported (especially in post-game celebrations) and cater for all ranges of ability, from absolute beginners to international players.

Top tip: Throw yourself into university life with full confidence. Be prepared to work hard and make an effort to socialise with nonmedics too!

Great things about Birmingham

- Fully integrated course with early clinical experience keeps your interest levels up.
- First class health care ethics and law teaching, beginning from year 1 and continuing throughout the course, which prepares students well for clinical and house officer years.
- The medical school is supportive of students learning about wider global health issues, and has introduced a global health SSM and is keen to start an international health BSc.
- Free printing in the computer cluster – no need to worry about costs!
- There are a diverse and active group of student societies within and outside of the medical school – something for everyone to participate in.
- There is little PBL teaching – most students appreciate this aspect of the course!

Bad things about Birmingham

- The excessive number of examinations in preclinical years can put unnecessary stress on students.
- The large intake of students can at times leave the medical school having difficulties coping with administration and timetabling, and hospital placements are at risk of becoming overcrowded.
- The wait for exam results, particularly in early years, can be rather long.
- The security guards are very diligent, so if you forget your ID card they won't let you into the medical school.
- There is a very poor welfare system within the medical school and too many students are often left without anyone to speak to regarding personal or academic problems, particularly apparent at crucial times of the year such as when exams results are released. It is pot luck if you get a personal tutor who will be prepared to meet with you regularly.
- There is little interaction with students outside of the medical school, because the medical school is physically separated from all other departments, though it is located on the main campus.

Further information

Professor C J Lote
Admissions Officer/Tutor
Medical School
University of Birmingham
Edgbaston
Birmingham B15 2TT
Tel: 0121 414 6888
Fax: 0121 414 7159
Email: c.j.lote@bham.ac.uk, med-admissions@bham.ac.uk
Prospectus requests: prospectus@bham.ac.uk
Web: http://www.medicine.bham.ac.uk

Additional application information	
Average A-level requirements	• AAB
Average Scottish Higher requirements	• AAAAB
Graduate entrance requirements	• 2:1 or better life sciences degree
Make-up of interview panel	• Two staff and one student
Months in which interviews are held	• October–April
Proportion of overseas students	• 8%
Proportion of mature students	• 10%
Proportion of graduate students	• 10%
Faculty's view of students taking a gap year	• No problem, provided constructive
Proportion of students taking intercalated degrees	• 25%

(*Continued*)

(*Continued*)

Possibility of direct entrance to clinical phase	• No
Fees for overseas students	• £10,700 pa (preclinical) • £20,300 pa (clinical)
Fees for graduates	• £1150 pa
Ability to transfer to other medical schools	• None, under any circumstances.
Assistance for elective funding	• The Arthur Thomson Charitable Trust can provide some funding to a few students each year. Extensive information is given to elective students in year 4 in preparation for funding and travelling
Assistance for travel to attachments	• None is available in preclinical years. Some is available in clinical years, due to the increased amount of travelling required
Access and hardship funds	• Access to Learning Fund is available to students, and the university has a number of bursaries too. Most hardship funds are not returnable and are income assessed
Weekly rent	• £50–£60 excluding most bills, in private accommodation
Pint of lager	• £1.35–£1.65 at local student-friendly pubs, and on student nights at clubs. It is unusual to pay more than £2.80 for a pint in Birmingham!
Cinema	• £3.50–£4.50
Nightclub	• From £3: Birmingham has a vibrant and diverse nightlife. All tastes are sure to be met. The clubs range from the hardcore dance clubs such as Godskitchen, to a more relaxed, chilled out evening listening to quality live jazz music at the Jam House, to the usual cheap student nights at regular nightclubs. Most of the bars and clubs are located in the city centre next to each other on the famous Broad Street

Brighton and Sussex Medical School

Key facts	Undergraduate
Course length	5 years
Total number of medical undergraduates	440
Applicants in 2005	2330
Interviews given in 2005	Information not available
Places available in 2005	136
Places available in 2006	136
Open days 2006	See www.bsms.ac.uk for details
Entrance requirements	AAB (340 UCAS points)
Mandatory subjects	Biology and chemistry
Male:female ratio	40:60
Is an exam included in the selection process? If yes, what form does this exam take?	No UKCAT in 2007
Qualification gained	BMBS

Fascinating fact: The University of Sussex Campus is actually set out in the shape of a cat … apparently!

The Universities of Brighton and Sussex were successful in their bid to host a medical school as part of the government's expansion plans for training doctors and the first cohort of 135 students started in autumn 2003. The Brighton and Sussex Medical School (BSMS) is a partnership between the Universities of Brighton and Sussex and the new Brighton and Sussex University Hospitals NHS Trust.

Students are members of both universities, and enjoy access to the academic and recreational facilities of each. The two universities have biomedical research interests recognised by grade 5 research ratings. Sussex has one of England's largest biological sciences schools, while Brighton has extensive and in-depth experience in the education and training of health professionals including postgraduate doctors, nurses, midwives, pharmacists, physiotherapists and medical laboratory scientists.

The two universities have adjacent campuses at Falmer, with fast rail and road links to central Brighton. Brighton, newly elevated to city status, has a vibrant social scene to which the universities' students (over 10% of the population) make a prominent contribution. The campuses also have direct pedestrian access into the planned new South Downs National Park, long recognised as an area of outstanding natural beauty.

Education €

Selection for interview is based upon the strength of an individual's grades and also, more importantly, the personal qualities that are shown in the personal statement section of the UCAS application form. If a candidate is said to be of good potential then that candidate will be called to an interview. If the candidate impresses at the interview then an offer is made. The standard offer for 2005 entry is AAB at A-level, although applicants that show good qualities at interview may be made an offer of ABB. The following is a statement from the BSMS website: 'Unfortunately it has proved necessary to change the BSMS standard offer levels for 2005 from those advertised in the prospectus. For example, most standard offers to A-level candidates will now be conditional on gaining 340 UCAS points in three A-levels (AAB) rather than 320 points (ABB or AAC).

A minority of conditional offers to candidates considered to demonstrate exceptional potential at interview will be made at 320 points.' For further advice consult the BSMS website.

In your first 2 years your academic and clinical studies will be based in new facilities at the Falmer campuses. You will start to gain direct experience of working with patients from the first term. Clinical experience at this stage will be mainly in primary care and community medicine settings, and you will carry out two individual family studies – in year 1 with a family looking after a new baby and in year 2 with a family including a dependant requiring continuing care. You will also experience medical practice in some hospital settings, including visits to a busy A&E unit. In parallel, you will develop your clinical and communication skills and study the normal and abnormal functioning of the human body using a system-based approach. The systems modules include the core material that every doctor must know, and are centred around weekly clinical symposia that employ a problem-based learning approach. They also include student-selected options that allow you to explore selected topics in greater depth, informed by the latest research.

During years 3–5 a balance between clinical and academic studies is maintained. While you gain progressively more experience in clinical contexts, the requirement to integrate your clinical experience with your understanding of the underlying clinical and social sciences and public health issues continues. You will maintain an individual clinical skills portfolio that will become an important element in the assessment of your progress, and a personal development portfolio to help you to reflect on how your personal strengths are developing along with your clinical experience. Your studies will now be based at the new medical education centre at the Royal Sussex County Hospital, Brighton. Year 5 is essentially an apprenticeship year to prepare you for your postgraduate year as a preregistration house officer (PRHO).

Teaching

A wide range of teaching methods is employed, with the emphasis on the small group academic and clinical teaching possible in a small and personal medical school. Individual patient studies, in which you will relate clinical findings and treatment to the principles of the underlying clinical and social sciences, will develop your understanding of the practice of medicine. We believe it is important to integrate information from different disciplines and sources, and this is emphasised throughout the curriculum.

The more detailed and more difficult topics in lectures are then considered in tutorial groups, which allows a great amount of time to be spent on a complex topic. Subjects that require visual aids (such as imaging lessons) are carried out in the new BSMS IT Suite. The study of anatomy is also enhanced by cadaveric dissection (of human tissues) in the state-of-the-art dissection room that is widely considered to be one of the best in the UK.

Your degree in medicine will equip you with the knowledge, clinical skills and attitudes that you will need to progress to the next stage of your training, the PRHO year. The student-selected options within the BSMS degree will equip you to progress either to a career in general practice or to undertake postgraduate specialisation to become, after further training, a medical consultant in a clinical specialty.

Your degree will also give you real insight into the astonishing pace of development of understanding in the biomedical sciences, and prepare you for the life-long learning to which all doctors must commit themselves to keep up to date. You will gain personal experience in medical research as a member of a BSMS, Brighton or Sussex research team through your year 4 *Individual Research Project*. On graduation, you will have the necessary academic background to practise evidence-based medicine and, if you wish, embark on a career combining medical practice with medical research.

Assessment

The integrated course has been developed so that both scientific knowledge and clinical skills are combined at an early stage. The first 2 years of the course consist of eight modules. The eight modules include: the foundations of health and disease; heart, lungs and blood; nutrition, metabolism and excretion; neuroscience and behaviour; reproduction and locomotion; and endocrine and immunity. These modules are assessed by both exams and coursework.

At BSMS, you are not only assessed by end-of-term tests but also through a number of essays. During the first term, you will work towards identifying areas of weakness in your academic ability. You are then offered advice on ways to develop your work and to strengthen areas that you feel you need to improve in. All written work is stored in an academic portfolio, which is added to over the 5 years of the course. This is a beneficial way of gauging the improvements that you make over time.

Students are not only assessed by written exams but also have objective structured clinical examinations (OSCEs) to show their competence in a clinical setting.

Intercalated degrees

Subject to your performance, you may also have the opportunity to extend this aspect of your study by including an intercalated BSc within your medical degree. This is usually carried out between years 3 and 4 of the BSMS course. Students who perform well in the exam at the end of year 3 are likely to be offered this opportunity.

Special study modules and electives

Student-selected components (SSCs) allow students to look at an area of the broader topic in greater detail. This allows you to develop in areas that you personally consider to be more interesting or beneficial to your medical training.

A list of SSCs is made available to students; you then select your top choices. A number of weeks later, you will be informed of which group you are going to be in. Group size is typically small, ranging between eight to twelve students in each. SSCs make up 25% of the module grade in seven of the first eight modules in years 1 and 2.

The elective is carried out in the first 8 weeks of year 4 at BSMS. You are given the opportunity to work in a different medical environment to that in which you normally work as part of your course. Some students may decide to travel abroad to observe how hospitals are different in Africa, while others may choose to see how medical access can affect treatment in places such as Australia by, for example, shadowing 'flying doctors'.

Erasmus

Unfortunately there is no Erasmus scheme currently at the Brighton and Sussex Medical School but it is hoped that one will be set up in the future as the school makes more links with other universities around the world.

Facilities

Library As a student at the Brighton and Sussex Medical School, you are a member of both the University of Brighton and University of Sussex. This means that you can use both universities' libraries, allowing you to have a large number of resources available to you. Medical students are also allowed to borrow books from the postgraduate medical library located at Brighton General Hospital too.

The libraries on campus also have computer rooms, quiet study areas, rooms available to hire for group work and also photocopying facilities.

Computers Similarly, as you are able to use both libraries, you will have access to the computer facilities on both campuses. In addition to this, a large computer room (with over 100 computers) is found within the medical school building at Sussex University. There are a number of 24-hour computer rooms at the University of Sussex. Another computer room is found in the medical school building on the Brighton campus.

Both universities' libraries have excellent computer facilities with a large number of computers, printers and scanners.

Clinical skills One of the real benefits of being a student at a new medical school is the fact that all the equipment is brand new. The medical school has invested heavily in 'patient-simulating' dummies, which are connected to computers. This allows the 'patient's' condition to be controlled and modified. For example, a patient simulator can be given a variety of diseases and students can then give a number of drugs and watch the effect that it has. On some models you can even feel the heart beating and a number of pulses!

Dissection is also used to back up what is learned in anatomy lectures; this is carried out in small groups in the BSMS dissection room. Located in the medical school building at the University of Sussex, this room has only been operational for a year. It has even been called one of the best dissection rooms in the UK! It is fitted with a number of dissection tables, teaching skeletons and also televisions so that the dissection can be demonstrated to the class before they begin their own hands-on work.

Attachments

Throughout the 5 years of the BSMS course, you will be attached to a number of GP surgeries and hospitals. Within the first few weeks, you will have early patient contact at the GP practice that you are attached to for the length of the first year. You also begin to rotate around different departments at both the Brighton General Hospital and Royal Sussex County Hospital throughout year 1. You continue to work your way around the different specialties over the length of the course.

During year 5 you will undertake periods of regional attachment in which you will experience a rotation of clinical placements in district general hospital and community settings in Sussex and its adjoining counties. During your regional attachments you will also spend periods shadowing a PRHO.

In the course of your studies you will develop the key personal skills and attitudes necessary for a successful professional career, in whatever direction it may develop. These include:

- learning how to learn – especially important in a field such as medicine where progress is so rapid that today's knowledge soon becomes obsolete;
- the communication skills necessary for effective engagement with patients and fellow health professionals;
- the ability to work effectively with others in multiprofessional teams to deliver first class health care to individual patients and to society as a whole and, where appropriate, to lead the team;
- the personal and ethical attitudes essential for good professional practice and an appreciation of your responsibilities to your patients, to your professional colleagues, to society as a whole, and to yourself;
- information technology skills – you will need to learn to use a wide range of IT applications to access information and diagnostic resources and to maintain patient records.

Brighton and Sussex
Medical School

Welfare 🏠

Student support

BSMS aims to give every student the most support that it possibly can. During the first year at the Brighton and Sussex Medical School you are assigned two tutors who will offer support and guidance throughout your stay at the medical school.

A 'parenting/buddy' scheme has been organised by MedSoc at BSMS. This is a programme in which students from year 2 help to show first-year students around during their first few weeks at the university.

As a member of both universities, and hence both student unions, you will be able to talk to members of both universities' student support teams if you ever feel the need to.

Accommodation

As a student at BSMS you are guaranteed first year accommodation on campus. There are student halls of residence on both the University of Brighton campus and University of Sussex campus. Most students choose to live on campus during their first year. You can decide as to whether you would rather live on the Brighton campus or Sussex campus. The halls can range between (on average) £50–£75 a week. All halls are self-catered and can range from basic to very elaborate, even including *en suite* facilities in some.

Lectures are held on the Sussex campus 4 days of the week, while 1 day is on the Brighton campus. However, it is only a 15-minute walk between the two campuses and this walk sometimes helps you to wake up, especially on winter mornings!

During the remaining 4 years of the course you will live off campus where student accommodation can vary in terms of quality and price. The two universities have housing lists of accommodation in town that students can rent, and BSMS students can apply for housing from both universities' lists.

Placements

During the first 2 years of the BSMS course you are attached to two GP practices located within 20 miles of the university. Most practices are in the city of Brighton though some can be further afield. The university provides taxis for people who have a long way to travel.

You will also learn clinical skills on the wards of the regions hospitals. In your first year you will visit both the Brighton General Hospital and Royal Sussex County Hospital a number of times. In later years you shall be based at other hospitals across Sussex.

Location of clinical placement/name of hospital	Distance away from medical school (miles)	Difficulty getting there on public transport
Brighton General Hospital	4	🚌
Royal Sussex County Hospital	5	🚌
Haywards Heath Hospital	18	🚗
Princess Royal Hospital	5	🚌

* 🚶: walking/cycling distance; 🚌 : use public transport; 🚗: need own car or lift; 🎈 : get up early – tricky to get to!

Sports and social

City life

Brighton is renowned as a lively city, full of clubs, bars and a number of other things that attract young people from around the country and the rest of the world. However, Brighton is not only an exciting city full of life, surrounding the city are large areas of countryside. The University of Sussex is even located in the picturesque South Downs Park. In Brighton you get the perfect blend of life by the coast as well as the natural beauty of the rolling hills and scenery of Sussex's South Downs Park.

Brighton caters for everybody, no matter what your outlook on life is. If you are an R'n'B loving guy or a rock chick then you can find a number of places suited to your personality. Similarly, if your perfect afternoon includes playing sport in the park with your friends or spending till you drop then this is the place for you. Brighton boasts the famous Laines, a cosmopolitan area containing a large number of shops, cafes, bars and restaurants.

If you are a fan of live music then Brighton has three popular venues: The Dome, Concorde 2 and the Brighton Centre. If you enjoy sporting events then you can watch basketball and ice hockey at the Brighton Centre or even see Brighton and Hove Albion play football at the Withdean Stadium.

Students make up a large proportion of the population in Brighton, making it a great city to live and study in. Summer by the beach on the south coast is fantastic and Brighton has everything on offer that a student could ever want or need.

However, if nothing takes your fancy locally then you can always catch the train to London for the day!

University life

The Brighton and Sussex Medical School is part of both the University of Brighton and University of Sussex. This means that as a BSMS student you are a member of both universities' Student Unions.

You can choose whether you want to live on either the Brighton Campus or Sussex Campus (or even live off-campus). Both of the universities' large libraries are available to BSMS students, this means that there is a huge number of resources at your fingertips. Another one of the great things about being a member of both universities is there are so many things to do, clubs to join and people to meet.

The University of Sussex has numerous bars and it even has its own nightclub on campus! Students can also stand as reps for different areas of the Student Union. Furthermore, a market can be found on campus 2 days a week.

Sports life

As BSMS is a new medical school and the class size is (on average) under 150 students in each year no medical-specific teams have been set up yet. However, with more students arriving over the coming years the MedSoc is keen to get teams set up as quickly as possible. Currently, BSMS students may join either of the universities' sports teams (but you cannot join both universities' teams for the same sport).

Some students choose to make their own 5-a-side football, hockey and netball teams and play against other teams from within the university. Staff can also enter their own teams! Both universities have a joint sailing club that proves to be quite popular, as do many other water sports. This is due to Brighton's excellent location by the sea.

On the Brighton campus you can find the Brighton Health and Racquet Club, which offers student membership to those students who live on the Brighton campus. The club's facilities include its own swimming pool, sauna, tennis and badminton courts, and weight rooms, as well as a number of other things.

> **Top tip:** Don't let the fact that the medical school is found on two separate sites deter you from applying to BSMS. The two campuses are located next to one another so whether you live on the Brighton campus, the Sussex campus or even off-campus you are all close to each other. Similarly, don't be put off by the fact that BSMS is a new medical school; this also has its advantages!

Great things about BSMS

- Brighton is a city of great diversity, there is always something to do and plenty of things to get involved with.
- Brighton and Sussex Medical School is only 1 year old and so has some of the most up-to-date and exciting technology in the medical world. Students are also among the first to use the new equipment!
- At the Brighton and Sussex Medical School you meet patients within your first 3 weeks at university! This allows you to develop communication and examination skills at a very early stage.

- BSMS students are members of both the University of Brighton and the University of Sussex. This means that you have the benefit of being members of both student unions, offering twice the support, twice the resources and twice the fun.
- Brighton and Sussex Medical School is proudly one of the smallest medical schools in the UK. This means that teaching is very personal and also gives the school a real community feel to it.

Bad things about BSMS

- Unfortunately the beach is not sandy; instead it is made up primarily of pebbles.
- The higher than average price of living in the south.
- The campus is located 5 miles outside Brighton.
- The fear of exams, and even worse … the fear of exam results!
- The fact that the wind makes it hard even to walk in the exposed areas of the Brighton campus during winter

Further information

Medical Admissions Office
Brighton and Sussex Medical School
BSMS Teaching Building
University of Sussex
Brighton
BN1 9PX
Tel: 01273 644 644
Email: medadmissions@bsms.ac.uk
Web: http://www.bsms.ac.uk – for further information about the Brighton and Sussex Medical School and its curriculum.
http://www.brighton.ac.uk – for general information on studying at the University of Brighton.
http://www.sussex.ac.uk – for general information on studying at the University of Sussex.

Additional application information

Average A-level requirements	• AAB
Average Scottish Higher requirements	• AAB
Make-up of interview panel	• Three panel members: see the medical school website
Months in which interviews are held	• November and February
Proportion of overseas students	• 7.5%
Proportion of mature students	• 25%
Proportion of graduate students	• n/a
Faculty's view of students taking a gap year	• Acceptable
Proportion of students taking intercalated degrees	• Not yet applicable
Possibility of direct entrance to clinical phase	• No
Fees for overseas students	• £20,000 pa
Fees for graduates	• £3000 pa
Ability to transfer to other medical schools	• N/A
Assistance for elective funding	• Elective is carried out in the first term of year 4 of the BSMA course. As yet very little is known as the first intake is just beginning its second year. Sponsorship is likely to be available to students
Assistance for travel to attachments	• Students are reimbursed for travel by train to GP practices. Students whose practices are found further afield have taxis provided for them
Access and hardship funds	• Both the University of Brighton and the University of Sussex have hardship funds available to BSMA Students
Weekly rent	• £54–£74
Pint of lager	• £1.50 (Union bars) at its cheapest. More expensive in town
Cinema	• £4.50 (with NUS card)
Nightclub	• Free or £1 (before 11 PM), up to £5 (in some clubs after 11 PM)

Bristol

Key facts	Premedical	Undergraduate	Graduate
Course length	6 years	5 years	4 years
Total number of medical undergraduates		c. 1000	
Applicants in 2005	272	1753	620
Interviews given in 2005	28	505	41
Places available in 2005	10	216	19
Places available in 2006	10	217	19
Open days 2006	Usually June		
Entrance requirements	AAB	AAB	2:1 and BBB
Mandatory subjects	Non-science	Chemistry and one other science	
Male:female ratio	1:2	1:2	1:2
Is an exam included in the selection process? If yes, what form does this exam take?	No	No	No
Qualification gained	MBChB		

Fascinating fact: Casualty is filmed in Bristol and cast members and on-location filming can often be spotted around the city. Watching the show can therefore be an opportunity to spot sights as well as catch up on revision!

Bristol is one of the old red-brick universities, but has a very modern and dynamic course. As well as a close-knit medical school, there are numerous opportunities to cultivate a wide circle of friends. The city centre provides an excellent and reasonably compact environment in which to work and play. The university itself has an excellent reputation, producing high-quality research and supporting good teaching. Bristol also offers a premedical year to a small number of students each year, in which the teaching is with predental students and provided by departments in the faculty of science. Since October 2003, Bristol has run an official (NHS-bursary eligible) 4-year fast-track course for graduates. There are only 19 places and the course is only available to Honours graduates in biosciences (see Chapter 4).

Education ▌

Selection is based on UCAS form and a short (10–15 minute) interview. A wide range of national and international qualifications are accepted with the normal offer being AAB at A-level. If candidates offer four subjects at A-level it is asked that at least one is a nonscience subject. Passes at A-grade in exams prior to A-levels are seen as advantageous but there is no minimum requirement. All candidates offered a place will have had an interview and short-listing for interview is based on evidence of motivation and dedication to a career in medicine and participation and achievement in extra-curricular activities. In interviews, admissions tutors look at a wide range of factors such as experience, breadth of personal interests, career aspirations, motivation, the report from your academic referee and your academic record.

Bristol introduced an integrated curriculum in 1995. The integrated course consists of three phases. Phase I, lasting two terms, acts as an introductory period and provides a basic understanding of the human body and the mechanisms of health and disease (molecular and cellular basis of medicine). Phase I also has a human basis of medicine component, where students learn medical sociology, ethics, and epidemiology. This is mainly taught in the school of medical sciences. Phase II lasts until the end of year 3 and consists of mixed clinical and theory-based systems-orientated teaching. Phase III includes teaching and clinical experience of specialty subjects (such as paediatrics, obstetrics, and gynaecology). In addition, phase III includes the elective period and senior clinical attachments in medicine and surgery. Clinical contact begins in general practices in year 1, and the first hospital attachment is in year 2. During phases II and III the whole year group is regularly brought together in Bristol for lectures and tutorial teaching.

Teaching

Teaching in the early phases consists mainly of lectures and practicals, supplemented by small group tutorials and some self-directed learning. No live animals are used in practicals, though occasionally some tissue, such as crab legs and guinea-pig ileum, is used in experiments. Topographical anatomy is taught by young medical demonstrators using cadaveric prosections. Students have the opportunity to do a short dissection project in anatomy in year 2. Anatomy is a popular and rewarding element of the medical degree course at Bristol.

Assessment

Regular assessments are made throughout the course. Many clinical attachments include projects or the preparation and delivery of a case presentation, whereas science teaching carries associated tutorial and practical work. There are usually exams at the end of each year, although continuous assessment contributes to the final-year mark. There are important exams at the end of year 3, and finals at the end of year 5.

Intercalated degrees

Undertaking a BSc is a popular option, with about a third of students opting to intercalate. The school positively encourages students to intercalate, usually after year 2, but it is possible to do so after year 3. There is a small range of conventional science subjects to choose from, although recently programmes such as bioethics have been introduced. There is the option to intercalate in other universities' degree programmes, but very few students take up this option and it has to be arranged and applied for independently. The honours year gives students an opportunity to try some 'real' science in the form of a potentially publishable original research project, as opposed to the rather structured medical course.

Student selected components and electives

Student selected components and electives (SSCs) are an important part of the new curriculum from year 2 onwards, allowing students to pursue subjects of special interest. Elective time is currently 8 weeks at the beginning of year 5. Year 2, 3 and 4 SSCs are marked internally and contribute to the assessment of the unit they are written for. One year 3 SSC and the year 5 elective are externally overseen by an SSC co-ordinator where students specify their own objectives.

Erasmus

There is the opportunity to take part in the Erasmus scheme in year 3 where you can study two of the four 9-week units abroad. There are two firmly agreed exchanges available in Paris and Vienna, while Strasbourg and Bordeaux are under negotiation. The university also has agreements with Rennes, Brussels, Oslo, Stockholm and Thessalonica though these opportunities are not as popular. To pass into year 4, students have to complete all year 3 units and SSCs in Bristol.

Facilities

Library The medical library is open until 9 PM on weekdays (5 PM or 6 PM during the long vacation) and on Saturdays. The main library has longer opening hours. Popular textbooks are available from the medical library on a short-loan basis. Medline, Embase and other databases are on open access on library computers, and email and internet connection are also available there and in the halls of residence. Students on placement are able to use their hospital library and computer facilities.

Computers Computers are available in the medical school (including the library) and in the main library. There are a number of 24-hour open-access rooms dotted around the university. Computer-assisted learning (CAL) packages are available in the medical library. Other terminals support internet access, email, word processing, and so forth. Information technology is supposed to be an integral part of the new course, but the quality of computing facilities is variable.

Clinical skills All the teaching centres have facilities, though the primary site is in one of the main teaching hospitals in Bristol, the Bristol Royal Infirmary. In year 2 adult life support is taught and students are examined and certified. The clinical skills laboratory is also used to teach venepuncture to year 2 students. As students progress through the course, other clinical procedures, such as intubation, may be learnt here or in the medical academies (see below).

Welfare

Student support

There is a personal tutor scheme in operation and it normally works well, the quality of the scheme depending on both the tutor (and the tutee). However, most students find a member of staff with whom they get on well and from whom they can seek help. The faculty tends to be supportive, provided they are informed of problems before they get out of hand. There is a staff–student liaison committee, but input does not often translate into immediate action. The university and the Students' Union both have counselling services. Access for students with disabilities may be difficult because of the layout of the university (on a steep hill). The secretary of Galenicals (the medical students' society) is also there to voice student opinions and views to the medical school.

Accommodation

Accommodation is guaranteed for all first-year students living outside the Bristol area so most of them live in university halls of residence. These tend to be comfortable enough and provide an excellent opportunity to bond with other freshers (medics and nonmedics) at the numerous organised events or in the hall bars. The main group of halls is located a 30–40-minute walk from the university precinct. It is possible to apply to stay in hall after the first year, but most people move into university flats/houses or into accommodation in the private sector. Weekly rents vary from between £55 and £75, but some pay more. It is usual to pay rent over the summer and the scrum for houses starts quite early in the year. The accommodation office provides some help, but a lot depends on individual initiative.

Placements

The first 2 years are spent mainly around the university campus in central Bristol. When you begin clinical specialty attachments you can be placed at one of the main Bristol hospitals or anywhere within a 50-mile radius of Bristol. Attachments start in year 3. Medical academies are being established in Somerset, Bath, Swindon, Weston-super-Mare Gloucestershire and North and South Bristol. The concept of an academy is a group of teachers and students (up to 80) focused on medical-school activities and with equivalent resources to the home university. Students will usually spend 6 months at each academy and, during the 3 years, half the time will be located in academies within Bristol. General practice attachments are also spread across the southwest. Accommodation is provided wherever it is essential for students to be away from Bristol. However, although some help is given with travel expenses, travel to and from these attachments can be an extra expense (especially if you want to come back every weekend). A car is a huge bonus, but trains or buses serve all the hospital attachments, but not all the general practice ones.

Location of clinical placement/name of hospital	Distance away from medical school (miles)	Difficulty getting there on public transport*
BRI, Bristol	0	
Frenchay/Southmead Hospitals, Bristol	8	
Bath	13	
Weston-super-mare	26	
Taunton	50	

* : walking/cycling distance; : use public transport; : need own car or lift; : get up early – tricky to get to!

Sports and social

City life

Bristol has a lot to offer both as a university and as a city. The university is a research-orientated institution with an excellent reputation but it does also provides good teaching. The city is just brilliant fun. Mainstream attractions abound and there is plenty of 'alternative' entertainment for those that want it. It is still reasonably safe (at least in the areas frequented by students), provided appropriate precautions are taken. It is certainly no worse than most other cities in this respect.

The city centre is reasonably compact and packed with things to attract all comers. The countryside (and the attractions of the West Country and Wales) is not far away. Students tend to congregate in the areas just around the university, such as Clifton. However, there is a shift towards areas a little further away which offer cheaper rents. Clifton is the most affluent part of Bristol, offering pleasant cafes and bijou shops. Shopping, theatre, museum and music lovers will all find something to their taste. There are plenty of pubs, restaurants, clubs, cinemas (including three 'art house' cinemas), plenty of parks and green spaces, and all the other things you would associate with a vibrant city like Bristol.

University life

Entertainment abounds in Bristol – sometimes there seems to be too much choice! A number of big acts play at the university and at other venues throughout the city. There is a huge range of societies to join at the Union. Halls and Galenicals lay on a range of entertainment, organise a number of sports teams, and represent students' views on a variety of committees. There are two revues for medics to take part in. The preclinical revue tends to be a rather drunken and disorganised affair, but the clinical one is a more organised and moderate event that runs for four nights in the Union theatre. Galenicals organises a lot of events for medics and has its own bar which students from all year groups use.

Sports life

The university has good outdoor facilities, a tennis centre, and a brand new indoor centre within the campus. Wednesday afternoons are usually free for sport, and there are teams at all levels in most sports. There are a number of medics' teams (including the infamous women's football team) organised through Galenicals, which tend to be a bit less competitive than the university teams. They have a considerable social component (and alcohol consumption, too!).

> **Top tip:** Don't worry about being out of Bristol in the new academy system. Lots of people are placed in each academy so it's a great opportunity to meet people from different years and have the social atmosphere of halls but in better accommodation! Most of the academies also have excellent facilities and you will have the opportunity to discover places outside of Bristol.

Great things about Bristol

- Friendly and close-knit.
- The generally high standard of teaching and the high quality of clinical experience, especially in peripheral hospitals.
- The city of Bristol itself, with its huge range of bars, restaurants and attractions.
- The opportunity to mix with plenty of nonmedics and medics from other year groups.
- A modern, clinical course in which student feedback is valued.

Bad things about Bristol

- The rather conservative nature of the university in terms of atmosphere and politics.
- The financial costs (high rents; long distance attachments in clinical years; expensive bus fares).
- Walking up all those steep hills (Bristol is one big hill)!
- Feedback on exams you have just taken can sometimes be a bit limited.
- Huge annual scramble for accommodation at a reasonable price.

Further information

Admissions Office
University of Bristol
Senate House
Tyndall Avenue
Bristol BS8 ITH
Tel: 0117 928 9000
Fax: 0117 925 1424
Email: admissions@bristol.ac.uk
Web: http://www.medici.bris.ac.uk
Prospectus requests: http://www.bris.ac.uk/prospectusrequest/

Additional application information

Average A-level requirements	• AAB
Average Scottish Higher requirements	• AAAAA
Make-up of interview panel	• Clinicians, medical scientists, GPs, nonclinician personnel
Months in which interviews are held	• November–March
Proportion of overseas students	• 5%
Proportion of mature students	• 10%
Proportion of graduate students	• 10%
Faculty's view of students taking a gap year	• Welcomed
Proportion of students taking intercalated degrees	• 30%
Possibility of direct entrance to clinical phase	• No
Fees for overseas students	• £12,400 pa (preclinical) • £23,100 pa (clinical)
Fees for graduates	• £3000 pa
Ability to transfer to other medical schools	• At any stage, assessed on a personal level. Not many do transfer, of course but help will be given to students having a genuine need to transfer
Assistance for elective funding	• Many bursaries available including Medical Elective Bursary, MedChi Prize, Medical/Dental prize, and external bursary funding from, e.g. Wellcome Trust
Assistance for travel to attachments	• Return travel paid for plus accommodation provided in clinical years
Access and hardship funds	• Available through student union, in line with other university arrangements
Weekly rent	• £65
Pint of lager	• £2
Cinema	• £4
Nightclub	• £2

Cambridge

Key facts	Undergraduate	Graduate
Course length	6 years	4 years
Total number of medical undergraduates	1298	83
Applicants in 2005	1408	254
Interviews given in 2005	Not known	Not known
Places available in 2005	273	20
Places available in 2006	273	20
Open days 2006	6 and 7 July	
Entrance requirements	AAA	2:1 or above
Mandatory subjects	Chemistry and two science/maths subjects	
Male:female ratio	45:55	Not known
Is an exam included in the selection process? If yes, what form does this exam take?	Yes BMAT	
Qualification gained	MB/BChir	MB/BChir

Fascinating fact: The teaching of medicine at Cambridge dates back to 1540 when Henry VIII endowed the University's first Professorship of Physic. Things moved quickly after that, and within only 320 years the number of medical students had reached double figures. Heady days indeed.

The standard 6-year medical degree at Cambridge comprises a traditional preclinical course followed by clinical studies. The 3-year preclinical course is a science degree in its own right: intercalation is compulsory unless you are already a graduate, and there is a strong emphasis on research. The clinical course continues that emphasis, and it is possible to intercalate an MPhil or a PhD. Until now the clinical course has been very intense and only 2¼ years long with finals in December, but from 2005 onwards it will be a 3-year course.

All Cambridge students are members of a college, and this is the focus of social life for most preclinical students. Despite the intensity of the course there is ample opportunity for extra-curricular activities, not just within the colleges but also in the university and within the city itself.

Cambridge also has a 4-year graduate-entry course which mixes elements from the standard preclinical and clinical courses with dedicated teaching; it is open to UK/EU graduates of any discipline. Graduate entry to the standard course is also possible, and is the only option for non-UK/EU graduate students.

Education

The Cambridge admissions procedure can be complicated, and prospective students are advised to contact the University Admissions Office (see Further information) and/or their sixth-form careers department for details well ahead of time. In particular, applicants to the standard 6-year course should be aware of the need to fill out the Cambridge Application Form (CAF) in addition to their UCAS paperwork, and of the requirement to sit the BioMedical Admissions Test (BMAT). Full information on the applications procedure (for both the undergraduate and the graduate course), is available on the website.

Preclinical and clinical medicine are taught separately at Cambridge, by the faculty of biology and the school of clinical medicine respectively.

All undergraduate preclinical students read for a BA – that is, they receive a BA degree on completing their first 3 years of study. In the first 2 years, students study anatomy, biochemistry, physiology, neurobiology, pathology, pharmacology and reproductive biology. Exams in these subjects count towards both the class (grade) of your BA, and the official 'Second MB' requirements for progression to subsequent years of the course. Smaller courses in medical sociology and statistics/epidemiology, and a brief clinical-contact program count towards the Second MB requirements only, while certain options taken in year 2 count towards the BA only.

The third intercalated year of the BA is compulsory, unless you already have a degree (in which case you receive your BA after 2 years and then go on to clinical study). It does not count towards the Second MB. Cambridge medics may intercalate in any undergraduate degree offered by the university – not just medical courses – so you could apply to study, say, law, or history of art, or philosophy, or indeed any other available subject that interests you. It should, however, be noted that most students are strongly encouraged to study one of the more scientific subjects. In many of these you get to spend some time on a project, usually with the chance to carry out some original research.

The preclinical course will give you a very strong grounding in the medical sciences, and a BA, plus the chance to study your choice from a very wide range of subjects in year 3. Do be aware though that patient contact is pretty minimal until you start clinical school.

If you have fulfilled the Second MB requirements in your first 2 years (and almost everyone does), you are guaranteed a place in clinical school at Cambridge, Oxford or London. Where you go depends on the preferences you express and the outcome of applications and interviews, but in most years everyone who applies to stay on at Cambridge gets to do so. Roughly half the students in the year stay on; the others go mainly to Oxford and London, but some choose to go to other compatible courses, such as the one in Edinburgh. Interviews for the clinical course take place in the February prior to entry. If you apply to the Cambridge clinical course after preclinical elsewhere, it is essential to complete a BA or BSc as well as equivalents of the Second MB before starting.

Currently the clinical course is intensive, lasting only 27 months. Most of the work is ward or clinic based and students are expected to be active in seeking out patients to clerk. **From 2005 there will be a completely new clinical program lasting 3 years** – at time of writing little information about it had been released, and the specifics in this article refer to the current course, but up-to-date details will be available from the sources listed at the end of the chapter.

Students on the 4-year graduate-entry course are admitted to the clinical school from the start and do not study for a BA. During the first 2 years their program of studies combines tuition for the Second MB with dedicated clinical teaching based at the West Suffolk Hospital, 30 miles east of Cambridge. For the third year they join the standard clinical course, and then return to dedicated teaching for the fourth year.

Teaching

Preclinical teaching is mainly in a traditional lecture-and-compulsory-practical (such as anatomy dissection) format. The lecturers often teach on their research area, and can go into considerable detail. The main occasions when students discuss and ask questions about the lectures are *supervisions*. These small group tutorials (usually two to four students, but sometimes more) are led by someone either involved with or familiar with the course, such as a lecturer (often a world-expert in their field), or a PhD or clinical student. They can be an excellent way of consolidating and testing your knowledge. Your supervisors will normally set and mark a few essays for you over the term.

Each part of the clinical course usually starts with a block of lectures, following which students are dispersed to attachments at Addenbrooke's or elsewhere within East Anglia. Teaching is still very much clinically based, so students get very good exposure to patients.

Assessment

On the preclinical course, you sit exams in May/June at the end of years 2 and 3. Each of the bigger subjects is assessed by a multiple choice/short answer paper and a practical paper (which count towards both your BA and your Second MB), and an essay paper (which counts towards your BA only). As mentioned earlier, you need to pass the Second MB in each subject to be allowed to enter clinical school. Your classes of BA in years 1 and 2 may be taken into account by your preferred clinical school in deciding whether or not to offer you a place, but are not a be-all and end-all. Again, graduate course students sit only the Second MB papers.

At clinical school, students will sit the new 'Final MB', to be introduced in 2005. This will cover medicine, surgery, and obstetrics and gynaecology, and will involve a multiple choice paper, an extended matching paper, a short answer paper and two OSCEs (objective structured clinical examinations – one on clinical skills and one on communication skills). Final MB pathology will still form a separate exam taken earlier in the course. There are also assessments at the end of each clinical attachment, which have to be passed before finals are sat.

Intercalated degrees

A full discussion of intercalated degrees at Cambridge is provided in the introduction to the Education section above. It is a requirement of the BA to be resident in Cambridge, so normally you cannot intercalate elsewhere. However, intercalation *is* allowed under the Cambridge – MIT (Massachusetts Institute of Technology) exchange scheme. This takes three medical students each year, who are then required to stay at Cambridge for their clinical studies.

Each year, eight or nine clinical students follow the MB PhD program, for which they apply after being accepted into clinical school but before starting the course.

Special study modules and electives

On both the standard-clinical and graduate courses there is a 7-week elective period. Ninety–five per cent of students go abroad. Limited funding (£80–£200) is available for electives from the clinical school (although students have to compete for this), and there may also be some assistance from your college and other sources.

Currently, neither the preclinical nor the clinical course have SSMs, although students are able to choose two options from a limited range of topics for studies in the final term of the second preclinical year. The graduate course *has* introduced SSMs, although only one is student-selected.

Erasmus

An Erasmus exchange is not normally possible during the preclinical course due to the requirement to be resident in Cambridge, and does not form part of the clinical course. Currently the only overseas travel opportunity apart from the elective is the MIT exchange scheme described above.

Facilities

Library Cambridge is not short of libraries! The Medical Library is based at the clinical school, and has multiple copies of many undergraduate clinical texts, as well as specialist books. The University Library, which is nearer to central Cambridge, is a copyright library, and so is entitled to a copy of every book published in the UK and Ireland, of which all the medical books should end up in the Medical Library. Clinical students can borrow books for up to 4 weeks at a time. In addition, each department (physiology, pathology, etc.) has its own specialised library. Finally, each college has a library, which is usually well stocked with preclinical textbooks in particular. Some of the college and departmental libraries have 24-hour access; the Medical Library is open from 8 AM–10 PM on weekdays. Cambridge also has a public lending library.

Computers There are computers everywhere in Cambridge and all students have an email account and access to central computing facilities. The colleges have networks which are available to their members, and many departments also have facilities which can be used by their intercalating students. Most college rooms have a network access point, and at least one college provides a computer (although not necessarily the most up to date model!) for all its students who are living-in.

The clinical school has computers reserved for the use of clinical students as well as others for use by anyone, and a wireless area network for those with suitably equipped laptops or palmtops. There is also a set of terminals spread around Addenbrooke's hospital, set up for students to access teaching resources while on the wards.

Welfare

Student support

All students are members of a college – it's where you'll live, eat, and socialise, at least to begin with, and it's where your supervisions are organised. The college allocates each of its students a tutor and a 'Director of Studies'. The tutor's academic subject may be unrelated to medicine, and they may be responsible for students from a wide range of courses. Their duties cover welfare matters such as finance and housing, and general pastoral care. The Director of Studies (in preclinical medicine) may be medically qualified or may be a scientist in one of the preclinical disciplines, and is responsible for students' academic progress and arranging supervisors in the various preclinical subjects. Directors of studies in clinical medicine are normally medically qualified and are appointed to provide academic guidance and support, plus advice on matters such as elective placements.

During the preclinical course there is a strong emphasis on the college as a focus for academic issues, although it is always possible to contact the various lecturers and course organisers for each subject, or even the *Director of Medical and Veterinary Education*, who oversees the preclinical course. During the clinical course the focus shifts to the Clinical School, and the *Director of Medical Education in the Clinical School* is normally a student's first point of contact over an academic issue.

Most colleges also have a nurse (and some also have a counsellor and a doctor-on-call), as well as a chaplain who is available for the pastoral support of students from any background. Most also have 'porters' – generally friendly staff who act as reception and security personnel for the college, and are on hand to deal with any emergencies 24 hours a day. There are also numerous university-linked organisations involved in student support, including the University Counselling Service, CUSU (Cambridge University Students' Union) and various student-run bodies.

Accommodation

Quality and cost vary with the college (and the wealth of the college), and can be difficult to determine before you apply. Most undergraduates can expect to live in college for at least 2 out of the 3 preclinical years, and have college-provided accommodation – often in college-owned houses around Cambridge – for the other year. One welcome hangover from the past is that most colleges continue to provide staff known as 'bedders', to clean student rooms – having to do your own cleaning if you move into privately-owned accommodation can be a shock! The standard of accommodation at its worst is definitely bearable and at its best can see you in some of the finest student rooms in the country.

Many colleges will also provide accommodation – albeit usually not in college – for the clinical years, and students joining these years from preclinical courses elsewhere can expect to have something provided for the first year at least. Many students who have already been at Cambridge for the preclinical years decide to rent a shared house in the private sector at this point, and many houses get handed on from one group of clinical students to another. This tends to cost between £50 and £60 per week for a middle-of-the-range house, usually shared by three or four people.

Placements

Lectures and practicals for the first two preclinical years are held on the science sites in the centre of Cambridge, and are within walking distance of most of the colleges. Supervisions usually take place in your college, but are sometimes at the supervisor's department building or another college.

All the teaching on the clinical course is based at Addenbrooke's Hospital, which is situated 2½ miles south-east of the city centre. Many students live close to Addenbrooke's and walk in, however it can easily be reached by bus or bicycle from anywhere in Cambridge. Parking on the Hospital site can be a nightmare.

On the standard clinical course there are regional attachments in up to a maximum of six out of the eleven Phase I and II placements. In Phase III, half of the time is spent at Addenbrooke's and half in a district general hospital. Accommodation at these placements is provided. Students are usually allocated attachments; however, if a student is heavily involved in a university sport they can arrange to remain in Addenbrooke's for the majority of firms.

Location of clinical placement/name of hospital	Distance away from medical school (miles)	Difficulty getting there on public transport*
Hinchingbrooke Hospital, Huntingdon	26	(need own car or lift)
Ipswich Hospital	58	(get up early)
James Paget Hospital, Great Yarmouth	87	(get up early)
Whipps Cross University Hospital, London	49	(need own car or lift)
Papworth Hospital	14	(use public transport)

* 🚶: walking/cycling distance; 🚌 : use public transport; 🚗—🚗 : need own car or lift; 💡 : get up early – tricky to get to!

Apart from these examples, there are another eight or so hospitals that provide regional attachments, all of which are within 50 miles of the medical school.

Sports and social 🏆

City life

With its undeniable beauty and rich history, Cambridge is an inspiring city to live and work in. Undergraduates (during term time), graduates and tourists (at all times) and, of course, the local residents, provide an ever-changing and colourful population superimposed on peaceful college cloisters, colonies of bustling student houses, and a busy town centre. On a more practical note, all the usual student needs are generally less than 15 minutes' walk away, and are certainly within a 15-minute cycle ride (with the exception of students at Girton College, who have to cycle into town from nearby Girton village).

Take your pick from the central market; the supermarkets and shopping centres; a wide range of chain stores; the excellent Arts Theatre; gigs at the Junction, Corn Exchange and Guildhall; countless pubs; several clubs; and loads of cinemas – college, art house and mainstream. The river soon meanders to open countryside in both directions and, finally, many routes lead out of Cambridge to London's many attractions, and the rest of the country. A 45-minute shuttle service runs up to every half-hour between London King's Cross and Cambridge train stations, and Cambridge also has good coach links, several city bus routes, plenty of taxis, and is close to Stansted international airport. Many students have bicycles but they're rarely essential.

Cambridge is not without the dangers of violence and crime and, like most places, these problems are often associated with last orders on a Friday or Saturday night. However, there are no very dangerous districts and students' property insurance premiums confirm Cambridge as one of the safest places in the country to live and study.

Local health care is excellent, and finding an NHS GP and dentist is not difficult.

University life

Cambridge life is a heady mix in terms of inhabitants and surroundings. The collegiate system means that in the preclinical years you get to meet students doing a wide variety of subjects, rather than just other medics. Although the course does place a significant workload on you there is time to do plenty of other things, such as sport – in particular rowing – and music, which are well represented throughout the university. There is much more of a 'medical school' feel to the clinical stage, with most students living nearer the hospital and away from their colleges. The small year-group sizes in these years mean that by the end of the course everyone gets to know one another.

Entertainment is provided at a variety of levels, and may be society, college, clinical school or university-based. If that's not enough, then there are many shows and concerts put on by nonuniversity establishments in the town. Cambridge is very different from other universities in that there is no central Student Union bar where everyone accumulates. Instead, and, arguably, much more pleasingly, there are bars in each college and student nights during the week at the various town and college hot spots.

'Formal hall' meals are a prominent feature of the Cambridge social scene. These are very merry three-course dinners in a college dining hall costing between £3 and £9. Students wear gowns, Latin benedictions are made and a gong sounds. It is hard to believe this becomes normality, but it's all light-hearted – great fun, just a nightmare when it's five minutes before graduation and you find 3-year-old food ingrained in your gown!

The MedSoc is the fourth largest student society and works to make sure preclinical medics have a good time. Every year there is a Christmas dinner, and other activities such as 'bops' (parties), barbecues and pub crawls are also organised. In addition, each college usually has its own medical society which hosts a number of dinners each year and provides ample occasion to chat on a less academic level with college fellows. The clinical students' society arranges its own social events, often sponsored by insurance societies hoping to get you to stay signed up with them post-qualification. On top of this, there are a whole host of opportunities to be involved in other societies, from drama (ranging from the famous Cambridge Footlights, to The Medics' Review comedy show, which travels to the Edinburgh Fringe every other year) and music to karate and gliding. There really is a society for almost every conceivable hobby and interest – be it caving or Canada, cocktails or Christmas, so the chances are you can find something you will enjoy doing.

Sports life

Almost every sport is catered for at the university level. Facilities at college level vary, but can often include huge playing fields, gyms and/or squash courts, plus the inevitable boathouse. Rowing, football, hockey, rugby, and cricket tend to have the largest shares of the college budgets. Thankfully, it doesn't really matter how good or bad you are, there is always an opportunity to take part in whatever you choose. During the preclinical stage sport is mainly college based and there is fierce intercollegiate rivalry. The clinical school has a sports society (known as 'The Sharks') and there is a sport and fitness centre situated on the hospital site to which all students are given free membership.

Finally, another popular – ahem – 'sport' in Cambridge is punting. Whether you prefer to do the active bit yourself or simply recline, enjoy the cool breeze and listen to punt chauffeurs tell elaborate lies to awe-struck tourists, you will love this very Cambridgey tradition!

> **Top tip:** Don't let any preconceptions put you off applying to Cambridge. Find out about the place for yourself, and then decide if it's for you – speak to the admissions offices and (most importantly) some current students, and visit a few colleges if you can. Interviews are friendly and fair; the workload is heavy but manageable; the city is modern; and the people are really, really friendly. Students of every background and personality tend quickly to feel at home here – we have one of the lowest drop-out rates of any university in the country.

Great things about Cambridge

- The social life in Cambridge is brilliant. Countless societies and the collegiate system mean that you get to meet students doing a wide variety of subjects.
- The preclinical course is regarded as one of the most comprehensive in the country – leaving you well-armed for clinical school and job applications. And you can choose from a huge range of intercalated degrees. And your BA gets automatically upgraded to an MA after 3 or 4 years!

- The supervision system aims to ensure that you are able to get help with any academic difficulties, helps to make sure that you are able to keep up with the course, and gives you substantially more individual tuition than most medical schools. It also makes sure you do the work!
- May week! Actually in June, after the preclinical exams. A week of celebrating, winding down, and college balls! After all this, you have over 3 months (in the preclinical years) to skip off into the sunset completely free of work worries.
- You get to live and study in truly beautiful surroundings – which make even Monday mornings a little more bearable. And yet, the cost of living is relatively low, especially for those in college accommodation, and the proximity of all the necessary amenities makes Cambridge an ideal place to spend life as a student. Finances are also helped by the many funds/bursaries available to all students for travel, study and extracurricular activities.

Bad things about Cambridge

- Cambridge is highly academic and can appear a very competitive learning environment, especially just prior to exams, which for many students can be rather stressful. Good time-management becomes key in warding off the lows known as '5th-week blues'.
- Living in college can be frustrating, as the rules and regulations the college enforces can make some individuals feel as though they are not being treated like adults. However, it's more than made up for by all the advantages of being part of an inclusive community, and by being able to get cheap accommodation without the hassle of such things as landlords and utility bills.
- The course is intensive and it is easy to fall behind. Although the preclinical terms are short (only 8 weeks of study) they can be very tiring, but this is made up for by longer holidays.
- The standard preclinical course is heavy on detail and can in some respects seem old-fashioned and resistant to change. In particular, be aware that you don't get to see patients for more than a few hours a year. However, if you wish to get a first-rate footing in high-level science sorted out before you start clinical school, the course will suit you.
- The tourists – who admittedly do generate a lot of income for the town and the colleges – manage to appear almost anywhere and at any time, including occasionally in lectures!

Further information

Cambridge Admissions Office (CAO)
Fitzwilliam House
32 Trumpington Street
Cambridge CB2 1QY
Tel: +44 (0)1223 333 308
Fax: +44 (0)1223 366 383
Email: admissions@cam.ac.uk
Web: http://www.cam.ac.uk/cambuniv/undergrad/

University of Cambridge School of Clinical Medicine
Box 111
Addenbrooke's Hospital
Hills Road
Cambridge CB2 2SP
Tel: +44 (0)1223 336 700
Fax: +44 (0)1223 336 709
Email: school-enquiries@medschl.cam.ac.uk
Web: http://www.medschl.cam.ac.uk/pages/admission/index.html

Additional information about applications and access issues is available from:
Cambridge University Students' Union
11–12 Trumpington Street
Cambridge
CB2 1QA
Tel: +44 (0)1223 356 454
Web: http://cususite.headporter.com

Additional application information

Average A-level requirements	• AAA
Average Scottish Higher requirements	• AAB
Make-up of interview panel	• Mixed clinical and nonclinical
Months in which interviews are held	• December
Proportion of overseas students	• 9%
Proportion of mature students	• 1%
Proportion of graduate students	• Information unavailable
Faculty's view of students taking a gap year	• Good
Proportion of students taking intercalated degrees	• 100%
Possibility of direct entrance to clinical phase	• No
Fees for overseas students	• £11,571 pa (preclinical) • £21,417 pa (clinical) plus £2000–£3000 college fees
Fees for graduates	• Please contact university for details
Ability to transfer to other medical schools	• About 50% of students transfer for clinical studies, moving mainly to Oxford and London • A small number of places exist for medics wishing to spend their intercalated year at MIT in the United States. Outside these schemes, transfer is not possible

(*Continued*)

(*Continued*)

Assistance for elective funding	• Limited funds are available from medical school/university sources, as well as from the Colleges and the Medical Society
Assistance for travel to attachments	• LEA-funded students will normally have one return trip/attachment outside Cambridge paid for. Students with an NHS Bursary or equivalent (i.e. most students in the second clinical year and above) claim their travel expenses from their NHS/Department of Health funding body
Access and hardship funds	• 'Isaac Newton' hardship bursaries are generous and are widely awarded. 'Access to Learning' funds of up to £3500 are also available. Both these grants are subject to financial assessment. Repeat awards are often made for each year of study. Many other sources of funding are available at college and university level
Weekly rent	• College average for 2003/4 was about £70 per week of term, including catering contribution
Pint of lager	• £1 OTC Bar • £2 or more in city centre pubs. Somewhere in between at college bars
Cinema	• From free (some college cinemas) to £4.50 (VUE multiplex) to £6.20 (Arts Picturehouse)
Nightclub	• From £2–£6

Derby

Key facts	Graduate
Course length	4 years
Total number of medical undergraduates	181
Applicants in 2005	1156
Interviews given in 2005	240
Places available in 2005	91
Places available in 2006	91
Open days 2006	April and September
Entrance requirements	2:2 Bachelors degree or better in any discipline
Mandatory subjects	N/A
Male:female ratio	65:35
Is an exam included in the selection process? If yes, what form does this exam take?	Yes, GAMSAT. Applicants are selected for interview based on highest scores from this exam.
Qualification gained	BMBS

Editors' note: If you are considering Derby it is worth your while to read the Nottingham chapter as there will be a large amount of highly relevant and applicable information due to the proximity of the cities.

The Graduate Entry Medicine (GEM) course at Derby is situated in a new, purpose-designed, medical school on the grounds of the Derby City General Hospital. Students study for 18 months in Derby and then proceed onto the same 30 months of clinical training that students from Nottingham receive. Successful students graduate with BMBS degrees from The University of Nottingham. Entrants are graduates of any discipline. The brand new building provides a comfortable learning environment, and being based on a hospital site gives a sense of vocation. Applications may be made to both the 5-year Nottingham course and 4-year Derby course without prejudice to either.

Education

The mainstay of education, during the preclinical months, is problem-based learning (PBL). This innovative programme was developed by the University of Sydney, Australia, and has been purchased for use in Derby.

Students are arranged into groups of seven, and each week a new case opens for the groups to discuss. Three sessions are held for each case. PBL is good fun but demands a great deal of private study to be effective. Lectures, specific to the current problem, accompany the PBL topic of the week. PBL topics are divided into successive blocks: foundation, musculo-skeletal, respiratory, cardiovascular, alimentary, renal, neuroscience, endocrine and cancer.

Anatomy, related to the current PBL topic, is taught by lectures and prosection. The highly thought of Personal and Professional Development (PPD) programme is composed of Clinical Skills workshops, lectures and GP placements. Clinical Skills workshops teach basic procedures, such as listening to heart sounds and taking blood pressure, as well as communication skills. There are nine GP placements during the preclinical months. The clinical course is as described for Nottingham.

Teaching

This is largely by clinicians practising in the Derbyshire area. There are a few in-house academics, while some travel from Nottingham to lecture.

Assessment

After the first 18 months of the course PBL, lectures and anatomy are assessed with a set of final written exams (short answer and multiple choice). Students also do an objective clinical examination (OSCE) at this time. A PPD portfolio must be submitted for review at the end of years 1 and 2. A formative exam is set at the end of each PBL block; the results of this are indicative only and do not contribute to the final degree mark. The clinical years, the final 30 months, are assessed as described for Nottingham.

Intercalated degrees

These are not available since all entrants are graduates. Unlike the 5-year Nottingham students, GEM students do not obtain a BMedSci degree.

Facilities

Access to the building is available 24 hours a day, 7 days a week. Only the library, lecture theatre, seminar room, clinical skills centre and anatomy suite have set hours of access. Walk-in access is available to anatomical learning aids throughout the day. Each group of seven students has exclusive access, via key code, to their own PBL room; each is equipped with two computers (with CD-Rw), tables, white boards, lockers and a set of core textbooks. Students also have their own common room with pool table and balcony.

Library The new library is very well stocked with the latest editions of many texts. All of the core texts are multiple-stocked in both the short and weeklong loan sections. There are few paper journals held but online access is available for most. Photocopying facilities and 10 computers, linked to a printer, are available. The library is open until 9:45 PM on weeknights and is also open at the weekends. GEM students have full access to the Greenfield Medical Library, at the QMC in Nottingham, and may also use the library of the Derby City General Hospital. There is a public library in the city centre.

Computers There are over 90 computers in the main computer room and 10 in the smaller one. There is a laser printer, colour inkjet printer and quiet work desks. All computers in the building are linked to the University of Nottingham network with fast broadband Internet access. PowerPoint™ lecture presentations are available from the GEM website, along with a vast amount of learning resources. The PBL scenarios, and all associated learning materials, are here also. Email is widely used for communication within the school, along with the bulletin board on the GEM website. Access is available to the computers at all times, and most have 250MB ZIP drives and USB ports.

Clinical skills Extra practice with medical equipment can be booked between 9 AM and 5 PM.

Welfare

Student support

The staff at the school are friendly and on first name terms with students. Each student is assigned a personal mentor: a member of staff available to help with both personal and academic issues. Students meet with mentors at the end of each PBL block to formally review progress; this also gives the opportunity to raise concerns of any kind. Meetings are relaxed and staff are very approachable. A new parenting scheme is being introduced where, in addition to the above mentor, newer students are given a mentor in a higher year group. All of the University and Students' Union services described for Nottingham are also available to GEM students.

Accommodation

Accommodation at Laverstoke Hall is available through the University. Laverstoke Hall is a large site of self-catering flats with seven students sharing. Usually about half the new intake opt for University accommodation each year and the rest usually share a house. There is a good availability of housing and private flats in the area.

Placements

These are the same as described for the Nottingham students.

Sports and social

City life

Bijou and quick to traverse, Derby caters for a spectrum of tastes. There is plenty of cheap entertainment, but there is less chance for lavish celebrations in exclusive surroundings. With well-connected train and bus stations, a return bus ticket to Nottingham is between £2 and £6.50 depending on time of travel and length of journey. Buses back from Nottingham operate through the small hours on Saturday and Sunday mornings, with a journey of about 20–30 minutes. Most major high-street names can be found and there are strangely almost as many banks as shops! There are a lot of bars, many late licensed, and a few clubs, and generally it's very lively. The medical school is about a 25-minute walk away from Laverstoke Hall. A retail park, with a Sainsbury's, Boots and B&Q, is a 20-minute walk from Laverstoke, and Tesco is within driving distance. Buses into the city centre from near the medical school or Laverstoke Hall are frequent and cost £1.80 return maximum. The city is a 20-minute walk from Laverstoke. Parking near the medical school costs £108 for a permit that lasts a year. The surrounding area of Derbyshire is very beautiful and rambling is popular.

University life

All students are automatically members of the University of Nottingham Students' Union but travelling can become tiresome without a car. Affiliate membership of The University of Derby Students' Union can be bought for a small fee and provides access to their societies and sports. GEMSoc is the in-house society for arranging social and sporting events. The Anatomy Society *GEM Cutters* provides an opportunity to perform dissection.

Sports life

Weekly sessions of football, Pilates, golf and squash are held, and cricket and climbing are also practised by some. A tennis coaching session is held weekly, and other sports are in the pipeline. With the school being new the attitude is very much *if it's not here already then set it up*!

Top tip: Thanks to the hard work of MedSoc there are brilliant discounts at many of the city's best bars, restaurants, and for that all important fancy dress! Make sure you track down your MedSoc card in Freshers' week to take advantage of these!

Great things about Derby

- Attractive new purpose-designed building.
- Excellent teaching and facilities, with dedicated staff.
- Wide mix of students with different degrees and life experiences.
- Close community atmosphere.
- Much of the teaching is by clinicians.

Bad things about Derby

- You can feel fairly isolated from the main University and Students' Union.
- Not many student societies are set up yet because the course is new.
- Everyone studies medicine, so there is not much integration with students of other disciplines.
- The small number of students means that you can get to know everyone, perhaps, too well.
- If you both work and live with medics you can get 'medicine overload syndrome'.

Further information

Nottingham

Admissions Officer
Faculty Office
Queen's Medical Centre
University of Nottingham
Nottingham NG7 2RD
Tel: 0115 970 9379
Fax: 0115 970 9922
Email: medschool@nottingham.ac.uk
Web: http://www.nottingham.ac.uk

Derby

Admissions Officer
GEM Course Office
The Medical School
Derby City General Hospital
Uttoxeter Road
Derby DE22 3DT
Tel: 01332 347141 Ext 2645
Email: Cath.Anderson@nottingham.ac.uk
Web: http://www.nottingham.ac.uk/mhs/gem

Additional application information

Average A-level requirements	• N/A
Average Scottish Higher requirements	• N/A
Make-up of interview panel	• Consultants, academics and lay people
Months in which interviews are held	• March–April
Proportion of overseas students	• Only open to EU students, no international students
Proportion of mature students	• All graduate students – age range 21+; an upper age limit of 45 will be set from 2005
Proportion of graduate students	• 100% (only graduates can apply)
Faculty's view of students taking a gap year	• Acceptable provided constructively used
Proportion of students taking intercalated degrees	• 0%
Possibility of direct entrance to clinical phase	• No
Fees for overseas students	• N/A
Fees for graduates	• £3000 pa
Ability to transfer to other medical schools	• Yes, usually after completion of BMedSci degree in year 3. Individual circumstances are considered separately
Assistance for elective funding	• Not directly, but students are invited to apply for elective prizes
Assistance for travel to attachments	• No, students must apply to their LEA and the medical school will validate the claim
Access and hardship funds	• Yes, but must be paid back in the future. All cases dealt with anonymously
Weekly rent	• £50 (self-catering halls) • £105 (fully catered halls) • £45–£65 (private)
Pint of lager	• £1.40 Union bar • £2.20 city centre pub
Cinema	• £4 with NUS card
Nightclub	• Free–£4 Monday–Friday, though posh clubs charge more at the weekends

Dundee

Key facts	Premedical	Undergraduate
Course length	6 years	5 years
Total number of medical undergraduates	6	770
Applicants in 2005	144	1813
Interviews given in 2005	14	469
Places available in 2005	Up to 10	154
Places available in 2006	Up to 10	154
Open days 2006	tbc	tbc
Entrance requirements	AAA	AAA
Mandatory subjects	Non-science	Chemistry
Male:female ratio	2:4	42:58
Is an exam included in the selection process? If yes, what form does this exam take?	No	No UKCAT in 2007
Qualification gained	MBChB	

Fascinating fact: Dundee is home to Professor Sir David Lane, ranked in the top ten biochemists in the world, and discoverer of the ubiquitous p53 cancer gene.

Dundee is a modern, friendly, progressive, and forward-thinking medical school with an international reputation. The new curriculum was introduced in 1993. Dundee medics have a reputation for being friendly, fun-loving and down to earth. Intake is approximately 40% Scottish, 35% Northern Irish, 5% Irish from the Republic of Ireland, 10% English, and 10% international. Dundee is extremely supportive of graduate/mature students and encourages applications from a wide variety of backgrounds. Over 16% of the students in every year are graduate/mature students, and each year also has about seven entrants from the premed course.

The curriculum offers good staff–student participation and has achievable learning goals with a realistic workload. Students first step onto the wards in the first week of their first year. Clinical teaching is phased in from year 2, and by year 4 the content is 100% clinical. Many aspects of the course at Dundee have received plaudits from the Scottish Higher Education Funding Council. The biomedical research programme is world renowned. Ninewells Hospital, the largest purpose-built teaching hospital in Europe, is built on a green park campus on the banks of the River Tay.

Education

The first cohort from the new-style course graduated in 2000 and the integrated course is well established. Teaching is structured around body systems. The first year (phase I) covers normal body structure and function and is taught on the main campus. First-year students also visit patients in the community as part of their General Practice placement, and do a basic emergency care course. During year 1 students are divided into groups for tutorials and practicals.

Groups change in year 2 for the Practising Medicine (clinical) programme, which helps you get to know more of your year. Phase II (years 3 and 4) and III (years 4 and 5) are based at Ninewells Hospital. Phase II concentrates on learning about abnormal structure and function and phase III deals with diagnosing and treating abnormal structure and function.

The course requires mastery (a pass grade of 75%) of relevant facts, clinical skills, and the correct attitude. Special study modules are a key component, but are assessed using different criteria.

Teaching

Phase I (year 1) teaching is organised into body systems. A syllabus is provided for each system, outlining core material that must be mastered along with beyond-the-core material that is useful to know. The teaching comes in the form of lectures covering physiology, biochemistry, anatomy, histology and behavioural science. In order to illustrate the clinical relevance of the teaching, patients are brought along to the lecture theatre to demonstrate examinations, signs and symptoms, and treatments. In addition, dissection classes follow the anatomy lectures to aid the integration of theory and practice. There are also physiology practical sessions once per week, which succeed in making physiology fun and interesting. The lectures and practical classes are supported by small group tutorials where students have the opportunity to clarify problem areas.

Important: there is no use of animals or animal tissues in practical classes.

Phase II (years 2 and 3) teaching takes place at Ninewells Hospital, where the medical school is based, and is organised into body systems (cardiovascular, respiratory, etc.). Teaching is delivered one system at a time. A study guide is issued at the beginning of each system course. This includes a timetable, core knowledge for the course, a summary of the clinical skills to be learned (e.g. taking blood, listening to the heart), questions for use in tutorials, problem-solving questions based around theme patients, a recommended reading list, and a list of online resources. The teaching is delivered through morning lectures and small group teaching. Afternoons are spent seeing patients on the wards and in an outpatient clinic setting, learning clinical skills in the Clinical Skills Centre, and in General Practice/Primary Care.

Multidisciplinary teaching takes place between the medical and nursing schools for ethics, and between the medical and midwifery schools for some parts of the Phase II obstetrics and gynaecology block.

At the end of each semester in years 2 and 3, there is a 4-week student-selected component (SSC). Students can either select a prearranged SSC provided by the medical school or arrange their own. The medical school provides a year 2 SSC in Medical French, followed by a clinical SSC in France during year 3. Some students arranging their own SSC choose to have them nearer home, and some use them as an opportunity to study abroad.

Phase III (years 4 and 5) is primarily clinical. Year 4 comprises ten rotations, each lasting 4 weeks. Students are able to choose their own rotations from a list. There are three surgical, three medical, one general practice, one obstetrics and gynaecology, one psychiatry, and one paediatrics/neonatology rotations. Study guides are provided for each rotation, and include information on Core Clinical Problems as well as information on travelling and accommodation. There is less formal teaching during year 4, but tutorials on the Core Clinical Problems are provided by rotation supervisors. Year 4 students also receive a 'Theme Therapeutics' study guide and can attend optional tutorials throughout the year.

Year 5 officially begins with an elective. This is a period of 10 weeks during which students are required to undertake 7 weeks of educational activity. Most people go abroad and use the other 3 weeks as a holiday. On their return students must submit an elective report. The remainder of year 5 comprises seven rotations of 4 weeks duration. Again students pick their rotations from a list, but there is also the option to self-propose a rotation. There are two clinical, two theme, two preregistration house officer (PRHO) shadowing, and one general practice rotation, with the option of an extended 3-month general practice rotation (the extra 2 months being in lieu of one clinical and one theme). The PRHO shadowing rotations allow students to become *au fait* with the jobs they will be doing when they graduate, and are usually spent in the hospital where the student has obtained a job for the PRHO year.

Teaching at Dundee has recently been rated excellent by the Scottish Higher Education Funding Council and is well thought of in GMC assessments.

Dundee has a very active peer tutoring programme, in which year 4 and 5 students hold tutorials for year 2 and 3 students to clarify difficult points and to go through case scenarios or example constructed response questions (CRQ). The junior students find this very valuable and the senior students enjoy teaching. The medical school provides support for the programme through the Curriculum Secretary, who posts sign-up lists, photocopies materials for the tutors, and organises the tutorial groups, tutorial times, and venues.

Assessment

There are computerised theory exams and an anatomy and histology exam at the end of each semester in year 1. In years 2 and 3, students sit two CRQ papers and 1 objective structured clinical examination (OSCE) at the end of the year.

The medical finals at Dundee are split into two parts. Part 1 is taken at the end of year 4 and comprises two CRQ papers and an OSCE. Part 2 comprises a portfolio examination at the conclusion of year 5.

Intercalated degrees

Most students wishing to complete an intercalated degree do so between years 3 and 4. However, it is also possible to take it between years 4 and 5. Subjects available include physiology, pharmacology and anatomy.

Dundee is the only medical school to offer BMSc courses in forensic medicine and orthopaedic technology. Some students take an intercalated degree at one of the London schools.

Student-selected components and electives

Over 42 SSCs are advertised on the medical school website, or you can design your own – overseas options are available. Staff are very supportive of individually designed SSCs arranged in their clinics/laboratories/wards. Year 5 kicks off with a 7-week elective (10 weeks if you tack on your 3-week vacation!). It's up to you to organise your own programme. Information and help regarding funding are widely available.

Erasmus

The medical school does not participate in the Erasmus scheme. However, SSCs provide an opportunity to travel abroad and the medical school offers an SSC in France.

Facilities

Library Year 1 books are housed in a large multifaculty library on the main campus. Years 2–5 books are housed at the Ninewells Medical Library. Normal opening hours are Monday to Friday 9 AM–10 PM; Saturday and Sunday 12 noon–5 PM. There is good availability of reference books, but be prepared to reserve some books in advance. Library opening hours increase as the academic year progresses.

Computers There is extensive computer access at both Ninewells (open 8 AM–11 PM all week) and the main campus. The computers in Ninewells are modern, with flat screens, and provide fast internet access. Facilities include computer-assisted learning (CAL) tutorials, microbiology laboratory summaries, multiple choice questions (MCQs), MRI/CT/X-ray imaging, and revision sessions. Classes in IT skills are laid on for the nervous!

Clinical skills The purpose-built Clinical Skills Centre opened in 1997. It provides multiprofessional teaching to small groups in areas such as communication and history taking; professional attitudes and ethics; physical examination and laboratory skills; diagnostics and therapeutics; practical skills and resuscitation. The centre is open 9 AM–5 PM for teaching and drop-in revision sessions. The clinical and administrative staff are extremely supportive and proactive, and run a book-in service for clinical skills revision sessions. Near exam time the Clinical Skills Centre opens at weekends, allowing students access to videos and other resources for revision sessions. Facilities in the Clinical Skills Centre include access to anatomical models and mannequins; diagnostic, therapeutic and resuscitation equipment; videos; simulated and real patients; and telemedicine links. Typical clinical skills sessions in Phase II (years 2 and 3) are generally good fun, last 2 hours, and allow students to develop confidence and competence in clinical skills before going on to the wards.

Welfare 🏠

Student support

The staff tend to be friendly, approachable, and supportive. They really do make an effort to ensure that students get the extra clinical training, core knowledge, and time for small group work required by the new curriculum. A new staff–student leisure facility at Ninewells was completed in 1998, and a Junior Doctor's mess was completed in 1996. The School of Nursing and Midwifery joined the Faculty of Medicine and Dentistry in 1997. Each student is assigned a personal and academic tutor. There is a Special Needs Coordinator based at Student Welfare on the main campus. The Dean is very approachable and student-friendly, and operates an open-door policy. Likewise, lecturers and clinicians are approachable, and typically put a lot of work into designing and teaching each systems block. All medical freshers are sent a student-produced *Student Survival Guide*, which covers academics, social, sport, local transport, etc.

The Dundee University Medical Society (DUMS) run a Senior–Junior scheme. All new students who want to participate are paired with a senior student who gives them academic advice, advises them which books on the book list they really need, and perhaps most importantly – introduces them to the social scene. There is also a very active Medical Students' Council (MSC), which regularly attends faculty meetings to voice student opinion. The faculty are very keen to receive student feedback and always strive to improve aspects of the course in response to this feedback. The MSC also runs a careers fair, women in medicine evening, annual symposium, electives evening, and PRHO meetings for students. A good indicator of staff–student relations is the number of staff who regularly attend Yearclub and medical school balls. The medical school has good wheelchair access.

Accommodation

There are two halls on campus. Belmont is a large 1900s catered hall of residence next to the Union, the sports centre, and the library. Airlie is a smaller self-catering hall on the other side of the Union and the library. Peterson House and Seabraes Flats are a 1-minute stumble from campus. They are both self-catering; the latter was built in 1996, and contains flats with *en suite* bathrooms. The West Park Centre is halfway between the town and Ninewells in the leafy west end of Dundee, and offers both catered and self-catering halls. This accommodation was also built in 1996. The self-catering accommodation comprises self-contained flats with phones, *en suite* bathrooms, colour TVs and computer links to the university internet. Most first years live in halls. Private accommodation costs about £40–£50 per week, generally in the west end of Dundee, and standards are pretty good.

Placements

The first year is based at the main campus with occasional visits to Ninewells. Years 2–5 are hospital based. Ninewells Hospital is about 3 miles from the town and main campus on the Firth of Tay. Wards have spectacular river views. Many students walk (30 minutes), cycle, or drive to the hospital but numerous buses run right to the front door (fare 95 pence) and there is now a free University bus running from Campus to Ninewells and back all day. Car parking is available but costs £1.50 per day or around £20 per month by direct debit if you get a key fob.

In years 2 and 3 ward teaching is at Ninewells Hospital. In years 4 and 5 you get a chance to travel around the UK and see how other hospitals work: up to 5 months of year 4 can be spent away from Dundee on out blocks if desired. Rotations in district general hospitals (DGHs) and general practices are set up around Scotland (including the Highlands and Islands) and the north of England, with free accommodation provided. For rural general practice rotations guesthouse accommodation or travel expenses are available depending on preference. A computer matching system allocates students to their peripheral attachments on a best fit basis, so most students can stay in Dundee if they wish, although for many the experience of peripheral hospitals/GP rotations is a highlight.

Location of clinical placement/name of hospital	Distance away from medical school (miles)	Difficulty getting there on public transport*
Perth	23	🚗
Queen Margaret, Dunfermline	45	🚗
Airdrie	78	🎈
Ninewells	3	🚶
Whitehaven	207	🎈

* : walking/cycling distance; 🚌 : use public transport; 🚗: need own car or lift; 🎈 : get up early – tricky to get to!

Sports and social 🏆

City life

Dundee is Scotland's fourth largest city and has a beautiful location on the Firth of Tay. Local sights include the riverside itself; the neighbouring seaside town of Broughty Ferry with its sandy beaches, castle, shops and pubs; Tentsmuir Forest Park and beaches; Carnoustie; St Andrews (15 miles away); numerous golf courses; and fantastic sunsets. As well as being spectacular to behold, the countryside offers skiing, hill walking, climbing, and numerous water sports. A new shopping centre, the Overgate, opened in 2000, vastly improving Dundee's shopping facilities.

The city is very student-friendly, and the area around the university is very much a student community. Taxis are affordable, and bars cater for students with drinks promos. Many new small shops, cafés, bars, and clubs have opened on the Perth Road in Dundee's west end over the past 18 months. There is constant building and renovation work in the town. Glasgow, Edinburgh, and Aberdeen are all within reach for a weekend, from 1–1½ hour's drive/train journey away.

University life

Dundee University Medical Society (DUMS) sponsors freshers' week events, and puts on many social bashes and trips throughout the year. DUMS tends to form a large part of a medic's social life, especially in the earlier years. Each year also has its own Yearclub which organises events. For example: end of year balls, fancy dress parties, nights out, pub golf and slave auctions – to raise money for charity. Ceilidhs (Scottish dancing) are very popular and are a great ice-breaker. Lessons are given for the uninitiated. Each Yearclub organises a halfway dinner (a weekend away at a hotel with a ball, and other entertainments) guess when – halfway through the course – and their own graduation ball (there is also a university graduation ball).

The Students' Union building is undergoing major refurbishment. The new Air Bar has recently opened and the existing bars and clubs have been dramatically overhauled. They were always good but are now better – very modern and trendy. Dundee Students' Union looks set to keep its position as 'probably the best union in the country!' It regularly hosts packed-out club nights through the week, and is very popular with medics and nonmedics alike.

Local pubs abound (some hosting live music) and the beer is cheap. The Dundee Repertory Theatre is active nationally, and hosts plays, musicals, and jazz festivals. The popular Dundee Contemporary Arts Centre (DCA) provides two screens for art house films, a large art gallery, café and wine bar, all right beside the university. There are also two multiplex cinemas, an Odeon and a UGC.

The Duncan of Jordanstone Art School is part of the main campus, adding diversity to the student population, and their summer degree show is always a sell-out. The university also has the usual wide variety of societies and sporting organisations.

Sports life

The sports centre now boasts the largest university indoor facilities in Scotland. Outdoor pitches are based at the scenic Riverside Drive. The university has a very active and varied sports scene, with a good level of competition at both Scottish and British university level. The medical school has its own teams in football, rugby, and netball. Competitions are organised against other Scottish medical schools. Medics often play for both the medical school and the university, with the medical school teams being a little less competitive in spirit than the university teams.

Top tip: Buy a Freshers' Pass for free entry to all freshers week events.

Great things about Dundee 👍

- Good teaching on an established new-style course with early patient exposure.
- Good social life based around DUMS and a friendly bunch of staff and students means that you can always find something to do.
- Dundee is a cheap, safe, and fun place to live.
- The clinical skills centre is excellent.
- Dundee is surrounded by beautiful countryside, with access to skiing, hill walking, water sports, and places such as St Andrews are close by for day trips.

Bad things about Dundee

- It can take some time to get used to the local accent.
- Dundee is not a great centre for shopping.
- There is no major airport in Dundee.
- It does get cold and windy over the winter.
- It can be difficult to park at Ninewells.

Further information

Information Centre
Admissions and Student Recruitment
2 Airlie Place
The University of Dundee
Nethergate
Dundee DD1 4HN
Tel: 01382 344160 (prospectus request)
01382 344032 (admissions)
01382 348111 (international)
Fax: 01382 348150
Email: srs@dundee.ac.uk
Web: http://www.dundee.ac.uk

Additional application information

Average A-level requirements	• AAA
Average Scottish Higher requirements	• AAAAB (premedical) • AAABB (undergraduate)
Make-up of interview panel	• Faculty members
Months in which interviews are held	• January–March
Proportion of overseas students	• 7.5%
Proportion of mature students	• 2.5%
Proportion of graduate students	• 13%
Faculty's view of students taking a gap year	• Will be considered
Proportion of students taking intercalated degrees	• 12%
Possibility of direct entrance to clinical phase	• No
Fees for overseas students	• £10,000 pa (premedical) • £12,500 pa (clinical)
Fees for graduates	• £1700 pa (premedical) • £2700 pa (clinical)
Ability to transfer to other medical schools	• Students are free to transfer to other medical schools if another school has a place for them
Assistance for elective funding	• Dependent on faculty funds
Assistance for travel to attachments	• No – responsibility of LEA/ELB/SAAS, but accommodation is provided
Access and hardship funds	• There is a university hardship fund available
Weekly rent	• £45–£50
Pint of lager	• £1.50
Cinema	• £3.50
Nightclub	• £3.50 with student ID card

East Anglia

Key facts	Undergraduate
Course length	5 years
Total number of medical undergraduates	520
Applicants in 2005	1500
Interviews given in 2005	500
Places available in 2005	130
Places available in 2006	141
Open days 2006	July and October
Entrance requirements	AABB
Mandatory subjects	Biology
Male:female ratio	Information not available
Is an exam included in the selection process? If yes, what form does this exam take?	No UKCAT in 2007
Qualification gained	MB BS

Fascinating fact: Mr Hugh Philips, consultant orthopaedic surgeon at the Norfolk & Norwich University Hospital, is the incoming President of the Royal College of Surgeons, and continues in the footsteps of Kenneth Mckee, a pioneer in hip replacement surgery in Norwich during the 1950s.

Education

Applicants apply via UCAS in the normal way, ensuring that their completed forms are returned by the deadline of 15 October. Applications received late may be considered but there is no guarantee. The Admissions Office is very pleased to receive enquiries and they will do their best to answer any questions. They will also provide detailed information on request. The application form is sent to the School via UCAS and it is checked thoroughly to ensure that all the relevant criteria are met. Once initial screening is performed, then detailed screening of the applications can take place. This involves two independent scorers examining the applications and awarding points to predetermined criteria. For example, the scorers look at the applicants GCSE results for evidence of English (at least a C), maths, and a science (6 A grades are awarded one point); similarly with A-levels, biology is essential but grades of AAA/AAB score two points, whereas ABB/BBB score one point. A total of 2 points is required to reach the second stage of the UCAS form screening. For applicants offering a degree, two points are awarded for a 2:1 and one point for a 2:2. An MSc or higher degree can override a 2:2. Again, biology to at least good A-level standard is essential. In the second stage of screening (personal statement and reference), three points are awarded for each of (1) the applicant's ability to work in a self-directed environment, (2) their ability to function as a member of a group and work in that team with their colleagues, (3) to take responsibility, (4) demonstrate evidence of motivation and (5) 'personal effectiveness'. The applications are scored by two independent scorers with a total of 30 points available. The top 500 applicants are invited to interview.

The interview is structured and full details are sent to candidates with an invitation to attend. Interviews are conducted by two interviewers, one a practising clinician and the other an academic at the school. The interviews are held between November and March and take place within the main Med Building. They last approximately 30–45 minutes and follow a set pattern. The interviewers aim is to select well-rounded individuals, people who will flourish in the UEA curriculum, who work well with others, who can deal with the ambiguity that pervades medicine, and to examine the candidate's motivation for a career in medicine, as well as checking for evidence of personal effectiveness. The interview also entails a discussion of two hypothetical situations which may involve ethical or empathic decisions. The candidates are scored independently by the two interviewers, the scores are summed and standardised and the highest-scoring individuals are offered places at UEA. The School of Medicine makes approximately 250 offers for the 130 places available.

This brand new medical curriculum follows the University motto, 'Do Different'. It's innovative, and in some respects, controversial structure places patients at the centre of all learning. Clinical exposure occurs right from the start of the course with integrated teaching at university, in general practice and in hospitals. Communication skills and an understanding of people are paramount to the way this course addresses disease. There is the same amount of clinical medicine, basic science, patient contact and psychosocial aspects in year 5 as there is in year 1. Thus the curriculum is a continuous one.

Teaching

The medical curriculum follows systems-based units throughout the 5 years, integrating theory, practical skills and clinical experience from the very start. University-based teaching fills two-thirds of the time, with problem-based learning (PBL) at the core. Students divide into small groups to discuss weekly case scenarios and with the guidance of a tutor/facilitator, formulate learning objectives for the relevant topics. The aim of the week is then to gather relevant information to 'solve' the cases, incorporating all aspects of medicine whilst maintaining a patient-centred approach. This is supported during the week by lectures and seminars designed to meet relevant objectives and delivered in the main by consultants and specialists. It is not possible to attend all the seminars that are scheduled during the week as they run concurrently. It is down to the students to decide amongst themselves which seminars to attend, and this provides another opportunity for students to feed back information to their peers gained from the seminars. This may take some getting used to by students more used to a didactic style of teaching.

All students are expected to attend the main lectures. Anatomy is taught through lectures and seminars, using cadavers to illustrate relevant clinical anatomy. Dissection is not routinely expected from students but those who wish to do so have an opportunity to dissect in the student-selected study sessions (see Special study modules, below).

During this university-based time, one day a week is spent in General Practice. These 'mini-placements' are a mixture of patient contact and small group teaching, consolidating the week's learning. These occur throughout all stages of the course and most students agree that this both reinforces and builds on current knowledge in a 'real-world' environment.

The other one-third of teaching time takes place during the block placement in Secondary Care that accompanies each unit. Learning occurs through following patients, a variety of clinics, teaching ward rounds and other clinical experiences. There is also a strong emphasis on inter-professional working, with time being spent with nurses, therapists, technicians and other hospital staff.

Both stages are supported with 'Blackboard', the medical school's 'virtual learning environment'. In essence, this is a vast online database comprising every lecture note, timetable and handout you will ever need! It is also used as a file exchange for group work, and for self-assessment with multiple choice questions (MCQs). The staff work very hard to ensure that all the lectures and seminars are posted on Blackboard in good time; however this does occasionally slip. Also, it is sometimes not possible to upload very image-intensive presentations.

Interprofessional practice is very highly regarded at UEA. In conjunction with the School of Nursing and Midwifery and the School of Allied Health Professions, medical students are obliged to take part in combined professional practice exercises. These occur once a week following a similar format to PBL scenarios and are aimed at promoting communication between, and an appreciation of, each profession in the health service. These sessions are now compulsory for medics in years 1 and 2.

Assessment

Each unit is assessed with a mini-objective structured clinical examination (OSCE), comprising 6 or so stations. These vary in content to assess communication, clinical skills and fundamental medical knowledge. Student-selected study presentations and paper appraisals (see Special study modules, below) are also conducted at the end of each unit for the first 3 years.

At the end of each year is an integrative period, where all previous learning is assessed. This takes the form of a large OSCE of between 18–24 stations, and a written paper containing extended matching questions (EMQs) and advance notice questions that are based upon several PBL-like scenarios provided prior to the assessment. Units from the previous years are also included in the integrative period after year 1. A formal reflective appraisal of the year must also be submitted for assessment. All assessed work during the units is awarded marks of a pass/fail nature. The integrative period assessments are awarded distinction/pass/fail and two distinctions are required for a distinction in the year overall.

Intercalated degrees

There are as yet, no students undertaking intercalated degrees at UEA. These are planned for the end of year 4 and will result in the completion of an MSc. The first intake is only in year 3 at present.

Special study modules and electives

All UEA students are obliged to take part in student-selected studies (SSS). There are two branches to this line of study, which assess a student's ability to gather, appraise and present information. During each unit students will study a topic of their choosing, selected from a list of domains (anatomy, biochemistry, epidemiology, ethics, health economics, law, physiology, psychology, sociology) and relevant to the current unit of study. This is then exhibited to clinical tutors and peers during a short presentation with question and answers. In later years, students will be expected to study an area of interest outside medicine. From year 3, students can choose from a range of areas that are unrelated to medicine including languages, archaeology, history, English literature and astronomy. These must be studied at a higher level than any previous qualification possessed by the student and must be passed in order to continue the course.

The second aspect of SSS runs concurrently with the university-based teaching. A series of lectures and support seminars equips students with the skills and knowledge required to appraise research papers. This is assessed through a formal written appraisal every unit during years 1– 3. There are also plans for later years whereby students will design and then conduct a research project for themselves.

An 8-week elective is planned for the end of year 4, with students free to choose the location and nature of clinical experience.

After Graduation

At the end of year 5, students will shadow the preregistration house officer (PRHO) job in which they will be employed after graduation. Where possible, the school intends this to be with one of their NHS partners in the region. During these posts in hospitals and general practice, the UEA will offer mentoring and postgraduate study throughout the PRHO period.

Facilities

The majority of teaching takes place in a purpose-built school on the UEA campus. This attractive centre is brand new, although unfortunately a little on the small side as most of the building is taken up by academic and research staff. This leads to overcrowding, especially when more than one year group try to converge between lectures and seminars. The seminar rooms in the Med Building are spacious, well presented and boast top-of-the-range interactive whiteboards and full audiovisual capabilities. As the school expands, there has been a requirement to utilise a large number of alternative lecture theatres, seminar rooms and other rooms for small group work. These often have the disadvantage of being spread across the campus. There is also extensive use of cutting-edge facilities at the Norfolk and Norwich University Hospital (NNUH), which has recently been relocated to modern, custom-built premises just a few minutes' walk from campus. A section of the NNUH has been designated to UEA and the medical school, with numerous rooms suitable for small group work, clinical skills and a ward designed for student learning experiences. Most students are impressed with this exciting facility.

In addition, teaching takes place at the James Paget Hospital in Great Yarmouth (which has recently gained a purpose-built education block with excellent facilities), and in GP surgeries across the region. The psychiatry module in year 5 will be taught in conjunction with Norfolk Mental Health Trust at their facilities across the county.

Library The UEA boasts a large library, suitably stocked with copies of all books on the reading list. A new £2m library extension is currently being completed. Students also have access to the hospital libraries at both teaching hospitals, which have a good collection of books on the entire range of medical specialities.

Computers With widespread use of the virtual learning environment, computer access is inevitably important to all students. The MED building on campus has a 24-hour access computer facility purely for the use of medical students although this can get a little busy, especially during lunchtimes. There is an additional, networked facility at the NNUH exclusively for students on placement, with both rooms having a combined 40 or so terminals. Students are also free to make use of the other campus facilities in the computer centre and the library. Network access is available in all campus residences.

Clinical skills As part of the joint venture programme, the school works very closely with the Norfolk and Norwich University Hospital. This has a designated 'ward', set aside for student teaching, which includes a well-equipped clinical skills lab with a variety of equipment. The James Paget Hospital, where some secondary care attachments occur, also has an excellent skills lab with dedicated technicians able and willing to assist.

There is a structured clinical skills programme extending across the 5 years, with gradual addition to the student 'armoury' each unit. These begin with basic observation skills and CPR, and progress during relevant units (for example, venepuncture during the haematology unit in year 2). It is hoped that students will complete advanced life support training at the end of year 5.

Communication skills are taught extensively in the first year, with supplementary training periodically thereafter, to add to and refresh students' proficiency. These sessions start with group work but rapidly develop to include trained actors who role play the parts of patients to a very high standard (these same actors take part in the OSCE stations during assessments).

Welfare 🏠

Student support

All the staff at the university, both academic and administrative, are very friendly and approachable, with everyone treated as an equal. That said, each student is assigned a personal adviser from the academic or clinical staff with whom they can discuss personal or academic issues.

The Mentor Scheme, organised by MedSoc and BMA on behalf of the medical school, is a scheme run by students for students. The aim is to ensure that every student has a supportive peer in the year above as a first line contact for general help and advice throughout their studies in Med School. The scheme has both educational and social elements, providing support to students and improving the integration of students between different academic years and indeed between schools.

It is hoped to extend this across the entire period of study, to create a student 'family'. Students are also on hand on the days freshers move in to their accommodation to provide support, advice or a friendly face in the bar.

The School of Medicine, Health Policy and Practice also makes use of the welfare services already provided by the UEA. The Dean of Students is responsible for welfare for the university but extensive services are also provided by the Union of UEA Students, including an advice centre and confidential help line out of hours. Problems for those living on campus can be addressed by resident tutors, senior students living in the halls to protect the welfare of residents. The chaplaincy is located on campus and Nightline is also run at UEA – both of these are available to lend assistance if needed.

Accommodation

The UEA has arguably one of the most attractive campuses in the country (you can even learn to love the original grey, concrete buildings!). There are trees aplenty, and copious open space for recreation or sunbathing. A large lake ('The UEA Broad') makes for a great revision environment on a sunny day. Residential accommodation on this attractive campus is guaranteed to first-year students, with a range of prices and facilities. On the one hand the *en suite* residences building has won architectural awards for brilliance; the other is described as the 'Swedish prison'. A new residence called Colman House has recently been completed, increasing the amount of university accommodation. The older Waveney Terrace is scheduled for demolition. The plush surroundings of the more expensive residences are certainly pleasant to live in, but many that choose more communal living comment on the excellent camaraderie of their halls. All facilities on campus are self-catering but there are a variety of places to eat. The costs of campus accommodation range from £48.30–£78.60 per week.

Norwich is well equipped to deal with student housing and there is a good provision of privately rented houses, flats and bed sits. The average rent is about £250 per month. Most of these are in the 'Golden Triangle' area about 30 minutes' walk from campus. New estates are being built in Bowthorpe, also about half an hour out, where many students choose to buy houses. This area is proving to be very popular with medical students (becoming known as Med Village) as it is equidistant to both UEA and the NNUH, and housing there is relatively affordable. There may be limited provision in hospital accommodation, but this is a little on the pricey side.

Placements

Location of clinical placement/name of hospital	Distance away from medical school (miles)	Difficulty getting there on public transport*
Norfolk and Norwich University Hospital	1	🚶
James Paget Hospital	32	🚌
General Practice Attachments	Across Norfolk and Suffolk	🚌

* 🚶: walking/cycling distance; 🚌 : use public transport; 🚗: need own car or lift; 💡 : get up early – tricky to get to!

Sports and social

City life

Famed 19th century linguist and traveller, George Henry Borrow coined the phrase 'Norwich, a Fine City' and this is still how most people are struck when arriving in the capital of Norfolk. It's large enough to be vibrant and exciting, yet small enough to still reflect its very rural surroundings.

Whilst still a bustling city, Norwich has managed to retain a relaxed and friendly atmosphere. It was once the second largest city in Britain and still proudly displays the castle and most of its other historic remnants in its medieval centre, including two magnificent cathedrals. In sharp contrast, Norwich continues to move forward with the recent opening of The Forum which holds a library, restaurants, and the local BBC services and looks out over one of the largest open-air markets in the country.

Norwich's surroundings are deeply attractive and distinctive. From the waterways of the Norfolk Broads (a National Park) to the vast expanses of the North Norfolk coastline, this is certainly a region worth exploring. With rail links to London, Cambridge and the Midlands, many students find it an irresistible environment to live in after graduation.

Norwich's club land becomes the centre of nightlife for East Anglia, although students used to the big city life often complain that it's still 'a bit quiet'. That said, Norwich's pub/club scene offers a whole range of student nights and low prices. The city used to be able to boast a pub for every day of the year. In the city centre there are over 200 pubs, many with their own unique character. There are also two breweries and real ale is extremely popular in many drinking holes.

Shopping is another attraction of this fine city. The large open-air market complements the facilities of the city centre shops in addition to the Castle Mall shopping centre. Holding over 70 shops The Mall is unlikely to impress die-hard shopping fanatics but is certainly one of the largest retail centres in the region, with a good mix of high street chains and local 'gems' worth exploring. A new retail shopping centre is currently being built in Norwich and promises to increase the opportunities for retail therapy by a huge margin.

University life

The UEA campus is well equipped to provide an almost self-contained environment for those who do not wish to venture from the university. Shops, a post office and of course, the bar, all provide a pleasant, relaxed atmosphere in which to live. There is free student access to the Sainsbury Centre for Visual Arts, the UEA's very own gallery and exhibition centre, for the more culturally inclined.

Last year, the student bar underwent a refit, providing a relaxed, pub-like section but also a contemporary, trendy bar hosting the occasional DJ. A second recent expansion and refurbishment has just been completed, costing £2.5m. Major sports fixtures are displayed on a huge screen at one end of the bar. The atmosphere is generally relaxed and the alcohol is cheap – ideal for a quiet night out, or for some drinking before heading upstairs to the LCR! This is the centre of entertainment at UEA, serving as discotheque, live music venue, comedy hall and mosh pit. The 'Ents' (short for entertainment) team works very hard to ensure that there are always things to do here, and on most weeks there is some sort of entertainment on offer every night. Some of the biggest names in UK and international music have played at UEA (Magnum, Coldplay, Mis-teeq, The Darkness, Motorhead, Toploader, Kosheen, The Levellers, Katie Melua, Jools Holland, Beth Orton, Beverley Knight... the list goes on!).

There are also plenty of opportunities to get involved away from the bar, and with over 100 clubs and societies to join, there is something on offer for everyone. If you are into something and a society doesn't exist, then gather up a few like-minded individuals and create your own. In addition to the rest of the university, the medical school is already finding *its* voice. With extra-curricular activities such as Medical Humanities and MedSIN and a dedicated MedSoc, the school is definitely making a name for itself within the UEA.

Sports life

UEA as a university is very into its sports. From korfball to lacrosse, there is something to suit most sports fans. In addition, the university runs its own inter-school competition called the Ziggurat Challenge. This is a series of events for all abilities and enthusiasms, from die-hard fanatics, to those who would rather just stroll round the campus lake. Unfortunately, medical sports teams are somewhat limited due to a lack of numbers, although the ultrakeen sports reps have great plans for the future. Presently, medical students also use their sporting energy against staff from the faculty and hospital.

UEA boasts 40 acres of dedicated sports field in addition to Astroturf, brand new tennis courts and local access to water sports. Other facilities include an Olympic sized swimming pool, indoor arena, gym, climbing wall, and a national standard athletics track in the sports park. Since opening in 2000, the sports park has attracted more than 1000,000 visits each year. All students are entitled to free access to the sports park and discounted activity rates. Off-peak use of the gym and swimming pool is set at £1.25.

> **Top tip:** Norwich is quite small and flat with few hills, which lends itself admirably to transport by bicycle. A cheap tatty-looking bike will enable you to get around simply and quickly, and should hopefully avoid the magpies that are attracted by the flashier looking ones. A good quality padlock is essential.

Great things about UEA

- Friendly and approachable staff and students; still small enough for everyone to know everyone.
- Clinical integration with patient contact from week 1.
- Excellent facilities at the teaching hospitals coupled with superb teaching.
- The campus is set in some gorgeous countryside and the social life is great.
- Innovation and participation are encouraged – there is always something exciting to be involved with and there is also ample opportunity to help develop/evolve the course.

Bad things about UEA ⏻

- The lack of a large medical school building leads to overcrowding and the necessity for groups to be placed at obscure locations across the campus.
- Many of the GP surgeries are some distance from the university, leading to increased travelling times.
- Car parking on campus is a significant problem.
- Constant review and refinement of the course leads to endless evaluation forms to fill in.
- Lots of concrete – either love it or hate it!

Further information

The Admissions Office
School of Medicine
University of East Anglia
Norwich
Norfolk
Tel: 01603 591 072
Fax: 01603 593 752
Email: med.admiss@uea.ac.uk
Web: http://www.med.uea.ac.uk

Additional application information

Average A-level requirements	• AAB
Average Scottish Higher requirements	• AAAAB (standard) AAB (advanced)
Make-up of interview panel	• One academic staff member and one active NHS practitioner/clinician
Months in which interviews are held	• November–March
Proportion of overseas students	• 7%
Proportion of mature students	• Information not available
Proportion of graduate students	• Information not available
Faculty's view of students taking a gap year	• Acceptable, but interested in student's plans for gap year
Proportion of students taking intercalated degrees	• None at present
Possibility of direct entrance to clinical phase	• No
Fees for overseas students	• £16,500 pa
Fees for graduates	• £3000 pa
Ability to transfer to other medical schools	• Due to the unique nature of the course, it may be difficult to transfer to other schools
Assistance for elective funding	• None as yet
Assistance for travel to attachments	• All transport is provided
Access and hardship funds	• Plenty of access through the main university
Weekly rent	• £48.30–£78.60, bills included for campus residences
Pint of lager	• £1.70–£2.10 on campus • £1.60–£2.20 city centre pub
Cinema	• Campus: £2.75 (or £12.50 for the year) • City: £3.60–£5
Nightclub	• £2–£6

Edinburgh

Key facts	Premedical	Undergraduate*
Course length	6 years	5 years
Total number of medical undergraduates		c. 1220
Applicants in 2005	226	2724
Interviews given in 2005		46
Places available in 2005	Premedical offers are made	218
Places available in 2006	to applicants who do not have the right subject combination, but who would otherwise be made an offer to the undergraduate programme	218
Open days 2006	No information	3 – see website
Entrance requirements	AAAB	AAAB
Mandatory subjects	GCSE maths, English, language or dual award combined science	A-level chemistry and one of biology/maths/physics
		Biology at least AS-level
Male:female ratio	No information	47:71
Is an exam included in the selection process? If yes, what form does this exam take?	No	No UKCAT in 2007
Qualification gained	MBChB	

Fascinating fact: Anatomy has been taught in Edinburgh since the 1700s and has an intriguing past. The anatomy department's museum still holds the skeleton of infamous 'body-snatcher' William Burke.

*Applications are welcomed for the five-year or six-year MBChB programme from non-medical graduates. Edinburgh Medical School does not offer a four-year fast-track graduate programme and graduate applicants are in competition with school-leaving and other applicants.

Although it is one of the oldest medical schools, Edinburgh has shed the traditional preclinical/clinical course for a new integrated curriculum that started in October 1998. With a strong research tradition (reflected by 40% of students taking an intercalated BSc), Edinburgh seems to attract high academic achievers and a lot of students from England and Northern Ireland. The recent opening of The New Royal Infirmary means that Edinburgh's medical students have the privilege of being taught in this state-of the-art facility.

Education

The new curriculum is taught in teaching hospitals, in district general hospitals (DGHs), and on attachment in GP practices. It is taught in an integrated fashion, with themes of clinical skills and communication skills running across all 5 years. Studying starts with the normal function of the body, building through to disease processes and clinical systems. Although there is some clinical involvement in the early years (particularly in general practice settings), the bulk of clinical placements are in years 3–5.

Teaching

The general trend is towards lectures and tutorials in the first couple of years, with formalised *en masse* teaching being replaced by ward-based teaching later on in the course. Although there is some problem- or case-based work, most of the teaching is by formal lectures and small group sessions. These are balanced between tutorials and group work, with facilitators, with the aim of gaining not only knowledge but also team-working skills. Anatomy is taught with prosected material and computer-assisted learning (CAL).

Assessment

Exams have traditionally been at the end of each term and count for at least 60% of the course mark. There is an increasing amount of continuous and modular assessment in the new curriculum.

Intercalated degrees

At Edinburgh there is a well-established Honours year programme and a large number of students intercalate every year; and if you choose to intercalate you would be taking the extra year with many year group colleagues. Acceptance onto an intercalated honours course is on a competitive basis (academic performance over the first 2 years is taken into account). The vast majority of intercalating students usually do so after year 2.

Special study modules and electives

Electives take place in year 5 and last for 2 months, and the faculty is very flexible about what you do and where you go – just as long as it's medically related. There are also several periods for special study modules starting in small groups in years 1 and 2 and leading to an independent research project for 14 weeks in year 4. This is a great opportunity to do your own ground-breaking research (in a subject of your choosing) at a university renowned for it!

Edinburgh

Erasmus

There is the opportunity to study part of some Intercalated BSc subjects in Leiden (Netherlands). Outside the Erasmus scheme, you are able to do your elective virtually anywhere in the world that you want, so long as the faculty approves it.

Facilities

Library The medical collections are found alongside those for most other subjects in the main library, which is situated centrally and easily accessible. There are also smaller collections of medical texts found in libraries at the main teaching hospitals. The availability of recommended textbooks on short loan is good. It is open 8.30 AM–10 PM Monday–Thursday, 8.30 AM–7 PM on Friday, 9 AM–5 PM Saturday and 12 noon–7 PM on Sunday. Holiday opening times vary.

Computer facilities There is a dedicated computer laboratory in the medical school with 100 PCs (and more in the library and throughout the university); word-processing, email, internet and specially designed CAL software are available. It is open 24 hours via a swipe card and can get very busy during the day. Many university-owned properties have computer facilities in them or on site.

Clinical skills There are laboratories at both the main hospitals, which are used for learning clinical skills. This facility is available to all medical students for personal practise outside timetabled hours.

Welfare

Student support

Faculty can seem a bit harsh and traditional when you first arrive. As each student has a director of studies responsible for monitoring his/her progress and providing pastoral care, this effectively acts as a safety net. The faculty tends to take a hands-off approach, which on one level gives you freedom and independence, but can leave you feeling like a small drop in a big ocean. However, if you have genuine difficulties then the faculty is extremely helpful and genuinely flexible. The faculty has good relations with the Medical Students' Council and a comprehensive *Student Handbook* is published jointly every year.

Accommodation

University accommodation in halls or flats is guaranteed in the first year. However, demand from all students for halls (which are of a good standard) is greater than the places available, and after the first year most students get a group together and rent a flat from a private landlord or the university. Some students also choose to take out a mortgage to buy their own flats, renting rooms to other students. An advantage of Edinburgh is that most of the student accommodation is very central for the university and the city, and almost invariably within 15–20 minutes' walking distance. However, the cold winters do raise your heating bills.

Placements

For the first 2 years medics are a real part of the university, with the medical school being centrally placed in George Square. It is very handy for all the library facilities, computers, unions, and halls. However, now that the New Royal Infirmary is open, services are gradually being moved there and it remains unclear how much of the school will remain on the university site and how much will move out. However the feel of things, particularly in the early years is bound to change. In the last 3 years of the course most time is spent in the hospitals and occasionally away from Edinburgh, so medics can begin to lose touch with their student roots and see less of their colleagues.

In year 1 students go into general practices for two well-received community-based practicals. Time in year 2 is spent in local GP practices learning clinical skills. In year 3 you have clinical rotations and may have the rare clinic outside the city. In years 4 and 5 a period of time may be spent on blocks in peripheral hospitals up to 80 miles from Edinburgh, as well as in general practices. There are normally at least two students on the placement, and accommodation is provided free of charge. As there are fewer students you get much more involved in the team, and the teaching is generally as good as (if not better than) in the central teaching hospitals. However, transport can be difficult if you don't have a car.

The two main teaching hospitals are the New Royal Infirmary and the Western General Hospital, which are both about a 25-minute bus ride away (about 80 pence) from the centre. Both have an atmosphere of pioneering, cutting-edge medicine and surgery. The facilities for students are adequate. There is a tremendous range of patients to learn from and ward groups are normally small (six or seven students in year 3 – but sometimes bigger – and two students per ward in years 4 and 5). If you put the effort in you'll get a lot out of it.

Location of clinical placement/ name of hospital	Distance away from medical school (miles)	Difficulty getting there on public transport*
New Royal Infirmary	7	🚌
Western General	5	🚌
GP placements in years 1 and 2	0–10	🚶 🚌
Peripheral placements in years 4 and 5	20–120	🚌 🚗 💡

* : walking/cycling distance; 🚌 : use public transport; 🚗: need own car or lift; 💡 : get up early – tricky to get to!

Sports and social 🏆

City life

Edinburgh, the city of festivals, is a great place to spend 5 years of your life. The university is centrally located, with the medical school at the heart of the university. Although it is the capital of Scotland, Edinburgh has more than its fair share of English and overseas residents, so there is a very cosmopolitan atmosphere. For the first 2 years you really blend into mainstream student life, but the time-consuming clinical years mean that you gradually drift away from the main student body. There is a strong community spirit within each year group, and no shortage of medic societies, sports clubs, and socialising opportunities.

Edinburgh has the advantage of being a compact and generally safe city where everything is within walking distance. It is a lively cosmopolitan capital city with a good pub and club scene, theatres, cinemas, shopping, and a lot of tourist attractions. Although it is a huge tourist trap (especially during the Military Tattoo and the International Festival and Fringe in the summer), the paths of tourists and students don't really cross. Between the three universities there is a large student population, which is very well catered for. Edinburgh has one of the highest concentrations of pubs in a city centre, and most are licensed to 1 AM (clubs open to 3 AM). Green space is found at the Meadows and Holyrood Park. Both are excellent venues for friendly football, rugby, hockey, American football and korfball matches. Edinburgh is well connected for getting to most other parts of the UK, and the great outdoors is not too far away if you want to get away from it all for some fresh air.

University life

The Medical Students' Council, Royal Medical Society (which has rooms open 24 hours to members) and each year's final year committee organise social events, talks, and balls. There is also a medics choir and orchestra, an active Christian Medics group, and the medical school magazine *2nd Opinion*. In short, if you want it, it is probably there (and if it isn't you can set it up)! Apart from traditional medic activities (various balls, plays, revue, academic families), most students find their own entertainment in the city itself rather than relying exclusively upon medical societies. The Union is one of the largest in the country, offers a good range of societies, and is an excellent venue. The Unions (as a group) do have lots of competition from the city itself.

Sports life

The medics' rugby team is well organised and successful, with a formidable reputation both on and off the field. A mixed hockey team and a netball team have recently been formed, and what they (sometimes) lack in skill they make up for in character. There are various year football and badminton teams. Medics tend to play a more active part in the wider university sports scene rather than just staying within the medical school. Most sports people who represent the medical school will also play for the main university and/or local clubs.

Top tip: At the start of the academic year you will be given a reading list of suggested books. Instead of rushing off to buy everything on the list it's a good idea to ask people in the years above who often sell their books (albeit a year old) at very cheap prices.

Great things about Edinburgh

- Edinburgh is a vibrant and lively university and city with excellent shopping, pubs, and clubs. The Festivals and Hogmanay are an extremely important part of the city's spirit, and the new Scottish Parliament has added to the city's charms.
- BOO! Edinburgh is renowned for its ghosts and is one of the most haunted cities in the world. There are many scary and exciting tours, many of which enter into the vaults under the city!
- Edinburgh hosts a lot of innovative and world-respected research projects in clinical medicine and surgery. You will be taught by some very big names!
- You can drink in pubs and restaurants 24 hours a day if you know how (and want to).
- The medical students have a very good collective spirit, especially in the first 3 years, without being too cliquey.

Bad things about Edinburgh

- Large numbers of tourists, festival luvvies and the New Year Hogmanay invasion.
- Peripheral attachments in the latter years mean that the year group doesn't meet up very often.
- The support network works well in a crisis, but you can feel a bit anonymous to the faculty at other times.
- Without a car, travelling to peripheral hospitals can be awkward.
- It gets very cold and windy in winter.

Further information

Admissions Office
College of Medicine & Veterinary Medicine
Room GU315
Chancellor's Building
49 Little France Crescent
Edinburgh EH16 4SB
Tel: 0131 242 6407
Fax: 0131 650 6525
Email: medug@ed.ac.uk
Web: http://www.mvm.ed.ac.uk

Edinburgh

Additional application information

Average A-level requirements	• AAA and B in fourth AS-level subject
Average Scottish Higher requirements	• AAAAB
Make-up of interview panel	• Interviews not normally held for school-leaving or overseas applicants
Months in which interviews are held	• tbc
Proportion of overseas students	• 6%
Proportion of mature students	• 7.6%
Proportion of graduate students	• 7.7%
Faculty's view of students taking a gap year	• Applications from undergraduates who wish to defer entry for a year are welcome. Deferred applications will not be accepted from graduate, mature or overseas applicants
Proportion of students taking intercalated degrees	• 40%
Possibility of direct entrance to clinical phase	• Yes for students from St Andrews, Oxford and Cambridge
Fees for overseas students	• £12,450 pa for premedical year, years 1 and 2 • £25,850 pa for years 3, 4 and 5
Fees for graduates	• £3000
Ability to transfer to other medical schools	• Unusual, however special circumstances will be considered by the faculty
Assistance for elective funding	• Funding and advice available through various organisations such as the Royal Medical Society
Assistance for travel to attachments	• Free buses run between city hospitals
Access and hardship funds	• Available – enquire through tutor system
Weekly rent	• £40– £80
Pint of lager	• £1.50– £3.00
Cinema	• Loads, most offering student discounts
Nightclub	• Huge variety– every taste catered for

Glasgow

Key facts	Undergraduate
Course length	5 years
Total number of medical undergraduates	c. 1200
Applicants in 2005	1944
Interviews given in 2005	1291
Places available in 2005	241
Places available in 2006	241
Open days 2006	6 September
Entrance requirements	AAB
Mandatory subjects	Chemistry and either maths, physics or biology
Male:female ratio	35:65
Is an exam included in the selection process? If yes, what form does this exam take?	No UKCAT in 2007
Qualification gained	MBChB

Fascinating fact: Dr Ian McDonald – pioneer of the ultrasound – and the neurosurgeon Professor Graham Teasdale responsible for the Glasgow Coma Scale, which is used worldwide, are both famous medics linked to Glasgow.

Glasgow medical school has historical origins in the 17th century and is a well-renowned centre for teaching and research excellence particularly for cardiovascular disease and cancer. It is currently housed in the new Wolfson medical school building situated on the main university campus. The building contains a study landscape, problem-based learning and vocational studies rooms, as well as a clinical studies suite. As with nearly all medical curricula in the UK, Glasgow has undergone some changes to fulfil the GMC's requirements and expectations of tomorrow's doctors.

Education

The new problem-based learning (PBL) course, now in its ninth year, has achieved a fine balance between teaching vocational and scientific aspects and well-equips the modern medical student with the skills necessary to pursue a career in medicine today.

Teaching

The mainstay of the course is PBL sessions. These involve groups of around eight students, guided by a facilitator, tackling two medical scenarios each week. There are also some supporting labs (fixed resource sessions) and lectures (plenaries). A week of lectures at the beginning of the year 3 has now been introduced to give students a better scientific grounding before they embark on their PBL sessions.

The traditional preclinical/clinical divide has been eroded – patient contact and practical skills are now taught from week 1. However, the bulk of hospital-based teaching still takes place in years 4 and 5.

Assessment

Continuous assessment occurs every 5-week block (in years 1 and 2) through coursework essays. There are also two formal written exams on the full curriculum at the end of year 1. An additional exam testing the student's ability to work through a problem is taken in year 1. This is the medical independent learning exam (MILE) in which a scenario is handed out and the student has 24 hours to work through it and produce a set of pertinent questions that he/she must answer along with a summary of the subject tackled.

An objective structured clinical exam (OSCE) is also part of the assessment from year 2 onwards. Years 4 and 5 are treated as a continuum consisting of ten 5-week blocks: three in medicine and surgery and one in general practice, child health, obstetrics and gynaecology and psychiatry. Formal modified oslers or 'observed portfolio cases' have been introduced at the end of each clinical block and form part of the overall assessment along with general supervisor assessment which will determine if the student has passed the block. If the student does not pass a clinical block, he/she must arrange a meeting with the head of the year and will also have to repeat the block before he/she can progress to the next year.

Intercalated degrees

There are both 1- and 2-year intercalated degree options. One-year courses are available in clinical or science subjects and lead to a BSc MedSci (Hons). Glasgow University is perhaps the only university in the UK which offers a special degree type open only to medical students: the BSc MedSci (Hons) in Clinical Medicine. Part of the degree involves choosing one of nine modules: cardiovascular studies, cancer studies, neuroscience, mechanisms of disease, developmental medicine, public health, sports medicine, immunology, and psychological medicine. These modules involve the teaching of the underlying science and the completion of a research project, which accounts for 60% of the degree mark. In addition the degree has a core curriculum which all students (regardless of the module they choose) undertake. This comprises statistical methods relevant to medical research, journal clubs presented by students and teaching on experimental procedures and techniques including advanced IT. The degree is designed to equip the student to understand and undertake medical research and to critically appraise research work. The 2-year BSc (Hons) option is available only in science subjects. The intercalated degree courses are undertaken between years 3 and 4.

Special study modules and electives

Special study modules (SSMs) cover a wide range of subjects and constitute about 20% of the overall course time (one 5-week block in year 2, and two in each year thereafter). Students choose from a list of options and may decide their own from year 3 onwards. Almost any topic can be proposed, including nonmedical subjects such as French or philosophy. It is also possible to take SSMs abroad in years 3, 4 and 5. There are two 4-week electives during the summers of years 3 and 4, which can also be spent abroad. An SSM can (timetable permitting) be amalgamated with an elective to provide a greater depth of study in a topic of interest.

Erasmus

There are no overseas travel opportunities because of the vast opportunities provided by the SSM and elective systems.

Facilities

Library The main university library, with an excellent range of reference books and journals, is open until 11 PM on weekdays and during the day at weekends. The new medical school building includes a purpose-built 'study landscape' well equipped with books and journals and is open 24 hours during term time. The study landscape has three floors of extensive library and computing facilities along with smaller seminar rooms, which can be booked for group study.

Additional study facilities are available on campus (24 hours in Unions) and in all hospitals, some of which are open 24 hours.

Computers There is good central provision of computers in the main university library, with over 300 PCs available. The medical school study provides over 100 flat-screen multimedia PCs that allow students to access a range of electronic learning facilities. Facilities are increasing and improving all the time, with about 20 PCs available for students in each of the main teaching hospitals, and peripheral hospitals gradually being linked to the campus network.

Clinical skills Students are taught clinical skills from year 1, including first aid and basic/advanced resuscitation training. The new medical school building includes a fully equipped ward and side rooms contain audiovisual facilities to enable students to study their own performance in a simulated clinical environment before being confronted with a real hospital situation. Other new facilities include a cardiology patient simulator (known as Harvey) which can mimic symptoms of up to 26 cardiac diseases.

Welfare 🏠

Student support

Glasgow is renowned for its friendly and relaxed atmosphere, and the medical school is no exception. Each student is allocated an Adviser of Studies to offer advice and support, and most tutors are approachable. The Medico-Chirurgical (the medics' society) operates a 'Mums and Dads' scheme for freshers with second-years acting as parents to guide the new first year intake! Glasgow has the usual university counselling and welfare services including a telephone nightline open from 7 PM-7 AM every night, which is operated by the Students' Representative Council.

Accommodation

Glasgow has a large number of local students, but it tries to guarantee accommodation to first-year students moving to the city. Thirty-five per cent of hall places are reserved for returning students. The vast majority of these places are in catered halls of residence. The university has little control over private sector flats but there is an accommodation office to help you. Average rents are £65 per week for full board in halls, £40 (plus bills) per week for a 52-week lease on a university flat, and £45–£65 (plus bills) per week for private flats.

Placements

Glasgow has a large, attractive campus in the west end of the city, 2 miles from the centre. Six large teaching hospitals within the Glasgow area and 13 district general hospitals (DGHs) provide the mainstay of the teaching. Hospitals used include the Glasgow Royal Infirmary, the Western Infirmary, Gartnavel, Southern General, and Stobhill Hospitals. Some of the DGHs used are some distance away, but free accommodation is provided and the facilities (although not quite the London Hilton) are clean and warm. Groups of students number between five and eight. This drops to two per ward by the final year.

For placements outside the university, peripheral attachments can take you to Paisley (8 miles) or as far as Dumfries (80 miles). However, there are many hospitals and general practices in the Greater Glasgow area and GP practices are likely to be local.

Location of clinical placement/name of hospital	Distance away from medical school (miles)	Difficulty getting there on public transport*
Royal Alexandra (Paisley)	8	🚌
Monklands and Wishaw	20	🚌
Ayr	40	🚌 🚗

Location of clinical placement/name of hospital	Distance away from medical school (miles)	Difficulty getting there on public transport*
Inverclyde	30	🏛️ 🚗
Dumfries	80	💡

* 🚶: walking/cycling distance; 🏛️: use public transport; 🚗: need own car or lift; 💡: get up early – tricky to get to!

Sports and social

City life

Glasgow is Scotland's biggest city and is truly international, with a large city centre containing all that you would expect to find. The main university buildings are among Glasgow's landmarks, with beautiful architecture and real atmosphere. The Gilbert Scott tower, the main university spire, is one of the highest points in the city. Lots of student accommodation is in flats in the west end, close to the university, great pubs, shops, and a lively club scene.

Glasgow was the 1999 City of Art and Design and 1990 European City of Culture, which reflects its interesting architecture and design history and cultural past and present. You are never short of something to see or do, from the well-established Kelvingrove Gallery (undergoing refurbishment but due to reopen in 2006), which houses one of the best art collections in the UK, to the new Museum of Modern Art. Glasgow also boasts some of the best shopping in Scotland and a leading club/pub scene.

If this isn't for you, how about an Old Firm game: Glasgow has the two largest Scottish football teams and many first-division rugby sides. The city also hosts many international athletic events. If you want a change of scene, getting out of Glasgow is easy enough, with access to some of the best hill walking, climbing, and skiing in the UK, a mere 1–2 hours away. Other Scottish cities are also close at hand, with Edinburgh and the new Parliament only 45 minutes away. Buses and trains leave every 15 minutes.

University life

The Medico-Chirurgical Society (Med-Chir) is an educational and social society set up and run by medical students. It meets every Thursday, with free beer and talks from a range of speakers on a variety of entertaining topics. It also arranges events, including trips abroad, the annual ball, the annual revue, and a musical culture night. Each year has its own year club to organise club nights, ceilidhs, balls, and to raise money for a massive graduation ball. Our medical students' magazine, *Surgo*, will also keep you updated on all the activities and gossip within the faculty. Unusually, Glasgow has two unions: Glasgow University Union (GUU) and Queen Margaret Union (QMU), both with bars, clubs, catering facilities, and a regular programme of bands, balls, and special events. The GUU has a Debating Chamber and Glasgow University has won the World Debating Championships more times than any other university. All the usual (and some unusual) clubs and societies are available for students to join.

Sports life

The sports centre at the heart of the campus has recently undergone a massive refurbishment programme. The facilities include a 25-m pool, sauna, weights room, squash courts, and sports hall. For only £20 per year you can have unlimited access to the sports facilities, as well as a wide range of daily classes in aerobics, muscle conditioning, and circuits. There is also a large off-campus sports facility housing tennis courts, floodlit hockey and football pitches and another new gym. A variety of sports clubs are on offer, from football and rugby through to swimming, squash, canoeing, and horse riding. Med-Chir also has medics' football and rugby teams.

> **Top tip:** All first-year students should consider buying a copy of *Principles of Anatomy and Physiology* by Tortora and Grabowski. It's an unpopular text with the faculty – probably because it holds the answers to most year 1 PBLs!

Great things about Glasgow

- Prime west end location, lots of shops, cafes and restaurants.
- Great facilities: two great unions, sports complex, main library, and a well-equipped new medical school building.
- Large number of teaching hospitals.
- Teaching by internationally acclaimed experts.
- Chance to mix with students from all corners of the world.

Bad things about Glasgow

- The weather: bring a brolley!
- Some of the district hospitals are far away.
- Little contact with students from other courses.
- Problem-based learning is not everyone's cup of tea.
- Traffic congestion around city centre and west end.

Further information

Admissions Enquiries
Wolfson Medical School
University of Glasgow
University Avenue
Glasgow G12 8QQ
Tel: 0141 330 6216
Fax: 0141 330 2776
Email: admissions@clinmed.gla.ac.uk
Web: http://www.medicine.gla.ac.uk

Additional application information

Average A-level requirements	• AAB
Average Scottish Higher requirements	• AAAAB
Make-up of interview panel	• Two doctors
Months in which interviews are held	• November–March
Proportion of overseas students	• 7%
Proportion of mature students	• 13%
Proportion of graduate students	• 13%
Faculty's view of students taking a gap year	• Acceptable if used constructively
Proportion of students taking intercalated degrees	• 24%
Possibility of direct entrance to clinical phase	• Yes – limited
Fees for overseas students	• £19,000 pa (2005)
Fees for graduates	• £1175 pa (2005)
Ability to transfer to other medical schools	• The faculty is usually keen to avoid this, unless it is in a format of an intercalated degree which is not offered at Glasgow
Assistance for elective funding	• The faculty invites students to apply for help with costs they might incur during their elective. Students are of course able to apply to the numerous external bodies which have funds available for electives and general education
Assistance for travel to attachments	• This is given through your local higher education funding body
Access and hardship funds	• The faculty every year does distribute a small amount of money via bursaries, but these are limited to postgraduate students only. There is a university-wide hardship fund, which all students can access if they are in need
Weekly rent	• £55
Pint of lager	• £1.60
Cinema	• £3.50
Nightclub	• Usually free entry but some may charge up to £3

Glasgow

Guy's, King's and St Thomas'

Key facts	Premedical	Undergraduate	Graduate
Course length	6 years	5 years	4 years
Total number of medical undergraduates	43	1800	24
Applicants in 2005	400	3500+	1300
Interviews given in 2005	140	1125	455
Places available in 2005	43	363	25
Places available in 2006	43	363	25
Open days 2006	July–August	July–August	July–August
Entrance requirements	AAB at A-level plus C at AS-level	AAB at A-level plus C at AS-level	2:1
Mandatory subjects	Biology	Chemistry or biology	None
Male:female ratio	67:33	35:65	63:37
Is an exam included in the selection process? If yes, what form does this exam take?	No	No UKCAT in 2007	MSAT
Qualification gained	MBBS		

Fascinating fact: Guy's Hospital, with its 30-storey 'tower' boasting spectacular views of Tower Bridge, the Tower of London, and St Paul's Cathedral, holds the record for being the tallest hospital in the world.

Guy's, King's and St Thomas' School of Medicine, popularly known as GKT, was formed in August 1998 by the merger of the United Medical and Dental School (UMDS) of Guy's and St Thomas' Hospitals and King's College School of Medicine and Dentistry (KCSMD).

The school combines two established medical schools, both with long histories, including older mergers. King's College is a multidisciplinary institution, part of the University of London, and had its own medical school at King's College Hospital in south London. Guy's and St Thomas' Hospitals had their own medical schools prior to the merger to form the United Medical and Dental Schools.

An intake of nearly 400 students makes the new school one of the biggest medical schools in the UK, and King's College as a whole the largest centre for health care teaching in Europe. Both King's and GKT emphasise personal academic development (for example a strongly supported intercalated BSc programme) and encourages students to participate fully in extracurricular activities.

Education

The course is split into two main sections. The first 2 years place an emphasis on the basic medical sciences. There is early clinical contact, with communication teaching taking place in a GP setting from year 1. The course is organised into systems, for example cardiovascular or musculoskeletal. All the core basic science teaching takes place at the Guy's Hospital campus.

Clinical disciplines are taught in the latter 3 years on the wards of St Thomas' Hospital, King's College Hospital, Guy's Hospital, University Hospital Lewisham, and also in the community. The long-established systems-based clinical course has been designed to complement the course structure from the earlier years. The core clinical subjects are delivered and examined during years 3 and 4. The final year consists of an 8-week elective, followed by attachments in the community and attachments shadowing medical and surgical house officers in district general hospitals.

GKT has a strong commitment to widening access to medical degree courses. A small number of places is available on an access programme which is designed to help bright and talented young people from low aspiration backgrounds become doctors. The programme will eventually allow for up to 50 extra undergraduate places in medicine and will be for talented pupils from South London who would not normally achieve the necessary grades to apply to study medicine. The course is based on a standard MBBS course but takes 6 years rather than five, because of the addition of special modules in the first 3 years.

A new graduate entry programme has been introduced and is designed to encourage access to medicine for graduates in the arts or other health care professionals. The course is shortened to 4 years and after a unique first year, the students join the regular 3-year clinical programme. From 1200 applications only 27 were successful in gaining places!

Teaching

There is a mixture of lectures, tutorials, and practicals, together with computer-assisted learning (CAL). Preclinical teaching has recently changed to a problem-based learning (PBL) format where diseases are studied as weekly themes. This mode of teaching is said to be more clinically relevant and so far students speak highly of it. Anatomical dissection is still a valued part of preclinical teaching.

The Guy's campus also houses the Gordon's museum which holds a unique collection of pathological specimens in pots. They are some of the only examples in the entire country and it is far more stimulating than learning from textbooks.

Assessment

Essays and short-answer questions are now rare during years 3–5. Written examinations during the clinical years are now mostly computer-marked multiple choice questions (MCQs). Objective structured clinical exams (OSCEs) are the main practical examinations during the clinical years, starting with a short communication skills OSCE in year 2.

Intercalated degrees

There are well-supported intercalated degree programmes at the college. There is a wide range of options to choose from, including many outside medicine and the sciences, sometimes even at other London Colleges.

Special study modules and electives

About 20% of each year is devoted to SSMs. There is a considerable range of subjects available and this is increasing every year. As the school is part of a multifaculty institution, many nonmedical SSMs are available, such as modern languages and the popular history of medicine. Students may also design their own SSMs if the subject they wish to study is not on offer.

The 8-week elective period is an opportunity to travel to far-flung destinations (or just down the road) to study in fields of medicine of your choosing. Assessment of how time is spent on the elective (to discourage the temptation to just lie on a beach for 12 weeks!), takes the form of a poster presentation. Various awards and sponsorships are available to help students fund their electives.

Erasmus

Despite the end of GKT participation in Erasmus schemes, the school has special links with numerous medical schools around the world, including the Johns Hopkins University in the USA, the University of Hong Kong, the University of West Indies, and Moscow Medical Academy. As GKT is twinned with these institutions, there are special allocations for GKT students who want to do their electives there. Accommodation will also usually be arranged for you, and extra bursaries may be available to help with travel costs to these colleges.

Facilities

Library Libraries at Guy's are open 9 AM–9 PM on weekdays, 9 AM–5 PM on Saturday, and 1 PM–5 PM on Sunday; there is also a large 24-hour study room. At King's College Hospital the library is open until 9 PM on weekdays and 1 PM on Saturday. Students also have access to the King's College London library at the old Public Records Office on Chancery Lane, which is open until 9 PM from Monday–Thursday, 6 PM on Friday, and 5.30 PM on Saturday and Sunday. All libraries have a good range of books and journals.

Computers All campuses have a large number of computer stations with access to email, the internet, and CAL programs designed in-house. There are 24-hour computing facilities at Guy's, Kings and St Thomas' campuses. The 'virtual campus' is a specialised area of the King's College London website for the GKT Schools of Medicine, Dentistry and Biomedical Sciences and enables students to download lecture notes, register for course components, or obtain details (but not the answers!) about their exams.

Clinical skills A new clinical skills centre opened at Guy's in 1999. It is the largest of its kind in Europe, and is available every weekday from 9 AM–5 PM. Students can book individual rooms in small groups or with their tutor. There are also various laboratories at the three main hospitals. These are great, with latex models of every imaginable part of the human anatomy on which students can practise their clinical skills, such as taking blood pressure or suturing (in the past, King's students on A&E attachments practised suturing pigs' trotters before being let loose on the population of south London!).

Welfare

Student support

Students are assigned to a personal tutor to support them throughout the course. Welfare and counselling services are available on the Guy's campus, where there is a welfare officer available every day. All sites are friendly environments with lots of support from the faculty and staff, as well as the Students' Union which provides student representation on a wide range of matters. The Student Medical Education Committee (SMEC) is a unique student committee that is actively involved in course development and provides feedback to course organisers on how things are going. It acts as a dedicated link between the medical school and the student body. There are six elected representatives in each year, and they will help students to deal with problems that arise with the course and address associated welfare concerns.

Multifaith pastoral care is provided on all campuses, as well as many student-run religious groups covering the main religious faiths.

Accommodation

College accommodation is available in many different parts of London. Some are on or near campuses (on-site accommodation is available on the Guy's campus), whereas others are much further away. The quality and cost of private accommodation can vary a lot in the central Guy's/St Thomas' area, but cheaper, good-quality accommodation is more readily available in the Denmark Hill area and at Hampstead. Students can opt for Intercollegiate University of London accommodation, although these tend to be some distance from any of the campuses.

Placements

Students in years 1 and 2 are taught at the newly developed Guy's Hospital campus at London Bridge. The campus is shared with other departments in biomedical sciences and dentistry. Most of the Guy's Campus has been refurbished to accommodate the large number of students, and many facilities are new. A large new building houses most of the disciplines, with state-of-the-art library and computing facilities. Most clinical teaching takes place at St Thomas' Hospital, King's College Hospital, Guy's Hospital, and University Hospital Lewisham. Students can also access King's College's other campuses, including the Strand campus and Waterloo campus. Psychiatry teaching is at the Maudsley Hospital and the Institute of Psychiatry, which has been awarded the status of 5 star top research institute in the United Kingdom.

As well as the central teaching hospitals in years 4 and 5, there are placements in district general hospitals (DGHs) in south-east England. This relieves some of the pressures at the central London teaching hospitals and provides access to high-quality teaching; clinical workloads tend to be lower, and consultants are able to devote more time to students. Peripheral placements also expose students to the more common conditions that are not seen at the large tertiary referral centres at the large teaching hospitals.

Location of clinical placement/ name of hospital	Distance away from medical school (miles)	Difficulty getting there on public transport*
Woolwich	5	🚶
Bromley	8	🚶
Canterbury	30	🚗
Brighton	50	🚗
Salisbury	90	🎈

* 🚶: walking/cycling distance; 🚌 : use public transport; 🚗: need own car or lift; 🎈 : get up early – tricky to get to!

Sports and social

City life

Most of the campuses are close to the centre of London, with all of London's attractions within easy reach by public transport.

University life

The old medical schools always had thriving social scenes, with numerous balls, weekly events, the annual revues, and RAG week. The social scene at GKT typifies this and GKT medical students still hold the world record for having the largest number of people naked on live TV! GKT also boasts that it has arguably the best university Diwali Show. There is a vast selection of clubs and societies to join including orchestras, bands, singing, dancing, drama and musical theatre groups. Everyone can usually find something that interests them, or comrades with which to start up a new society. The Students' Union runs its own bars, shops, cafes, nightclubs and gym. Student bars are present on all campuses and there is the main medics night spot in the basement of Guys Hospital. If that's not enough, all students have access to the University of London Union (ULU) with its own range of facilities.

GKT gives students access to a large multidisciplinary institution while retaining the friendliness of a medical school. With its almost enclosed courtyard, promenade, and grass park at London Bridge, the Guy's campus is regarded as the closest thing to a campus university in central London. There is a wide cultural mix of students at GKT and with access to University of London Union facilities there will be plenty of opportunity for integration. Students are also encouraged to get involved in Community Action volunteering programmes, working with homeless and disadvantaged people within the local area.

Sports life

Particularly strong sports include football, hockey, netball, tennis, badminton, rowing, and squash, alongside the oldest rugby team in the world at Guy's. There is also a strong karate scene. GKT has sports grounds at Honor Oak Park in south London, Dulwich, and Cobham in Surrey, which provides facilities for rugby, football, and hockey. King's College also has sports grounds in Surbiton. There are gyms at the Guy's and St Thomas' campuses, and also at the Stamford Street halls of residence. For swimmers, there is a pool at Guy's.

Top tip: Students are allocated a 'mum' and a 'dad' from the year above. Make the most of them, they can pass on their books and notes and also give invaluable exam advice.

Great things about GKT

- GKT hospitals are all world renowned.
- Excellent range of learning and social facilities at the medical school campuses, with more on the way.
- The new school is part of a multifaculty institution. Students will have the opportunity to mix with a variety of students from other courses, and have access to a wide range of facilities.
- Good sports clubs with lots of history and traditions.
- Welfare and student support mechanisms are well established and are effective.

Bad things about GKT

- Cost of living in London and travelling to far flung clinical placements.
- Student accommodation can be a long way from your campus.
- Large number of medics in each year group can lead to it being a bit cramped and impersonal.
- The medical school can be a bit bureaucratic.
- Some feel there is a lack of teaching on pharmacology.

Further information

Student Admissions Officer
The Hodgkin Building
Guy's Hospital Campus
King's College London
St Thomas' Street
London Bridge
London SE1 9RT
Tel: 020 7848 6501
Fax: 020 7848 6969
Email: gktadmissions@kcl.ac.uk
Web: http://www.kcl.ac.uk

Additional application information

Average A-level requirements	• ABB/C
Average Scottish Higher requirements	• Premedical: ABB/B or AB/AAB Undergraduate: AA/BBC (Advanced Highers/Highers)
Graduate entry requirements	• 2:1 degree
Make-up of interview panel	• Chair and interviewer (sometimes an observer also)
Months in which interviews are held	• December-May (Premedical) November-May (Undergraduate) February-March (Graduate)
Proportion of overseas students	• Information not available
Proportion of mature students	• Information not available
Proportion of graduate students	• 19%
Faculty's view of students taking a gap year	• Encouraged
Proportion of students taking intercalated degrees	• Please contact university for more information
Possibility of direct entrance to clinical phase	• Yes (start of year 3)
Fees for overseas students	• Premedical: £12,405 (years 1, 2 and 3) £23,070 (years 4, 5 and 6) • Undergraduate: £12,405 (years 1 and 2) £23,070 (years 3, 4 and 5) • Graduate: £12,405 (year 1) £23,070 (years 2, 3 and 4)
Fees for graduates	• £3000 pa
Ability to transfer to other medical schools	• Yes, for Intercalated BSc or for clinical years
Assistance for elective funding	• Good – both college awards and advice for external sources
Assistance for travel to attachments	• No – and some attachments are far away
Access and hardship funds	• Excellent student support and hardship facilities
Weekly rent	• £80 (London prices!)
Pint of lager	• £2.00 (ditto)
Cinema	• £5 upwards
Nightclub	• Free–£15

Hull York Medical School

Key facts	Undergraduate
Course length	5 years
Total number of medical undergraduates	420
Applicants in 2005	2023
Interviews given in 2005	700
Places available in 2005	130
Places available in 2006	141
Open days 2006	Please see University of Hull and University of York websites for details
Entrance requirements	AABB (excluding general studies at AS-level)
Mandatory subjects	Chemistry, biology (or human biology)
Male:female ratio	47:53
Is an exam included in the selection process? If yes, what form does this exam take?	No UKCAT in 2007
Qualification gained	MBBS

Fascinating fact: Hull is the home of the world's smallest window which can be found in the George pub in the land of green ginger.

September 2003 saw the long-awaited opening of the Hull York Medical School (HYMS) and its first 136 students take up their places on a new and exciting programme of medical education. Students are now in its second year. The school is a collaboration between the long-established and well-respected universities of Hull and York. Both universities have a wealth of experience in health and bioscience education and the medical school is very much a natural progression in their development.

Hull York Medical School is forward looking. It aims to accommodate the growing need for doctors in the UK and to set the pace in delivering a curriculum and education that will equip them for the realities of 21st century practice and ensure they truly are 'tomorrow's doctors'.

Education

Students are divided equally between two campuses at Hull and York universities. Despite the physical separation for years 1 and 2, staff and students work hard to ensure complete continuity in teaching, resources, timetables and indeed, social activities at the respective locations. Both locations have new custom-built facilities and the constant movement of faculty between the two locations guarantees that students have good access to all members. The running of parallel timetables and employment of moderators assures HYMS students receive the same education and opportunities regardless of where they are placed. In years 3, 4 and 5 Hull and York groups combine and together follow a programme of community and hospital-based study in centres throughout east and north Yorkshire and northern Lincolnshire.

The course content is organised around the study of body systems and the 5-year course is divided into three phases. In phase I (years 1 and 2), basic sciences are studied in the context of clinical medicine. In phase II (years 3 and 4) the course becomes multicentred with teaching in hospitals, general practices and community placements across north and east Yorkshire and northern Lincolnshire. Clinical teachers deliver the programme and students benefit from low student–teacher ratios and plenty of opportunity for hands-on learning in hospital and primary care settings.

Phase III, the fifth year and the preregistration year, gives students extensive clinical experience in medicine, surgery and general practice. After graduation, in the preregistration year, close supervision and educational support continues.

Teaching

The curriculum at HYMS is designed to make education interesting and exciting. In phase I, virtual patient case studies are used each week as a framework in which to conceptualise and explore the science. Clinical placements provide the opportunity to transpose the theory into medical realities.

A broad range of learning methods are used at HYMS to meet the variety of learning objectives set by the curriculum. Methods include problem-based (PBL) and self-directed learning, lectures, and a staff-supported resource laboratory, which contains visual aids such as anatomical models, radiographs and computer packages. A new anatomy museum provides use of prosections. Typically, a lecture is delivered by a speaker at either Hull or York and beamed into the other end by an impressive video conferencing link. Technological teething problems have now all but subsided and likewise, stage fright, as students across campuses regularly engage in discussion via the video system. There are also biopracticals, which consist of some teaching where students learn about different aspects of physiology through performing experiments, for example values of lung function by spirometry. Workshops are an innovative way of expanding gained knowledge in clinical contexts, for example the use of ethics in clinical practice.

Patient contact is made from day one. Clinical placements start from the beginning of the first year with weekly half-day attachments within a small group. In year 2, a full day per week is spent with patients and in the second and third phases clinical experience becomes much more intense with the majority of the final year spent on placements. The early placements are arranged not only to make the science and transition to the role of doctor easier, but also to supplement several curricula themes by highlighting the responsibilities and duties that come with being a doctor. The importance of engaging with your patient and considering the psychological and social effects of their illnesses is given strong emphasis at HYMS and reflected in the fully integrated course where complementary disciplines are learned together.

Assessment

Assessment addresses the 'learning outcomes' of each stage of the course using a combination of factual tests; multiple choice questions (MCQs), modified essay and short answer and practical patient-based assessments (OSCPE). Exams are conducted at the end of the summer term. Students also keep a computer-held portfolio of learning and reflective writing as a record of progress. Formative assessments – self-test papers and examinations to assist learning but not included in the final degree – occur at the beginning of the summer and spring terms. These help students to recognise their strengths and weaknesses and to guide their work objectives accordingly.

Intercalated degrees

Selected students may devote an optional year, usually between years 2 and 3, to study for an honours degree in the biomedical or health sciences or another appropriate scientific subject. These can be taught or research based. They take the form of 120 credits whereby 40 are research based and the remaining 80 are taught based. Out of the 80 taught-based credits 20 are at level 2 and 60 credits at level 3 (requiring more critical analysis). Entry for the degree is competitive and is based on having done well in the previous exam. A maximum of five students over the two sites was allowed to take the degree in its inaugural year.

Special study modules and electives

Special study modules called student-selected components (SSCs) provide an exciting opportunity to pursue new interests or develop existing ones. Comprising about a fifth of the course they are highly valued by HYMS students and can cover a broad range of disciplines. These could be basic or social sciences, medical specialities or nonmedical subjects such as languages or the arts. Students in years 1 and 2 take one SSC per term.

The elective is an opportunity to spend 8 weeks experiencing any medical speciality in any part of the world between July and September of year 5.

Erasmus

There is no opportunity to participate in an Erasmus program at Hull/York although students can travel abroad for their elective.

Facilities

Both Hull and York have custom-built or modified buildings and bear testimony to a substantial budget well spent. Within the buildings are the PBL rooms, which constitute the students' favourite resource.

Everyone that sees them agrees: we are spoilt. Students are divided into groups of eight for problem-based learning sessions and allocated a PBL room which contains a high-tech, networked computer for each group member, a large and incredibly useful array of interactive learning packages, wall-to-wall white boards and most importantly the learning support of peers in your group. Friendships and learning relationships develop quickly and strongly within these groups. PBL members have access to their own room 24 hours a day. This is where students do the majority of their study, securing it as a respected learning environment, a source of note sharing and (rumour has it) a pizza delivery place for those working into the night!

Library The library resources are abundant and joint access to the both Hull and York libraries, regardless of your home campus, translates to access to over two million books. This is before the surrounding hospital and local affiliated libraries are considered! There is a substantial collection of medical and health-related books, papers and periodicals at both universities. Students also have access to a large number of electronic journals, multimedia CDs, videos and the Cochrane database. At York, the medical library is part of the University's JB Morrell library. Term time opening hours are from 9 AM–10 PM and at weekends from 11 AM–6.00 PM. Hull's Brymore Jones library is open Monday–Thursday from 9 AM– 10 PM, Friday and Saturday 9 AM–9 PM and Sunday 1 PM–9 PM.

Computers In addition to the HYMS buildings, medical students have full 24-hour access to other computing resources across both Hull and York campuses. University and HYMS email accounts are provided. IT training and language courses are open to students at both campuses.

York runs an excellent information literacy course, ILIAD, the Languages for All Programme enabling students to learn a foreign language whilst studying for their degree; two vocational skills-based programmes and the York award. The latter comprises a range of courses designed to improve students' employability of which the ILIAD and Languages for All can be a component.

Hull gives all students the opportunity to develop or gain language skills and hosts the Language Institute; one of the largest and best equipped learning centres in Britain.

Clinical skills Students take part in weekly clinical skill sessions in which students learn communication skills whilst taking medical and social histories from simulated patients. They perform clinical examinations on healthy volunteers. Skills learnt from these sessions can be transferred to real life patients in clinical placement sessions.

Welfare

Student support

Student welfare and a caring supportive environment are at the heart of the ethos at HYMS. We are acutely aware that the most valuable commodity we have is each other and a formidable support network comes from fellow students and the academic support gained by close contact with staff.

In additional to departmental and academic support, both Hull and York offer a range of specialist services. At the beginning of term you are introduced to the support facilities rather than having to seek them out when you need them most. These include chaplains, counselling staff, health professionals and disability services. York has the added bonus of strong support via the College network and all HYMS welfare services are supplemented by the welfare work of the Student's Union.

A buddies scheme is now in operation at HYMS; first-year medical students are allocated a second-year medical student 'buddy'. This informal relationship allows the first-year student to gain the benefit of the experience of other students and to integrate the two year groups.

Accommodation

Accommodation is guaranteed for all medical students at both campuses. Most students are offered rooms in halls of residence on campus; however a small number of off-campus places are within easy reach of the medical school. Students can indicate which hall they would prefer to be in on their application form.

Placements

Clinical placements start from the beginning of year 1 with weekly half-day attachments within a small group. Attachments increase in frequency and duration throughout the course. In years 3, 4 and 5 Hull and York groups will combine to follow a programme of community and hospital-based study in regional centres throughout east and north Yorkshire and northern Lincolnshire. Accommodation is provided during regional placements by the Trust where your home base is. Accommodation is not provided for students during years 1 and 2 as partner hospitals are all in close proximity to the medical school.

Location of clinical placement/ name of hospital	Distance away from medical school (miles)	Difficulty getting there on public transport*
York NHS Services Trust	Varies	
Hull Royal Infirmary	3	
Castle Hill Hospital Hull	4	
Primary and secondary care placements near three partner hospitals	Near to medical schools	

* : walking/cycling distance; : use public transport; : need own car or lift; : get up early – tricky to get to!

Sports and social

City life

Hull, once a hideout for beatniks and intellectuals, is now a living catwalk for the super cool and the terminally trendy. Indeed, Hull is the focus of a recent multimillion urban regeneration project. Unfortunately, it suffers from preconceptions which are far wide of the mark. Students love to live and study here. Graduates gush with praise and fondness and the new HYMS intake are already displaying ferocious loyalty and affection for the place. The nightlife at Hull is nothing short of legendary, with numerous venues in the city centre and its very own on-campus nightclub recently voted the best university venue in the UK. Hull is unbelievable value for money. Lower accommodation costs will be difficult to come by at another university and if you are coming from London, expect another three pints for your fiver!

Hull University holds a global reputation not only for academia, but also for friendliness. Its graduates are consistently among the top ten UK universities for graduate employment and it places strong emphasis on students excelling both in and out of the classroom.

York is a beautiful city. Steeped in history and encircled by ancient walls, it boasts some remarkable architecture including its landmark Minster, the largest Gothic cathedral in Northern Europe, and winding medieval streets. A strong tourist industry ensures it bustles with life throughout the year and hosts a remarkable array of shops, restaurants, pubs, bistros and sights. York has a distinctly cosmopolitan feel, catering for every interest. The Theatre Royal, Grand Opera House and a wide variety of live music venues enrich the staple student regime of clubs and kebabs. The university has a collegiate system; ensuring friendships can run far beyond the medical school. Socialising tends to take place in the college bars or the city centre, but York's proximity to Leeds and Manchester ensures there are bigger nights out not too far away.

Hull and York are both located in some of the most spectacular countryside in England. Surrounded by the Pennines, Dales, North Yorkshire Moors and the seaside towns of Whitby, Robin Hood's Bay and Scarborough there are many opportunities to explore and appreciate the area. York also has the advantage of being placed half-way between Edinburgh and London, both of which can be reached in less than two hours by train. The regular and cheap ferries running from Hull to Amsterdam require little promotion.

University life

With the array of extracurricular opportunities existing between Hull and York and HYMS, social calendars require some organising. The enthusiastic MedSoc, a body of eight students from both campuses who arrange events ranging from visiting speakers to charity pub-crawls, does this. Enthusiasm and talent is not in short supply and all students are working hard to bring to life plans for unisex sports teams, a medics band, a Christmas revue and a HYMS newspaper. As a new school, clubs and projects are evolving to reflect students' interests and talents and we eagerly await the new intake to supplement and enrich the current stream of activity.

Links with the BMA and other medical schools are growing and HYMS is eager to establish itself in the wider community of medical students and health professionals. HYMS has been shown a warm welcome by York Medical Society and the local trust. Outside lectures, close contact is maintained between both students and staff by the web-based discussion boards and regular social activities

Common rooms provide a place for a coffee, chat or break should one be needed and are great for socialising.

Sports life

The sporting facilities at Hull are excellent with gyms, jacuzzis, an astroturf, and squash courts. The

Athletic Union currently has around 50 different sporting clubs. A magnificent new sports stadium and 'The Deep', an innovative ocean discovery centre, are just two of the exciting new developments marking out the future face of the city. In York, there is an abundance of facilities, accommodating the golfer, cyclist, swimmer, climber, gym fanatic and hardened gambler – we do have one of the finest racecourses in the country!

> **Top tip:** Bring your old biology and chemistry books if you have recently taken-levels (AS A2) as they will still come in handy in the first year. The pub the Gardeners has beer/lager £1.09 a pint on Mondays (a short walk from the university).

Great things about Hull and York

- You are spoilt with the huge amount of resources available to students.
- Clinical placements from the very beginning of the course are invaluable.
- Hull's Asylum nightclub was voted the best student union venue in the UK.
- Dr Menos Lagopoulos and Professor Paul O'Higgins, our eminent tutors in anatomy. They are an unmissable double act.
- The students – HYMS is a close community where a culture of cooperation not competition reigns.

Bad things about Hull and York

- Self directed and problem-based learning requires adaptation from A-level style syllabus and teaching.
- Although students state a preference for the campus they would like to be placed at, allocation is largely by ballot. Only exceptionally are individual personal circumstances taken into account.
- Student and staff refusal to accept that the video link is not TV and no, your mum cannot see you wave. Will the novelty ever wear off?
- The consequences of freshers' week or to be more specific, *3* fresher's weeks are far reaching. Hull starts term a little earlier than York does and HYMS fits into the former's timetable. What this translates to is a freshers' week at HYMS, one at Hull University and a later one at York University.

Further information

Admissions and Schools Liaison
University of York
Heslington
York YO10 5DD
Tel: 01904 433 533
Fax: 01904 433 538
Email: admissions@york.ac.uk
Web: http://www.york.ac.uk

Student Recruitment and Admissions Service
University of Hull
Kingston upon Hull
Hull HU6 7RX

Tel: 01482 466 497
Email: admissions@hull.ac.uk
Web: http://www.hyms.ac.uk

Additional application information

Average A-level requirements	• AABB
Average Scottish Higher requirements	• AAAAB
Make-up of interview panel	• Two people: one clinician and one non-clinician
Months in which interviews are held	• November–March
Proportion of overseas students	• 7.5%
Proportion of mature students	• 39%
Proportion of graduate students	• 32%
Faculty's view of students taking a gap year	• Encouraged
Proportion of students taking intercalated degrees	• 5%
Possibility of direct entrance to clinical phase	• No
Fees for overseas students	• £20,000 pa
Fees for graduates	• £3000 pa
Ability to transfer to other medical schools	• Transfer to other medical schools is not available
Assistance for elective funding	• There is no assistance but there are many places to apply to for funding although it is not always guaranteed
Assistance for travel to attachments	• The first-year medical students are currently provided with a free taxi service to their placements. Second-year medical students find there own way usually by bus or car and are reimbursed at public transport rate
Access and hardship funds	• There is a contact number to apply to if any student is having financial hardship
Weekly rent	• £47–£80
Pint of lager	• Carling £1.40 and Stella £1.60 Student Union • £2.00–£2.50 city centre pub
Cinema	• UGC and the Odeon cinema entrance cost approximately £3.50
Nightclub	• £2–£5 – the Asylum in the University has been voted best university nightclub in the UK. There are many others as well

Imperial College London

Key facts	Undergraduate
Course length	6 years
Total number of medical undergraduates	2000
Applicants in 2005	3000
Interviews given in 2005	900
Places available in 2005	326
Places available in 2006	326
Open days 2006	15 February and 5 July
Entrance requirements	AAB (graduates need 2:1 degree and three Cs at A-level)
Mandatory subjects	Biology and chemistry
Male:female ratio	44:56
Is an exam included in the selection process?	Yes
If yes, what form does this exam take?	BMAT
Qualification gained	MBBS/BSc

Fascinating fact: The triangular teabag was invented at Imperial College!

Imperial College School of Medicine (ICSM) was established in 1997 and was the product of a merger between Charing Cross and Westminster and St Mary's Schools of Medicine. The Faculty of Medicine at Imperial College is one of Europe's largest institutions – in terms of staff and student population and research income. The first intake of the new course graduated in 2004 and there are now no students from the original medical schools. ICSM has created a new identity while maintaining the spirit and traditions of the original schools.

Research at both medical schools has traditionally been strong, and this has been aided by incorporation into Imperial College. The Sir Alexander Fleming building at the Imperial College site in South Kensington is very central and only 200 m from Hyde Park. All first-year halls of residence are close to this site. Imperial is now one of the largest medical schools in the country, and the noncourse elements such as sport and music are flourishing in their new environment. Which other medical students graduate in the Royal Albert Hall?

Education

Imperial offers a 6-year course which incorporates an intercalated Honours year (BSc) for everyone except appropriately qualified graduates. Nongraduate mature students are expected to undertake 6 years of study. It combines the best of the traditional medical courses with more emphasis on communication skills, medical ethics and law and IT. There is integrated teaching from year 1, which includes early exposure to general practice on a weekly basis combined with laboratory and clinical skills sessions. There is a term-based structure for years 1 and 2 (see prospectus). A wide variety of clinical experience is offered, at many sites. The course takes advantage of the large number of hospitals in west London. New courses have been introduced, including a business course and an introduction to graduate medical practice. The integrated course has now matured and adapted to the comments of the pioneering students. This has made it a well-tailored and enjoyable one.

Teaching

A mixture of exams and continuous assessment is used to monitor students' progress. Problem-based learning (PBL) in small groups is a part of the teaching at Imperial, but lectures remain the mainstay of teaching. Students are encouraged to use the computers and clinical skills laboratories that are located at all the main campuses. Lectures and ward attachments occur during all parts of the course, but as you progress more time is spent on hospital attachments. Anatomy is taught from year 1 by dissection of cadavers as well as use of predissected cadavers, which you are guided through by an anatomist. These are fun weekly sessions if you can stand the 'unpleasant for some' smell!

Assessments

End-of-year exams form the basis of assessment in the first 3 years, with more regular assessments after most firms as you progress into the clinical years. Formative exams in year 1 are useful to gain an idea of what is expected at medical school, as it is very different from what most have experienced before. Retakes are offered after all end-of-year exams if things don't go to plan and are traditionally held in the September before the following academic year. Vivas (oral examinations) have been phased out at Imperial, which many students have welcomed as they were sometimes not very standardised.

As a BSc is a compulsory inclusion to the Imperial course, this is assessed by exams, throughout the year via in-course essays, and on the BSc project, which is usually of your choosing.

Intercalated degrees

A compulsory BSc, normally undertaken in years 4 or 5, has been built into the new course. The

BSc is a modular degree programme and there is a wide range of subject choices; for example, genetics, psychology, biochemistry and management (taught at the Imperial College Management School alongside MBA students). Some introductory modules that count towards the final BSc are undertaken in year 3. Students are also free to apply to other universities for courses not offered by Imperial College.

Special study modules and electives

There is an 8-week elective in year 6 where you are encouraged to learn and explore how medicine is practised abroad. Imperial College offers many grants each year to students undertaking valuable study abroad, which helps ease the cost. An SSM in the final year covers a 3-week block in a topic of your choice. There is a wide range of specialties to choose from, ranging from alternative medicine to sports medicine to radiology.

Erasmus

The college participates in the Socrates and Erasmus schemes. Currently, all Socrates-Erasmus participants who are assessed as eligible (usually through eligible European nationality), receive a mobility grant courtesy of the European Union. Europe is the main area where students pursue the various types of placement abroad. The College has an extensive network within the European Union's Socrates-Erasmus programme of study abroad exchanges. These cover whole year and shorter placements. The Imperial College Union has an Erasmus Club which aims to help with and improve your preparation. You can obtain further information from Admissions Tutors. Alternatively, you can contact the International Liaison Office by telephoning +44 (0)20 7594 8044 or emailing exchangestudents@imperial.ac.uk.

Facilities

Library There are libraries at all sites (including peripheral ones), of which most are open from 9 AM–9 PM on weekdays and also on Saturday mornings. A 24-hour opening trial at the central library on the South Kensington campus has just been successfully completed, and there is a possibility of this becoming permanent. The libraries do hold reference copies of all recommended texts, but loan copies generally disappear quite quickly. All libraries also hold videos of clinical lectures, so that if you miss one or don't understand one, you can always review it at your leisure – you can't always make every 9 AM! Centrally given lectures are also 'beamed' out to the peripheral hospitals so that you never miss important lectures if you are on an outside placement.

Computers There is a considerable emphasis on IT in the Imperial course. To sustain this, the number of computer facilities has expanded considerably, and IT training is also provided formally in the first year. The Charing Cross campus has recently installed new machines, with CD-writers and DVD playing facilities. There are computer facilities for Imperial College medical students at all peripheral attachments as well. Printers are available at all sites using a prepay card system that is convenient and easy to use.

Clinical skills There are clinical skill labs at all central hospitals and at many peripheral hospitals too. Students are encouraged to use them as part of their training in both timetabled and student-arranged sessions. They are very well equipped and good fun to use – many are supervised so that you can obtain help if you need it. You can practise everything from taking blood to doing a rectal examination on latex dummies. These help you build confidence before doing procedures on real patients.

Welfare

Student support

Students in the first years, who are based at South Kensington, can feel remote from the medical environment. Soon after starting at Imperial, each fresher is allocated a 'mum' or 'dad' student from the years above. These 'parents' are able to help you adjust to university and medical school life. They also help you to ease into the social life and can offer advice and tips about the course; they will probably even cook you dinner and show you why medic life is so renowned!

Each student is also allocated a tutor, who should be available for personal and academic problems and advice. However, the reality is that some students may go through 6 years without ever meeting him/her. This is in the process of being improved, so that future years should feel more supported, and there is a head of pastoral care who can be contacted in the event of your tutor not being available. Imperial College has counselling and welfare services available to all students. The medics' students' union has a welfare officer who can be contacted in times of need.

Accommodation

First-year students have a guaranteed place in halls from £50 (triple room) to about £85 per week for a single and higher rent for rooms that come with *en suite* bathrooms. Halls are 2–30 minutes from one of the three main hospitals, and no more than an hour from all the peripheral sites. Private sector accommodation is expensive if you want to live near to Imperial College in South Kensington (£85–£100 or more per week). However, as you will spend the majority of your time from year 2 onwards based in the Hammersmith hospitals, most students live in and around Hammersmith where rent is less expensive but still quite high, between £85 and £100 or even more.

Placements

The school uses a wide range of centres across central and west London for teaching. The main teaching hospitals – Charing Cross (Hammersmith), Chelsea and Westminster (Fulham), and St Mary's (Paddington) – are supplemented by peripheral district general hospitals (DGHs) and teaching hospitals in Middlesex and Surrey. The Sir Alexander Fleming building at the main Imperial College site is used for basic biomedical sciences, which constitutes much of year 1. There are good public transport links between all sites, and a London Transport discount scheme has reduced the travel costs. However getting home from some of the peripheral hospitals can be difficult so accommodation is generally provided if this is the case.

Students experience a wide range of clinical attachments, starting with a GP practice placement in year 1. Initially many attachments will be near to Imperial College, but as you proceed into your specialist clinical studies (years 4–6) they may be further afield (outside London). You are generally offered a shortlist of hospitals to choose from.

Location of clinical placement/ name of hospital	Distance away from medical school (miles)	Difficulty getting there on public transport*
Charing Cross	4	🚶 🚌
Chelsea	1.5	🚶
St Mary's	1.5	🚶
West Middlesex	6	🚌 🚗
Northwick Park	9	🚗

* 🚶: walking/cycling distance; 🚌 : use public transport; 🚗: need own car or lift; 💡 : get up early – tricky to get to!

Sports and social

City life

Nothing written in a small paragraph could do justice to the multitude of activities, events, venues, clubs, and locations that London offers. Suffice to say that if you went to a different restaurant, cinema, ice rink, museum, or club each day for the 6 years you are here, there would still be more to see!

University life

The medical school has made a name for itself by incorporating the best of both its parent schools. The central London setting and the wide range of people have assisted this process. Opportunities for nonmedical pursuits abound, but the traditional medical student lifestyle is in no danger of disappearing. The medical school's own Students' Union and societies help Imperial medics maintain a separate identity from the rest of Imperial College students.

However, medical students are still able to take advantage of Imperial College Union and its teams and clubs. There is a newly refurbished student bar at the Charing Cross campus, which holds regular events including video nights, comedy nights, console tournaments as well as ICSM's renowned 'bops'. These produce a good turn-out of students from all the years, often in amusing fancy dress. Highlights of the year include the freshers' roadshow, the interyear rugby match, Rag week, including the Circle line pub crawl, and many balls which vary from being at top London night clubs to 5 star hotels. There are plenty of medical student events spread through each term organised by either the medical school union or individual clubs and societies to ensure that everyone plays hard, as well as working hard.

Sports life

Imperial College medical school teams have grounds at Teddington (previously home to England RFC), as well as pitches and an Astroturf at Gunnersbury. Harlington is the largest of the sports grounds and also serves as the training ground of Chelsea Football Club. Students can also use one of three Imperial College-owned sports centres, with an additional centre scheduled to open in autumn 2005 that will provide the South Kensington campus with some of the best sporting facilities in London.

The Imperial medics' rugby team (old boys include J.P.R. Williams) has already made a name for itself at a European level, and the school frequently holds many United Hospitals trophies. A substantial financial rugby scholarship is also awarded annually to the fresher who has made the greatest impression at the club. Rowing at Imperial College is world class, having produced Olympic gold medallists, and the training facilities reflect this. Women's sports are well established, with hockey and netball being among the most popular. The men's cricket team pride themselves on their post-match celebrations. Other sports include water polo, mountaineering, surfing, and mixed lacrosse, to name but a few. The variety of sporting choice is paralleled only by the mixture of abilities: from the social players to the semiprofessionals and internationals; all are welcome and encouraged.

Top tip: With its many campuses and sites things can get a bit confusing at times – the student union website is brilliant to get up-to-date news about social and educational matters so that you're not left behind!

Great things about Imperial

- The opportunities available here will ensure you leave with the greatest of experiences.
- State-of-the-art audiovisual system, meaning that if you are at one site and the lecture is at another it can be beamed to your site; this reduces the need to travel and hence cost.
- You can choose between the close-knit medical community at the medical school, the larger Imperial College environment, or metropolitan city life.
- A brand new building for biomedical sciences, at the South Kensington Imperial College site, as well as Chelsea and Westminster Hospital (known as the 'Hilton Hospital') means salubrious surroundings.
- Large city with a huge range of cultural activities – anything you want can be found.
- Most students live in the lively, safe, cosmopolitan area of west London – and halls in the first year in South Kensington make celebrity spotting a frequent occurrence.

Additional application information

Average A-level requirements	• AABB
Average Scottish Higher requirements	• AAABB + AAB in Advanced Highers
Make-up of interview panel	• Chair, two members of the selection panal and a senior medical student
Months in which interviews are held	• January–April
Proportion of overseas students	• 6%
Proportion of mature students	• 7%
Proportion of graduate students	• 7%
Faculty's view of students taking a gap year	• Welcomed - applicants must state in UCAS personal statement how they propose to spend their time. Deferred applications not normally accepted from graduate, mature or overseas applicants
Proportion of students taking intercalated degrees	• 100% (Suitably qualified students may apply for exemption from BSc year and if granted exemption will follow a five year course to be awarded MBBS degree only)
Possibility of direct entrance to clinical phase	• No (Apart from an agreement with Oxford and Cambridge to fill quota of transfer places)
Fees for overseas students	• £15,150 (years 1, 2 and 3) • £24,900 (years 4, 5 and 6)
Fees for graduates	• Same as undergraduates – please contact university for details
Ability to transfer to other medical schools	• If the student has the agreement of the Head of Undergraduate Medicine in exceptional circumstances
Assistance for elective funding	• Based on contribution to medical school and/or hardship reasons
Assistance for travel to attachments	• None available
Access and hardship funds	• Several funds are available to all students
Weekly rent	• £50 (triple room in halls) – £120 (private with *en suite* bathroom)
Pint of lager	• £2.80
Cinema	• £7.00
Nightclub	• Free–£20

Leeds

Key facts	Undergraduate
Course length	5 years
Total number of medical undergraduates	1230
Applicants in 2005	2626
Interviews given in 2005	696
Places available in 2005	238
Places available in 2006	238
Open days 2006	June and September
Entrance requirements	AAB
Mandatory subjects	Chemistry
Male:female ratio	43:57 (for first year)
Is an exam included in the selection process? If yes, what form does this exam take?	No UKCAT in 2007
Qualification gained	MBChB

Fascinating fact: You can fit a mini into the lifts in the med school.

The course at Leeds underwent a major overhaul several years ago, at which point the old, subject-based teaching of anatomy, physiology, then biochemistry, etc., was abandoned in favour of modules that each focused on one, complete system of the body (anatomy, physiology, diseases and treatments all at once). Some clinically oriented teaching takes place from year 1, and hospital-based teaching starts in year 2. Staff and departments have been receptive to feedback and this has generated a very student-friendly atmosphere.

The medical school itself has a real mix of students from up and down the country, as well as overseas and mature students. Medics can sometimes feel a little separated from the rest of the student population, but most get a chance to mix in halls of residence and through sports clubs. An excellent Medical Students' Representative Council (MSRC) has been instrumental in designing the new-style course and is in constant contact with the staff to ensure that it continues to run smoothly. A large and enthusiastic MedSoc ensures all medics have a great time and tries to cater for all of its members by organising a wide spectrum of events.

Education 📖

The course is systems based; including clinical experience from year 1. Modules progressively cover all of the systems of the body and then primary care and the various medical and surgical specialties. In addition, students are simultaneously taught personal and professional development skills. Leeds offers a huge range of student-selected modules (SSCs) where individuals can create their own projects or explore particular areas of interest in depth. These can range from foreign languages, to working with the police, giving sex education, learning teaching skills, and from medical ethics and law, to scientific and community projects.

Teaching

Teaching at Leeds is well integrated, with a mix of problem-solving exercises, small group teaching, and lectures. The use of computer-based learning (CAL) is increasing rapidly, with experiments, tutorials, and practice test questions being placed on the intranet. Anatomy is still taught using dissection of human cadavers in years 1–3. Ward teaching begins in year 2.

Assessment

Assessments include integrated examinations consisting of multiple choice question (MCQ) papers and extended matching questions (EMQs) with a chance to do a formative exam to help students see how much they need to revise! Student-selected components count towards a major part of the course and objective structured clinical examinations (OSCEs) occur in years 3, 4 and 5.

Leeds has the largest teaching complex in Europe and ward-based teaching is split between the Leeds General Infirmary, St James' Hospital and Bradford Royal Infirmary.

Intercalated degrees

Leeds is one of the universities where students still have the choice of whether or not they want to do an extra year to gain a BSc. These can be taken after years 1, 2, 3 or 4. The number of places available for intercalating has recently been increased and there is a range of scholarships available.

Special study modules and electives

Student-selected components run throughout the course and the staff at Leeds have received awards for the range of SSCs offered. In year 1, the emphasis is on learning how to access medical literature and conduct a scientific investigation. In year 2, students undertake a literature review and also have the opportunity to study medical ethics in detail. Year 3 offers students the opportunity to design their own project. This has resulted in many published articles for Leeds students (very useful on your CV!) In year 4 there are three SSCs and in year 5 there are four.

A 10-week elective is timetabled at the beginning of year 5 for the first week in August until the first week in October. Many students travel overseas for this, and recent destinations have been Canada, Australia, Africa, and Barbados.

Erasmus

There is no Erasmus scheme.

Facilities

Library The medical school has its own library and this is well stocked with the latest publications, core textbooks and internet access. The library is open 7 days a week and stays open until midnight near exams. Medical students also have access to the other two libraries in the university as well as hospital libraries

Computers There is an excellent provision of computers throughout Leeds University. The 200 in the medical school have recently been updated to flat screens and medical students are also granted access to computer clusters in the local hospitals. An IT course is run at the beginning of the first year to help those who need to update their computer literacy. There is also a 24-hour computer cluster on-campus.

Clinical skills There are clinical skills laboratories at St James' Hospital, Leeds General Infirmary (LGI) and Bradford Royal Infirmary. These offer the opportunity to practise on the same equipment that will be used in the exams.

Welfare

Student support

There is a wide level of support at Leeds including the highly successful student-mentoring scheme, the individual personal tutor scheme and the counselling services available in the university. The student-mentoring scheme means that every new medical student has two 'parents' from the year above to show them around and answer questions that they may not want to ask the staff. If you would prefer to speak to a member of staff, each student is also allocated a doctor who is a point of contact for personal and academic issues. Students in years 1 and 2 have the opportunity to meet with the academic deans to discuss their progress and highlight any fears or anxieties they may have. The MSRC also provide a direct link with staff and are available to accompany you to any meetings that you might arrange with the staff, should you wish. The Students' Union and the university also have excellent counselling services.

Accommodation

Most first-year students live in university accommodation (either halls or flats). These can be costly, but standards are generally good and this can be a good way to meet nonmedics. In the second year, many move out to back-to-back houses in Headingley. Rents start at about £50 per week, but most pay a little more. Insurance is pricey, and burglary can be a problem. The locals can sometimes be a little antistudent, but your mates all live in the next street. There is help in finding accommodation available from the university Unipol scheme.

Placements

The medical school is on campus but is also attached to the Leeds General Infirmary (one of the main teaching hospitals). The city centre is less than a 10-minute walk from the school, and free shuttle buses run from the LGI to St James' Hospital and to other hospitals that students may need to attend. Facilities in the teaching hospitals are generally of a high standard. The three main teaching hospitals are St James', LGI and Bradford Royal Infirmary.

A lot of district general hospitals (DGHs) are also used, including York, Harrogate, Ilkley, Halifax, Scunthorpe, Otley, Hull, Huddersfield, and Wakefield. A few year 3 students spend a term in the Yorkshire Dales. In years 4 and 5 attachments can be even further afield. All accommodation and transport is provided for residential attachments. Travel costs are variable and are to a certain degree supported by the university although students may occasionally be expected to carry the bulk of the cost. Free buses are provided to some placements. Associated DGHs incorporate the majority of west and north Yorkshire (although this may change as the Hull/York school develops), with Sheffield Medical School serving South Yorkshire.

Location of clinical placement/ name of hospital	Distance away from medical school (miles)	Difficulty getting there on public transport*
Leeds General Infirmary, City centre	0	🚶
St James' University hospital	2.7	🚌
Bradford Royal Infirmary	15	🚌 🚗
Seacroft Hospital	7.2	🚌
Wharfedale Hospital	12.9	🚗

* 🚶: walking/cycling distance; 🚌 : use public transport; 🚗: need own car or lift; 💡 : get up early – tricky to get to!

Sports and social

City life

Leeds is the fastest-growing city in the UK outside London. The main city centre has all the shopping and nightlife your bank account can take, and is within a 10-minute walk from the main campus.

Theatre, Opera North, museums, and galleries cater for the culture vultures. Sport is big in Leeds, especially football, cricket, rugby union and rugby league.

Possibly the shopping capital of the north! The city centre boasts the first Harvey Nichols outside London, and with the many other shops there is everything anyone could want. The Yorkshire Dales are a short bus journey away and a fantastic place to walk and get away from the hustle and bustle of life in Leeds. There are good road links and Leeds is on the fast, GNER rail network to London.

University life

The Students' Union has had a huge cash injection and comprises four bars, a nightclub and a supermarket. Leeds MedSoc is the largest and probably the most active society of the union and organises endless events, including two annual balls, bowling nights, pub-crawls, ice-skating, quizzes, ballet trips, and lots of general drinking nights – something for everyone. The university also has a wide range of clubs and societies.

Sports life

Medics' rugby, football, hockey, netball, cricket, and racket games are all supported by MSRC. The university has a large sports centre, loads of gym equipment, aerobics classes, yoga, kickboxing, and more. The main university also runs many sports teams.

> **Top tip:** At Leeds, students get the basic science needed for medicine out of the way in the first term and this can be disheartening but stick with it; once the clinical side of things gets underway, it's much more fun!

Great things about Leeds

- You get to learn the anatomy on real bodies, not just textbooks and videos (great for would-be surgeons).
- The city centre is right on your doorstep and everything you could want from a multitude of shops to banks to bars to clubs is all in one place.
- The Medical Students' Representative Council is highly respected by the staff and so the course is very student-oriented.
- Proximity to the Yorkshire Dales – a city in the country!
- The staff go out of their way to make sure the transition from school life to medical school life is as easy and gentle as possible.

Bad things about Leeds

- Leeds University does not have a swimming pool.
- Medics always seem to have exams and holidays when the rest of the university hasn't, and vice versa.
- Most medics struggle to make friends outside of the medical school.

- There is not enough parking on-campus.
- Leeds has no major concert venue.

Further information

Admissions Office
School of Medicine
University of Leeds
Leeds LS2 9JT
Tel: 0113 343 7194
Fax: 0113 233 4375
Email: ugadmissions@leeds.ac.uk
Web: http://www.leeds.ac.uk

Additional application information	
Average A-level requirements	• AAB
Average Scottish Higher requirements	• AAAAB plus 2 Advanced Highers
Make-up of interview panel	• Two staff members from university or affiliated hospitals or local GP plus one medical student
Months in which interviews are held	• January–March
Proportion of overseas students	• 16%
Proportion of mature students	• 5%
Proportion of graduate students	• 4%
Faculty's view of students taking a gap year	• Encouraged for those wishing to gain work experience, voluntary work or travel
Proportion of students taking intercalated degrees	• 10%
Possibility of direct entrance to clinical phase	• Yes but only for dentists wishing to gain a medical degree for Maxillo-Facial career
Fees for overseas students	• £11,400 pa for years 1 and 2 • £21,300 pa for years 3, 4 and 5
Fees for graduates	• In 2005: £1658 pa for years 1 and 2 • In 2005: £2848 pa for years 3, 4 and 5 2006 fees tbc
Ability to transfer to other medical schools	• This option is not encouraged because of the integration of course
Assistance for elective funding	• Yes, although applications with projects are more successful than those for clinical attachments
Assistance for travel to attachments	• Shuttle buses and coaches are provided for some attachments but not others. In addition, students can apply through their LEA
Access and hardship funds	• Yes. See http://www.leeds.ac.uk/welfare/access.html
Weekly rent	• £50–95 (halls) • £50–75 (private)
Pint of lager	• £1.40 Union • £2.50 city centre pubs
Cinema	• £3–£5
Nightclub	• £3–£6

Leicester

Key facts	Undergraduate	Graduate
Course length	5 years	4 years
Total number of medical undergraduates	1000	171
Applicants in 2005	2000	450
Interviews given in 2005	1400	250
Places available in 2005	175	64
Places available in 2006	175	64
Open days 2006	5 July	
Entrance requirements	AAB	2:1 in health science degree
Mandatory subjects	A in Chemistry	–
Male:female ratio	50:50	
Is an exam included in the selection process? If yes, what form does this exam take?	No UKCAT in 2007	No UKCAT in 2007
Qualification gained	MBChB	

Fascinating fact: The university administration building used to be an asylum.

Leicester is a young medical school whose first students graduated in 1980. It is a friendly place, with teaching for phase I on the university campus in the Maurice Shock Building (MSB), around 15 minutes' walk from the city centre. Most halls are further out in one of the nicer areas of Leicester, and have beautiful gardens. The later phases of the course are largely based at the Clinical Sciences Building (CSB). This is part of Leicester Royal Infirmary and is also close to the city centre. The Students' Union provides many good nights out, with a wide range of alternative nightlife and other events organised by the medical student society (including balls, outings, and skiing trips).

In 2003, the 5-year course in Leicester was joined by a new 4-year course in medicine for health science graduates. The 4-year accelerated course is the second of the Leicester–Warwick Medical Schools programmes to offer graduates a specialised programme of study.

Approximately 10% of students on the 5-year course are mature students and there is a good representation of international students from a variety of countries.

Education

In common with most other medical schools, Leicester has largely done away with the traditional preclinical/clinical divide. The 5-year course is now separated into two phases, each lasting 2½ years. Phase I is taught in the MSB and is structured around tutorials and lectures. There is, however, an introduction to clinical skills and you are let loose on wards in November of year 2. Anatomy is taught using dissection and prosections. Phase II is mainly clinical, with ward teaching in different specialties, and includes an elective period in March of year 4. Progression between the two phases is subject to passing examinations.

The graduate course at Leicester has just admitted its second intake of 64 health science graduates. The students include nurses, physiotherapists, radiographers and psychology graduates to name but a few. Ages range from early twenties to early forties. Most students reside in Leicester but some commute.

The first 18 months (phase I) of the course covers the same material as the first 2½ years of the 5-year course. This makes the course intense but rewarding. Formal teaching time is around 25–30 hours per week plus your own self-directed learning time. The intensity of the timetable makes doing paid work difficult, although there is one long summer break at the end of year 1. Exams take place in January and June, and clinical contact starts in January of year 1. Phase II (clinical phase) of the course sees the 4- and 5- year programmes merge.

In written examinations, extra time is given to those with specific educational needs such as dyslexia.

Teaching

For Phase I, teaching students are placed in a group of eight for tutorial work and will remain with this group throughout the phase. Four tutorial groups share a room and tutor. Phase II teaching is on the wards, but it is backed by some lectures in the form of an academic half-day each week. Students are placed with a clinical partner of choice and attendance is registered and contributes to passing each clinical attachment. There are 13 8-week blocks, which rotate through disciplines and include an elective. For each block, the pair of clinical students is attached to two consultant teams of different specialities.

Assessment

Module examinations are mainly written short-answer questions or assessed essays. There is a 15-station objective structured clinical and practical exam (OSCPE) at the end of semester two. Assessment in phase II includes patient portfolios (case studies) and clinical skills (histories and examinations); students also receive formative grading from their consultants on completion of each clinical attachment to help assess their progress. Finals have a clinical component and written examinations.

Intercalated degrees

Any student wishing to do an Honours year is encouraged to do so. Honours degrees can be science based or clinical and there are a wide range of subjects to choose from, usually comprising either a research project within the Faculty of Medicine, or more rarely students may join the final year of a course within the Faculty of Medicine and Biological Sciences to pursue further study. Students have the option of intercalating after either the second or third year of study assuming their academic performance is good enough.

Special study modules and electives

All students have a 2-month elective module, which can be carried out in the UK or abroad and which takes place during March of year 4.

Two special study modules (SSMs) are taken in phase I, and one in phase II. It is compulsory to study one science SSM, although other subjects such as languages are available for the second.

Erasmus

Leicester has recently entered the MedSIN/IFMSA exchange programme which is organised by the MedSIN National Officer for Professional Exchanges. This allows clinical students to switch places directly with a foreign student for a 4-week period. There is no promotion of this scheme and it relies on interested students to contact the relevant people. Furthermore, there is an opportunity in year 3 to spend 10 weeks on a short Erasmus exchange to Germany. Some knowledge of the native language is advisable when applying for Erasmus programmes. A disadvantage is that upon returning from exchanges in December, students must sit the phase I examination in January. However, the staff are supportive if asked for help with revision. Plans are being considered to move the Erasmus programmes to the clinical phase of the course in future years.

Facilities

Library The main university library is on campus, near to the MSB, and is open until midnight Monday–Friday and until 6 PM Saturday and 9 PM on Sundays. There are also medical libraries at the three main teaching hospitals. The CSB library at the Leicester Royal Infirmary is the largest of these and opens 24 hours, making it popular around examination times! It is staffed between 9 AM and 10 PM on weekdays. The staffed hours are shorter on Saturday (9 AM–6 PM) and Sunday (2 PM–9 PM).

Computers There are computer facilities for all university students on the main campus in the main library, Charles Wilson and Kenneth Edwards buildings. The MSB has a computer room for medical students, which has recently been refitted with new computers. There are also PCs available at the clinical sciences libraries at all three University Hospitals of Leicester sites. Course work (case studies and essays) must be word-processed. The medical school is gradually introducing on-line assessments in some modules.

Clinical skills Clinical skills at Leicester begin during year 1 of study. This initially takes the form of interviewing 'simulated patients' as well as practising physical examination skills on volunteers. These skills are examined at the end of year 1 in the form of OSCPEs. This progresses in year 2 to clinical placements one morning per week in one of the Leicester hospitals, where the skills learnt in year 1 are revised and put into practice.

Welfare

Student support

Each tutor group is allocated a personal tutor; these are nominated faculty members with a pastoral role. Overall, the faculty staff at the MSB are very approachable and supportive. Each hospital has a student facilitator to deal with queries and problems. There is always a member of staff available (24 hours) if there are any major problems or emergencies. Leicester University has a self-referral counselling service and the university Nightline offers support and guidance to students (including telephone numbers for taxis and late night food delivery!). Most areas of the medical school and university have standard disabled access facilities, such as ramps and lifts. Anyone with specific requirements would be advised to check with the university.

Accommodation

University accommodation is available throughout the degree, and some medical students stay in university accommodation beyond the first year. In the first year it is popular – and advisable – to live in catered halls, as there are loads of activities and great end-of-term balls and parties. Privately rented accommodation is inexpensive but variable in quality. It is best to shop around in advance for a good deal. A union-run accommodation office can help you find places and there are many notices on the medical school notice boards for house shares.

Placements

Phase I is based on the university campus in the MSB, and phase II is based in the Robert Kilpatrick Building at the Leicester Royal Infirmary (LRI). The LRI is only a 10-minute walk from the MSB, and everything is in reasonable proximity. Teaching also takes place at the Leicester General and Glenfield General Hospitals, which are both a short bus ride or, for the energetic, a cycle ride away. There is no student parking available at either the university or the LRI, but there is plenty of free parking at either Glenfield or the General. The medical school is currently undergoing an investment programme that will see a new multidisciplinary medical sciences teaching building being built with an expected opening date in 2008. In addition, district general hospitals (DGHs) are used in Kettering, Northampton, Boston, Lincoln, Burton-on-Trent and Peterborough, where free accommodation is provided. GP attachments are in Leicester and the surrounding area, with the furthest away being in Rugby.

Location of clinical placement/name of hospital	Distance away from medical school (miles)	Difficulty getting there on public transport*
Leicester Royal Infirmary	0.5	🚶
Leicester General Hospital	2.5	🚶 🚌
Peterborough District Hospital	40	🚗
Pilgrim Hospital, Boston	65	🚗 💡
Queens Hospital, Burton-on-Trent	34	🚗

* 🚶: walking/cycling distance; 🚌: use public transport; 🚗: need own car or lift; 💡: get up early – tricky to get to!

Sports and social

City life

The city centre is about a 45-minute walk from halls, or 10–15 minutes from the university campus. There is a regular bus service between halls, the town centre, and the university during term time and a student bus pass available to buy giving discounted travel. A good range of cinemas, a theatre, pubs, clubs, bars, and shops manages to reflect the city's diverse ethnicity. There are plenty of restaurants, and curry lovers in particular have a wide choice. There are popular clubs in town and late bars to suit all tastes. Many top bands come to Leicester on tour visiting De Montfort Hall and De Montfort University. The 'Charlotte' is also a renowned venue for smaller events and is frequented by several popular bands. Leicester has all the facilities of a city as well as some of the homeliness and friendliness of a smaller town.

The city is reasonably small, but has all the shops you could want. There is an excellent fruit, veg and fish market for fresh food (cheaper than the supermarkets). If you have your own transport, the Leicestershire countryside is attractive and makes a pleasant escape from the city. There is first division football and world-class rugby on the doorstep.

University life

At the Students' Union there are club nights every Wednesday, Thursday, Friday, and some Saturdays. There are also university events at local clubs – such as the exotically named Zanzibar – every week. The Redfearn bar is open all day weekdays and food is available – it proves a popular place to relax after lectures or exams. 'Elements', which is found in the union building is open from 10 AM serving coffees and snacks. LUSUMA arrange social events every term, such as Halloween parties, a medics' revue, a 'Stars in their Eyes' show and an annual medics' ball. There is a large variety of university societies to choose from, you will be spoilt for choice and it is a great way to meet students from other courses. Many medical students are involved with university societies. The university provides safe transport for all students with its night mini buses, which take students from the campus to anywhere within the city limits. The buses run from approximately 6 PM in the winter (7 PM in summer) until the union closes at 2 AM. There is a minibus card available to buy which gets you a 'free ride', or each journey currently costs £1.

Sports life

Medical students have the opportunity to join University sporting teams (of which there are many) as well as the wide range of medic sporting teams available. Thanks to team captains and the sporting secretaries there have been vast improvements in recent years in the organisation of the teams. Many teams receive sponsorship from local businesses. There are often sports days at home and away against other medical schools. The university has sports fields at Stoughton Road, two sports halls, two gyms, where there are circuits and aerobic classes, and an athletics track. There are plenty of swimming pools in town, or one near the university halls in Oadby. The medical school adheres (during phase I) to the nonscheduling of afternoon lessons on Wednesdays when matches take place. Due to timetabling commitments the 4-year course students are not released from teaching on Wednesday afternoons.

> **Top tip:** Hold off buying all the text books on the reading lists until you have seen what the years above have to offer. Or checking out http://www.unilot.co.uk for student auctions on books and equipment.

Great things about Leicester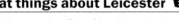

- Students and staff are friendly and welcoming.
- There are wide-ranging activities available for all organised by LUSUMA, the Students' Union, and other societies.
- Great improvement in Leicester's nightlife in recent years, with many new bars, clubs, and restaurants for varying tastes.
- Leicester was ranked number 1 in the 'Guardian' teaching league tables in 2003.
- Clear module objectives to assist with self-directed learning.

Bad things about Leicester

- The location of placements can present you with travel problems.
- Lack of temperature control in lecture theatres.
- Phase II students are spread about the region.
- Not near the sea – in fact, Leicester is about as far from the sea as it is possible to be.
- No student car parking at the University and Leicester Royal Infirmary.

Further information

Dr Kevin West
Maurice Shock Medical Sciences Building
Leicester University
University Road
Leicester LE1 9HN
Tel: 0116 252 2969/2985
Fax: 0116 252 3013
Email: med-admis@le.ac.uk
Web: http://www.le.ac.uk/medicine

Additional application information

Average A-level requirements	• AAB
Average Scottish Higher requirements	• AAB
Graduate entry requirements	• 2:1 in health science discipline
Make-up of interview panel	• One senior staff, one final year medical student
Months in which interviews are held	• November–February
Proportion of overseas students	• 5%
Proportion of mature students	• Not known
Proportion of graduate students	• Not known
Faculty's view of students taking a gap year	• Neutral
Proportion of students taking intercalated degrees	• 10%
Possibility of direct entrance to clinical phase	• No
Fees for overseas students	• Please contact university for details
Fees for graduates	• £3000 pa
Ability to transfer to other medical schools	• Transfers to other medical schools are not encouraged, but if necessary are allowed
Assistance for elective funding	• There is a £250 interest-free loan which all students are eligible to apply for towards electives. Students are also able to apply for £100 bursary
Assistance for travel to attachments	• Not available
Access and hardship funds	• Administered through the university welfare service. Students are required to fill in an application form which is submitted to an assessment panel. The panel meets every week and so decisions can be made rapidly
Weekly rent	• £51–£90
Pint of lager	• £1.90–£2.20 with many promotions, meaning available a lot cheaper the majority of the time
Cinema	• £4.50 with NUS card
Nightclub	• Generally offer free entry before 10.30 PM weekdays. Thereafter £5–£7. Student nights in the week often only cost £2–£3

Liverpool

Key facts	Undergraduate	Graduate
Course length	5 years	4 years
Total number of medical undergraduates	1402	94
Applicants in 2005	1988	650
Interviews given in 2005	1033	90
Places available in 2005	283	32
Places available in 2006	292	32
Open days 2006	29 March	29 March
Entrance requirements	AABB	BBB and 2:1 degree in life sciences or health sciences
Mandatory subjects	Biology and chemistry	Biology and chemistry
Male:female ratio	40:60	28:72
Is an exam included in the selection process? If yes, what form does this exam take?	No	No
Qualification gained	MBChB	

Fascinating fact: The Liverpool Medics Students Society is the oldest in the country and its current record for downing a yard of ale is only 12 seconds!!

In 1996 Liverpool Medical School introduced a brand new curriculum, in accordance with GMC guidelines. So far it is proving to be a success. August 2001 saw the first PBL (problem-based learning) students to graduate from Liverpool starting on wards as preregistration house officers (PRHOs). The school is growing in size with around 1200 undergraduates and the introduction of the new graduate entry programme, but a strong Medical Students' Society ensures there's always a friendly face around. The city is the European Capital of Culture for 2008 – a well deserved honour – which has bought massive investment and is helping to continue to transform this great city. In the words of Roger McGough a local Liverpool poet – 'I used to have to defend the city, but now the city speaks for itself'.

Liverpool

191

Education

Since the introduction of the new PBL course, subjects are no longer taught in lecture theatres day in, day out: instead different areas of medicine are presented to students as problems to research for themselves. Students discuss the issues and formulate learning objectives in small groups with tutor guidance, then go and research the topics independently. From the beginning of year 2 an increasing proportion of time is spent on hospital and community attachments. Studies follow the human lifecycle, from conception and birth through adulthood and into old age.

Teaching

The new course contains little in the way of formal teaching. In the first 2 years, plenaries (lectures) are given that are designed to provide an overview only of each problem, in a newly built state-of-the-art lecture theatre (plenary theatre?!). Anatomy is demonstrated using models and prosections in a recently refurbished and improved multimillion pound Human Anatomy Resource Centre. Clinical skills and communication skills are taught throughout the course.

During the clinical years, teaching is arranged during hospital placements with excellent standards in a variety of bedside and small group teaching in addition to ward rounds and clinics. The teaching main hospitals are well respected centres of excellence at the cutting edge of modern research and practice.

The new graduate entry course provides an accelerated course for graduates in which the first 2 years of the traditional course are merged into one.

Assessment

Assessment is continuous, designed so that everything you learn (including practical skills) will be recognised and recorded. Formative exams occur at the end of each year for the first four years, with no exams in the final year! The final year comprises five, 8-week rotations consisting of two selectives plus general practice, emergency medicine and shadowing designed to prepare students for the realities of the house job. Consultant assessment of performance takes place at the end of each of the rotations.

Intercalated degrees

It is possible to study for an intercalated degree at the end year 4 in a wide variety of subjects with BSc, BA or Masters Degrees available dependent on the course taken. It is possible to transfer to undertake the degree and then return to complete the medical course at Liverpool. Limited funding is available to some students wishing to study for an intercalated year.

Special study modules and electives

There are five 4-week SSMs spread through the first 4 years of the course covering a wide range of subjects. The fifth special study module (SSM) in year 3 allows a more in-depth study of a topic lasting one day a week for two-thirds of the year, providing the opportunity for students to arrange their own module. Topics from any specialty can be chosen, with a 2500 word essay for each module. Some students are able to get their work published in medical journals.

In addition, in the final year there are the two SAMPs – selectives in advanced medical practice. These are 8-week placements taken as part of the final year, spent in a specialty chosen by the student.

The elective takes place at the end of year 3 from June to the start of September. This is widely regarded as the most exciting prospect of most medical students' courses. Applications are aided by a wide network of contacts all over the world.

Erasmus

Two exchange schemes – Socrates and Erasmus – allow students to study at a participating European medical school for a period of 16 weeks during the final year. Current exchanges are set up with schools in France, Spain, Germany, Holland, and Sweden. The scheme has recently been expanded to include Eastern European countries.

Facilities

Library A short-loan system operates for the books most in demand. The library is open until 9.30 PM most weekdays and 5 PM at weekends (if you feel the need!!). All hospitals in which students have placements have their own libraries with varying borrowing arrangements. The books stocked are directly influenced by the demands of the students so the latest books are always available complemented by an increasing array of electronic resources and journals.

Computers The university and hospitals have ample 24-hour computer facilities available for students, with free use of email and the internet. Free work-related printing is available for students at some of the hospitals.

Clinical skills One of the real highlights of the new course has been the introduction of the clinical skills centre, where students are able to master a whole range of practical clinical skills, from taking blood and suturing wounds to advanced life support. There are weekly sessions in year 1, with an objective structured clinical examination (OSCE) at the end of the year.

Welfare

Student support

Students generally mix well and there are good relations within and between year groups. There is a long-standing mentoring system set up by the LMSS (Liverpool Medical Students Society), so that each first-year student is given a second- or third-year 'tutor'. The role of the tutor is to introduce the fresher to the joys of all aspects of medical school life in Liverpool. In recent years Liverpool has enjoyed a very constructive and student-friendly atmosphere within the faculty. In addition to facilities provided by LMSS, the Students' Union has the standard welfare and counselling services.

Accommodation

Most students only live in university accommodation for their first year. This is a good opportunity to meet other students, but it is more expensive than renting privately. There is a wide variation in the standard of private accommodation, but there is plenty of choice. The university has no input into regulating the private sector, but the accommodation office can offer advice.

Placements

Liverpool University was the original redbrick university. The campus dominates a large area adjacent to the city centre. The main University Hospital is adjacent to the university campus, and the medical school is well placed near to all the main university and hospital departments.

The medical school is part of a large teaching hospital, the Royal Liverpool University Hospital. In addition the city boasts the largest specialist Women's (LWH) and Children's (Alder Hey) hospitals in the country, plus the Cardiothoracic Centre, University Hospital Aintree and the School of Tropical Medicine.

Students are also placed in local district general hospitals (DGHs) – all of which have high standards of teaching and are very popular with many students. In year 4, some students spend the year in Lancaster or Barrow. General practice and community placements are spread throughout the course.

Location of clinical placement/ name of hospital	Distance away from medical school (miles)	Difficulty getting there on public transport*
Royal Liverpool Hospital	0	🚶
Alder Hey	3	🚶 🚌
Whiston	10	🚶 🚌
Chester	25	🚗
Lancaster	70	💡

* 🚶: walking/cycling distance; 🚌 : use public transport; 🚗: need own car or lift; 💡 : get up early – tricky to get to!

Sports and social

City life

Liverpool is a thriving multicultural city. It extends a warm welcome to students. It is a proud city, with its world-famous accent, sense of humour, two cathedrals, football teams and maritime history. It was once the biggest port in the British Empire. Having fallen on hard times in the 1970s and 1980s, Liverpool is now very much on the up and investment in the city has never been higher! Many students, from all courses, stay in the area after graduation.

The medical school and the student residential areas are well placed for all the attractions and are adjacent to the many surprisingly beautiful parks within the city. Like many other cities there is crime about, but a common sense approach will ensure that the good times aren't spoilt. Police statistics show that Liverpool is, in fact, one of the safest cities in the UK.

Liverpool has an excellent social life – with every taste catered for, excellent pubs, several cinemas, sports complexes and nightclubs of all hues. It has a great sporting tradition and is home of the Grand National steeplechase, two premiership football clubs and numerous other great sporting teams. It is also the birthplace of the little known band *The Beatles* and the Cavern club still thrives with Beatle-maniacs. The city is only a short distance from Manchester, North Wales, Chester, and the Lake District.

University life

The LMSS is a major plus for studying medicine in Liverpool. It covers all aspects of medical student life, from interaction with the faculty to weekly meetings with guest speakers. There are regular balls, dinners, and social parties, as well as the medics' own orchestra, choir, sports teams, play, and the annual Smoking concert. The university also offers a wide range of societies. LMSS has its own website at http://www.lmssonline.co.uk. There is also a very active and expanding branch of MedSIN.

Sports life

The Medical Society has football, rugby, hockey, netball, basketball, squash, badminton, and cricket teams. Recent additions to the sports teams include Chinese martial arts and a celebrated tiddlywinks team! The university has all these and more. The university sports hall, complete with swimming pool, has recently been renovated.

> **Top tip:** Some of the events at the students' guild in the first week are basically the normal nights at three–four times the price! Explore the city nightlife instead which will have plenty of introductory student offers on.

Great things about Liverpool

- The PBL course is self-directed and self-motivated and allows you to adapt your learning to your pace. During the early years this allows students to make time to pursue other interests – in effect, the course is on flexitime.
- Students have a real say in the course at Liverpool and course organisers are receptive to their suggestions.
- The course prepares students to work effectively as PRHOs through early patient contact and clinical skills training.
- A diverse syllabus allows all aspects of medicine and those affected by illness to be appreciated.
- The LMSS provides a strong backbone to all activities in Liverpool Medical School, from academic issues to social and welfare issues.

Bad things about Liverpool

- The necessary approach to course work at Liverpool can be very different from A-level studies: PBL is not for people who want to be spoon-fed in lectures.
- Hospital placements can be some distance from Liverpool, and travelling by public transport can be time-consuming and expensive.
- The Medical Student Society President traditionally strips at the Freshers' Initiation ceremony – which is never a pretty sight!
- The social life within the medical school can be so good that sometimes it is difficult to get to know students from other courses.
- The weather – it can be cold and wet, particularly in winter.

Further information

Admissions Administrator
Faculty of Medicine
2nd floor Duncan Building
Daulby Street
Liverpool L69 3GA
Tel: 0151 706 4266
Fax: 0151 706 5667
Email: mbchb@liv.ac.uk
Web: http://www.liv.ac.uk

Additional application information

Average A-level requirements	• AABB
Average Scottish Higher requirements	• AAABB and two Advanced Highers in biology and chemistry
Make-up of interview panel	• Two interviewers
Months in which interviews are held	• November–March (undergraduate) January–February (graduate)
Proportion of overseas students	• 8%
Proportion of mature students	• 4%
Proportion of graduate students	• 6%
Faculty's view of students taking a gap year	• Acceptable
Proportion of students taking intercalated degrees	• 10%
Possibility of direct entrance to clinical phase	• No
Fees for overseas students	• £16,250 pa
Fees for graduates	• Please contact university for details
Ability to transfer to other medical schools	• A supportive faculty will try their best to facilitate any transfer if there are exceptional circumstances
Assistance for elective funding	• Limited number of bursaries available, which are allocated based on the elective by the Faculty. Of course your bank is always there!
Assistance for travel to attachments	• Only through LEA, nothing specific available
Access and hardship funds	• Guild is supportive in applications although remember to keep all those bank statements, it may be the only way to pay for your elective
Weekly rent	• £40 in the main student areas • £60 if you prefer the comfort of the increasingly popular purpose-built student flats
Pint of lager	• £1 (Raz) • £1.20 (AJ – on campus) • £2 Concert Square and Albert Docks
Cinema	• £4 at local Odeon and UGC plus an excellent art house cinema FACT newly opened
Nightclub	• Numerous new clubs and bars in the city centre and docks which cater for all the tastes plus the old favourites like the Raz

Manchester, Keele and Preston

Key facts	Premedical	Undergraduate
Course length	6 years	5 years
Total number of medical undergraduates	20	1977
Applicants in 2005	407	2701
Interviews given in 2005	42	1022
Places available in 2005	20	336
Places available in 2006	20	340
Open days 2006	Three – please contact university for details	Three – please contact university for details
Entrance requirements	ABB	AAB
Mandatory subjects	Three arts subjects or two arts subjects and one science subject	A-level chemistry and one other science
Male:female ratio	1:1.25	1:1.25
Is an exam included in the selection process? If yes, what form does this exam take?	Yes, BMAT UKCAT in 2007	Yes UKCAT in 2007
Qualification gained	MBChB	

Fascinating fact: Kellogg's cornflakes, Patak's curry sauce and Boddington's beer are all made in Manchester.

Medicine has been taught in Manchester since the early 19th century. The city plays host to the University of Manchester, the Manchester Metropolitan University (MMU), and the University of

Manchester Institute of Science and Technology (UMIST). The University of Manchester and UMIST are set to merge to create the largest university in the UK, with the size and resources to compete on a global scale.

As a result there is a student population of over 50,000. The merger will mean world-class teaching and research equal to only a handful of UK institutions, and the new institution will compete with the best in the world. The medical school is part of the University of Manchester and is the second largest in the UK. The campus is located in the heart of a busy cosmopolitan city.

Manchester was the first UK school to introduce the systems-based, problem-based learning (PBL) curriculum, following the publication of the GMC document Tomorrow's Doctors, and has over 8 years' experience in PBL. Although a preclinical/clinical divide exists, the basic sciences are studied within a clinical framework of patient cases, which are used to direct learning each week. The newly implemented 'early experience' scheme will also ensure that students have some clinical contact from year 1. Manchester is unique in that students are joined in year 3 by an intake of students from St Andrew's. In addition, students may choose to undertake part or all of their training at the new teaching centre of Keele.

Preston, a base hospital of the Lancashire Teaching Hospital NHS Trust, welcomed its first group of year 3 students in September 2003. This new base hospital is a permanent addition to the Manchester Medical Schools and will provide additional medical education posts in the north west.

Education

The course is 5 years long, with two preclinical years followed by three clinical. The preclinical course is structured around weekly cases that are studied through a mixture of group discussion, practical anatomy and pathology laboratories, computer skills sessions, lecture theatre events, and personal study. The course is organised into four semesters, so that cases relate to the four themes of nutrition and metabolism, cardiorespiratory medicine, abilities and disabilities, and lifecycle. Years 3 and 4 continue the case-based approach in a clinical setting, and the four themes are repeated. Four days per week are spent in one of the five teaching hospitals, and 1 day per week in general practice surgery. Year 5 works on a four-block rotation system, whereby an equal number of students will be on an elective, at a teaching hospital, a district general hospital, or in the community at any one time. Because of the high attendance demands on final-year students, free hospital accommodation is provided during attachments, which allows students to shadow house officers and gain practical experience to prepare them for their preregistration house jobs.

The Premedical Programme, lasting 1 year, is available for those who do not have the required science qualifications for entry into year 1, but have achieved good A-levels grades in mainly arts subjects. Around 20 students are taken onto this programme yearly with entry to the next year of the medical course automatic on satisfactory completion. The programme is problem-based, in line with that offered in subsequent years. The patient case studies will include the relevant areas of physics, chemistry, biology and mathematics.

Students can apply to enrol on the European Studies Option during the first semester of year 1. Linguistic ability is required to A or AS-level standard or equivalent in French, German or Spanish. During years 1–4, language skills will be maintained and enhanced by weekly tuition in the selected language. For students following this option, there is the opportunity to study in a European country during one of the special study modules in years 3 or 4, and in year 5 a 16-week placement will be undertaken at one of our partner universities in Europe. Our current European partners include the University of Rennes (France), Faculte de Medecine Xavier Bichat (France), University of Saarland (Germany), University of Lausanne (Switzerland) and University of Hannover (Germany). Good working relationships with these universities have been established over a number of years and it is known that students receive a good quality educational experience on their placements. Further partnerships in France and Spain are being explored with links being created with a teaching institution in Alicante.

Selection criteria information is on the website. Selection is based on application and interview. Resits are considered but students are advised to have applied to Manchester the first time.

Teaching

Year 1 and 2 teaching focuses on a weekly case study with supplementary group discussions, lectures and practical sessions; including microscopy, basic clinical skills, computational skills, and anatomy sessions using cadavers. Manchester offers hands-on demonstrator-led dissection supplemented by prosections. Students work in PBL groups to create and subsequently discuss weekly learning objectives; these are fulfilled in their own time with the aid of the above resources.

Years 3, 4, and 5 continue to base teaching around a case setting, but students now fulfil learning objectives within a clinical setting. Whereas in year 1 the study objectives in the case of a person with lung cancer would involve learning about the pathology of lung cancers from a textbook and pathology specimens, in clinical years students would have the opportunity to attend chest clinics and talk to and examine people with the actual disease. In the clinical years, students also receive bedside teaching. In years 3 and 4 there is a maximum of 12 students per firm. Unfortunately, it is not uncommon for sessions to be cancelled, or for sessions to be rescheduled owing to patient commitments of the medical staff.

Assessment

In years 1 and 2 there are exams at the end of each of the four semesters. They comprise multiple choice questions (MCQs) and a slide-based exam forming one component and two papers on clinical case studies forming the second component. There is also an exam which requires the interpretation of scientific prose into lay language and summarising a scientific publication, an objective structured skills examination (OSSE) and a computer skills exam. At the end of each semester groups are assessed and marked for communication skills and teamwork. For those studying the 'European option' there are weekly lessons with homework and yearly exams.

Assessment in years 3 and 4 occurs twice a year and consists of a progress test (single best answer format) and an objective structured clinical examination (OSCE). The OSCE sees students rotate through up to 15 5-minute stations, where they are presented with various tasks and challenges appropriate to the area they are being assessed upon. For example, students may be asked to interpret laboratory results, examine patients, or deal with ethically challenging situations. In the final year, students take one set of exams in May comprising an OSCE, a patient management paper (PMP) and a final true/false paper.

Intercalated degrees

Intercalated BSc (or MSc) courses are offered at the end of years 2 and 4. There is a wide range of basic bioscience subjects available to study, as well as more unusual subjects such as health care ethics and law, and history of medicine, which have proved extremely popular over recent years. Students can choose to intercalate at another institution (including Keele), but only in a subject not offered at Manchester.

Traditionally, students wishing to intercalate would have been expected to have an above-average academic record, but the faculty encourages access to any student wishing to intercalate. Some funding, including bursaries, is available and is allocated according to academic merit. Some scholarships are also available from businesses, depending on the subject studied.

Special study modules and electives

In years 1 and 2 there is one 4-week special study module (SSM) per year, whereas in years 3 and 4 there are two per year. These modules can be on practically anything, and there is talk of allowing students to do one SSM in a topic unrelated to medicine to encourage the pursuit of other hobbies and interests. Another point to note is that in the clinical years one of the SSMs must be in a district general hospital (DGH) and one in the community.

Many students do SSMs at Preston; the Families and Children module has been run at Preston for several years now. Both Chorley and South Ribble DGH have a good record in providing year 5 placements in hospital and community for the Preston course.

In the final year there is an elective period, where students are encouraged to go abroad to appreciate medical education in a foreign health care setting. The elective officially lasts 8 weeks, but students often piggyback their time on to an adjacent holiday such as Christmas to increase their time away. Students cover costs for electives, so a great deal of organisation and planning is often needed. In addition, a report must be submitted upon returning to Manchester.

Erasmus

Overseas students Socrates-Erasmus students are selected by the home university. Students must first approach the Erasmus coordinator at the International Centre at their own university where they will be provided with an application form/learning agreement and a copy of their Study Abroad Handbook containing details of the Manchester course. Alternatively, forms can be requested from the European Officer. Manchester University does not accept 'free-movers', i.e. students moving outside an Erasmus agreement – such students must apply as an EU Visiting Student.

Students should have a high level of English sufficient to follow courses alongside UK students. The Cambridge Certificate of Proficiency in English is recommended.

Tuition fees are waived for incoming Erasmus students. For living expenses it is suggested that students will need about £623 per month to cover accommodation, food, travel in the UK and essential items.

Full year students are guaranteed a place in University housing as long as they apply before the deadline.

UK students Eligible Manchester students are offered the chance to pursue the 'European option'. Students who successfully complete this element of the course are awarded a degree which recognises their medical training in the context of a foreign language and health care system. Uniquely to Manchester, at the end of year 4 students undertake a 12-week research project. Students are allocated a supervisor and have the opportunity to pursue a topic that particularly interests them. This period provides an excellent introduction to medical research, and allows students to get to grips with medical statistics. Some students even go on to have their work published. Students may also interrupt the course to complete a PhD.

Facilities

Library The Medical Faculty library is well equipped with the basic textbooks, but demand is high and it is often busy. It is open 9 AM–8 PM during term time, weekdays only. The John Rylands University Library across the road stocks most of the major journals. This library is open from 9 AM–9.30 PM weekdays, and 9 AM–6 PM and 1 PM–6 PM on Saturday and Sunday, respectively. The opening hours in holiday times are shorter. Hospital libraries vary in size and standard.

Computers There are excellent computer facilities in the medical school and John Rylands Library, with internet access and email for all. A number of computer-assisted learning (CAL) programs are available, and computer laboratories in the medical school are open from 9 AM–7 PM. Hospitals have computer and email facilities as do the computer cluster in Fallowfield student village and Manchester Computer Centre on Oxford Road.

Clinical skills More and more emphasis is being placed on the use of skills laboratories, and facilities in the clinical years of the course are being improved. There has been a tremendous influx of cash into the skills laboratories over the past 2 years and there is a variety of mannequins for practising CPR, injections, blood taking, and so forth, and video resources on clinical skills. Students are required to buy stethoscopes by the start of year 3.

Welfare 🏠

Student support

Faculty staff are approachable and student feedback is consistently encouraged. Elected student representatives sit on all major faculty committees, but have in the past complained about a lack of clarity of communication from the medical school. Three staff–student liaison meetings are held in each academic year, which give an opportunity for students to raise issues close to their hearts. Good relationships between students and tutors are fostered through tutorials. Students are also allocated a member of staff who acts as a pastoral tutor, and a mentor from the year above to act as

Bad things about Imperial

- The course is highly academic – however, expect the demands to be great and the rewards high.
- Travel between sites adds to the expense of studying and can be stressful.
- Split teaching at different sites can divide up the year group.
- Imperial College is sometimes pictured as boring and academic. However, that's **not** the medics!
- Expensive, polluted, overpopulated, time-consuming, dirty old London …

Further information

School of Medicine
Imperial College
London SW7 2AZ
Tel: 020 7594 8001
Fax: 020 7594 8004
Email: admitmed@imperial.ac.uk
Web: http://www.med.imperial.uk
Students' Union website: http://www.icsmsu.com

social support. There are both faculty and Students' Union-based counselling services, which are highly regarded.

Accommodation

University accommodation is guaranteed for first-year students, and although most students choose to move into the private sector after this, many do stay. Halls may be catered or self-catering, and vary in price and standard. There is a lot of private sector accommodation, ranging in price from £37–£60 per week. Most accommodation is within a short bus ride from the University and town centre. The past few years have also seen the rise of a number of large commercial accommodation blocks aimed at students, a number of which offer rooms with *en suite* facilities, and even onsite gyms and swimming pools!

Placements

In years 3 and 4, 4 days per week are spent at the base hospital and 1 day in the community. However, as in most other medical schools, getting to and from placements can be very time consuming without a car. In theory, base hospitals (excluding Keele and Preston) are all within 45 minutes of the university by public transport.

Location of clinical placement/ name of hospital	Distance away from medical school (miles)	Difficulty getting there on public transport*
Manchester Royal Infirmary	0	
Hope Hospital	6	
Wythenshawe Hospital	6	
Preston	39	
Keele	45	

* : walking/cycling distance; : use public transport; : need own car or lift; : get up early – tricky to get to!

Sports and social

City life

With such a huge student population, Manchester offers an endless choice of things to go and places to go. There is a wide variety of pubs, bars, clubs, stores, theatres, and restaurants, each with a different character, theme, or style. However the student holidays leave Manchester's nightspots noticeably less vibrant during the week, unlike London, for example.

The city is truly multicultural and there is a good mix of home, overseas, mature, and postgraduate students, as well as a vibrant gay and lesbian scene. For those interested in music or comedy, Manchester is a fantastic place to study. As well as the local scene, most of the big-name tours include Manchester gigs. However, should all the excitement get too much for you, the Peak District, Pennines, Lake District, and North Wales are not far away for a little peace and tranquillity, along with Liverpool, Leeds, and Sheffield!

University life

The Medical Students' Representative Council (MSRC) is the focus of medical school social life. The 12-strong committee is elected each year by students and organises a number of medics' events throughout the year, including the infamous 'pyjama pub crawl' and the annual winter ball. There are also year clubs, which organise trips, parties, and one graduation ball for each year. The medics' dramatics society organises an annual pantomime, and a revue. In addition, the medical school magazine *Mediscope* is published three times a year (on paper and the web) and provides a journalistic forum for the medical student population. The recent revival of Manchester's branch of MedSIN, the body bringing together the collaboration of international medical schools on global issues, has been a great benefit to Manchester Medical School.

Along with faculty events, a huge range of clubs and societies are run from Manchester Students' Union, which is opposite the medical school.

The campus has its own cultural attractions too: the internationally-renowned Whitworth Art Gallery, Contact Theatre and Manchester Museum. Students can drop in to gaze at a Hockney, marvel at ancient Egyptian mummies or see the best in contemporary theatre. Medical students normally take part in social gatherings in Rusholme – The Curry Mile, to introduce themselves and meet other medics for a 'PBL group curry'. It's a great way to get to know each other!

Sports life

Being home to the most famous football team in the world is only the start for Manchester. United's games can be a little pricey, Manchester City offers cut-price tickets to students for home games. This is probably a blessing in disguise, as the majority of locals living in the student areas are City fans! There is also a discount price for students at Sale Sharks Rugby Club.

Manchester's sports scene has seen huge benefits from the opening of many facilities built to cater for the 2002 Commonwealth Games, which has left a legacy of world-class sporting facilities. Developments include a campus-located Olympic swimming pool, as well as the creation of the national cycling, squash, and netball centres. The centrepiece of the Commonwealth Games is the 37,000-seat City of Manchester stadium, which in 2003 became the new home of Manchester City.

Within the medical school, Manchester has a thriving sporting community. There are medics' rugby, hockey, tennis, netball, rowing, and football teams, which actively encourage participation and socialising. The main university also has countless sports clubs, but medics tend to play for the medics' team if one exists in their sport. Most of the medics sport teams have an annual tour which is not to be missed.

Keele

The universities of Manchester and Keele won funding to provide training and education for undergraduate medics from October 2000 onwards, and also to establish the full 5-year course at Keele from September 2003. Keele University is a campus university situated in north Staffordshire, just outside Stoke-on-Trent, the home of Robbie Williams. The area is referred to as 'The Potteries' by the local inhabitants, reflecting its industrial background for the world famous production of pottery, including Wedgwood and Spode. In the past a major source of employment, but now a common source of the locals' health problems.

Students studying at Keele will undertake the Manchester medical course and therefore its details will not be repeated, except for subtle differences. Students who wish to study at Keele have the following options.

1 5-year course at Keele.
2 5-year course, with years 1 and 2 at Manchester and the final 3 years at Keele.
Currently students from St Andrews can also study at Keele after completion of the BSc course; however, the number of students from Manchester and St Andrews completing their clinical training in Keele will be reduced as of 2005. There is currently no premedical year option available at Keele.

All short-listed applicants will have a short 15-minute formal interview – no candidate will be offered a place without an interview. The applicant will be assessed on their UCAS personal statement, interview, intellectual achievements, skills (communication, teamwork, and so on) and other extracurricular activities. For more detail regarding selection criteria you are referred to the Keele School of Medicine web page: http://www.keele.ac.uk/dept/ms/undergrad.htm

An intercalated degree can be incorporated with either of the above options. A BSc can be taken at Keele. It may still be possible to intercalate in Manchester – it is presently possible to intercalate in London but special permission is required; it would only be granted if the BSc is not available locally. Depending on your choice of the study options listed above, you should apply to either Manchester or Keele. Students undertaking the full 5-year course at Keele will spend years 1 and 2 based primarily on the Keele campus site in the new, very well equipped, purpose-built Health Sciences complex.

Years 1 and 2 will spend the vast majority of their time on the Keele University campus. It is a large attractive campus university with restaurants, sports and social facilities, as well as library and academic buildings. Students are guaranteed accommodation on campus for their first year of study, currently costing about £53 per week.

The clinical years at Keele will be spent predominantly at the North Staffordshire NHS Hospital Trust, only 3 miles away from Keele. This is a very busy hospital offering the full range of clinical services and an excellent place to gain clinical experience. Also available on the hospital site is the new Clinical Education Centre (CEC), opened in September 2004. This attractive building is a multidisciplinary centre catering not only for medical students but for others including nursing and physiotherapy students. Within the building is the new Health Library with up-to-date IT facilities, excellent clinical skills labs and the usual seminar and lecture theatres. Students will also spend some time at Stafford and Shrewsbury District Hospitals, both of which have received additional funding to expand their resources for medical students, including education and accommodation. Keele is conscious that a medical course can be challenging and at times very stressful and have therefore – in addition to the standard university welfare services – provided a mentor system which students can choose to take advantage of. This involves each student being given a designated doctor in the local hospital or community who they can approach for support, advice or just a general chat. There is something similar for years 1 and 2, known as pastoral tutors.

Many students decide to live off-campus, especially during their clinical training, locally in Newcastle-under-Lyme or Stoke-on-Trent. The cost for private accommodation ranges from £28–£60 per week. The area offers a variety of shops, takeaways, bars, nightclubs and restaurants. There is also a gym 3 minutes from the hospital. Owing to the nature of the course students will spend time in the community during their GP and psychiatry placements. A car is very advantageous, but not essential as local public transport is adequate. Currently students are provided with free accommodation in year 5, on campus and at the DGHs depending on their placements.

The Keele/North Staffordshire area is ideally located as it is approximately halfway between Manchester and Birmingham, which are only minutes away by train. It is also located very close to Alton Towers; in fact a regular bus service is available from Stoke-on-Trent during the open season. The location is also ideal, as students can take advantage of the Manchester medic nights out, however for practical reasons it is advised that you make a few friends in Manchester so that you have somewhere to stay the night!

Keele has its own Medical School Committee run by elected year 3 students. It is responsible for representing the student body and organising social events, such as the ball. The students can also represent themselves through the staff/student committee meetings, both at Keele and Manchester.

Generally, the structure of the course and the assessments are the same for both Keele and Manchester students. Students in years 1 and 2 will find that there are slight differences between Manchester and Keele. Essentially both Manchester and Keele students in years 1 and 2 are doing the same course, but Keele is responsible for Keele students' admissions, exams, progress and so forth, and thus can make minor alterations without any difficulty. The first students for Keele and North Staffordshire arrived in October 2002, having started in Manchester and St Andrews in October 2000 and September 1999, respectively. Some students complained at being sent to Keele in year 3 after having studied at Manchester or St Andrews, so students must be aware of this possibility from day one to avoid confusion. Keele has an advantage in being a new medical school: the patients have not been exposed to endless interrogation by students and are therefore more than happy to help with our education, and the local consultants and staff in partner DGHs are extremely enthusiastic about teaching.

In 2007 Keele will 'break away' from Manchester and run independently with its very own medical course. Those students already at Keele will continue with the Manchester Medical degree, which they receive. The 'new' Keele students will receive a Keele Medical degree after undergoing a very different course which, as already mentioned, is in the process of production. Until 2007 at the earliest, Keele can only consider applications from UK and EU students.

Preston: Lancashire teaching hospitals

Preston forms part of the Lancashire teaching hospitals and was created in August 2002 by the merger of two well-established hospitals. Royal Preston Hospital has a long history and is now a modern building with good transport access. Chorley and South Ribble DGH was extensively rebuilt and enlarged in 1994. Both hospitals have an excellent record in providing placements for Manchester students.

Since September 2003, 30 places per annum have been available for Manchester students to study at the Lancashire teaching hospitals; from 2007 this will increase up to 80 places.

There is a modern education unit at the Chorley site and a new education and training unit under construction at Preston to provide state-of-the-art facilities for learning and teaching. Both centres will have excellent library and IT resources in addition to a well-provided clinical skills unit.

Student accommodation is available within a reasonable distance from the main base hospital at Preston. Access to Manchester is reasonable; journeys are 30–40 minutes by car. Trains are frequent and provide access to central Manchester in 30–40 minutes. Blackpool, Preston and Wigan have an active nightlife and Preston has a large student population linked to the University of Central Lancashire.

For further information Dr Simon Wallis, Director of Medical Education and Hospital Dean, may be contacted on 01257 245 600 or email simon.wallis@LTHTR.nhs.uk

Great things about Manchester

- Enthusiasm for medicine is maintained by a course that emphasises clinical problems from day 1.
- The faculty staff are very approachable and open to change. There are plenty of opportunities to give feedback on both course and staff.
- The social life is excellent. There are loads of events organised by the MSRC (Medical Students' Representative Council) and there is generally lots going on at reasonable prices.
- The sheer size of the multifaculty universities in Manchester and the 2002 Commonwealth Games has ensured top-level academic and sporting facilities.
- In year 3 a load of new people arrive from St Andrews, which spices things up a bit!

Bad things about Manchester

- Adjusting to self-directed learning can be difficult for some students who are used to being spoon-fed, although this is becoming the case at all UK schools with new courses.
- Differing interpretations of self-directed learning can often mean students perceive a lack of teaching.
- Some hospital placements are quite a distance away and can be difficult to reach on public transport.
- As with all major cities, Manchester does have a higher than average crime rate and insurance premiums can be high.

- Communication from the medical school is often lacking in clarity with students hearing about changes through rumour and speculation.
- It has a habit of raining!

Further information

Manchester
Ms L M Harding
Admissions Officer
Faculty of Medicine
Stopford Building
University of Manchester
Oxford Road
Manchester M13 9PT
Tel: 0161 306 0200 (general enquiries)
0161 275 5025 (undergraduate admissions)
Fax: 0161 275 5584
Email: ug.admissions@man.ac.uk
Web: http://www.manchester.ac.uk

Keele
Admissions and Recruitment Office
School of Medicine
Keele University
Staffordshire ST5 5BG
Tel: 01782 583937
Fax: 01782 584637
Email: medicine@hfac.keele.ac.uk
Web: http://www.keele.ac.uk

Additional application information

Average A-level requirements	• ABB (premedical) AAB (undergraduate)
Average Scottish Higher requirements	• AAAAB
Make-up of interview panel	• Please contact university for details
Months in which interviews are held	• November–April
Proportion of overseas students	• 7%
Proportion of mature students	• 11%
Proportion of graduate students	• 10%
Faculty's view of students taking a gap year	• Gap year students considered equally
Proportion of students taking intercalated degrees	• 10%
Possibility of direct entrance to clinical phase	• No
Fees for overseas students	• Check current fees with university student services
Fees for graduates	• Check current fees with university student services
Ability to transfer to other medical schools	• Students welcome to intercalate at other universities with equivalent learning opportunities
Assistance for elective funding	• Prizes and bursaries available are updated annually on the Manchester Medical School website
Assistance for travel to attachments	• GP placements are usually within 10 miles of your base hospital and information about public transport to each place is sent out with your placement pack
Access and hardship funds	• As for electives
Weekly rent	• £30–£50
Pint of lager	• £2 upwards
Cinema	• £3–£5
Nightclub	• £5 upwards

Newcastle and Durham (Queen's Campus, Stockton)

Key facts	Undergraduate	Graduate
Course length	5 years	4 years
Total number of medical undergraduates	1100	40
Applicants in 2005	3000+	1000+
Interviews given in 2005	500	100
Places available in 2005	326	25
Places available in 2006	326	25
Open days 2006	Please see website for details	
Entrance requirements	AAB (will be AAA in 2007)	2:1 degree
Mandatory subjects	Chemistry or biology	–
Male:female ratio	38:62	43:57
Is an exam included in the selection process? If yes, what form does this exam take?	No UKCAT in 2007	No UKCAT in 2007
Qualification gained	MBBS	

Fascinating fact: Newcastle Medical School might have expanded with the creation of its link with Durham, but in fact the medical school started off in Durham. In a moment of insanity about 50 years ago Durham actually gave it away to Newcastle, and has regretted it ever since.

Newcastle is a friendly city and the university is very centrally situated. The medical school is 5 minutes away from the main campus, very near to the halls of residence. As in the rest of the university there is a diversity of students, both national and international, from many different backgrounds. The staff are generally approachable and supportive, and well liked by students. Building work continues and the medical school is proud to have a brand new, state-of-the-art 400-seat lecture theatre and a starship enterprise entrance foyer.

At Newcastle early patient contact comes from hospital and GP visits in the first 2 years, and the course attempts to break down the traditional preclinical/clinical divide. There are opportunities for extended contact with patients by way of the 'family' and 'chronic illness patient' studies. The medical school is well established and highly regarded. Its graduates find they are well placed to get the jobs they want, and although many students want to spread their wings after qualifying many also chose to stay in the north east or to come back there later in their careers. The social life, centred on both the university and the city itself, is excellent, with something to appeal to everyone. Newcastle, the northernmost English university city, gives a warm welcome to its students.

In addition to the traditional 5-year medical degree at Newcastle there is now the opportunity for graduates to apply for the accelerated 4-year course at Newcastle which is demanding but has the obvious advantage of being a fast track to qualification.

The new medical school at Durham University is based at Queen's Campus Stockton (some 20 miles from Durham, and 40 from Newcastle) in brand new facilities set along the regenerated Tees riverside. As the result of a partnership between Durham and Newcastle Universities, Stockton students spend the first 2 years of their Newcastle medical degree being taught at this campus as members of Durham University before being transferred and integrated with the much larger numbers of Newcastle students in years 3–5. The course in Stockton has been developed alongside that in Newcastle and aims to produce a cohort of students with levels of skills and knowledge the same as those produced via the more traditional route in Newcastle. Although the two courses work to similar terminal objectives, there are some key differences on the Durham course, which we have highlighted in the profile.

Stockton is a small and friendly place, with the town centre 10 minutes' walk from Queen's campus, Although it might not boast all the attractions of a traditional university city it has all the facilities you would expect of a big town, and has become student-friendly with new café-bars and clubs, and an international summer art festival. For nights out partying then Middlesbrough is on the doorstep

Durham University at Queen's Campus has developed strong links with schools and colleges of education in the local area through a programme of open days and visits and has promoted a 'widening access' policy the benefits of which can be seen in its nontraditional student intake. Its medical students have qualifications ranging from the usual three science A-levels to first and second degrees in arts as well as sciences, and professional qualifications from worlds as diverse as law and nursing. Mature students are well represented and their presence has contributed to a genuinely interactive style of teaching with staff that are less didactic and more open to discussion than in many medical schools.

Students who start at either Newcastle or Durham quickly develop an affection for their communities whether it is the vibrant Newcastle, or the rapidly developing campus at Stockton. At both centres the large student presence makes for an excellent social life.

Education

The courses at Newcastle and Stockton are divided into two major phases based on the traditional preclinical/clinical model.

In phase I (years 1 and 2) the course is case-led and systems-based, with an emphasis on the clinical approach from the start. There are several opportunities for early patient contact in the form of project work (a family study of a pregnant mother and her baby and a study of a patient with a chronic illness), and hospital and GP visits. Clinical skills are introduced, but really just to give a flavour of relevance to the systems being studied, although communication skills are given a high priority from the very beginning. The systems the course covers include cardiovascular, respiratory and renal, gastro-intestinal, endocrine and the metabolism in year 1. In year 2 clinical sciences and investigative medicine are taught, with immunology, haematology, and neuromuscular skeletal. In both years personal and professional development and medicine in the community are taught in addition. There are differences between the Newcastle and Stockton phase 1.

At Stockton students do a 60-hour community placement in a local voluntary sector organisation and are assessed on this in year 2. In addition, the Stockton students are required to maintain a personal and professional development portfolio over their two Stockton years and they undergo an interview about this before moving on to phase 2. These aspects of the course reflect a greater emphasis on the social and cultural aspects of medicine at Stockton. A more traditional curriculum in Newcastle in the first 2 years presents the students with more emphasis on science-based subjects such as medical genetics in year 1, and a larger medical school means the Newcastle students have more consistent training in clinical skills in their first 2 years.

The accelerated course, which is available only in Newcastle, not Stockton, aims to combine the essential elements of years 1 and 2 into one intensive year which it achieves by teaching core material over a 45-week year (rather than two years of 31 weeks) and in which a problem-based learning (PBL) method is largely used. Lots of tutor support is available with students being taught in groups of 8–10. This accelerated phase began to run for the first time in 2002, and feedback from the students has been very positive

With the creation of the accelerated phase I, and the Stockton phase I which only began to run in 2001, the outcomes for the different entry routes have yet to be seen. However it can be said that medicine in Newcastle is now being taken by a much more diverse population of students than ever before. In September 2003 the Newcastle phase II (years 3 and 4) contained Stockton students and accelerated course students, all brought together as one cohort for the first time.

Teaching

Phase I teaching is lecture based (40%–50%of the time) for the Newcastle and Stockton students, except for the accelerated course students, who follow a pattern of structured tutorials and anatomy classes with prosected specimens followed by self-directed study. All students on phase I have small-group seminar work, practical sessions, clinical skills sessions, and undertake self-directed study.

Both universities protect Wednesday afternoon from teaching to allow time free for sport and leisure (or just plain sleeping) across the universities.

In phase II the students are allocated for their entire year 3 to a 'base unit' which comprises a cluster of hospitals located within the sizeable northern region as follows:

- **Teesside** (Middlesbrough, Stockton, Bishop Auckland, Darlington, Hartlepool)
- **Wear** (Sunderland, Durham, South Tyneside)
- **Tyne** (Newcastle hospitals and the Queen Elizabeth Hospital in Gateshead)
- **Northumbria** (North Tyneside, Ashington, Hexham, and Carlisle).

There is a degree of choice over which base unit students are allocated to, and 60% of students end up with their first or second choice. Extenuating circumstances may guarantee a particular base unit, but for the majority of students decisions have to be made about whether to try to hold out for one of the closer hospitals or whether to opt for a more distant one. There are advantages to both. Almost all students opt to commute rather than stay in hospital accommodation where possible. Phase II sees the emphasis shift significantly to clinical experience. There is an introductory 'Foundations of Clinical Practice' course, lasting 16 weeks, which introduces students systematically and thoroughly to clinical history taking and examination, and is one of the best received parts of the course by students. After this, students embark on a series of essential junior rotations which takes them through to the end of year 3. Students spend time in reproductive and child health, chronic illness and rehabilitation, mental health, public health and infectious diseases. Throughout the year students spend one morning per week with a GP practice, which many students say is the highlight of the week as they have the opportunity to work in small groups of three and get a very individual and personalised experience.

Year 4 starts with another 16-week block, this time in 'clinical skills and investigative medicine', based back at Newcastle (their first direct experience of Newcastle University for some of the Stockton students) and this is the followed by three 7-week student-selected components (SSCs) and at the end of year 4 by the 9-week elective period (to which 2 weeks' holiday can be added to extend your trip away).

Year 5 comprises essential senior rotations in the major clinical specialties; acute and chronic hospital care, primary care, critical care and mental health. Placements can be throughout the north from the west coast of Cumbria to Northumberland and down as far as Teesside. Final-year students spend 5 days a week in hospital and are expected to become part of the team to which they are attached, including being around during some evenings. The emphasis is on taking responsibility for your own self-directed learning, and therefore time is often left deliberately unstructured.

In terms of actual teaching, different students prefer different teaching styles, and there's something for everyone at Newcastle/Durham. For the first 2 years a student should consider carefully the various phase I options, all of which have quite a different emphasis. A mature or local student might prefer the community spirit of Stockton. Someone coming straight from school and wanting to be at the heart of the action might think Newcastle is more their scene. Either way, make the choice carefully because it might then determine your feelings about where you want to be in year 3. After that you start to be directed by what you want to chose to study yourself in year 4 and then you head into your final year, year 5.

Assessment

Phase I exams consist of a multiple-choice question (MCQ) paper, a data interpretation/problem solving paper, and a clinical-based objective structured clinical examination (OSCE). In phase I exams are midyear, and at the end of the year; and about 6 weeks into the first year there is a short exam that gives students a chance to see how they're doing. There are also several in-course assessments which are essays, literature reviews, project work, presentations and posters, and an SSC.

Phase II exams consist of data interpretation/problem-solving papers, MCQs, and OSCEs. In-course assessment is by way of in-course marks for the junior rotations and SSCs in year 4. Final exams at the end of the fifth year consist of data interpretation/problem-solving, an OSCE, and a 'long case'.

In all exams there are vivas for borderline or distinction students.

Intercalated degrees

Students may wish to intercalate, after either year 2 or year 4. This means they study for a further year for the additional degree of BSc (various science subjects) (Newcastle), or BSc Health and Human Sciences (Durham). They then slot back into their medical degree the following year, joining the year behind them. In addition the options when intercalating at the end of year 4 include study for a research masters or an MPhil. Research projects available in the intercalated year are wide ranging, from clinical to laboratory-based work, and topics in the social sciences. Until recently at Newcastle intercalation led to a BMedSci. It is not yet known how the change to BSc will affect the number of students wanting to intercalate. Traditionally about 10% took this route.

Special study modules and electives

The SSCs in year 4 can be followed virtually anywhere across the northern region, and it is possible for a student with a burning interest in a particular subject to set up an SSC themselves with the University's approval, either within the region or beyond. For those who don't want to go to the trouble of this there are 300 modules on offer by the university, some hospital-based, some community and some in investigative medicine.

Electives are entirely up to the individual to dream up and arrange. The University has a database of information from previous student electives, but the idea is to think creatively, and be adventurous if you wish.

Erasmus

There is no formal Erasmus programme in the medical school, but options exist to do languages as SSCs and to use these on electives for example.

Facilities

Library The Newcastle Medical Library is situated within the medical school and is open in the evenings during the week, but more limited hours at weekends. It is well stocked with books and videos, but does get busy at exam time. Students may also use the University Library, which is also close to the medical school (5 minutes' walk). Durham students have full use of the Newcastle library facilities

There are more limited library facilities at Stockton, where emphasis is put on using web-based resources such as Medline in addition to text book resources.

Computers These tend to be very good, and much information is passed on to students via email. Computer courses are held as part of the course, specifically in word processing and the use of email/internet to search databases.

There are well over 100 PCs in Newcastle Medical School, ten of which are library-based. . If all of these are busy, there are numerous quieter clusters throughout the university available for use.

Stockton has 200 computers on campus, with a significant number being library-based. All facilities at the university in Durham itself are available to Stockton students as well as Newcastle University facilities.

Clinical skills The clinical skills laboratories at Newcastle and Stockton are available for private revision sessions as well as for timetabled teaching sessions.

Welfare

Student support

All students are assigned a personal tutor for pastoral support, and faculty staff are friendly and approachable. Occasionally there may be some tutors who are too busy to see their tutees, but there are other members of staff that students can approach. Both universities and the Students' Unions have welfare officers and counselling services, including Nightline. All fresher medics join a peer family (often with five generations!) to help get themselves orientated. Those at UDSC have peer families in Newcastle as well, to encourage integration of the courses.

Mature students have an increasing presence at the medical school. Newcastle University has a mature students' officer for advice on issues like finance and childcare. At Stockton free kids club places in half terms are available.

Accommodation

Newcastle freshers' accommodation is guaranteed in halls or self-catering flats, although not all are centrally located. The housing office offers help and advice to students renting in the private sector, as most do from year 2. Popular student areas for renting are Jesmond, Heaton, and Fenham. Renting is easy and low-cost in Newcastle compared to many other universities.

At Stockton first-year students tend to chose to live in halls which are all within 5 minutes of the medical department, and which offer an outstanding standard of accommodation because of the newness of the buildings. Most rooms have internet access, and prices are reasonable. In the second year students tend to live out. Stockton has a lot of low-priced but reasonable quality accommodation all close to the University.

Placements

The Newcastle campus is situated very close to the city centre and includes the Royal Victoria Infirmary (adjoining the medical school). The facilities within the medical school are good – even including a gym. In the first 2 years students will visit hospitals close to the medical school, but all the lecture-based teaching happens at the medical school. This gives cohesion to the first 2 years which students appreciate.

At Stockton the smaller numbers lead to good opportunities for integration with both other Stockton students and those from the rest of Durham University. In the first 2 years the majority of the teaching is based at the medical school, but some courses are taught in hospital teaching centres in the Tees and Durham area hospitals. This is generally enjoyed by the students who get to experience teaching from a number of clinicians in a range of different hospital and primary care settings from the very beginning. Travel expenses for the students are not refunded by either university for Stockton students in phase I.

During phase II, attachments may be much further afield such as at the base units in year 3. There is usually accommodation available in hospitals if students wish. Reimbursement of travel expenses is limited.

Students often find that the inconvenience of commuting to distant attachments is outweighed by the fact that the smaller district general hospitals (DGHs) further afield usually have fewer students than the central teaching hospitals. The welcome given to students and the commitment to quality of teaching is generally excellent.

Location of clinical placement/ name of hospital	Distance away from Newcastle medical school (miles)	Difficulty getting there on public transport*
Newcastle hospitals	4	🚶
Durham and Sunderland	18	🚗
Ashington	18	🚗
Carlisle	50	🚗 💡
Middlesbrough	45	🚗 💡

* 🚶: walking/cycling distance; 🚌 : use public transport; 🚗: need own car or lift; 💡 : get up early – tricky to get to!

Sports and social

City life

Newcastle is a very lively city within easy reach of the hills of Northumberland and the unspoilt north-east coast of England. In recent years, Newcastle was voted eighth best 'party' town in the world, with no shortage of bars and pubs, and an ever-increasing club scene. The medical school has good access to the city centre shops, theatre, cinema, museums, art galleries, and music venues. More shops are to be found at the Metrocentre, just across the River Tyne in Gateshead. The locals are generally very friendly and eager for everyone to have a good time.

Stockton is nestled between the bustle of Middlesbrough and historic Durham, with easy access to both, and to other cities in the north east. In Middlesbrough pubs and clubs abound, and you can quickly get out to beautiful coast and moors of North Yorkshire. It's just as easy to visit the world heritage site of Durham Cathedral and lunch in one of the cosy cafés tucked away in Durham's narrow streets. In Stockton itself there is a shopping complex with a multiplex cinema and bowling alley just minutes from the campus, and many student bars and night clubs throughout the town.

University life

MedSoc is a great melting pot of all the years in the medical school and provides an opportunity to meet up with friends every week. MedSoc events take place in Newcastle every Friday evening, and usually consist of a guest speaker or show followed by a free bar. Previous events include karaoke nights and even a blind date evening. The annual MedSoc–DentSoc challenge is a regular favourite. Other highlights include the 'Metro line' pub crawl and exotic trips away to far-flung foreign cities like Edinburgh. Stockton's MedSoc has been up and running for 3 years now and has quite a repertoire of events held throughout the year.

The third-year students annually stage a Medics' Revue in May, and there are numerous medics' balls and dinners throughout the year. The medics' summer ball is organised by the Newcastle Medical and Dental Student Council, which is a student committee primarily concerned with support and welfare for medics and dentists. It is this organisation which runs the peer parenting scheme and organises events to support a wide range of charitable organisations

Other organisations such as MedSIN provide a campaigning link to international medical student organisations like The International Federation of Medical Students Associations (IFMSA); dedicated students forge links with the community, working with local schools providing sex education for example, and with disadvantaged groups such as asylum seekers. Regular student BMA meetings are held for those students who are politically minded.

A huge range of other clubs and societies are available through the Students' Unions of both universities.

Sports life

At Newcastle medics' rugby, netball, and hockey teams compete in leagues, and there are also football, volleyball, cricket, squash, and other sports clubs for medics, and innumerable other university-run clubs. The medical school in Newcastle has its own gym (£7 per year), and the university sports facilities are good and close by around (£55 per year).

At Stockton there is a great deal of interest in sport at all levels with rowing and canoeing being very popular, utilising the nearby Tees Barrage canoeing facilities. Sport in Durham is taken seriously at college and university levels

For the enthusiastic spectator there are Newcastle, Middlesbrough and Sunderland Football Clubs locally as well as rugby, basketball, athletics, cross-country, and more.

Top tip: This is a great school, but make your mind up in advance that you don't mind being moved from Newcastle to Tees for a whole year in your third or final year.

Great things about Newcastle

- The locals are friendly – adding to this vibrant, rapidly developing city where the atmosphere is never impersonal.
- Cost of living is relatively low.
- If you need a break from city life, it's easy to escape to the country or the coast.
- New pubs, clubs, and restaurants spring up all the time, with the Quayside and Jesmond being student favourites.
- Free beer at MedSoc (for life!).

Bad things about Newcastle

- There is some trepidation about how the increase in student numbers in recent years might affect course organisation and the student body.
- Travelling around the region can be time consuming without a car and costly with one.
- Timetable planning is sometimes late in being communicated to students.
- The tutor system doesn't work for everyone and so the amount of pastoral support students receive is variable.
- Some consultants mutter bitter words to the effect of 'Of course, the students at Newcastle don't know any anatomy these days ...' You'll get sick of hearing it!

Great things about Durham (Queen's Campus, Stockton)

- Brand new state-of-the-art facilities, with very committed staff.
- Small (190 medical students in the department in total).
- Most of the teaching is delivered by a wide range of clinicians who come from many different hospitals and primary care centres in the region.
- Access to both Durham and Newcastle University facilities, e.g. libraries.
- Patient-centred course with high emphasis on communication skills.

Bad things about Durham (Queen's Campus, Stockton)

- The library is noisy and lacks the comprehensive stock of a more established medical school library.
- The number of staff permanently in the medical school is very small.
- Stockton is a small town.

- The transition for Stockton students to Newcastle's curriculum in phase II is not yet fully tried and tested.

Further information

The Medical School
University of Newcastle
Framlington Place
Newcastle Upon Tyne NE2 4HH
Tel: 0191 222 7005
Fax: 0191 222 6521
Email: medic.ugadmin@ncl.ac.uk
Web: http://www.ncl.ac.uk, http://medical.faculty.ncl.ac.uk/

The Department Of Medicine
University of Durham, Queen's Campus
University Boulevard,
Thornaby
Stockton-on-Tees TS17 6BH
Tel: 0191 334 2000
Web http://www.dur.ac.uk

Additional application information

Average A-level requirements	• AAB
Average Scottish Higher requirements	• AAAAB
Graduate entry requirements	• 2:1 degree
Make-up of interview panel	• Two selectors
Months in which interviews are held	• November–March
Proportion of overseas students	• Quota 26
Proportion of mature students	• Not known
Proportion of graduate students	• Not known
Faculty's view of students taking a gap year	• Must use year constructively to gain experience
Proportion of students taking intercalated degrees	• Not known
Possibility of direct entrance to clinical phase	• No
Fees for overseas students	• Please see website for details
Fees for graduates	• Please see website for details
Ability to transfer to other medical schools	• Not unheard of, but rare • Depends on personal circumstance, among other things
Assistance for elective funding	• Students can apply for a bursary if in financial difficulty
Assistance for travel to attachments	• Limited help – travel bursary for Tees, Northumbria and Wear Base Units
Access and hardship funds	• Available, but don't bank on them.
Weekly rent	• £40–£60 or more
Pint of lager	• £2.00 at the popular Tiger Tiger on a Saturday night • £1.50 in the Union • £ 1.30 at some pubs
Cinema	• £3.50–£5.00
Nightclub	• £1.00–£3.00 during, the week, more at weekends

Nottingham

Key facts	Undergraduate
Course length	5 years
Total number of medical undergraduates	1155
Applicants in 2005	2104
Interviews given in 2005	464
Places available in 2005	246
Places available in 2006	246
Open days 2006	30 June, 1 July, 13 September
Entrance requirements	AAB
Mandatory subjects	Biology and chemistry
Male:female ratio	36:64
Is an exam included in the selection process? If yes, what form does this exam take?	Yes UKCAT
Qualification gained	BMedSci and BMBS

Fascinating fact: Emeritus Professor Sir Peter Mansfield designed the first MRI scanner at Nottingham. He has received the Nobel Prize for his pioneering work.

Nottingham is a campus university with a community atmosphere in a vibrant city. Medics and nonmedics mix in the first year in superb halls of residence on a beautiful campus built around a lake. There is plentiful off-campus accommodation, mostly located in the Lenton area between the campus and the city. This area is very student orientated, so that many of your friends will live within walking distance of your home(s) throughout the course. The cost of living compares favourably with other university towns, and the city is very multicultural.

The medical school is a part of the massive Queen's Medical Centre (QMC) hospital at the city end of the university campus. The course is systems-based, with emphasis on the early introduction of clinical skills. Outside placements are accessible and the quality of teaching is high. All students do a BMedSci degree within the 5-year course, and there are growing opportunities to study abroad. Clinical attachments are assessed individually and within themselves. The elective period follows finals, which is a great idea as it means less worry and you have assimilated more knowledge than on courses where the elective comes much earlier. Most graduates choose to find preregistration house officer (PRHO) jobs through the matching scheme and stay in the Nottingham area.

Education

Nottingham offers a blend between traditional and modern-style courses. Throughout the 5 years the subjects are split into four themes: Cell, Person, Community, and Doctor – learn this for the interview!

The first 2 years are integrated clinically, with systems-based teaching arranged in four semesters. One morning every fortnight is spent seeing patients, either in general practice or in hospital; clinical skills are taught and examined in both years.

Year 3 is split into two halves: the first involves a research project leading to a BMedSci degree for everyone; the second marks the beginning of full-time clinical study, with general medical and surgical attachments after a brief introductory course.

The final 2 years are spent on clinical attachments in a variety of specialties, e.g. paediatrics, obstetrics and gynaecology and psychiatry before returning to general medicine and surgery. Throughout the course there is significant and appropriate emphasis on personal and professional development including communication skills, ethics, and career advice.

Teaching

Lectures form the basis of most year 1 and 2 courses and the main lecture theatres were renovated earlier this year and have new comfy seats. Lectures are supplemented with a limited number of tutorials (about ten students) and seminars (about 25 students). Anatomy is taught by group dissection (ten students) and clinical problem solving in the newly renovated dissection laboratories. Practical classes are taught in large tele-linked laboratories.

Assessment

The course is examined by continual assessment instead of a single final exam after the 5 years. Depending on your outlook, this either reduces or spreads the inevitable stress. Warning! You sit over 40 exams like this in the first 2 years of the course. For the first 2 years, exams take place in January and June, often using multiple choice questions (MCQs), which employ negative marking on true/false questions (these can be more challenging than they sound). The BMedSci is assessed mainly from a 10,000–15,000-word research-based project. In the clinical years logbook assessment and practical exams follow each attachment, with MCQ exams twice a year. In year 5, the finals are clinically orientated, involving medicine, surgery, orthopaedics, and clinical laboratory sciences. The final year was redesigned relatively recently to allow several practice attempts at finals before the real exam.

Intercalated degrees

Despite being a 5-year course, everyone does a research-based BMedSci (Hons) degree in year 3. The exam results of the first 2 years contribute 50% of the final degree mark. Students who leave the course after this have the benefit of a degree qualification. This is a comfort, but not many students leave midcourse. Many students use their projects to publish scientific papers or present them at conferences. These projects often involve hard work but provide excellent analytical and self-directed learning skills for clinicals. There is an element of chance in what you end up studying, but the vast majority of students are happy with their project in the end.

Special study modules and electives

The 8-week elective is at the end of all clinical attachments and final exams in year 5. However, if you have failed any clinical examinations in years 4 and 5 you may have to resit them in this period. Most people choose a mixture of work and play; a short report is expected from everyone.. There are two periods of 4-week special study modules (SSMs). One is in year 4 and the other in the final year. The choices are varied and Nottingham currently offers 30 SSM places throughout Europe.

Erasmus

Nottingham medical school no longer takes part in the Erasmus scheme. However, there are several opportunities to study abroad. A limited number of students have had the opportunity to complete their BMedSci project overseas. This is dependent on which department you are placed in and whether such an opportunity is available that year. As mentioned above it is possible to study one of the SSMs in Europe. In year 4 two students from the year have the opportunity to spend 6 months in Norway, completing their child health and obstetrics and gynaecology attachments at the University of Oslo.

Facilities

Library The medical library is on the ground floor of the medical school; it is large and the staff are friendly. It is well stocked with core texts and journals, but can become busy around exam times. It opens until 11.15 PM weekdays, and during the day at weekends for most of the year.

Computers IT facilities are good, with over 200 terminals in the medical school. There is unlimited and free access to email, the internet, teaching CD-Roms and computer-assisted learning (CAL) packages for teaching and revision. The recently redesigned Networked Learning Environment allows internet access to lecture handouts, slides, and learning aids from outside the medical school. The main computer room is open 24 hours a day. Facilities at outlying hospitals are improving.

Clinical skills There are a series of newly built rooms dedicated to teaching clinical skills such as examining patients. The laboratory is staffed and resources have rapidly expanded to an excellent level. The rooms are used on a casual basis and have many self-teaching aids – suturing practice kits, models of eyes, ears, arms (for blood pressure), videos, and so on.

Welfare

Student support

As a whole the university has a friendly and open feel. Student welfare is now taken very seriously. In the medical school every student is allocated a tutor who can address academic or personal problems. Unfortunately, the amount of 'actual' support given varies from tutor to tutor. The students organise a mentoring system in which first-year students are allocated individual second-year 'parents'. Whether or not you meet regularly with your 'parent' depends on how well you get on; however, a high rate of adoption leaves most people happy! The university and Students' Union have welfare, legal, financial, and counselling services, along with an active Niteline (night-time counselling service) run by students.

Accommodation

Almost all first-year students are housed in good-quality university accommodation; these are mostly catered halls, though some students opt for self-catering flats. There are 12 medium-sized halls on the main campus, each with its own bar. A further three large halls are found on the recently built Jubilee campus, about 15 minutes' walk from the main campus or QMC. In subsequent years you can apply to stay in halls, though most students move into private rented houses: 80% choose to live in Lenton, which is a relatively safe student area that is 20 minutes' walk from the campus and town. House hunting begins very early after Christmas; most students organise it themselves without university vetting. The Union organises house hunting for first-year students wanting to live out before their first term.

Placements

The teaching hospitals are all located within one rush-hour drive of Nottingham. The smaller hospitals are generally friendlier (as they have more time to talk to you), but sometimes more work is expected from you. Accommodation is provided free of charge in Mansfield and Lincoln depending on which placement you are doing. Otherwise you are expected to travel daily. At Nottingham, students can state preferences for where their attachments are. It is unlikely, that any student will have all their attachments in Nottingham itself, so a degree of travelling is inevitable.

Clinical visits in years 1 and 2 often require some travelling, but transport or suggested routes are provided. Students usually organise to share car lifts as some hospitals can be very difficult to travel to via public transport. In addition to the main hospitals where students are placed, there are other, smaller, hospitals where you may be based for short periods. These are generally within Nottingham and are easily accessible by public transport.

Location of clinical placement/ name of hospital	Distance away from medical school (miles)	Difficulty getting there on public transport*
Nottingham City Hospital	5	🚌 🚗
Derby Royal Infirmary	20	🚗
Derby City General Hospital	25	🚗
Mansfield Hospital	30	🚗
Lincoln Hospital	45	🚗 🚌 💡

* : walking/cycling distance; 🚌 : use public transport; 🚗: need own car or lift; 💡 : get up early – tricky to get to!

Sports and social 🏆

City life

The city centre is attractive, compact, and has good shopping facilities. Nottingham is renowned for its inexpensive and diverse bars, clubs, pubs, and restaurants. The theatres are good, but there are few live music venues. The city centre is within walking distance of most off-campus accommodation, and a 10-minute bus ride (£1) from campus. Because of its central location travel to most other cities is quick and easy. The Peak District and surrounding countryside provide a welcome escape where students can enjoy themselves, far away from anatomy revision.

University life

Student life is rich and varied, and there is plenty of time to enjoy it while doing a medical degree. The student medical society (MedSoc) provides a good range of social events such as cocktail parties, balls, and guest lectures. MedSIN is also very active in Nottingham, so it is easy to get involved in projects such as Sexpression, WaterAid, Heartstart and Marrow. Nottingham has one of the largest student rags in the country, called 'Karni'. This raises about £230,000 for charity from activities in the first term. On-campus entertainment revolves around hall life, and includes bars and themed parties. In later years the pub and club scenes of Lenton and the city dominate. There are also hundreds of university clubs and societies facilitating much interaction within the student body from Unifilms to MutantSoc!

The main distinguishing feature of Nottingham medics' social life is the extent to which medical students are mixed with the whole university population. After the first year many medics live with their nonmedic friends from halls. Lenton, the main student area, is well equipped with cheapish pubs, launderettes, late-opening shops, takeaways, video rental shops, and buses. Although the campus accommodation is excellent, the university could take more responsibility for off-campus housing.

Sports life

Nottingham has good-quality, accessible sporting facilities including a swimming pool on campus and a newly refurbished fitness centre. Medics' teams play against the hall teams; they are particularly strong in hockey, rugby, tennis, and football. Most sports and standards of ability are represented somewhere in the university. The clubs provide a focus for excellent social lives.

> **Top tip:** Thanks to the hard work of MedSoc there are brilliant discounts at many of the city's best bars, restaurants, and for that all important fancy dress! Make sure you track down your MedSoc card in freshers' week to take advantage of these!

Great things about Nottingham

- You get a bonus degree (BMedSci) without having to do an extra year; this is very useful later in your career.
- Good social life for students, with variety, value, and accessibility along with many active and friendly student societies.
- Beautiful campus, with good community spirit and healthy interhall rivalry.
- Integration of medics with nonmedics in halls broadens social circles and reduces the cliqueyness that medics are sometimes accused of!
- After the first year all your hall friends remain within walking distance by moving to the student area (Lenton).

Bad things about Nottingham

- Because of the poor Union bar and lack of a campus venue for top bands there is little to attract medics back to campus after their first year.
- It is felt that the university attracts students from similar backgrounds, leading to a lack of diversity within the student population.
- House-hunting begins too early (January) and can be stressful.
- The preclinical course is very lecture based.
- Nottingham tends to like using computer-matching schemes to allocate students to BMedSci projects, PRHO jobs and other parts of the course. Students often feel as though they have little control over their future – it's almost like a lottery!
- The med school is notorious for not confirming where your next attachment is until the week before it starts, so keep a sharp eye on the 'Networked Learning Environment'!

Further information

Admissions Officer
Faculty Office
Queen's Medical Centre
University of Nottingham
Nottingham NG7 2RD
Tel: 0115 970 9379
Fax: 0115 970 9922

Email: medschool@nottingham.ac.uk
Web: http://www.nottingham.ac.uk

Additional application information	
Average A-level requirements	• AAB with grade As in biology and chemistry and a B in a third subject (excluding general studies)
Average Scottish Higher requirements	• AAB
Make-up of interview panel	• Consultants and academics
Months in which interviews are held	• November–March
Proportion of overseas students	• 10%
Proportion of mature students	• 2%
Proportion of graduate students	• 2%
Faculty's view of students taking a gap year	• Acceptable, provided it is used constructively
Proportion of students taking intercalated degrees	• 0%
Possibility of direct entrance to clinical phase	• No
Fees for overseas students	• £12,160 pa for years 1 and 2 in 2005. • Years 3, 4 and 5 will be set at the clinical rate applicable when student reaches year 3. For guidance, clinical rate for 2005 was £20,900 pa
Fees for graduates	• £3000
Ability to transfer to other medical schools	• Yes, usually after completion of BMedSci degree in year 3. Individual circumstances are considered separately
Assistance for elective funding	• Not directly, but students are invited to apply for elective prizes
Assistance for travel to attachments	• No, students must apply to their LEA and the medical school will validate the claim
Access and hardship funds	• Yes, but must be paid back in the future. All cases dealt with anonymously
Weekly rent	• £50 (self-catering halls) • £105 (fully catered halls) • £45–£65 (private)
Pint of lager	• £1.40 Union bar • £2.20 city centre pub
Cinema	• £4 with NUS card
Nightclub	• Free–£4 Monday–Friday, though posh clubs charge more at the weekends

Oxford

Key facts	Undergraduate	Graduate
Course length	6 years	4 years
Total number of medical undergraduates	900	120
Applicants in 2005	1076	250
Interviews given in 2005	425	90
Places available in 2005	150	30
Places available in 2006	150	30
Open days 2006	28 and 29 June, 15 September	Easter and summer
Entrance requirements	AAA	2:1 or better; GPA above 3.5; 2 science A-levels (including chemistry)
Mandatory subjects	Chemistry and one other science/maths	Bioscience or chemistry degree and A-level chemistry
Male:female ratio	45:55	70:30 (2005 entry)
Is an exam included in the selection process? If yes, what form does this exam take?	Yes, BMAT UKCAT in 2007	Yes, BMAT UKCAT in 2007
Qualification gained	BMBCh	

Fascinating fact: One lucky person every year at the clinical school will have the traditional honour of playing the rear end of a large pink elephant in the medical school pantomime!

Oxford is a unique place. If you wish to mix a sense of history with a centre renowned for cutting-edge research; the choice of living in modern student accommodation or 15th century, wood-panelled rooms; meet students of all backgrounds; have the double benefits of a small college and a large university; with a traditional yet innovative medical course, then Oxford is for you!

As with most medical schools the course has undergone some changes recently and the intake was increased in 2001 but Oxford still retains the ethos of a 'small' medical school, which is a real advantage. The addition of an accelerated course for bioscience graduates is another innovation.

Some may criticise the lack of clinical involvement during the first 3 years of the 6-year undergraduate course. However, the firm scientific basis of medicine strongly emphasised on the Oxford course is of vital importance clinically and the acquisition of skills, such as the critical evaluation of papers and an understanding of research, is rightly given very high priority. In the early years a real effort is also made to highlight the clinical relevance of the 'basic science' being taught. Three years before significant patient contact may seem like a long time, but the knowledge and skills gained during the preclinical course will be of use for the rest of your career, and having an 'extra' science degree is no bad thing when applying for medical jobs.

The course demands the very highest level of academic ability and commitment. However, your college tutor, who selects you in the first place, has a vested interest in your success and, in most cases, works very hard on your behalf – no-one is left to struggle. The short terms and long holidays also make the hard work survivable and enjoyable.

Education

Oxford Medical School was recently assessed by the QAA as a single 6-year course, but for practical purposes there remains a clear-cut division between the preclinical and clinical courses in Oxford. In the preclinical school the first five terms are spent studying the basic medical sciences (anatomy, biochemistry, physiology, pharmacology, pathology, and neuroscience). Some clinical contact is introduced through the 'Patient–Doctor Course' by spending 2–3 afternoons a term with a GP tutor. The final four terms are spent working towards an Honours degree (BA in Biomedical Sciences). After finals, preclinical students 'stay on' for a clinical anatomy course. The anatomy taught is relevant to clinical practice, and practical skills such as examination of cranial nerve function are worked into the teaching. Application to the clinical school is competitive, with about 55%–65% of the Oxford preclinical students staying on. The rest go mainly to London or Cambridge, and there is an influx of students – most from Cambridge and some from London medical schools.

The clinical course lasts 3 years and aims to deliver the best teaching of both scientific principles and clinical practice. It is in a particularly good position to do so, because of the combination of its small size (about 150 per year, including the graduate entry intake) and the very high quality of its academic and clinical staff. Year 4 starts with a 6-week introductory foundation (Patient–Doctor II) course, a fortnight of which is dedicated to teaching by the final year students doing a 'Medical Education' Special Study Module. This is always greatly enjoyed, and offers a gentle and sympathetic introduction to clinical practice, without the pressures of being assessed by clinicians! The remainder of year 4 consists of an 8-week laboratory medicine (pathology) course, general, medicine and surgery rotations, a residential general practice attachment and a placement at a district general hospital (DGH). Courses on medical ethics and law, communication skills, complementary therapy, evidence-based medicine and basic life support are 'threaded' into the year. Special study modules (SSMs) are an exciting addition to year 4. These can be taken in subjects such as philosophy, theology, chronic illness, and foreign language, where students are free to explore their interests.

Year 5 contains all the specialist rotations: paediatrics, obstetrics and gynaecology, A&E, orthopaedics, general practice, neurology, neurosurgery, ENT, ophthalmology, psychiatry, public health, geratology and palliative care. Some of these rotations will be spent partially at a DGH outside Oxford; for example, Reading, Milton Keynes, Swindon, Northampton or Banbury, but most of the time is spent in Oxford itself. Year 6 focuses again on medicine and surgery. Students also undertake 'clinical options' and a DGH attachment before clinical finals in January. After this, there is a 10-week elective period, the chance to complete ALERT and ALS courses and several weeks of special study modules. All students complete a 'Preparation for Practice' module comprising a taught course and a house officer shadowing attachment. There is a requirement to produce a portfolio during year 6, with reflective reports on the attachments or work completed, which is developed in conjunction with a supervisor, whom students select individually. In addition, an extended essay is written. Throughout the clinical course there is a great deal of ward-based teaching, with both consultants and the more junior doctors (all of whom are keen to practise being teaching hospital consultants!)

The graduate entry programme at Oxford is a 4-year course currently restricted to graduates in bioscience and chemistry. This is an intensive programme with emphasis on academic science, both medical and clinical. The first year focuses on the basic sciences in a clinical context with the introduction of essential clinical skills such as history taking and physical examination. Teaching in year 2 begins to be integrated with first-year clinical students on year 4 of the standard medical course. Emphasis here is on clinical teaching with a smaller science component. The final 2 years are fully integrated with the existing clinical course. Informal assessments are held at several points during the first year. Assessments are also held towards the end of each clinical attachment throughout the course. Formal university examinations take place at the end of years 1 and 2, and again towards the end of the final year.

Teaching

In the preclinical years the basic medical sciences are taught by means of lectures and practicals, supplemented by college tutorials 2–3 times a week. In the clinical years, teaching practices vary between departments, with some lectures/seminars and some ward-based teaching. Some colleges provide clinical tutorials in addition to the central, medical school-based teaching.

Assessment

Currently, assessments are at the end of year 1 and before Easter in year 2, and consist of essay papers, short notes, and problem-solving questions. The practicals are assessed continuously and practical books must be kept up to date.

In the clinical years, assessment is largely by objective structured clinical examinations (OSCEs) and the odd written paper. In year 4, assessment is largely formative; whilst in year 5, exams after each 8-week specialty rotation are pass/fail. The modular form of the specialist rotations means that there is no easy fifth year, but the pressure at finals is much reduced.

In the final year, assessment comprises a written exam, clinical exam, an extended essay and satisfactory completion of a portfolio.

Intercalated degrees

All students spend the last terms of the preclinical phase working for an Honours degree in Biomedical Sciences (unless they are already graduates). The degree course has a large amount of flexibility, and students are encouraged to follow courses that interest them. It is a quirk of the Oxford system that the degree awarded is a BA (and, after a few years, it can be upgraded automatically to an MA), rather than a BSc!

Special study modules and electives

There is a 10-week elective in year 6 and most go abroad. Some of the colleges can help financially. In addition, there are opportunities to undertake other placements abroad, for example during the paediatrics and obstetrics and gynaecology modules. The 14 weeks of special study modules (SSMs) in the final year are more clinical in nature than the modules of the first clinical year. There are over 60 options, ranging from the traditional (such as cardiology, anaesthetics or general practice) to the innovative (creativity in health care, medical publishing, medical anthropology, or even a language), and can be either purely clinical, research, or a mixture of both. If the extensive list does not cover the one subject that you desperately want to study, you are free, with the medical school's permission, to arrange your own. This can on occasion be undertaken outside Oxford and even abroad.

Erasmus

Whilst it is more challenging to arrange study abroad during the preclinical part of the course, there are plenty of travel opportunities during the clinical years. The year 5 placements in paediatrics, and obstetrics and gynaecology can both be partly undertaken abroad. In addition, the 10-week elective scheme in the final year enables experience of medicine anywhere in the world. As well as these opportunities, it is possible to arrange an SSM in a foreign country (or partly abroad).

Facilities

Library Oxford is very well catered for with respect to libraries. At preclinical level, the Radcliffe Science Library (RSL) and college libraries are the most useful and used. College facilities vary but are in general good to excellent. The RSL has an incredible number of books and journals, but rather limited opening hours out of term. The Cairns Library is located at the John Radcliffe Hospital, and is the library used during clinical years. It is very well stocked and open 24 hours a day, 365 days a year. It has any book you need!

Computers The computing facilities are very good in colleges, departments, libraries and, at clinical level, in Osler House and the Cairns Library, where a large number of computers are reserved exclusively for medical students. Computer-assisted learning (CAL) is gradually being introduced, and all lecture notes and resources for courses such as the laboratory medicine course are available electronically. The new 'Weblearn' system is entirely computer-based, with up-to-date timetables, information about SSMs and clinical school notices all being posted electronically.

Clinical skills There are two large and recently renovated skills laboratories for teaching of medical and surgical skills. Two automated dummies (both called Harvey!) have also been purchased for skills teaching.

Welfare

Student support

Oxford students are bright yet friendly and very social. There really is a niche for everyone. The collegiate system enables the pastoral care provided by tutors to work very effectively in the preclinical years. In clinical years, when links with the college are not as strong, the system does not work so well but is supplemented by good support, be it academic or pastoral, from the medical school. Colleges provide significant financial assistance, ranging from subsidised accommodation, meals and entertainment, to elective funding and hardship grants. Oxford University has welfare and counselling facilities, in addition to the provision by the medical school and colleges. In clinical years, an 'informal, but structured' peer support system operates.

At preclinical and especially clinical levels medical students tend to know each other very well. Depending on your viewpoint, this can either be an advantage or a disadvantage, but most seem to enjoy the camaraderie and banter, whether in the bar or in the dissection room! One of the great things about Oxford is the collegiate system: this broadens your horizons and makes it very easy to make friends with nonmedics. At the clinical level, Osler House Club (the Students' Union) provides a very relaxed way of meeting people and making friends.

Accommodation

Preclinical students will find their life completely integrated with that of students in other subjects and will live with them in college accommodation. Many of the college buildings are old and beautiful, but do bear in mind that sometimes the accommodation you will actually live in will either be 1950s or private lodgings. All the accommodation is of a reasonable to excellent standard.

Things are very different for clinical students, however. Very few live on college sites, as the majority of graduate accommodation is in nearby annexes. The exception is Green College, which was established for medical students and is still largely populated by them. Many prefer to live out during their clinical training, as it affords more independence than college can provide, and there is plenty of good-quality private accommodation in Oxford.

Placements

The early years are spent studying basic medical sciences in and around the centre of Oxford. This is amid the Oxford colleges, with their long traditions of study and learning. The clinical school is based at the John Radcliffe Hospital (JR), which is a large teaching hospital situated in Headington, two miles east of Oxford city centre and easily accessible by bus or bike. It is modern, large, and contains all of Oxford's acute medical and surgical services. The Churchill Hospital is increasingly becoming a specialist centre for certain services, such as transplants, oncology, and soon diabetes and endocrinology. The Radcliffe Infirmary contains services for neurology, ENT, ophthalmology, and plastic surgery. It is due to be closed down and relocated to the JR site within the next 5 years. The Nuffield Orthopaedic Hospital, the Warneford and Littlemore psychiatric hospitals are smaller centres used for specific modules of the course. All the hospitals are easily reached by bike, bus, or car (although parking is almost impossible!).

Although other hospitals in Banbury, Reading, Swindon, Northampton, and Bath are used, the majority of a student's time will still be spent in Oxford. Many find this very useful, as it allows them to be involved in university and college life, whether sports, drama, music, or other activities. On residential placements outside Oxford students are provided with free accommodation and travel expenses are reimbursed. There are also, ample opportunities to travel (in addition to the elective) for those who want to: for example, several of the specialties (such as paediatrics, and deliveries in obstetrics) can be studied in other parts of the country or world.

Location of clinical placement/ name of hospital	Distance away from medical school (miles)	Difficulty getting there on public transport*
Banbury	27	
Aylesbury	25	
Reading	27	
Swindon	30	
Northampton	42	
Milton Keynes	39	

* : walking/cycling distance; : use public transport; : need own car or lift; : get up early – tricky to get to!

Sports and social

City life

Oxford, the 'city of dreaming spires', is a small city with easy access to the rest of the country, and London in particular (only 50 minutes by train and 90 minutes by coach). Many preclinical students survive the first 3 years without needing to travel more than 5 minutes on foot from the centre of the city, but at clinical school you are forced to move a little further afield. The town centre has the usual core of shops, and you will find it sufficient for most needs. Having said that, Oxford can't compare to what many cities offer in terms of variety. Culturally there is a lot going on, particularly if you like theatre and music. It has to be said that the club scene in Oxford is not comparable to that in the larger centres such as London or Manchester, so it wouldn't suit the more dedicated punter! However, the clubs are getting better, and you can always get to and from London on buses leaving every 12–15 minutes, 24 hours a day.

University life

There are numerous university and college-based clubs and societies dedicated to ensuring that students get the most they can out of their time in Oxford. At preclinical level these often form a prominent part of most people's social life, with the medical society (MedSoc) supplementing this. The societies range from the sublime to the ridiculous, and you will find that talents you never realised you had are catered for.

The clinical school social life tends to revolve around Osler House, a 1920s house in the grounds of the John Radcliffe run for and by clinical students. There is a bar, a television room, computing facilities, pool table, and a pleasant garden, with lunch served daily. The Osler Committee organises many events – social, sporting, and cultural. However, many clinical students also remain involved in other aspects of university life, be it at their college or elsewhere. The clinical school pantomime, *Tingewick*, deserves a special mention. This occurs every year and is a great chance for the students to get their own back at their consultants and anyone else who deserves parody.

Sports life

Oxford is famous for its rowing and rugby, but other sports are well represented too. In particular, the collegiate structure means that there are both facilities and opportunities for involvement in sport at any level of ability. All the colleges have sports pitches and boat houses, and many can provide squash and tennis courts as well. Intercollegiate competitions (Cuppers) form one focus for the competitive energy, and the very committed can find themselves competing at the highest levels – the Varsity competitions. Even if you lack speed, strength, skill, accuracy, or talent in general, you will still be able to find a team of your level and skill! In the collegiate events the clinical school is represented by the Osler–Green teams, who regularly manage to field competitive sides.

Top tip: Before applying to Oxford visit as many colleges as possible. Speak to current medical students to find out what the college is really like. Teaching and facilities are generally good everywhere but this can be variable. Each college has a unique atmosphere and differs in what they can offer in terms of tutorials and financial support. Try to meet with the college medical tutors at each college to see if you would get on. This is important as you will be directly under this tutor's care for at least 3 years.

Good things about Oxford

- The collegiate system and relatively small size of the medical school means personalised teaching and allows you to meet students sitting a variety of subjects. This not only means you get to know people well but are also exposed to a wide range of interests and education.
- The tutorial system – having one-to-one or two-to-one tuition, with the academic support that this offers. Consequently, very few students fall behind in their work.
- The influx of up to 50 new students from other medical schools in year 4 creates a fantastic opportunity to make new friends when you begin your clinical training.
- Excellent scientific and clinical teaching, together with a stimulating environment in a university with a first-class, worldwide reputation.
- Oxford is a beautiful city in which to work. Together with its traditions, this makes student life here a unique experience.

Bad things about Oxford 🖐

- The public perception of Oxford is behind the times and relies too much on stereotypes. These are inaccurate and unhelpful – don't be discouraged from applying!
- Some students at Oxford are incredibly hard working, so the pressure can build up at times.
- The scientific nature of the course, particularly during the preclinical years, does not suit everyone.
- The nightlife in Oxford is limited, but London is nearby and easily reached.
- The preregistration house officer (PRHO) matching scheme doesn't work well.

Further information

Oxford Colleges Admission Service (undergraduate admissions)
The University Offices
Wellington Square
Oxford OX1 2JD
Tel: 01865 270207
Fax: 01865 270208
Email: undergraduate.admissions@admin.oxon.ac.uk
Web: http://www.ox.ac.uk

Clinical Medical School Offices
John Radcliffe Hospital
Headington
Oxford OX3 9DU
Web: http://www.medsci.ox.ac.uk

Additional application information	
Average A-level requirements	• AAA
Average Scottish Higher requirements	• AAAA plus at least chemistry at Advanced Higher
Make-up of interview panel	• Undergraduate: Two interviews by those teaching the course, one of which will include a practising clinician. • Graduate: Two or three (typically one clinician and one college tutor)
Months in which interviews are held	• December
Proportion of overseas students	• 3% (undergraduate) 2% (graduate)
Proportion of mature students	• Not known
Proportion of graduate students	• 1%
Faculty's view of students taking a gap year	• Supportive if constructive use is made of the time

(Continued)

(*Continued*)

Proportion of students taking intercalated degrees	• 100% (the Honours degree is part of the course)
Possibility of direct entrance to clinical phase	• Yes, Honours graduates only with preclinical qualification undertaken in the UK
Fees for overseas students	• £16,500 pa (preclinical) • £23,500 pa (clinical).
Fees for graduates	• £7,500 pa (2 preclinical years) £2,000 pa (3 clinical years)
Ability to transfer to other medical schools	• Yes. Possible after completing the 3-year preclinical component of the course, but only to other schools (mainly Cambridge and some London medical schools) that run nonintegrated courses
Assistance for elective funding	• Yes – there are a variety of funds available. Each college has its own travel bursaries, as does the medical school itself
Assistance for travel to attachments	• With placements out of Oxford, the medical school will reimburse travel costs in full (where accommodation is provided, only one return journey per week)
Access and hardship funds	• Administered through individual colleges, and always available, but vary in value and criteria for application. Usually very generous, worth finding out about from the colleges/websites before deciding which college to apply to
Weekly rent	• £65–£105 (varies with college)
Pint of lager	• £1.50 (college bars) upwards!
Cinema	• About £5 – there are great cinemas though, including great Arts ones
Nightclub	• Lots to choose from (contrary to popular belief, there are actually some decent ones); £5 entry for students with cheap(ish) drinks. There are always student promotions Most colleges have 'entz' and 'bops', basically music (which is generally pretty good) and alcohol at very cheap prices

Peninsula

Key facts	Undergraduate
Course length	5 years
Total number of medical undergraduates	634
Applicants in 2005	1917
Interviews given in 2005	691
Places available in 2005	167
Places available in 2006	181
Open days 2006	23 and 24 June
Entrance requirements	AAA + 1 AS-level (370–400 points)
Mandatory subjects	One subject grade A
Male:female ratio	38:62
Is an exam included in the selection process? If yes, what form does this exam take?	Mature students are asked to sit the GAMSAT examination, UKCAT in 2007
Qualification gained	BMBS

Fascinating fact: We are the most southern medical school in the country. Some students have a chance to have placements with GPs on the Isles of Scilly!

Peninsula Medical School is the result of collaboration between the Universities of Exeter and Plymouth and NHS hospital trusts across the south-west. The three main bases of the medical school are Exeter, Plymouth and Truro and students are expected to spend some time at each site. It is a new and vibrant medical school that is passionate about medicine. The first undergraduate students started in 2002 and are now in year 4.

Plymouth, Exeter and Truro are very different cities and provide students with sometimes very contrasting experiences. All are pleasant to live in and the 'medicine' seen on each site is very different, with different specialities and contrasting populations of patients. Exeter is fairly affluent and Plymouth significantly poorer. Truro and Cornwall is an interesting mixture of both.

The school has an exciting approach to medical training with students having extensive exposure to primary and community medicine, the aim of which is to develop an understanding of patient care at all levels. Students are taught through self-directed learning in a supportive environment. The course is split into preclinical and clinical years and students are based at hospital sites from year 3. Practical clinical skills are taught from year 1 in brand-new clinical skills suites across the south-west. Special study modules (SSMs) are offered from year 1.

Education

The course at Peninsula is taught in three phases. Phase I is largely based at Exeter and Plymouth, with some clinical placements accompanied by lots of clinical skills teaching. Phase II is hospital-based in Exeter, Plymouth or Truro. Phase III is the 'apprentice preregistration house officer (PRHO)' year, and consists of shadowing junior doctors in hospitals across the south-west, including Barnstaple and Torbay. Life sciences are a theme throughout all phases. Clinical and communication skills are timetabled from the first week of the course.

In phase I, students learn about issues relating to different stages in the life cycle of a human being. Each stage of human life, from conception to old age, is covered in a 2-week long case unit of which there are ten in years 1 and 2. In year 1 emphasis is placed on the normal functions of the body; year 2 emphasises pathology. The lectures, clinical skills and placements during a case unit aim to supplement learning objectives for that case unit. For example, during the 'conception' case unit, students research topics such as the menstrual cycle, reproductive system and fertility, while also learning how to carry out appropriate clinical examinations such as vaginal examinations and listening to the baby's heart in a pregnant patient. Students will also visit a community clinical placement, which could be a local GP or a visit to a family planning clinic and have a chance to discuss the issues arising from this visit in a small group session.

In phase II, students follow one of three 'pathways' each term, and have a 'trigger case' each week on which to base their learning, Examples of trigger cases may include 'the confused drinker', 'shortness of breath', and 'the new baby'. Students are split into very small groups (2–3) and have several placements during each week, including a protected, timetabled 2-hour teaching sessions with the consultant in charge of each week.

Teaching

Along with other new medical schools the course at PMS relies on problem-based learning (PBL), which involves students working in small groups to determine learning objectives, researching these objectives and sharing information obtained in subsequent sessions. In phase I these sessions are co-ordinated by a member of staff who acts as a facilitator and ensures that the sessions run smoothly. In phase II, students are supported in learning life sciences with clinicopathological conferences and have access to the full resources of the life sciences facilities. One day of each week in phase II is an 'academic day' based at the hospital teaching centre, with lectures, small group work and clinical skills sessions.

Assessment

Students are assessed in four major areas; applied medical knowledge (AMK), clinical skills, special studies units (SSUs) and personal and professional development (PPD). Four times a year, all students sit a 'progress test', a multiple choice question (MCQ) exam which assesses AMK. The exam is not based directly on previous work – rather, it aims to assess progress across the board in all aspects of AMK and all year groups sit the same exam at the same time. This might mean that students in year 1 get very low marks, but are deemed satisfactory within their year group. By year 5, students are expected to get very high marks.

Judgements of PPD made by staff are collected together and form a portfolio, and this element is assessed by completing a reflective portfolio analysis written by the student. Assessment of clinical skills is carried out at the end of year 2 by an objective structured clinical examination (OSCE). Students must pass all four modules at the end of year 2 to commence on to phase II of the course (years 3 and 4). Assessment in phase II may vary slightly, as each of the consultant-contact sessions will be used to form a summative assessment, similar to those described above.

Intercalated degrees

Intercalated degrees are still in development and are likely to be available for students after year 4. There is also the possibility that students will be able choose between intercalating a traditional BSc degree or a nontraditional BA degree.

Special study modules and electives

Peninsula offers SSUs from year 1 of the course. During phase I, these are mostly short, 2-week placements providing each student with the opportunity to research medical issues and topics of personal interest ranging from clinical (e.g. stroke management) or scientific (e.g. psychoneuroimmunology) to alternative medicine and community (e.g. shiatsu and yoga). In phase II, SSUs are mostly in specialist clinical settings, but also include themes such as 'doctors as managers' and medical humanities. The units vary in length from 2 weeks to a month, during which students are required to attend contact sessions with the SSU facilitators and to prepare a report and/or a presentation on their research topic.

Since Peninsula is a new medical school, no PMS students have undertaken an elective as yet. The elective is planned for the first part the final year.

Erasmus

No information about Erasmus – this hasn't been set up. The option is a possibility if someone really wanted to (although we don't know if they would be credited with the study during this time).

Facilities

Library Students have access to the University libraries at Exeter and Plymouth, as well as hospital libraries across the south-west and various postgraduate centres and specialist libraries such as public health. There is not a separate, 'Peninsula Medical School' library, although students are well supported by library staff at each site and have access to extensive internet resources. The medical school also has several 'life sciences' centres across the sites and these have open access facilities including books, databases and models, although resources cannot be removed from the allocated rooms.

The medical school makes extensive use of an online learning environment, known as 'Emily', where everything from timetables to anatomy texts can be found. Most of the lectures are also put onto 'Emily', sometimes in advance.

Computers At all sites, including both Universities and all three hospitals, students have 24-hour access to brand-new, dedicated IT suites exclusively for the use of medical students. These suites are generously equipped and there always seems to be a computer free to use at any time.

Email is used heavily to communicate with students. Teaching sessions are provided on the use of computers, and specialist support is also available.

Clinical skills Students attend a clinical skills session in brand-new, purpose-built clinical skills centres, based in each main hospital site. Core skills taught include basic and advanced life support, taking blood, measuring blood pressure and physical examinations. Teaching facilities include mock-wards and clinical kit such as defibrillation machines. Development of communication skills is also a key teaching theme which starts with 'initiating a consultation' and includes practising patient interviews with actors. These may vary from the 'patient' with a sore tummy to a 'patient' with suspected schizophrenia. The actors are remarkably convincing! Facilities for recording these 'patient' interviews onto CDs are used so that students can have lasting, take-home records of how cringe-worthy their first attempts at interviewing 'patients' were! Attempts to educate 'patients', this time other students, on how to use condoms can be particularly amusing viewing!

Welfare

Student support

Students have access to pastoral tutors, who are one or two members of staff appointed to each phase and each site. This is a new system and staff are keen to provide appropriate support to students who need it during their time at the medical school.

As students of the universities of Exeter and Plymouth, PMS students have access to the student support services available in their locality. This includes the welfare and equal opportunities offices, student counselling centre, student advice centre, education unit and 'Nightline', a student support hotline. For students with families, support is also available from the student–parent department and family centre.

One of the challenges for the medical school is providing comparable student support for students based in Truro and other outlying hospital sites. However, the senior staff are working hard to remedy this and are developing support mechanisms, including 'buddying' systems for staff and students.

Accommodation

Accommodation is provided for all first-year students in Exeter and Plymouth and third-year students in Truro. In Exeter the accommodation is within walking distance of the campus, hospitals and many of the GP surgeries that students will visit for their placements. It is also conveniently located next to a number of restaurants and banks as well as a chemist and grocery shop which is open till late. In Plymouth, accommodation is central to both the University and city centre. At Plymouth students are housed in a large new building, which is part of a planned development giving new arts' space to the university and city.

Placements

While Peninsula is split across three main sites, Exeter, Plymouth and Truro, students are mostly based in Exeter and Plymouth for the first 2 years with community-based placements across the city. Clinical skills are also taught in the hospitals and in Plymouth and a shuttle bus is provided to get the students from the University to the hospital.

In the subsequent years, students are moved around the south-west and may have a year based in each of the three hospital sites that have their own locality base for students. Each student is allocated a GP practice to visit for a week at a time, three times across the year. In cases where transport to these GP placements each day is an issue, the medical school is in the process of negotiating appropriate accommodation for students and the cost of this will be met by the medical school. Several students volunteer to go further afield, as placements include the seaside towns of Dartmouth and Torquay, moors towns like Tavistock – in short some of the most beautiful areas of the country!

Location of clinical placement/ name of hospital	Distance away from medical school/University campus (miles)	Difficulty getting there on public transport*
Royal Devon & Exeter Hospital	0.5	🚶
Placements in Exeter	0–4	🚶
Derriford Hospital (Plymouth)	6	🚶
Placements in Plymouth	0–4	🚶 🚌
Placements across the south-west	Up to 100	🚗 💡

* 🚶: walking/cycling distance; 🚌 : use public transport; 🚗: need own car or lift; 💡 : get up early – tricky to get to!

Sports and social

City life

Exeter is a city packed with a blend of modern and historical attractions for students. These range from popular nightspots in the city centre and on the waterfront to the magnificent Exeter Cathedral, cobbled alleyways and catacombs.

Plymouth is an interesting mixture of the traditional Devon appeal (think clotted cream teas) and modern edge. Part of the city centre is being redeveloped and will provide great new shopping and city centre venues. Many sailors and surfers live in Plymouth and it's not far from Dartmoor, which provides stunning scenery and the opportunity for fantastic outdoor pursuits. There are plenty of cinemas, good places for eating and drinking, and the infamous Union Street for late-night going out.

Truro is a beautiful cathedral city, surrounded by amazing Cornish countryside. They say that nowhere in Cornwall is more than 16 miles from the sea – so the beach isn't far! Truro is full of good places to drink and eat, although the clubbing scene is rather limited and there is only one small cinema. Truro tends to also be a bit more expensive than the other cities, as there aren't as many students based there.

University life

Plymouth and Exeter provide rather different student experiences. In Plymouth, medical students are integrated into the student population – the halls in the first year are mixed and many second-year medics live with other nonmedic students. By contrast, medical students in Exeter are mainly based on a separate campus from the other Exeter students and are hence less integrated into the wider university. The Medical Society (MedSoc) on both sites have similar aims and provide similar social events such as themed evenings and trips out, sometimes with the aim of charity fundraising. Plymouth MedSoc also has an 'academic' arm; organising lectures and study sessions – and it is planned to expand this to Exeter in the near future. There is also development of (less alcoholic) events that involve families, as there are a fair number of mature students with children. A highlight is the MedSoc balls; at the time of writing Exeter hosts the Christmas Ball and Plymouth the Summer Ball.

MedSIN groups in Exeter and Plymouth are rapidly growing and have started to attract attention from other student societies and students. MedSIN offers students the opportunity to run and participate in numerous different community projects such as Marrow, Sexpression and CPR in schools.

Students also have the opportunity to set up new societies. There is an active drama and music society supported by the medical school, which provides funding for arts and humanities in medicine. Plymouth has a student union whereas Exeter has a student guild. Both do essentially the same job, although no doubt some argument could be made over who has the best socials!

Sports life

Both the main campus and St Luke's campus in Exeter have well-maintained sports halls that include a gym and swimming pool as well as basketball, badminton and squash courts. The Athletic Union in Exeter has over 40 sports clubs (including seven different kinds of martial arts) ranging from archery to windsurfing. Water sports (such as subaqua and surfing) are extremely popular as there are regular trips on the weekends to the coast and nearby beaches.

Plymouth University has its own sailing and diving centres running courses at a small cost. The number of sports clubs is enormous – and if they don't have what you want you can set up your own club! There is also a university gym which is open to all students for a small annual fee. Intraschool sports competitions are also being developed. The first two annual football matches (Plymouth vs. Exeter) have taken place (with both boys and girls teams) and rugby is planned to follow soon.

> **Top tip:** Particularly in the more clinical years of the course, having a car comes in handy; as although Devon and Cornwall are famous for their beauty, they aren't famous for their good transport links! Some placements can be interestingly – and widely – spread across the peninsula.

Great things about Peninsula

- Students learn clinical skills from the first week.
- It's always only a short drive/train ride to the beach.
- Small year groups on each site so no one is a stranger.
- Living costs in both Plymouth and Exeter are relatively inexpensive – Plymouth is particularly cheap.
- The brand-new medical school buildings, with brand-new facilities, exclusively available to medical students are excellent.

Bad things about Peninsula

- No student parking provided at medical school sites.
- After years 1 and 2 on both campuses, students are rotated around various Peninsula Medical School locations in Devon and Cornwall (Exeter, Plymouth, Truro, Barnstaple, Torbay). A downer if you're looking to settle down in one place!
- Peninsula doesn't have an assessment based approach – this may not be good if you are not self-motivated.
- You may never get to meet other students in your year if they move to a different campus from you.
- You may move to a different site after phase I and away from your friends.

Further information

Peninsula Medical School
Tamar Science Park
Research Way
Plymouth
PL6 8BU
Tel: 01752 247 444
Fax: 01752 517 842
Email: pmsenq@pms.ac.uk
Web: http://www.pms.ac.uk

Additional application information

Average A-level requirements	• 320 points from three A-levels including one science subject grade A, plus one further subject at AS-level grade B
Average Scottish Higher requirements	• 320 points from three Advanced Highers including one science subject grade A and one further subject at Higher Level grade B. • Or two Advanced Highers grade A including one science subject plus ABB at Higher level. • Or AAAA (including science) plus a further grade B at Higher level
Make-up of interview panel	• Three: one clinician and two from the following – healthcare professionals, non-clinical academics, lay community members
Months in which interviews are held	• November, December and March • January for mature applicants
Proportion of overseas students	• 7.5%
Proportion of mature students	• 18.7%
Proportion of graduate students	• 23%
Faculty's view of students taking a gap year	• Encouraged
Proportion of students taking intercalated degrees	• 9.6% of year 4 students
Possibility of direct entrance to clinical phase	• No
Fees for overseas students	• £11,000 pa (years 1 and 2) £19,500 pa (years 3, 4 and 5)
Fees for graduates	• £3000 pa
Ability to transfer to other medical schools	• No information
Assistance for elective funding	• No information
Assistance for travel to attachments	• Available
Access and hardship funds	• Available
Weekly rent	• £45–£55 Plymouth • £65 Exeter
Pint of lager	• From £1
Cinema	• £3–£4
Nightclub	• £5

Royal Free and University College London

Key facts	Undergraduate
Course length	6 years (graduates 5 years)
Total number of medical undergraduates	1700
Applicants in 2005	2141
Interviews given in 2005	850
Places available in 2005	330
Places available in 2006	330
Open days 2006	April
Entrance requirements	AAB + AS (2:1 for graduates)
Mandatory subjects	Chemistry at A-level, plus biology AS-Level
Male: female ratio	45:55
Is an exam included in the selection process? If yes, what form does this exam take?	Yes BMAT
Qualification gained	MBBS (BSc)

Fascinating fact: The new University College London Hospital building is set to be the most technologically advanced hospital in Europe, if not the world!

One of the largest medical schools in the UK lies in an exciting, attractive and vibrant part of London. The Royal Free and University College London Medical School (RF&UCMS) is the combined product of two previously separate world-class institutions: Royal Free Hospital School of Medicine (Hampstead) and University College London Medical School (Bloomsbury). The schools are now completely integrated from top to bottom, and incorporate a number of world-famous institutions with excellent reputations for teaching and research. These include the Institute of Child Health (Great Ormond Street), the Institute of Neurology (the National Hospital for Neurology and Neurosurgery), the Institute of Laryngology and Otology (the Royal National Throat, Nose and Ear Hospital), and the Institute of Ophthalmology (Moorfields Eye Hospital). RF&UCMS offers a modern course which is taught by respected academics and clinicians, as well as some very friendly students.

Education

The new curriculum started in 2000. It is a 6-year integrated systems-based course, including a mandatory intercalated BSc for nongraduates. Clinical experience starts from the first day, and although full integration is close to completion, the preclinical/clinical divide has not entirely been abandoned.

Teaching

The core curriculum is traditionally arranged into three distinct phases, although these are becoming integrated. Phase I consists of sequential systems-based learning modules which cover all basic medical subjects. Phase II (science and medical practice, years 3 and 4) consists of a series of sequential clinical attachments, reflecting and building on the systems-based modules of phase I. In year 3 there are eight clinical attachments each comprising a core medicine and surgery teaching course half a day a week (including basic science), half a day of professional development (such as communication, ethics, law and so on) and 1 week of pathology per two attachments . In year 4 there are nine clinical blocks which have varying degrees of formal teaching integrated within them. In phase III (professional development, year 5) there are clinical attachments in general practice, A&E, oncology and district general hospital medicine and surgery, as well as selective specialist clinical or research attachments and a period of elective study.

RF&UCMS prides itself on its professional development spine (PDS). This is a series of themes, integrated through the years, which cover topics including society and the individual, ethics and law, communication skills and evaluation of evidence. Students are allocated a PDS tutor early on in the course, and the greatest legal, ethical and sociological minds are drawn in to lecture.

Assessment

Assessment in phase I of the course is mostly by multiple choice questions (MCQs), and some objective structured clinical examinations (OSCEs), with an emphasis also placed on coursework. By phase II, students are heavily involved in clinical work, and the assessments change to reflect this with the introduction of extended matching questions (EMQs), more OSCEs and a logbook for the recording of clinical firm grades. The phase II, year 4 exams are technically finals exams for the clinical specialties, but the main 'finals' are in medicine, surgery and general practice at the end of phase 3, year 5. These exams consist of 'long station' OSCEs and 'short station' OSCEs, as well as written papers.

Intercalated degrees

All nongraduate students are expected to complete an intercalated BSc. Although the majority of students will intercalate between phases I and II, some will choose to do so later in the medical degree programme, especially if they wish to pursue a BSc programme designed for students with greater clinical experience. The range of subjects to choose from is impressive and new intercalated BSc course units and degree programmes in 2002 were extended to include medical ethics and law, forensic archaeology, and space physiology and medicine. Unfortunately competition for some BSc courses is high, and some students may have to settle for their second choice. Information on the intercalated BSc is given to students in year 2.

Special study modules and electives

In addition to the core curriculum there are special study modules to permit the study of selected aspects in depth. In phase I, several are undertaken and these tend to be nonmedical and can include law, history of medicine, arts and modern languages. A further two are undertaken in phase III, and are almost all clinical or research-oriented. Many of the SSMs are offered at world-class institutions and hospitals such as Great Ormond Street, the National Orthopaedic Hospital, and the London Heart Hospital, giving RF&UCMS students opportunities often unavailable to many other students nationwide.

An elective period of 8 weeks is offered in the final year, although many of the elective rotations border on a holiday period that can also be used to extend the elective time. The minimum time that must be spent in clinical practice is 6 weeks (or whenever you can get your supervisor to sign you off for 6 weeks!). Most take their electives abroad, although help in finding placements abroad is extremely limited, and contact opportunities are limited to your own, or those of friendly clinicians. A limited number of competitive bursaries are offered, although quite hard to acquire, though University College London will reimburse some small costs.

Erasmus

There are currently no opportunities for exchange under the Erasmus programme, and travel overseas is generally restricted to the elective period, although some people have been known to sneak off to Trinidad for their paediatric rotations.

Facilities

Library There are large medical and clinical science libraries on the Bloomsbury campus, a well-stocked and spacious library on the Hampstead campus, and a new and well-stocked library on the Archway (Whittington Hospital) campus. In addition, the many postgraduate medical institutes associated with UCL have specialist libraries within easy walking distance of Gower Street. The

Royal Free and
University College

British Library is a stone's throw away from the Bloomsbury campus as is the Wellcome Institute, the Institute of Neurology, the School of Pharmacy and the London School of Hygiene and Tropical Medicine.

Computers There are clusters of networked computers throughout all RF&UCMS campus sites and in many halls of residence. When they are not booked for formal teaching, students have free access on a first-come first-served basis. Most networked computers are Windows PCs, although there are some Apple computers. All students have free internet and email access, although the university has recently initiated an unpopular move to charge for printing above a certain quota (which medical students almost certainly exceed). IT skills are assessed at the beginning of the course, and there is a scheme for peer tutoring.

Clinical skills There are clinical skills laboratories on all three 'home' campuses, and in addition to timetabled sessions, students may arrange access at other times. They are all well liked by students, allowing such diverse activities as suturing sponges, cannulating plastic arms and catheterising plastic penises – what fun!

Welfare

Student support

In phase I all students are assigned a PDS Tutor, normally a basic scientist who oversees their personal and academic development and provide pastoral care. In phases II and III students are currently assigned personal tutors who are clinically qualified. In addition, the faculty tutorial team provide regular 'walk-in surgeries', and most academic staff in UCL have an open-door policy or clearly advertised hours when they are available to students. UCL has a wide range of welfare, support and counselling services available for students.

Student feedback on course quality and teaching is actively sought through questionnaires, faculty education committees and staff–student consultative committees. Courses will be changed in the light of (valid) student comments. Organisation is generally fairly good, with comprehensive lecture notes being provided by lecturers. Lectures and formal tutorials still form an important part of the new course.

Accommodation

Practically all first-year students stay in UCL or University of London halls. Halls are generally acceptable, although of lower value-for-money than non-London halls. A second year in halls is occasionally available during the BSc or final year. The accommodation office at Senate House offers help and legal advice to London students. To find better-value accommodation, many students choose to travel into central London from places like Finsbury Park and Camden, though it has been known for some students to pick up reasonable rents in central London locations.

Placements

There are three 'home' campuses which make up the Royal Free and University College Medical School. The Bloomsbury site (UCH – a brand new hospital, and the UCL facilities), the Hampstead site (Royal Free), and the Archway site (Whittington). Most teaching in phase I occurs at the Bloomsbury site, except teaching for the PDS which is split across the three.

Most clinical teaching placements in phase II, year 3 and about half in phase II, year 4 are at UCH, Royal Free and Whittington Hospitals, all of which are in central London and are easily accessible by public transport. In the other half of phase II, year 4, and in almost all of phase III, year 5, placements are at more distant district general hospitals (DGHs), which take anything from 30 minutes to a few hours to commute to depending on their location and your location. It is generally possible to either select, or swap DGHs most of the time to ensure you shouldn't have to travel an inordinate amount of time. In addition accommodation is usually provided, given the travelling time, and where accommodation is unavailable, travel costs are reimbursed.

Location of clinical placement/ name of hospital	Distance away from medical school (miles)	Difficulty getting there on public transport*
UCH/Middlesex	0	🚶 🚌
Royal Free	0	🚶 🚌
Whittington	0	🚶 🚌

*: walking/cycling distance; 🚌 : use public transport; 🏎: need own car or lift; 💡: get up early – tricky to get

Sports and social 🏆

City life

The central London location of UCL places students very close to some of the finest theatres, concert halls and museums in the world. The Royal Free campus has both the cosmopolitan atmosphere of Hampstead and the green scenery of Hampstead Heath. In nearby Camden there are opportunities to see live music and visit Camden Lock market. The famous areas of Soho and Covent Garden are only a short walk away from the Bloomsbury campus. Furthermore, you can't walk down a street in Central London without coming across a nightclub.

University life

Students of the medical school are, like all UCL students, members of University College London Union, and they enjoy all the facilities and services that the Union provides. Medical students form a very large group within the total student population, and their special needs are provided for by medical student Union officers on all three sites. As a community we call ourselves 'RUMS' (**R**oyal Free and **U**niversity College **M**edical **S**tudents).

The family-like community of medical students here is encouraged from day 1, when freshers are allocated to a 'set' which they then stay in for social events and competitive sports. Throughout the year the RUMS officers organise various events, including balls, theme nights and shows, beginning with the 14-day extravaganza of RUMS freshers' fortnight. As well as organising a Rag week and running more than 30 clubs and societies, the RUMS officers also represent medical students to the school on educational and welfare-related issues.

UCL Union operates several bars around its central sites, and traditionally medical students have thrust themselves upon the (newly refurbished) Huntley Street bar as their venue of choice, although a new medical student bar is now also opening at the Royal Free Campus. The Whittington Hospital also has a small bar, usually frequented by the doctors, or more often the porters, of the adjacent hospital. The excellent University of London Union (ULU) is directly adjacent to the Bloomsbury campus. This means there is an unparalleled variety of sports and social facilities available, with opportunities to meet students from other disciplines.

Your motto will become 'work hard, play hard' and there is something for every RUMS student to enjoy: there are medic societies as well as the hundreds of Union societies to choose from. We also have our traditional medics' 'comedy' revue company, which puts on an annual Christmas show for the benefit of charity, not to mention legendary balls, together with the official Union entertainment. All dramatic, musical and operatic performances are shown in the college's own renowned West End venue on campus, the UCL Bloomsbury.

One of the most anticipated events is Rag week, which is a high-spirited event that collects money for charity. You'll get up at 5 AM to shake a tin at a tube station and go to bed at 3 AM having exhausted yourself at a party or pub crawl. The societies organise social events ranging from 'civilised' dinners to rather less civilised initiations, and put on plays and musical shows alongside gigs and choral performances. Don't forget that at RUMS you are not confined to socialising within the medical school – you also have the varied clubs and societies of UCL to explore.

Sports life

You can play for RUMS in most sports, but you are also entitled to play for the UCL Union and ULU teams if you wish. They all compete in both national and local competitions in most sports. RUMS teams play at UCL's sports ground in Shenley, Hertfordshire. This is a 60-acre site catering for most sports and is the home ground of the UCL Union teams as well. When not in use for such important fixtures Watford FC is permitted to train there! UCL has a very strong tradition of water-based sports. We row from the University boat house in Chiswick. One highlight of the sporting year is the United Hospital Bumps for eights on the Thames.

The swimming pool in the basement of John Astor House is available to medical students, as are the weights room, gym, squash courts and billiards rooms. Somers Town Sports Centre is a new and important venue for UCL sports and is situated near the Bloomsbury campus. It offers excellent facilities for a number of the RUMS teams, including the basketball, netball, hockey and football clubs. The Union also provides an impressive gym complex, the Bloomsbury Fitness Centre.

Finally, UCL students have full access to ULU facilities and societies and there is a large swimming pool, jacuzzi and sauna in the nearby Malet Street buildings. Of special interest are the various United Hospital sports clubs in which all members of our students' society are encouraged to participate.

Top tip: Look around hard for accommodation when not in halls. Try agencies, notice boards and websites. If you search hard enough and check up several times a day, you might just find that perfectly located, bargain cheap apartment you have always dreamed of!

Great things about RF&UCMS

- One of the top-ranking universities in the UK for research in basic medical sciences and clinical medicine, with a school truly integrated into the multifaculty institution of UCL and associated benefits in terms of sporting, cultural and social facilities.
- The central London location places students very close to some of the finest theatres, concert halls and museums in the world. The Royal Free campus has both the cosmopolitan atmosphere of Hampstead and the green scenery of Hampstead Heath.
- Plenty of opportunity to mix socially and academically with nonmedics at a multifaculty university with many BSc opportunities.
- A major centre of biomedical research, with opportunities to work alongside world leaders in research at a school renowned for its teaching system, with plenty of small-group tutorials, a superbly equipped dissection suite and new teaching and learning facilities.
- Medics are members of their own Union, the UCL Union and the University of London Union, so there is no shortage of student activity even though the opportunities of central London are on your doorstep.

Bad things about RF&UCMS

- Central London can be a little daunting at first if you're not used to living in a big city; and crossing Euston Road every day can't be good for your health with its combination of pollution and dangerous drivers!
- The need to travel around London to get to different campuses: Bloomsbury (UCH), Archway (Whittington) and Hampstead (Royal Free), and the fact that you probably won't be able to avoid a 20-minute tube journey into college after you leave halls.
- Year group sizes are steadily rising (we must be trying to beat GKT!) and are currently around 400. It can be easy to feel isolated and not meet all of your fellow students, especially in the early years. As UCL is a 16,000-strong college you can feel like a very small fish in a very large pond when you first arrive.
- The visible signs of poverty, such as the homeless on the streets, can be depressing.
- Tough retake policy.

Royal Free and
University College

Further information

Faculty Tutor
Faculty of Life Sciences
University College London
London WC1E 6BT
Tel: 020 7679 5487/5494
Email: medicaladmissions@ucl.ac.uk
Web: http://www.ucl.ac.uk/medical school

Students' Union: Medical Students' and Sites' Officer
25 Gordon Street
London WC1H 0AY
Tel: 020 7679 7949
Email: mss.officer@ucl.ac.uk
Web: http://www.uclu.org.uk

Additional application information	
Average A-level requirements	• AAB
Average Scottish Higher requirements	• AAB
Make-up of interview panel	• Three: two UCL staff (one clinical, one life sciences) and one other (student or teacher)
Months in which interviews are held	• November–March
Proportion of overseas students	• 7.5%
Proportion of mature students	• 15%
Proportion of graduate students	• 15%
Faculty's view of students taking a gap year	• Positive
Proportion of students taking intercalated degrees	• 100% (excluding graduates)
Possibility of direct entrance to clinical phase	• Yes – Oxbridge only
Fees for overseas students	• £20,500
Fees for graduates	• £3000
Ability to transfer to other medical schools	• Not normally, extenuating circumstances required, although students transfer into the school from Oxford and Cambridge after their year 3
Assistance for elective funding	• Yes, a few hundred pounds of costs will be refunded to most students
Assistance for travel to attachments	• Travel outside of zone 2 is refunded. If accommodation is provided, only one return journey is paid per week

Access and hardship funds	• There is a large access fund available to all its students throughout the year. Remember there are over 10,000 undergraduates at UCL so it is advisable to get your application in early
Weekly rent	• The minimum you can expect to pay is £65, but you'll fight with commuters for 40 minutes every morning. Most RF&UCMS students pay £80–£100 per week to live in zone 2
Pint of lager	• Only 99 pence on Monday nights at the union! Most other week nights you can expect to pay at least £1.65
Cinema	• The Odeon cinema chain across London offers discounts to student – £5 for latest releases • UCL Union Film Society offers movies you may have missed the first time round for £2
Nightclub	• Big name clubs regularly charge £10–£15 but there are many smaller clubs with lower admission charges. Drinks are expensive

Royal Free and
University College

St Andrews

Key facts	Undergraduate
Course length	3 years (followed by 3 years at Manchester Medical School to obtain MBChB)
Total number of medical undergraduates	424
Applicants in 2005	991
Interviews given in 2005	267
Places available in 2005	124
Places available in 2006	124
Open days 2006	See website for details
Entrance requirements	AAB
Mandatory subjects	Chemistry (plus one of physics, biology or maths at A-level). GCSE English at B or better
Male:female ratio	45:55
Is an exam included in the selection process? If yes, what form does this exam take?	No UKCAT in 2007
Qualification gained	BSc (Hons) in Medicine; MBChB completed at Manchester

Fascinating fact: Dr Susan Whiten, a lecturer in the Bute who is heavily involved with first-year students, both in an educational and pastoral capacity, was selected as Higher Education Science Teacher of the Year in 1999 by the Royal Institution of Great Britain and the Times Educational Supplement.

Established in the 15th century, St Andrews is the oldest university in Scotland. It is set in a small picturesque town on the east coast of Fife. In September 2004, the course was radically changed so that students graduate with a BSc (Med Sci) at Honours level in 3 years (medical students gain direct entry into St Andrews University at the second year level of a 4-year Honours degree programme for which the first year does not exist!). During the 3 years, students are taught a system-based curriculum, where important concepts are frequently revisited and consolidated.

On graduation from St Andrews, the vast majority of students head south for Manchester, where they complete their clinical studies (a further 3 years). The uniqueness of such a course provides a great opportunity for students to experience studying both in an ancient university town and in a big vibrant city. The faculty is small and students socialise with medics and nonmedics alike.

Education

St Andrews University is the oldest university in Scotland, which explains the traditions and customs that surround being a student here. However, always keen to keep up with the needs of a modern doctor in training, the course has been overhauled so that students are taught an integrated curriculum instead of the traditional pure preclinical sciences, like anatomy and physiology. Year 1 is spent learning about the foundations of medicine, in which cellular and molecular processes are emphasised as the starting point for disease, along with other biological sciences, leading to a good understanding of the structure and function of the body. The Honours programme begins over the next 2 years and takes the form of an integrated review of all the main body systems. The final semester consists of two modules. Applied Medical Science links the medical sciences through a series of clinical seminars and patient cases. The final Honours module is a significant student-selected component (SSC) of the course. This may take the form of a course of advanced study, a laboratory based project or a library project.

Students graduate in Medical Sciences, and then progress to a clinical school for a further 3 years before graduating as a doctor. Students are guaranteed a clinical place at the University of Manchester, the largest medical school in Europe, with outstanding clinical facilities. Students are based in one of its three big teaching hospitals, or at Preston or Keele campuses. Clinical relevance is emphasised throughout the course in the form of a series of patients, which the students work on in small groups. The small class size for tutorials and dissection gives a great opportunity to develop good relationships between students and with staff. Some aspects of the course mimic the problem-based learning (PBL) approach in operation at Manchester, and integration between the two schools has improved greatly over the last few years. One of the benefits of the course structure at St Andrews is that students leave here with a degree whether or not they continue medical studies.

Teaching

Throughout the course a wide range of teaching methods are used, including lectures, laboratory-based practicals, computer-based resources, small-group tutorials and problem solving. The medical curriculum is delivered via the university's new web-based managed learning environment, and students are taught how to use these extensive online resources at the start of their course. From here, students can access interactive timetables, and most importantly, are given a set of detailed learning objectives. Unlike in some institutions, students have the increasingly rare opportunity to learn anatomy by careful regional dissection of the whole body. Scheduled classes occupy approximately 15 hours per week, with 6 additional hours set aside for guided study.

Assessment

The learning objectives are the basis of assessment, and students are encouraged to focus their learning in light of these learning objectives. Exams are varied and include a mixture of multiple choice questions (MCQs), short-answer questions, case studies, and objective structured practical examinations (OSPEs). Midterms and practical work done throughout the year contribute a small amount towards the end of year mark.

Intercalated degrees

All students graduate from the University of St Andrews with a BSc in Medical Sciences at Honours level.

Special study modules and electives

The electives are taken at the clinical school you attend. Different types of student-selected components (SSCs) exist throughout the course, with a major component in the final semester that can take the form of laboratory-based research projects, taught modules (such as reproductive biology, cancer biology, health psychology or ethics) as well as library projects using current medical literature, based on a topic of interest selected by the student.

Erasmus

There are no opportunities for Erasmus or study abroad at St Andrews.

Facilities

Library A reasonable range of books is available, with students allowed to borrow up to 25 at any one time, but many students buy the core texts because of the restricted availability of some titles. There are also some titles available in smaller departmental libraries around the university. Books are available on short loan (4-hour/overnight/weekend slots for the most popular titles), 3-day and long loan. St Andrews students are also allowed to borrow books from Dundee medical library. Opening hours are increased during exam periods and shortened over the vacations: Monday–Thursday 8:45 AM–10 PM; Friday 8:45 AM–6 PM; Saturday 9 AM–5 PM and Sunday 1 PM–7 PM.

Computers There are several computer rooms available, including within the Bute Medical building itself, and within halls of residence. The university runs a 24-hour service in computer laboratories scattered around town.

Clinical skills Clinical skills training begins in year 1 and continues throughout the course. Access to the laboratory is good and the staff are helpful. Skills like examining radiographs, taking blood, taking blood pressure and neurological examination of patients are incorporated into the course. There are strong links with the community and the opportunity to gain wider clinical experience through hospital visits, GP attachments and other primary care initiatives in Fife.

Welfare

Student support

This is an area of major strength at St Andrews. In such a small town, the medics are well integrated into the university, and you will have the chance to get to know everyone at the school and make friends outside the faculty. The Dean and faculty are good and very supportive, and tend to get to know everyone by name quite quickly. The Students' Union provides welfare and counselling services, including a free confidential and anonymous 'Nightline' service for students in need of advice. The locals tend to be student-friendly, if only because the university is the biggest local employer and as students make up a third of the town's population. However, when the revelry surrounding some of the ancient traditions still upheld by the university gets a bit over the top (for example, during the infamous Raisin Weekend in November), 'town-and-gown' relations can become a little strained.

Accommodation

All students can spend their first year in university accommodation (halls and flats), and there are often rooms available for further years. Rooms are often shared for first-year students and the standard of flats is generally good. Students can opt to be catered for or self-cater within university residences. Some halls are better than others, but none are bad. Other privately owned accommodation is available, facilitated by a housing office at the university. Rents average £55–£100 a week. Parking is difficult if you want to live in the town centre.

Placements

The medical school consists mainly of the Bute medical building, referred to by students as 'The Bute'. Some other buildings in St Andrews may be used, but they are all within walking distance of each other. St Andrews is very small for a university town, so there is no problem getting around.

The new curriculum provides opportunities to increase the amount of early training and experience in communication skills through a series of family interviews. Using primary care facilities in Fife, students visit a number of different clinics to see clinical teams at work and learn about public health medicine in practice. Thus, strong links are formed with the community from the very start of the course. For clinical placements, please refer to the Manchester chapter.

Sports and social 🏆

City life

St Andrews is a beautiful coastal town, famed for its golf courses, with a population of around 18,000, one third of which is students. Being the oldest of Scotland's four ancient universities, it has more than its fair share of traditions and some of the oldest student societies. The students all live very near the centre of town, so it is never far to walk to meet a friend. There is a very good atmosphere among the students, with plenty of chances to mix with medics and nonmedics, and enough things going on in the town, at the Union and with the societies to keep you as busy as you want to be. Tourists and golf followers can make the town bustle a bit too much at times, but you can go celebrity spotting with some success!

The town has an excellent pub and café culture and there are easily enough pubs, restaurants, and cafés to keep most people happy. Ravers needing something more than the cheesy Union 'bop' every Friday will have to travel to Edinburgh or Dundee for some real action, along with equally die-hard shopaholics. Outdoor types have easy access to the Grampian Mountains, and the nearby sea and beaches can be good fun. There is no railway station at St Andrews; the nearest being Leuchars, which has regular bus services, or taxis costing around £8.

University life

The Union is good – especially for freshers getting to know the place – and alcohol is reasonably cheap, but the club scene is lacking. There are weekly coaches to nightclubs in Dundee, 30 minutes away, which offers clubbers the chance to visit some of the busiest clubs in Scotland. The price for these buses is £5, which includes entrance to the club and a bus back to St Andrews. St Andrews' Medical Society is known as the Bute Medical Society, and has good socials, including a famed annual ball as well as a raucous revue. There are many different types of societies, from the very sensible to the downright silly (the Tunnocks' Caramel Wafer Appreciation Society anyone?). Social life tends to focus around balls and events run by these societies. There is normally something each and every week, giving students plenty of opportunity to meet people both within and outside of the medical faculty, and to keep up with the 'work hard, play hard' adage that medics are famed for.

Sports life

Most sports are supported, especially hockey and rugby, and there is a medics' competition every year called the 'Hypertrophy'. Medical school teams do not play every week, and keen players often get involved with their hall teams or the main university clubs. Interhall competitions are also popular. The facilities have been improved in recent years, such as the gym and athletics union. There is no university swimming pool though one is located within the town. It is, of course, golf heaven, with the Royal and Ancient offering excellent deals for students. Membership is around £100 a year, which includes the Old Course.

> **Top tip:** Try to wait before buying your textbooks. There are usually a lot that you will be told to buy, and you will also be given a lot of choice. It is best to wait to see which books you work best with, which the lecturers tend to recommend, and which you can cope without! You may also find you can grab a bargain from older years selling on their textbooks by keeping an eye on the noticeboards around the Bute.

Great things about St Andrews

- Small year group and good integration with nonmedics and between medics in all 3 years.
- Excellent pastoral and education support, with most lecturers getting to know you on first name terms (can be a good or bad thing!)

- Numerous social activities organised by the Medical Society – there is a different ball to go to practically every week.
- Gives you the opportunity to study medicine in two different institutions.
- St Andrews has its own beach and there is dirt-cheap membership on the best golf courses in Scotland.

Bad things about St Andrews

- Having to leave to pursue your clinical training – you can get very attached to the place!
- No nightclubs, unless you count the Union bop.
- Not many shops – you will probably shop in your home town or travel to Dundee (only 30 minutes' bus ride away).
- It can get a bit cold and windy.
- Relatively small student numbers and the small size of the town can make it difficult to 'get away from it all'.

Further information

Admissions Application Centre
Old Union Building
North Street
St Andrews
Fife KY15 9AJ
Tel: 01334 462 150 (Schools Liaison Service); 01334 476 161 (switchboard)
Fax: 01334 63388
Email: admissions@st-andrews.ac.uk
Web: http://www.st-andrews.ac.uk

Additional application information

Average A-level requirements	• ABB (if physics, biology or maths are not offered at A-level or AS-level, each must normally have been passed at GCSE grade B or better. A good pass in combined or dual science at GCSE will be accepted instead of GCSE Physics)
Average Scottish Higher requirements	• AAAAB
Make-up of interview panel	• Two panel members – mix of teaching and honorary staff
Months in which interviews are held	• November–March
Proportion of overseas students	• 8.5%
Proportion of mature students	• 4%
Proportion of graduate students	• 4%
Faculty's view of students taking a gap year	• Positive, provided relevant to medical career
Proportion of students taking intercalated degrees	• 10%
Possibility of direct entrance to clinical phase	• No
Fees for overseas students	• £15,700
Fees for graduates	• £2700
Ability to transfer to other medical schools	• Guaranteed transfer to Manchester/Preston/Keele for clinical training. Although you can theoretically apply to any university for clinical training
Assistance for elective funding	• N/A
Assistance for travel to attachments	• N/A
Access and hardship funds	• Financial department supplies a means-tested bursary – several different ones available
Weekly rent	• £55–£100
Pint of lager	• £1.50 Union
Cinema	• £3.65
Nightclub	• £3 at Union nightclub

St George's

Key facts	Foundation for medicine	Undergraduate	Graduate
Course length	1 year	5/6 years	4 years
Total number of medical undergraduates	16	1000	280
Applicants in 2005	160	1746	1427
Interviews given in 2005	50	700	300
Places available in 2005	20	187	70
Places available in 2006	20	187	70
Open days 2006	Last Wednesday of every month at 2 pm (except July and September)		
Entrance requirements	Open to mature students	380 UCAS points	2:2 in any discipline and GAMSAT
Mandatory subjects		Chemistry and biology	–
Male:female ratio	50:50	40:60	45:55
Is an exam included in the selection process? If yes, what form does this exam take?	No	No UKCAT in 2007	Yes, GAMSAT UKCAT in 2007
Qualification gained	Undergraduate certificate	MBBS	MBBS

Fascinating fact: St George's Hospital Medical School boasts the longest student bar in the country!

St George's Hospital Medical School (SGHMS) is located in the heart of Tooting, in south London, 5 minutes' walk from Tooting Broadway underground station. It genuinely is a very welcoming school, with plenty of atmosphere and a wide variety of clinical experience available. St George's Hospital itself is one of the largest teaching hospitals in Europe, situated in a heavily populated part of London with pressing health needs. The school offers two medical degree programmes: an established 5-year course and a 4-year graduate-entry programme.

As well as medics, there are nursing, midwifery, physiotherapy, radiography, pharmacy, social work, paramedic and biomedical science students at St George's. While the courses are run separately, the Students' Union runs events available to all. Staff, students and the Students' Union are friendly and welcoming, which creates a strong feeling of community within the hospital. It is this, in particular, that makes SGHMS a great place to study. Most will thoroughly enjoy the atmosphere, and will, at the very least, appreciate what is has to offer.

Education

Teaching

For the 5-year course, the first year begins with the common foundation module, in which much of the teaching is shared by all the first-year health care courses (nurses, physios, radiographers, biomeds, etc.) for the first term. The rest of the teaching is then divided into two core cycles: 1 and 2. In core cycle 1 (years 1 and 2) students study systems modules integrated with some clinical experience and undertake two special study modules (SSMs). In core cycle 2 (years 3–5) students get general clinical experience in hospitals and GP surgeries covering a very wide range of medical and surgical areas. At all clinical attachments structured teaching is provided, in addition to on-going lecture programmes at St George's. Students also complete three more SSMs in core cycle 2, the last of which is the elective. Clinical skills are taught from the beginning of year 1 by students from older years as well as dedicated clinical teaching fellows. They are also taught again at the beginning of year 3 before clinical attachments start.

On the 4-year course, the first 2 years are spent in problem-based learning (PBL) across six modules: life cycle, life support, life maintenance, life control, life structure and life protection, which together cover the whole of basic and clinical science. Within these modules, objectives are listed under four different themes: basic clinical science, community and population medicine, patient and doctor, and personal and professional development. Most 'teaching' is self-directed, but some lectures and seminars are provided. The final 2 years are spent gaining clinical experience with general clinical attachments (GCAs) and specialties. SSMs are also a requirement for this course.

Both courses offer an abundance of communications skills teaching – some would say to the detriment of more 'traditional' subjects such as anatomy. This teaching is, however, very comprehensive and offers the opportunity to meet patients and practise history-taking before entering the clinical years proper and covers some of the hot potatoes such as breaking bad news, before doing it for real.

Assessment

On the 5-year course, exams take place every term for the first 2 years, and term exams contribute to the end-of-year synoptic exams. These must be passed to progress to the next year. At the end of year 3 students take an exam which accounts for 20% of the final MBBS qualification. Three exams taken in year 4 from topics covered in the preceding clinical firms provide 10% each towards written finals, which come at the end of year 4. Electives and clinical finals are in the final year. Written assessment takes the forms of: multiple-choice questions (MCQs), which are negatively marked; extended matching items (EMIs), which are essentially long lists from which the correct answer must be chosen; and short-answer questions (SAQs). In major exams essays make up the bulk of the examination. Practical skills are assessed with objective structured practical examination (OSPEs) or 'spotters', which are predominantly anatomy-based and objective structured clinical examinations (OSCEs), which test clinical skills using actors as patients.

On the 4-year course, exams are after every module for the first 2 years (every 4–7 weeks!), formative in the first and summative in the second. The only requirement in year 1 is to pass the SSM. Exams take a similar format to the 5-year course with MCQs, EMIs and SAQs. In year 2, the 'mini-case' is introduced, taking the form of a clinical scenario given out progressively during the exam, requiring the investigation and diagnosis of a medical or surgical complaint from initial presentation onwards. Year 2 also sees the introduction of OSCEs to assess clinical skills, history taking and ethics. Year 3 is assessed at the end of the year with written papers and OSCEs, with electives and final exams taken alongside 5-year course students.

Intercalated degrees

An intercalated BSc can be taken after the years 2, 3 or 4 on the 5-year course. The later the degree is taken the more clinical in nature it can be. Study may be at St George's Hospital, other London colleges/medical schools, or further afield if you wish. A wide range of courses is available – choices are not restricted to medical or science subjects. Intercalation is currently not offered to 4-year medical students.

Special study modules and electives

SSMs can really provide an opportunity to study an area that is of specialist interest. On the 5-year course, the first two (in year 2) must be undertaken at St George's, but from then on the choice is very open, with the option to study abroad. Many St George's students follow the pattern of taking the first three at St George's and using the fourth as a 'mini-elective' before the main elective, which counts as the final SSM. The 4-year course is more prescriptive: the first SSM is an obstetrics family attachment with an essay to hand in, the second a research project culminating in a poster presentation, the third a clinical mini-elective, and the fourth is the main elective period. All electives at St George's last just over 2 months, and the only requirements are to get signed off by the host institution and hand in a short (1500 word) report.

Erasmus

The IFMSA exchange scheme (handled by the MedSIN group) has recently been introduced to St George's and allows medical students from across the world to swap places for a few weeks. The exchanges scheme is huge and involves over 100 countries, so possibilities are immense. The 4-year course offers the opportunity for some people to swap for a term with students from Flinders University in Australia, which runs a similar course. Places are allocated by lottery.

Facilities

Library The library has just undergone a multimillion pound refurbishment. Facilities are extensive, with about 40,000 books, 800 journals on current subscription, and a total of 77,000 journals available.

Other facilities include interlibrary loans, photocopying, a large history and archive collection, and an audiovisual room with a large variety of video material. Students also have access to the library at the University of London for anything that cannot be found at St George's.

Computers There is an excellent range of computing facilities available, with networked database, CD-Rom and writers, ZIP and interactive media. This can get busy at peak times, but queues are usually short-lived; the provision of free wireless access in the library and student bar has helped, and is a boon for laptop users. The library has an electronic catalogue that allows searching for books and other publications; this can also be used to renew and reserve books, and is accessible over the internet. There are over 100 workstations for network access, Microsoft Word and Excel and a few computers are set aside with scanning facilities and Photoshop. Printing is provided for with monochrome and colour laser printers that are operated using the library copier cards, available from a vending machine. There is also a large 24-hour access computer room in the medical school with about 30 terminals and printing facilities. Good online teaching facilities are available, especially for anatomy. Key topics pages for problem-based learning cover the basic knowledge for the 4-year, and increasingly 5-year, courses.

Clinical skills These facilities have been hugely improved in recent years, with an incredible range of realistic models for students to practise on before being faced with real patients. The rooms housing these gadgets are open 9 AM–5 PM from Monday–Friday, so students can walk in any time they have a free moment. In addition, the clinical skills facilitator is usually on hand to offer guidance on technique. It is a very valuable resource, which students are encouraged to take advantage of.

Welfare

Student support

Students at St George's tend to be friendly and easy-going by nature. There is a strong spirit and students support each other. All freshers are assigned a 'mother' or 'father' student to look after them in their first year. There is normally no problem in borrowing lecture notes and getting useful advice. The school has counselling services on-site, and students can use all ULU (University of London Union) facilities. Relationships between the two medicine courses were a little tense to begin with, but most students now get on very well, and students from all courses are involved with every aspect of St George's life.

The medical school is part of the main teaching hospital but occupies its own distinct area. There are six floors containing the library, computer rooms, teaching theatres, clinical laboratories, Students' Union, NatWest Bank, school shop and offices. The Students' Union, on the second floor, comprises the student bar, Students' Union offices, a coffee shop, school bookshop, games room, music room, and snooker room. Many students and staff go there to relax for lunch and coffee breaks, and many of the extracurricular activities are held there.

Accommodation

All first-year students are guaranteed a place in halls but they are open to all years. The main accommodation costs only £57.50 a week, which represents superb value. It is self-catered and about 10 minutes from the medical school. There is a downside in that rooms are a bit on the small side, and baths, toilets, and kitchen facilities may have to be shared between six or eight people. A small computer room is provided, and wireless networking with direct access to the school network is currently being installed. Catered accommodation is also available, the same distance from the medical school but costing £95 per week, however the rooms are significantly bigger and bathroom/kitchen facilities are shared between three or four. It is also an intercollegiate hall so one is able to meet students from other London colleges. Wireless internet access is provided for a small fee (£15/term at the moment) but this does not connect directly to the school network.

Tooting itself is filled with eager landlords waiting to accommodate local medical students, and rents in the area are more favourable than in many other parts of London, the average per week is about £70–£80. Watch out for estate-agent managed properties, where the landlord may be difficult to track down, and 'hidden' fees (such as contract renewal) may appear.

Placements

From year 3, students are placed at a variety of other hospitals for specialty training. Approximately half of the training takes place at St George's, and there is usually a choice of where you go. Travel expenses may be reimbursed depending on distance, and accommodation is provided for the more distant attachments. Travel to hospitals other than St George's may take from 30 minutes to 2 hours by public transport. The distance to attachments increases in the final year, as you reach the end of your training, with the furthest being Darlington.

Location of clinical placement/name of hospital	Distance away from medical school (miles)	Difficulty getting there on public transport*
Bolingbroke	2	🚶
Springfield	0.5	🚶
St Helier's	4.5	🚗
Kingston	6.5	🚗
Epsom	10	🚗

* : walking/cycling distance; 🏢 : use public transport; 🚗: need own car or lift; 💡 : get up early – tricky to get to!

Sports and social 🏆

City life

St George's students contribute much to the vibrancy of culturally diverse Tooting. Many restaurants, cafes and a huge variety of shops add to its cosmopolitan feel, and the cost-of-living is significantly more affordable than other London locations. We're close to Wimbledon, Clapham and Kingston; 25 minutes from central London and one hour from the south coast.

University life

First and foremost, St George's is now the only free-standing medical school in the UK. All of the students here are studying health care subjects or biomedical science. There is a great feeling of camaraderie in the college: you will get to know most people in your year and many others. There is much mixing between year groups and with students of the other disciplines, which can be an immense benefit whenever you have questions about the course, etc. This is partly because there are so many social events organised by the Students' Union. The medical school itself encourages students and staff to take as positive an attitude to their extracurricular interests as it does to studying.

St George's bar is one of the biggest and cheapest in the country, and is the scene of many a great night for many students. Discos are frequent, comedy nights and bands are well attended, and much fun is had by all. There is big-screen TV with satellite, films, and main football and international rugby matches, etc., are regularly screened. There is a colossal range of societies and clubs to join, from all the conventional sporting ones to a parachuting club and a hill-walking society. There are various religious societies, and a number of performing groups. The Students' Union is supportive of new clubs and societies, or students are welcome to join with those at ULU.

Sports life

St George's is selling its sports ground at Cobham, Surrey. Use of the facilities has been guaranteed until 2006, by when alternative provision has been promised. The rowing teams use the Boat House at Chiswick, where many other London colleges row. The Robert Lowe Sports Centre is on site in Tooting, with six squash courts and three general fitness rooms with exercise bikes, treadmills, rowing machines, and step machines. There is also a weights room and a large sports hall for team sports, such as five-a-side football, badminton, volleyball, netball and basketball. There are regular circuit training and aerobic lessons.

Top tip: Make use of your George's 'Mum' and 'Dad' for information on friendly students, multicultural Tooting and cosmopolitan London.

Great things about St George's

- It's a close-knit community, with many easy-going, fun-loving people for company.
- Location, location, location! The medical school is part of one of the biggest teaching hospitals in Europe, giving easy access to loads of weird and wonderful pathologies.
- If you do have to travel to a distant site expenses are reimbursed or accommodation provided.
- Much support from both staff and students to help you along your way.
- Freshers' month lasts a month-and-a-bit. Yes, that's right, St George's offers 5 weeks of continuous freshers' events, from the St George's Ball to a three-legged pub crawl. Numerous discos and nonalcoholic events also feature.

Bad things about St George's

- Although you are at a London medical school, St George's cannot pretend to be central London. Tooting to Leicester Square is about 30 minutes on the tube and 50 minutes on the night bus.
- Lack of students studying anything apart from health sciences can limit the conversation!
- The small size can mean that if you don't get on with someone you're unlikely to be able to avoid them!
- Parking at or even near the hospital can be difficult and expensive (no charge at halls – 15 minutes' walk)
- St George's does not have the capacity to offer an intercalated BSc to all its students, although most of those who want to pursue this course of study usually manage it.
- The hospital canteen food can leave a lot to be desired!

Further information

St George's Hospital Medical School
Cranmer Terrace
London SW17 ORE
Tel: 0208 6729944
Fax: 0208 7252734
Email: medicine@sghms.ac.uk
Web: http://www.sghms.ac.uk

Additional application information

Average A-level requirements	• 380 UCAS points
Average Scottish Higher requirements	• 380 UCAS points
Make-up of interview panel	• Three interviewers and a student
Months in which interviews are held	• November–March (undergraduate) March–April (graduate) February (premedical)
Proportion of overseas students	• 7.5%
Proportion of mature students	• 30%
Proportion of graduate students	• 25%
Faculty's view of students taking a gap year	• Encouraged
Proportion of students taking intercalated degrees	• 40%
Possibility of direct entrance to clinical phase	• Yes (undergraduate only)
Fees for overseas students	• £15,000 pa (years 1 and 2) £23,000 pa (years 3, 4 and 5)
Fees for graduates	• £3000 (for 2006)
Ability to transfer to other medical schools	• Yes – for clinical years 3, 4 (and 5)
Assistance for elective funding	• Some, limited. Although good resources and help with applications to other funding bodies available
Assistance for travel to attachments	• Most are close, public transport predominates; limited funding provided for more distant attachments
Access and hardship funds	• Hardship funds (currently only for home students) available on application
Weekly rent	• £60 (self-catered halls) • £95 (catered halls) • £70–£80 (apartments in Tooting)
Pint of lager	• £1.35
Cinema	• £5 (Wimbledon)
Nightclub	• £2.50–£4 at St George's • £2–£4 student nights in Wimbledon and Kingston

Sheffield

Key facts	Premedical	Undergraduate
Course length	6 years	5 years
Total number of medical undergraduates	18	1300
Applicants in 2005	396	3938
Interviews given in 2005	42	644
Places available in 2005	18	241
Places available in 2006	18	241
Open days 2006	Eight – please see website for details	Eight – please see website for details
Entrance requirements	AAB	AAB
Mandatory subjects	–	Chemistry and another science
Male:female ratio	1:2.6 (2005 intake)	1:1.5 (2005 intake)
Is an exam included in the selection process? If yes, what form does this exam take?	No	Yes UKCAT in 2007
Qualification gained	MBChB	

Fascinating fact: Professor Anthony Weetman, the Dean, is an internationally renowned thyroid expert.

Sheffield is a city built on seven hills – like Rome – and is almost, but not quite, as scenic! The university has a very large undergraduate population (over 15,000) and Sheffield is reputedly one of the best student cities in Britain (see The Virgin Alternative Guide to British Universities), and that included the big place down south. It was also given the title of UK University of the Year for 2001.

The majority of students live and work in the scenic – i.e. hilly – parts of town, but there is a wide variety of areas to choose from. The medical school attracts students from all walks of life and there is a good mixture of backgrounds. It uses a systems-based teaching scheme, running since 1994, which is under regular review. In general the curriculum can be seen as a hybrid of the traditional science-based course and the newer problem-based learning (PBL) approach, with increasing emphasis on self-directed learning. There tends to be one set of exams at the end of each year, and some project work is undertaken in groups throughout the year.

The medical school is based at the Royal Hallamshire Hospital, which is situated adjacent right next to the main university campus. The early years teaching mainly takes place at the medical school, biomedical sciences building and the auditorium within the university union. The clinical years are taught on the wards of the various Sheffield and district general hospitals.

Lecture blocks for the whole year group are held in the medical school and the excellent Union cinema, but smaller groups attend the Northern General Hospital Medical Education Centre. This provides much better teaching facilities, but is situated on the other side of town (20 minutes from the university).

Education

The course is divided into six phases. Phases Ia and b are essentially years 1 and 2 and span the first 2 years, consisting mainly of systems-based lectures, some clinical demonstrations and fortnightly integrated learning activities (ILAs). Clinical skills such as history-taking from actual patients are included from year 1 onwards. A new, unique feature of year 1 is that following the Christmas vacation there is a 3-week block consisting of early patient contact with a doctor, nurse and nursing home staff in separate 1-week blocks. This is called 'intensive clinical experience' (ICE).

Phase II lasts for only 6 months and involves an introduction to clinical medicine, consisting of such things as history taking, examination skills and professional behaviours. The phase finishes with a set of objective structured clinical exams (OSCEs) in January. There are no written papers at the end of this phase. Phases IIIa and b follow this and last for 2 years. During this period, you rotate around clinical specialties, special study modules (SSMs), and undertake the elective. Phase IIIa is assessed with both OSCEs and written exams. At the end of phase IIIb you sit your final written papers, for the MBChB. Phase IV starts with 6 months of purely clinical work, and the final OSCEs for the MBChB are taken in the summer.

The clinical course has been redesigned to increase the number of ward attachments, but has reduced the time spent on each attachment. These changes have given students a broader range of experience and teaching, but have reduced the opportunity to settle into a placement.

Teaching

The emphasis at Sheffield is on teaching broad concepts rather than detailed facts. This relies on the students' desire to look things up for themselves and hopefully produces doctors who are committed to lifelong learning. There is a lot of anatomy dissection, with plenty of opportunity to get 'hands on' experience, as well as practicals in physiology and biochemistry. Animals are not used in the lab, although animal products are. The number of lectures has been reduced to allow time for small-group project work and self-directed learning. Clinical years consist mostly of ward-based attachments, interspersed with lecture blocks and tutorials in year 3.

Handouts outlining timetables and course objectives are provided at each stage. The elected year representative is extensively involved with the academic staff and is supposed to be the first port of call in times of poorly organised teaching. Formal teaching sessions are rarely cancelled. Ward-teaching is variable, with some excellent and some poor teaching, depending largely on the clinician doing the teaching.

Assessment

Assessment of preclinical students is mainly by the end-of-year exams, which comprise written multiple choice question (MCQ) papers and practical spotter exams. The practical exam consists of dissection specimens to test anatomy, physiology, biochemistry and physiology, but there is some continuous assessment through projects and practical write-ups. There are also brief anonymous tests at the end of each module, which are used as a means to monitor your own progress – otherwise known as formative assessment. In the clinical years, objective structured clinical examinations (OSCEs) are added as well as written papers, and used to examine clinical skills.

Intercalated degrees

The option of spending an extra year studying for a Batchelor of Medical Science (BMedSci) is open to anyone who has passed all their preclinical exams. Funding is available for most places, which are generally research and/or laboratory-based. There is little competition for places and students can 'design' their own degree. The faculty publishes a list of projects open to BMedSci students, and staff are very keen to recruit students. However, owing to Sheffield's unique course format, which runs January to January, students wishing to study away from Sheffield will have to apply to the medical school for permission to leave midway for the BSc/BMedSci which is usually no problem (typically Honours degrees run September to September).

Special study modules and electives

There is one 8-week elective period during year 4 which (if approved by faculty) is usually completed abroad. Some help with funding is available.

Many clinical students get involved in their own special study modules (SSMs) by helping a relevant consultant in their chosen expertise either as research, audits and the like.

Erasmus

Sheffield does not participate in the Erasmus scheme as the course is completely integrated and does not allow sufficient flexibility. Students who nevertheless are keen to experience medicine in a different country are encouraged to do so through the elective or SSM.

Facilities

Library Libraries are situated around the university and in all hospitals used for teaching. The two main medical libraries have been refurbished and have on-site computer access, including access to the internet and Medline. Core texts and places to sit are increasing, but be prepared to fight for them at exam time. Opening hours are reasonable, but are limited during weekends.

Computers There are widespread computer facilities throughout the university and in the Royal Hallamshire, but be prepared to wait at peak times. One site is open 24 hours. Software provided includes email, internet access, and an increasing number of computer-assisted learning (CAL) packages that students are encouraged to use.

Clinical skills There are two new labs, one at the Northern General and one at the Royal Hallamshire. Others exist at each of the peripheral hospital and although they're not as extensive, they're excellent nonetheless.

Welfare

Student support

First-year students are eased into the course fairly gently and there are usually plenty of people around to help you with problems. Most lecturers are willing to help solve academic problems, and the undergraduate deans are very approachable. Each student is allocated a social tutor and medical students from the years above as part of a social group to help out with any problems and offer advice, but support tends to be patchy and dependent on the involvement of individual tutors. The scheme is currently under review. The Students' Union and the university have counsellors and provide welfare support. A new 'buddy scheme' has been initiated whereby a couple of medics in year 2 act as 'parents' for a couple of medics in the year below. The point of this is not as it may first seem, as an extension of the nanny state! Instead it serves to provide a source of information, help and so on for first-year students in case they are unwilling to approach academic staff.

Accommodation

All first-year students are guaranteed university-owned accommodation, either in a catered hall of residence or in self-catering accommodation. The standard is pretty good, a major plus being that it is all within easy walking distance of university and in the better part of town. Most (but not all) students move into the private rented sector for their second year. Plenty of housing is available, mostly on 12-month contracts.

Placements

Throughout the clinical phase there are peripheral attachments in hospitals throughout South Yorkshire and Humberside (up to 50 miles away). There is also a 10-week attachment at a GP practice in or around Sheffield, to which students commute. First-year students shadow a patient suffering from a chronic illness, to assess the impact of disease on daily living. This is known as the community attachment scheme (CAS), and takes a different approach to most of the medical course because it emphasizes the social effects of disease, rather than how to treat it.

On-call rooms are available in Sheffield, with more permanent (free) accommodation in district general hospitals (DGHs).

Location of clinical placement/ name of hospital	Distance away from medical school (miles)	Difficulty getting there on public transport*
Royal Hallamshire Hospital, Sheffield	0	
Rotherham DGH	11	
Chesterfield and North Derbyshire Royal Hospital	16	
Doncaster Royal Infirmary	27	
Hull Royal Infirmary	68	

* : walking/cycling distance; : use public transport; : need own car or lift; : get up early – tricky to get to!

Sports and social

City life

The city centre is compact and not terribly well laid out, but has a good collection of small shops and restaurants, while Division Street has lots of trendy student shops and many trendy bars. Eccleshall Road boasts many trendy cafes and shops but is situated in the more scenic part of Sheffield, not far from the centre. (Real shopaholics go to the huge purpose-built out-of-town Meadowhall Centre, accessible by bus, train and tram, with every high-street store under the sun.)

Sheffield is famous for having the most bars and pubs in one city outside London. There are an ever-increasing number of new nightclubs, café-bars and live music venues. With so many clubs there is a student night nearly every day of the week, with cheap entry, drinks promotions, and a free bus to and from the venue. There are two theatres and five cinemas, which all have student discounts for those after a bit of culture: the UGC cinema contains the biggest screen in Europe, appropriately called The Full Monty.

The crowning glory of Sheffield is the Peak District. This attracts many active outdoor types (especially climbers) to the university, as well as those who like to relax over a pint in a nice country pub. Just 10 minutes' drive from the university you can walk, cycle, climb, admire the stunning scenery, and forget about medicine. The local people are generally friendly and it is very easy to settle in at Sheffield quickly.

University life

Sheffield University Union is considered to be one of the best in the country, and has just been refurbished again. However, if you are looking to be part of a medical clique, Sheffield may not be for you. The school is keen to recruit away from the stereotypical medic and a wide range of backgrounds is represented. Medics are very much part of the university as a whole and the city has such a small, friendly feel to it that settling in is quick and easy.

The Medical Society organises regular social events; the annual November Ball (be prepared to save up for it) and the legendary Medics' Revue are particularly well supported, as well as the annual fancy dress three-legged pub crawl and loads of guest lectures involving free pizza. The society is also excellent in representing you academically and in welfare and is the largest student society at both Sheffield and Sheffield Hallam University!

The Students' Union organises cheap and cheerful events every night of the week, including Pop Tarts if you like your culture 'dumbed down'. There is a huge variety of clubs and societies available to join: anyone fancy the Warhammer Assassins' Guild or Star Trek the Whistling Society? Those interested in the more altruistic side to medicine can join the Marrow Appeal set up by medical students, or MedSIN, which are both active in Sheffield.

In addition, people from all religious denominations are catered for through their respective religious societies. Muslim prayer rooms can be found within the medical school and the Student Union.

Sports facilities

The city of Sheffield has inherited a large range of world-class sports facilities after hosting the World Student Games, including the Olympic swimming pool at Pondsforge and Don Valley athletics stadium. Unfortunately, the free university facilities are on the disappointing side; consisting mainly of a pool and several Astroturf pitches. All sports are well catered for, but the dry ski slope and indoor climbing wall are particular attractions. The medical school has numerous sports teams, with the rugby, football and hockey clubs all being particularly active.

> **Top tip:** Join the Medical Society! £37 for 5-year membership may sound loads but the discounts for white coats, stethoscopes and dissection kits from the Freshers' Fair and the free BNF in the Clinical Fair gives you most of the money back! Plus, membership guarantees you application to the annual ball, which is incredibly popular, as well as cheaper entry for all society events. Over a 5-year period you'll save loads – especially if you want to get stuck in with the medics lifestyle!

Great things about Sheffield

- The course allows individuals to learn things at their own pace. Lecturers are very accessible and are usually happy to help with any problems.
- There is still dissection and on-hands practicals instead of prosections which are beginning to turn up at all new medical curriculums. Definitely a dying breed.

- There are endless clubs for all music tastes, bars and coffee shops for the trend setters, and just about every type of entertainment under the sun.
- Student accommodation is in the nicer parts of town, within easy (and safe) walking distance of the university and all local amenities. Sheffield was voted the Safest Student City in the UK in 2001.
- Sheffield medics are down-to-earth and represent a wide cross-section of society. Medical students are part of the university as a whole and not just the medical school. This enables them to make use of all the facilities available, and to escape from medicine when they want to.

Bad things about Sheffield

- Students complain of faculty's lack of organisation and inability to provide up-to-date information on the continually changing curriculum.
- Self-directed learning is hard if you are a poor self-motivator and leave things to the last minute; with formal assessment only at the end of the year, it's easy to fall behind.
- According to the consultants, they don't teach anatomy like they used to ... or physiology, or biochemistry, etc.!
- Some of the peripheral attachments are to slightly less than glamorous towns – Hull, Grimsby, Rotherham, Scunthorpe and Barnsley.
- Hills – good practice if you're training for Everest!

Further information

Sub-Dean for Admissions
Medical School
University of Sheffield
Beech Hill Road
Sheffield
S10 2RX
Tel: 0114 271 3349 (medical school reception)
0114 271 3727 (medical admissions)
Fax: 0114 271 3960
Web: http://www.shef.ac.uk
Email: medadmissions@sheffield.ac.uk

Additional application information

Average A-level requirements	• ABB (in two sciences, one of which must be chemistry)
Average Scottish Higher requirements	• AAAAB and Advanced Higher at grade AB in chemistry and another science subject
Make-up of interview panel	• Medically qualified senior staff, biomedical scientist and medical student or lay person
Months in which interviews are held	• November–March
Proportion of overseas students	• 5.3%
Proportion of mature students	• 17.4%
Proportion of graduate students	• Not known
Faculty's view of students taking a gap year	• Acceptable
Proportion of students taking intercalated degrees	• 3%
Possibility of direct entrance to clinical phase	• No
Fees for overseas students	• £10,500 (preclinical 2005 figure) • £19,350 (clinical 2005 figure)
Fees for graduates	• £3000 pa
Ability to transfer to other medical schools	• Yes, if other medical school consents
Assistance for elective funding	• Yes, bursaries and loans available
Assistance for travel to attachments	• None
Access and hardship funds	• Available
Weekly rent	• £49–£100 (halls) • £40–£70 (private)
Pint of lager	• £1.30 Union bar • £2 city centre
Cinema	• £1.50–£3.80
Nightclub	• £3–£9

Southampton

Key facts	Premedical*	Undergraduate	Graduate
Course length	1 year	5 years	4 years
Total number of medical undergraduates	30	1050	80
Applicants in 2005	232	3029	1297
Interviews given in 2005	110	172 across both programmes	
Places available in 2005	30	206	40
Places available in 2005	30	206	40
Open days 2005	tbc	tbc	
Entrance requirements	200 UCAS points. Selection based on academic and non-academic criteria	ABB – selection based on academic and non-academic criteria. See www.som.soton.ac.uk for full details	2:1 in any discipline – selection based on academic and non-academic criteria. See www.som.soton.ac.uk for full details
Mandatory subjects	Biology/human biology and chemistry	Chemistry	Chemistry
Male:female ratio	40:60	37:63	37.5:62.5
Is an exam included in the selection process? If yes, what form does this exam take?	No	No UKCAT in 2007	No UKCAT in 2007
Qualification gained	BM Medicine	BM Medicine	BM Medicine

*Six-year widening access programme with Year 0 – this programme offers a guaranteed place on the BM5 programme (conditional upon satisfactory completion of the Year 0).

Fascinating fact: *Young Doctors* was filmed here!

The medical school at Southampton University is modern and student-friendly. It is a young medical school, with a well-developed modern course. Southampton pioneered the new integrated curriculum now in operation in most UK medical schools. As such, it has had more experience than most schools at settling in to the new ways of learning medicine. In the first 2 years a significant amount of time is set apart for interprofessional learning, a programme that involves working with other health science fields such as nursing, midwifery and rehabilitation sciences. Southampton has just about everything city life has to offer, but on a scale which is easy to cope with, and, of course, it's by the sea!

Education

The fully integrated course has an increasing clinical component throughout the 5 years. During the first 2 years, each term deals with the basic science and clinical aspects of a major organ system, and includes clinical sessions in general practice and in the labour ward. Year 3 is the first clinical year, and students work in the Southampton area. Exams at the end of this year integrate basic science and clinical knowledge, a feature that is valued by students. Year 4 comprises clinical experience in the minor specialties, plus a research project. This educational innovation enables students to study an area of their choice for 8 months, finishing with a dissertation and presentation. Some are fascinated by their project, but others are not and feel they forget a lot of the first 3 years' teaching. Final-year students are spread throughout the Wessex region in large teaching hospitals and smaller district general hospitals (DGHs). Southampton has complied with GMC recommendations to limit the amount of factual knowledge that is required, and as a result the examinations are not structured to make you regurgitate thousands of facts but to test your ability to solve clinical problems, that is, to be a good doctor!

Teaching

In the early years students spend most of their time on the main university campus with other, nonmedical, students learning in lectures, tutorials, and laboratory practicals. Southampton has also been introducing computer-assisted learning (CAL) into the curriculum.

Assessment

The major exams are at the end of years 1 and 3 and throughout the final year.

Intercalated degrees

Between 5% and 15% of students take the opportunity to spend an extra year between years 3 and 4 to study for a BSc, usually in biomedical science. Only a few students do this, because of the extra expense, and because all students spend time in research during year 4. Students who already have undergraduate research experience may skip the year 4 project and take an accelerated course, qualifying 6 months earlier.

Special study modules and electives

At the end of year 3 students have an 8-week elective during which they may decide to spend time working in a hospital abroad.

There are SSMs during year 3, where students may choose to study a particular area in depth, and in year 5 there is a 5-week block when students choose which specialty to gain additional experience in.

Erasmus

The medical school has no Erasmus programme, but you always have your elective.

Facilities

Library Students have access to the biomedical sciences library on the main campus and the health sciences library at the General Hospital. Library facilities are good, although the most popular books are always in demand and students find it more convenient to buy core texts.

Computers The computer facilities are very good and are updated regularly. Workstations are available all over the campus, at the General Hospital, and in some halls of residence.

Clinical skills This is an excellent facility and used in the medicine in practice course in years 1 and 2, as well as in some of the clinical attachments in years 3 and 4. It is also used for revision during the final year.

Welfare

Student support

Most people are struck by the friendliness of the staff and students at the medical school when they visit. A scheme has recently been set up whereby students run minitutorials for newer students in order to pass on the most relevant information: which books to buy, books not to buy, consultants with nice yachts who often need crew on trips round the Channel Isles – all the really important stuff. Southampton University has a counselling service, and the Students' Union has welfare services.

Accommodation

Students are offered a place in halls of residence for their first year only. There are a range of options, from a small self-catering room with no sink, to a large *en suite* room with breakfast and evening meal. Which option you choose is governed mostly by your bank balance! A limited number of places is available in halls for subsequent years, but most people move into private rented houses in the Highfield and Portswood areas. Most halls are within a mile of the medical school.

Placements

The main university campus is in the Highfield/Bassett area of Southampton and is close to most of the halls of residence. The General Hospital, where most of years 3 and 4 as well as 1 or 2 days a week in years 1 and 2 are spent, is about 1 mile away in Shirley. There is a reliable university bus service connecting all sites.

Clinical attachments may be in local Southampton hospitals though in year 3 and in the final year, they can be in several hospitals and GP practices as far afield as Guildford or Portsmouth. In these final-year placements there are fewer students per hospital and, consequently, more individual attention;

students give excellent feedback from these placements. Accommodation and travel expenses are provided on peripheral attachments.

Location of clinical placement/name of hospital	Distance away from medical school (miles)	Difficulty getting there on public transport*
Winchester	14	🚗
Portsmouth	20	🚗
Isle of Wight	10	🚗
Salisbury	24	💡 🚗
Guildford	60	💡 🚗

* 🚶: walking/cycling distance; 🚌: use public transport; 🚗: need own car or lift; 💡: get up early – tricky to get to!

Sports and social 🏆

City life

Southampton has been widely rebuilt, having been heavily bombed during the Second World War. There is a wide range of shops and restaurants, and most of the amenities you would expect of a city are evident. There are over 35,000 students in the city, which has a range of clubs, pubs, cinemas, and eateries. The New Forest is popular for nature lovers, cyclists and 'pub-lunchers', and the Solent and the Isle of Wight are popular with sailors. The proximity to Bournemouth beach is a bonus for sun and sand lovers. London is close enough for a day or night out by car, coach, or train.

University life

The Students' Union runs every club you could ever imagine wanting to join, and quite a few others besides! The Union building hosts nightclub events and bands. The on-site theatre and concert hall host lots of nonmainstream acts and performances. The medical school is renowned for its strong social life, and has a number of sporting and other societies. There is an annual ball, which is the most popular in the university, and an extravagant Christmas revue, which never fails to entertain.

Sports life

The University of Southampton has excellent water sports teams. The facilities are accessible to everyone, from those who have never sailed/rowed/canoed in their lives to those who wish to compete at an international level. Southampton has teams in most sports.

Top tip: Buy a bike – you can travel all over the city much more easily than on any other form of transport, and the entire wider area (Isle of Wight, New Forest) is also easy to reach!

Great things about Southampton

- Excellent course, which is well liked by students.
- Good patient/doctor to student ratio on attachments.
- Students are part of the main university, not just the medical school.
- Staff are very student-friendly and approachable and there is a great support network if you experience problems.
- It's on the south coast, therefore relatively warm – and it's by the sea!

Bad things about Southampton

- As it's one of the newest medical schools, some of the older consultants tend to be sceptical about any 'newfangled' ways of doing things.
- Too many distractions – university social life, medical school social life, good lectures, beautiful countryside.
- The city's nightlife isn't what it could be.
- Having the elective after just 1 year of clinical work makes you less useful in a hospital abroad.
- Some of the year 5 attachments can leave you feeling isolated and away from Southampton (for example Isle of Wight), but this doesn't last too long – maximum 8 weeks.

Further information

Admissions Office
University of Southampton
Biomedical Sciences Building
Bassett Crescent Building
Bassett Crescent East
Southampton SO15 7FX
Tel: 02380 594 408
Fax: 02380 594 159
Email: prospenq@soton.ac.uk, bmadmissions@soton.ac.uk
Web: http://www.som.soton.ac.uk

Additional application information

Average A-level requirements	• ABB
Average Scottish Higher requirements	• AAAAB
Graduate entry requirements	• 2:1 in any discipline
Make-up of interview panel	• Two members of medical selection committee (where appropriate)
Months in which interviews are held	• February–April (premedical) January–April (undergraduate and graduate)
Proportion of overseas students	• 9.5%
Proportion of mature students	• 5%
Proportion of graduate students	• 7%
Faculty's view of students taking a gap year	• Encouraged if used constructively
Proportion of students taking intercalated degrees	• 18%
Possibility of direct entrance to clinical phase	• No
Fees for overseas students	• £10,800 pa (years 1 and 2) • £19,800 pa (years 3, 4 and 5)
Fees for graduates	• £1175 pa
Ability to transfer to other medical schools	• If the other medical schools consents
Assistance for elective funding	• Some bursaries are available, but not many
Assistance for travel to attachments	• For those without a car efforts are made to arrange attachments within the city limits if possible. Some though will have to be on attachment to hospitals in the region, but usually at least one person will have access to a car. Reimbursement for travel is provided
Access and hardship funds	• Through the central university
Weekly rent	• £50–£60
Pint of lager	• £1.50 Union • £2.15 city centre pubs • 50 pence certain places and nights
Cinema	• £4.50
Nightclub	• Several, prices vary

Wales College of Medicine

Key facts	Premedical	Undergraduate	Graduate
Course length	1 year	5 years	4 years – at Swansea University
Total number of medical undergraduates	15	1500	108
Applicants in 2005	226	2600	501
Interviews given in 2005	22	773	175
Places available in 2005	15	305	70
Places available in 2006	15	305	70
Open days 2006	April and July	April and July	April and July
Entrance requirements	ABB plus AS minimum C, from 21 units	ABB plus AS minimum C, from 21 units	2:1 degree in any discipline
Mandatory subjects	One science A-level	Biology and chemistry (one A grade). Minimum B at AS level	Maths, English and Biology/Chemistry to GCSE
Male:female ratio	40:60	40:60	
Is an exam included in the selection process? If yes, what form does this exam take?	No	No UKCAT in 2007	Yes, GAMSAT UKCAT in 2007
Qualification gained	MBBCh		

The University of Wales College of Medicine has merged with Cardiff University and together they have a link institution with the University of Wales. Within the new merged institution there is a new Wales

College of Medicine made up of the Schools of Medicine, Dentistry, Nursing, Health care Studies, Postgraduate Medical and Dental Education, Psychology, Optometry, Pharmacy and Biosciences; this provides a unique opportunity for interprofessional health education. The university has strong links with all hospitals in Wales, offering clinical placements across the Principality. Students from all walks of life – mature, overseas, Welsh and non-Welsh – make a varied student body, providing a peer group for almost any person. The university is ideally located for the leisure/recreation/social facilities available in this small, yet friendly capital city.

Education

The course has been following the new curriculum since October 1995. It is guided by five themes and delivered through 11 subject panels, with practical experience gained through clinical modules. Year 1 is the foundation year, introducing basic clinical and scientific skills and knowledge, with years 2 and 3 developing them further. Years 4 and 5 place a greater emphasis on clinical experience in preparing for the role of house officer. Teaching is provided through core and student selected components.

September 2004 saw the first intake into the new 4-year graduate entry programme. The first 2 years of the course follow a problem-based learning style, and is based at Swansea University. At the end of these 2 years the students will have to meet the same learning outcomes as the year 3 students in Cardiff and then they will all enter the same final 2 years of the course based in Cardiff.

Teaching

A combination of lectures, tutorials, small group sessions, and self-directed learning makes up the bulk of the learning. Anatomy is learnt by hands-on human dissection and taught using demonstrated dissection and prosections. Various computer-assisted learning (CAL) programs are used, mainly as a revision medium and for tutorial support. Firm sizes vary depending on the hospital: five to six in the main teaching hospitals, and usually two in the district general hospitals (DGHs) (varying from one to four).

Assessment

Examinations take place at the end of years 1, 3, 4 and 5, with resits being available in years 1 and 3. Continuous assessment and the satisfactory completion of all coursework and student selected components are a feature of the examination process.

Intercalated degrees

Intercalated degrees are available to one-third of the year, and can be done after years 2, 3, and 4. There is a choice of subjects, including basic medical sciences (anatomy, physiology, biochemistry), or more clinically orientated modular degrees in medical sciences.

Student selected components and electives

Special study modules make up 24%–30% of the timetable throughout the 5 years. An 8-week period of elective study, either in the UK or abroad, is undertaken at the start of the final year as part of the normal block rotation. Students pursue an original research project on any subject of personal interest and provide a written report of their elective experience.

Erasmus

The College participates in the Erasmus exchange programme which is funded by the European Union. Opportunities exist for students to study for 3 months in France, Germany, Finland, Holland, Italy, Sweden and Romania.

Facilities

Library The library facilities in the main teaching hospital consist of three separate libraries, two 24-hour reading rooms and a 24-hour computer room containing 40 computers. The availability of texts and journals is excellent. Students also have access to the library and computing facilities of the University of Wales, Cardiff University, and many other libraries in most hospitals.

Computers There are adequate computer facilities on site, and in most outlying hospitals. Some tuition is given initially, and all submitted work is expected to be word processed and in some cases submitted electronically.

Clinical skills Cardiff has a new skills laboratory which is heavily used. It is a key focus for the new curriculum.

Welfare

Student support

The school of medicine at Cardiff University is very student friendly and actively encourages and acts upon the views of its students. Weekly meetings between student reps and the deanery staff occur where students' grievances are voiced in an informal setting. Students are also represented on all the curriculum planning committees. Being part of the Cardiff University allows students access to its general counselling and welfare services, as well as pastoral care within the faculty.

Accommodation

Accommodation is provided in the first year by Cardiff University. There is space for all year 1 students in halls. The standards are high, with over 50% of accommodation being less than 5 years old, and two-thirds is *en suite*. There is ample good-quality private housing for rent, with prices ranging from £45–£55 a week. Cardiff Council runs a house renting registration scheme, which aims to monitor and license rented accommodation in the city.

Placements

The medical school is based on two sites approximately 1½ miles apart: the Cardiff School of Biosciences (a part of Cardiff University Cathay's Park campus) and the Heath Park Campus jointly occupied with the University Hospital of Wales. Community-based teaching in practices in and around Cardiff forms a substantial part of the course. Hospitals throughout Wales are used for teaching, ensuring an excellent student–patient ratio. It also provides an opportunity for students to see all of the different parts of Wales, and gain more of an idea where to apply for jobs a few years down the line. Bangor is the most distant of the district general hospitals (DGHs) used, being 260 miles away from Cardiff. Attachments in general practice include some time spent at a rural practice somewhere in Wales. Travel subsidies are available from the college, and accommodation is provided in all DGHs that are not within a reasonable commutable distance from Cardiff.

Location of clinical placement/ name of hospital	Distance away from medical school (miles)	Difficulty getting there on public transport*
University Hospital of Wales, Cardiff	0	
Royal Glamorgan Hospital, Llantrisant	12	
Princess of Wales Hospital, Bridgend	20	
Singleton Hospital, Swansea	40	(onsite accommodation provided)
Ysbyty Gwynedd, Bangor	260	(onsite accommodation provided)

* : walking/cycling distance; : use public transport; : need own car or lift; : get up early – tricky to get to!

Sports and social

City life

Cardiff is a very student-friendly city. Cardiff University, UW Institute Cardiff, and the Welsh College of Music and Drama combine to make a student population of over 26,000. Most clubs/pubs/theatres host student nights/special rates for NUS card holders. The city also has plenty of parks and open spaces, so there is always somewhere to relax and sunbathe, especially in the summer. As the capital of Wales, Cardiff has all the attractions that you would expect of a large city, while being small enough to make you feel at home. The local countryside is very beautiful, and all outdoor activities are available. The development of Cardiff Bay and the Welsh Assembly has given added excitement to the atmosphere in the city.

University life

Medical students are members of their own Students' Club, which provides sporting facilities/teams, its own fleet of minibuses, and its own bar, where drinks are often the cheapest in Cardiff! The Students' Club organises one staff/student dinner a year, six balls, and many other social events, ranging from top-name bands, comedians, long-distance pub crawls, and tours around the UK – all attended by a mix of medics, dentists, nurses, radiographers, and physiotherapy students. A wide range of clubs and societies are available, including climbing, orchestra, canoeing, and martial arts. There are also religious groups such as the Islamic Society and the Christian Medical Fellowship. Each year the students organise a charity revue called 'Anaphylaxis' and *Medrag* to raise money for local charities. In 1992 the Students' Union started its own charity, BACCUP. Each year a limited number of health care students from Cardiff University have the opportunity to travel out to Belarus to work in an orphanage for children with special needs. Students also have access to all of the facilities offered by Cardiff University and its Students' Union.

Student life can be very hectic, juggling work commitments with the variety of sports and clubs offered by the Students' Club. The majority of teams, clubs, and societies are fully funded by the Club, including the provision of minibuses for the use of its members. 'Medclub' provides a friendly/social/cheap venue for the post-match celebrations and a very cheap source of alcohol for those not partaking in the sporting scene! It is also the venue for some of the craziest scenes you're likely to find during freshers' week. There is also the impressive Cardiff Students' Union, with its two bars, 1800 capacity nightclub, live music venue, and snooker/pool hall. As a capital city, Cardiff also offers excellent sport, leisure, and recreational facilities. The Millennium Stadium hosts the FA Cup and the Worthington Cup Finals, the Six Nations rugby, as well as a number of live music gigs. Cardiff also has a great range of shops, pubs, clubs, and a redeveloped seafront at Cardiff Bay. Living in Cardiff also allows easy access to beautiful and varied scenery, including the Brecon Beacons National Park.

Sports life

The Club has a large number of teams, some of which gain great success far beyond that expected of a small university. Our rugby team has won the Med Schools Cup nine times in its 10-year history and also won the BUSA shield in 2004! Most teams compete in the various BUSA interuniversity competitions, intermedical school competitions, and some local leagues. The Students' Club also has pool, tables. Besides the facilities on offer by the dedicated Students' Union of WCM, students have the benefit of using the sports and Union facilities of Cardiff University.

Top tip: If you enjoy playing sport get involved with the medic sports teams; they cater for all levels and it's a great way to meet people from other disciplines and years. Friends in higher years are very helpful when it comes to exams and coursework!

Great things about Cardiff

- Students are members of the Students' Unions at Cardiff University, allowing access to both Med Club and the bars and nightclub at Cardiff University. This also allows medical students to socialise with nonmedics as well as medics.

- A lot of interactions (socially and academically!) between students of all years, and with dental, nursing, physiotherapists, etc.
- All the advantages of living in an expanding and vibrant capital city without the usual costs.
- Using all Welsh hospitals keeps firm sizes low and student/patient ratios high.
- An excellent course with a great balance between problem-based learning, lectures, and clinical experience.

Bad things about Cardiff

- The large year group size means it can be difficult to get to know all fellow students individually.
- The wait for coursework to be returned is often long.
- Distances between hospitals and the accessibility of some rural hospitals make travelling very awkward/time consuming, unless you have a car.
- Clinical placements in years 4 and 5 can make it hard to see your nonmedic friends (and medic friends not with you on placement) regularly.
- The weather!

Further information

Undergraduate Admissions Officer
University of Wales College of Medicine
Heath Park
Cardiff CF4 4XN
Tel: 029 2074 2027
Fax. 029 2074 3690
Email: uwcmadmissions@cf.ac.uk, medical-school@cardiff.ac.uk
Web: http://www.uwcm.ac.uk

Additional application information

Average A-level requirements	• AAB
Average Scottish Higher requirements	• AAAAB to include chemistry
Make-up of interview panel	• Undergraduate: three to include one clinician and one current 4/5 year student • Graduate: one academic and one clinician
Months in which interviews are held	• November–March (undergraduate) February (graduate)
Proportion of overseas students	• 7%
Proportion of mature students	• Not known
Proportion of graduate students	• 7%
Faculty's view of students taking a gap year	• Acceptable if student is spending time in a positive way
Proportion of students taking intercalated degrees	• 15%
Possibility of direct entrance to clinical phase	• No
Fees for overseas students	• See website for details
Fees for graduates	• See website for details
Ability to transfer to other medical schools	• Applications to transfer will each be considered in their own right. Financial and family health reasons are usually accepted. However, transfers require a mutual acceptance from the receiving medical school
Assistance for elective funding	• Several bursaries available to compete for
Assistance for travel to attachments	• Free transport provided to placements in year 3, clinical placement costs reimbursed in years 4 and 5. A car-sharing scheme is in the pipeline!
Access and hardship funds	• Financial contingency funds available to those in serious financial difficulty
Weekly rent	• £50–£60
Pint of lager	• £1.50
Cinema	• £5
Nightclub	• £5

Wales College
of Medicine

Warwick

Key Facts	Graduate
Course length	4 years
Total number of medical undergraduates	650
Applicants in 2005	900
Interviews given in 2005	300
Places available in 2005	164
Places available in 2006	164
Open days 2006	Please see website for details
Entrance requirements	Biological science related degree
Mandatory subjects	N/A
Male:female ratio	1:2
Is an exam included in the selection process? If yes, what form does this exam take?	MSAT and selection centre
Qualification gained	MBChB

Fascinating fact: Warwick University has recently been selected to be the leading institution to go into partnership with the new NHS university.

The Universities of Leicester and Warwick joined up in 2000 to offer an accelerated 4-year medical degree course to graduates in biomedical sciences. The course started with 67 students who began studying in 2000 and have just graduated. Now in its fifth year, any early problems have been ironed out, resulting in a well-run and organised curriculum delivered by enthusiastic teachers.

As a relatively new medical school there has been much investment in student facilities with brand-new buildings and learning resources. A new university hospital is currently being built in Coventry, which is due to be completed in 2006. Warwick Medical School was formally established as a faculty at the University of Warwick in January 2003 and provides a friendly environment with rapidly growing courses for many health care professionals. This gives the medical school a great feeling of innovation and an atmosphere of cutting edge health care research.

Education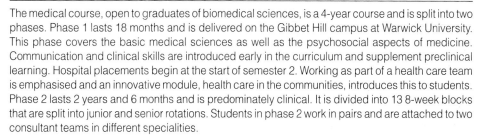

The medical course, open to graduates of biomedical sciences, is a 4-year course and is split into two phases. Phase 1 lasts 18 months and is delivered on the Gibbet Hill campus at Warwick University. This phase covers the basic medical sciences as well as the psychosocial aspects of medicine. Communication and clinical skills are introduced early in the curriculum and supplement preclinical learning. Hospital placements begin at the start of semester 2. Working as part of a health care team is emphasised and an innovative module, health care in the communities, introduces this to students. Phase 2 lasts 2 years and 6 months and is predominately clinical. It is divided into 13 8-week blocks that are split into junior and senior rotations. Students in phase 2 work in pairs and are attached to two consultant teams in different specialities.

Teaching

Phase 1 of the course is run over three semesters. Most learning in this phase occurs through a balance of lectures and group work. Students are placed in groups of 8 for group work and stay in this group until the end of phase 1. Each module session lasts for approximately 3 hours and involves a mixture of lectures and group work. The lectures offer an overview of the topic, which is then developed further in group work by working through cases or discussion of issues. Anatomy is integrated in each of the modules and is supplemented with dissection sessions at Leicester. Clinical skills are taught at the beginning of the course in semester 1 and then further developed by weekly placements in hospitals in semesters 2 and 3. DISC (developing interviewing skills in consultation) is a strand of the course that helps to develop communication skills and is first taught using highly convincing actors. Following this you spend four sessions in GP practice.

Phase 2 is clinical and mainly taught in hospital, with community teaching where appropriate. Weekly academic half-days supplement ward learning.

Assessment

Assessment in phase 1 of the course is varied with a mixture of short answer questions(SAQs), multiple choice questions (MCQs), essays and case studies. The musculoskeletal module also includes a viva voce exam. Students are graded as excellent, satisfactory, borderline satisfactory or unsatisfactory. Clinical skills are assessed at the end of semester 1 with a 12-station objective structured clinical practical exam (OSCPE) testing a variety of skills gained during the year. The Introductory Clinical Course is assessed in November of semester 3 by attendance, patient portfolios and a clinical exam. Also in phase 1 is the integrated medical sciences assessment (IMSA). This is a MCQ exam that covers all modules taught up to the point of the exam and tests integration of knowledge. At the end of phase 1 there is an over-arching IMSA, a 3-hour paper that tests learning objectives from all modules taken in phase 1. A 7500 word dissertation to be written on a clinical topic of your choice is also a component of phase 1.

Phase 2 assessment contains a mixture of clinical and written assessments. The main clinical assessments are the Intermediate Clinical Assessment (ICE) in year 3 and the clinical finals in year 4. Eight-week rotations require students to produce written portfolios for each block with a total of 36 portfolios to be completed.

Intercalated degrees

All students are graduates and intercalated degrees are not offered.

Special study modules and electives

One SSM is taken in phase 1. Topics include advanced anatomical studies, prehospital trauma medicine, sleep medicine, current research topics in medicine, a variety of languages as well as other skills such as counselling and sign language. The elective is taken in year 3 of the course. Students can choose to go anywhere and are required to fill in a report about their experience.

Facilities

Library Warwick has a huge library on the central campus with a well-stocked medical section. Many resources are available electronically and at the Leicester site where books can be ordered and delivered to you. However lecture notes and module handbooks contain the majority of information required for self learning.

Computers Computer facilities are excellent within the medical school with 24-hour access. There are also many clusters located around the Warwick campus.

Clinical skills The medical school is equipped with 3 clinical skills rooms that contain all the required resources needed for practising and developing clinical skills. Seminar rooms also contain a range of equipment from full body skeletons to blood pressure instruments. There is also a resource room containing many anatomical models, books and DVDs/videos that aid learning. All of the main teaching hospitals have well-resourced clinical skills centres that are staffed by friendly teachers, which all students can use.

Welfare

Student support

Students can access the main university counselling and welfare services, as well as those available through the Students' Union. A personal tutor scheme operates in the school and interyear relations are good, so there is always someone you can ask advice from about the course. First-year students are allocated a student mentor in the above year to provide informal support and information about life at the medical school.

Accommodation

Accommodation in university halls is not guaranteed but can be available. Most prospective first-year students are accommodated in nearby university housing in the Earlsdon, Canley, and Tile Hill parts of Coventry. In the second year most students choose to live in private accommodation in

Leamington Spa, Kenilworth or one of the areas of Coventry adjacent to the university. All student accommodation is a bus or car ride away from the main university campus.

Placements

The medical school building is located on Gibbet Hill, a quiet part of the campus, a short walk away from the main centre. Most phase 1 teaching occurs here and in local hospitals. The main teaching hospitals are George Elliot (Nuneaton), Walsgrave, Warwick Hospital, and the Coventry and Warwick Hospital. Phase 2 teaching is at the main teaching hospitals and hospitals in Rugby and Redditch. Accommodation is provided at both Rugby and Redditch hospitals. GP placements are located all over the Midlands. It is worth noting that public transport to clinical placements is limited and a car is an advantage.

Location of clinical placement/ name of hospital	Distance away from medical school (miles)	Difficulty getting there on public transport*
Walsgrave	5	🚶
Coventry and Warwick	3	🚶
George Elliot (Nuneaton)	20	🚌
Warwick	8	🚌
Alexandra (Redditch)	30	🚗 🚌

* 🚶: walking/cycling distance; 🚌: use public transport; 🚗: need own car or lift; 💡: get up early – tricky to get to!

Sports and social

City life

Warwick might have been named Coventry University when it was founded. It may be in Warwickshire, but it is really a part of Coventry. Coventry suffered terribly in the Blitz and much of the centre was unimaginatively rebuilt. One notable exception is the new cathedral, which was built within the remains of the old one. It does, however, have almost everything you might expect of a medium-sized city: theatre, museums, good shopping, restaurants, and travel links. It was the centre of the British car industry and, retains Land Rover and Peugeot plants. A short journey in any direction can get you into pretty countryside, and places to visit in Warwickshire include Kenilworth Castle, Warwick and Warwick Castle, and Stratford-upon-Avon.

Warwick

University life

In spite of its relative youth, Warwick has a busy MedSoc, which runs regular events for medics. Freshers' week 2004 was a huge success and included 'mums and dads', doctors and nurses, medics' revue, freshers' ball and many other events. There are many medical student-run societies with one of the most successful being MedSIN. Students at Warwick can take advantage of a wide range of facilities on campus. A large Students' Union provides a wide range of entertainment: bands, balls, and student theatre are all regular events. A large and busy arts centre hosts many touring theatre and dance companies, as well as music of all types. There are loads of student societies with every possible activity imaginable. Banks, shops, and a post office are all part of the campus.

Sports life

There are many sports facilities at Warwick, including an athletics track, swimming pool, playing fields, and sports centre. All the main sports are catered for, as well as many less popular ones with facilities open to all. Medical students have their own teams in football, rugby and netball. There is also a popular squash ladder.

> **Top tip:** Warwick University and the Students' Union have loads of opportunities to become involved with a wide range of activities, from hundreds of student societies and sports clubs to life-skills courses and community volunteering, so take the time to have a look at all that is on offer to make the most out of your time here.

Great things about Warwick

- A well-run and organised course with excellent new facilities and resources available 24 hours. All lectures and course material are placed on the web giving students easy access.
- A brand new state-of-the-art teaching hospital is currently being built, with a fantastic new clinical sciences building. Upgraded clinical skills facilities at all the hospitals used for teaching also means students are never short of things to do whilst on placements.
- Significant clinical content from early on in the course and clinical application of what is learnt is constantly emphasised. In clinical years, a pair of students is allocated to a pair of consultants keeping staff–student ratios low. This allows students to fully integrate into each attachment and feel as though they are part of the firm.
- Friendly staff, who are always willing to help, in all parts of the medical school. You can even get post delivered to the medical school and the security guard will sign for it!
- Warwick campus has a great range of student facilities with a nationally renowned arts centre that attracts top names. The surrounding Warwickshire countryside is beautiful and is easily accessible to escape to when revision is looming. Birmingham is only a 20-minute car or train journey away and is great for a night out and shopping.

Bad things about Warwick

- Access to clinical placements is difficult without a car or friends with a car.

- The course is intense and the workload is high, meaning students have to be well organised to enjoy a full social life. However there is a large sense of satisfaction in passing each stage of the course and that everyone else is in the same boat!
- At the end of a long day it is often a tiring journey home if you live off campus.
- Car parking during the day on campus is expensive, and you sometimes feel as if Warwick University exists purely to make money.
- The main centre for shopping is Coventry, which, whilst having all that you need, it is not the most attractive of city centres. However, die-hard shopaholics have easy access to the new Bullring in Birmingham which is only a 20-minute train journey away.

Further information

Student Recruitment and Admissions Office
University House
University of Warwick
Coventry CV4 8UW
Tel: 02476 528 101 (medical admissions)
Fax: 02476 573079
Email: med-admis@warwick.ac.uk
Web: http://www.lwms.ac.uk

Warwick

Additional application information

Average A-level requirements	• N/A
Average Scottish Higher requirements	• N/A
Make-up of interview panel	• N/A
Months in which interviews are held	• February–March
Proportion of overseas students	• 7.5%
Proportion of mature students	• 100%
Proportion of graduate students	• 100%
Faculty's view of students taking a gap year	• N/A
Proportion of students taking intercalated degrees	• 0%
Possibility of direct entrance to clinical phase	• Yes – limited circumstances
Fees for overseas students	• £1000 (year 1) £20,000 (years 2, 3 and 4)
Fees for graduates	• Likely to be £3000
Ability to transfer to other medical schools	• Yes; requests are dealt with on an individual basis. Reasons can be financial, personal or health related
Assistance for elective funding	• There is at present no financial assistance for electives by way of scholarships or bursaries but students may take a loan from the school, which has to be paid back at graduation
Assistance for travel to attachments	• Travel to clinical attachments is covered by NHS bursary in years 2, 3 and 4 for English and Welsh students. Scottish students do not receive an NHS bursary but can claim from start of course for travel to clinical placements
Access and hardship funds	• There is access to the Access to Learning Fund (ALF) as hardship funds no longer exist at any HE institution. Students are required to see the University Student Financial Adviser to state their case before a decision is made
Weekly rent	• £45–£55 (halls) • £55 (private)
Pint of lager	• £1.20 Union bar • £1.70 city pub
Cinema	• £2.80 with NUS card
Nightclub	• Free–£10

Appendices

Mikey & Michelle's quick compare table

Mikey & Michelle's quick compare table

University	No. of applicants (2005)	No. of places (2005)	% interviewed (2005)	Entrance req. /(UCAS points)	Mandatory subjects	M:F	% Intercalated year	% Mature	% Overseas	Graduate course
Aberdeen	1900	175	66	AAB	Two science or maths	1:1.3	15	18	10	No
Barts	2500	277	36	AAB	Chemistry and biology	40:60	6	30	8	Yes
Belfast	650	262	8	AAA + A at AS-level	Chemistry, biology to at least AS-level	45:65	7	No info	5	No
Birmingham	2700	370	33	AAB	Chemistry and either biology, physics or maths	30:70	25	10	8	Yes
Brighton & Sussex	2330	136	No info	AAB (340)	Chemistry + biology	40:60	0	25	7.5	No
Bristol	1753	216	29	AAB	Chemistry and one other science	1:2	30	10	5	Yes
Cambridge	1408	273	No info	AAA	Chemistry and two further maths/ sciences	45:55	100	1	9	Yes
Derby	1156	91	21	2:2 degree	N/A	65:35	0%	100	N/A	Yes
Dundee	1813	154	26	AAA	Chemistry	42:58	12	2.5	7.5	No
East Anglia	1500	130	33	AABB	Biology	No info	N/A	No info	7	No
Edinburgh	2724	218	2	AAAB	Chemistry and either biology, physics or maths. Biology at least AS-level	47:71	40	7	6	No
Glasgow	1944	241	66	AAB	Chemistry and one other science/ maths	35:65	24	13	7	No
GKT	3500	363	32	AAB + C	Chemistry or biology	35:65	No info	No info	No info	Yes
Hull & York	2023	130	35	AABB (excluding general studies)	Chemistry and biology	47:53	5	39	7.5	No
Imperial	3000	326	30	AAB	Chemistry and biology	44:56	100	7	6	No
Leeds	2626	238	27	AAB	Chemistry	43:57	10	5	16	No
Leicester	2000	175	70	AAB	Chemistry	50:50	10	No info	5	Yes

(Continued)

Mikey & Michelle's quick compare table (continued)

University	No. of applicants (2005)	No. of places (2005)	% interviewed (2005)	Entrance req. /(UCAS points)	Mandatory subjects	M:F	% Intercalated year	% Mature	% Overseas	Graduate course
Liverpool	1988	283	52	AABB	Chemistry and biology	40:60	10	4	8	Yes
Manchester/Keele/Preston	2701	336	38	AAB	Chemistry and one other science	1:1.25	10	11	7	No
Newcastle/Durham	3000	326	17	AAB (AAA in 2007)	Chemistry or biology	38:62	No info	No info	8	Yes
Nottingham	2104	246	22	AAB	Chemistry and biology	36:64	0	2	10	No
Oxford	1076	150	40	AAA	Chemistry and one other science/maths	45:55	100	No info	3	Yes
Peninsula	1917	167	36	AAA + one AS-level (370–400)	One science	38:62	10	19	7.5	No
Royal Free & UCL	2141	330	40	AAB + one AS-level	Chemistry and biology	45:55	100	15	7.5	No
St Andrews	991	124	27	AAB	Chemistry and either biology, physics or maths	45:55	10	4	8.5	No
St George's	1746	187	43	(380)	Chemistry and biology	40:60	40	30	7.5	Yes
Sheffield	3938	241	16	AAB	Chemistry and another Science	1:1.5	3	17	5	No
Southampton	3029	206	no info	ABB	Chemistry	37:63	18	5	9.5	Yes
Wales	2600	305	30	ABB + one AS-level	Chemistry and biology	40:60	15	No info	7	Yes
Warwick	900	164	33	Biological sciences degree	N/A	1:2	0	100	7.5	Yes

Glossary

Medicine is full of jargon and abbreviations. Estimates suggest that students' vocabularies double over the course of a 5-year medical degree. Unfortunately, it is such a part of life for medical students and doctors that they sometimes forget to speak in plain language to the general public. The following is a very brief list of words pertaining to medical education that you are likely to come across in this guide, and perhaps in medical school prospectuses. Our apologies for any jargon we have used in the guide not listed here!

Anatomy: The study of the structure of the body. While this used to be taught by dissection, prosections (predissected specimens) are more commonly used nowadays.

Attachment: The term given to clinical placements. The student is placed under the supervision and guidance of a hospital consultant and his/her team (firm) or a GP for a period in the course.

Biochemistry: The study of the structure and functioning of the body at the molecular level.

British Medical Association (BMA): The doctors' professional association and trade union, providing representation and services for doctors and medical students.

BSc (Honours): *see* Intercalated degrees.

Clerking: Taking a history from and examining a patient on admission. A very useful learning experience if you are the first person to see the patient.

Computer-assisted learning (CAL): Computer programs are sometimes used to teach a topic more interactively than a lecture/tutorial, and let the student set his/her own learning pace. They may also give the opportunity for self-assessment on a topic.

Consultant: The senior specialist doctor, usually based in a hospital.

Core curriculum: Under GMC directives the medical course is split into a core curriculum (in which all students must cover the same key topics to a high standard) and Special Study Modules (in which the student can go in his/her own direction and study an area of interest in more depth), which may not be covered by all students.

District general hospital (DGH): A regional hospital which treats a broad spectrum of patients but refers more specialist cases to a teaching hospital. Medical students are taught by NHS staff, not university-employed consultants and registrars.

Elective: A period (usually 6–12 weeks in the latter years of the course) when students can choose an area of interest to study independently outside their medical school, either in the UK or, more often, abroad.

Endocrinology: The study of the hormonal function of the body.

Epidemiology: The study of the pattern and causes of diseases in society.

Foundation programme: New 2-year training and education programme taken up immediately after graduation from medical school, to be introduced in August 2005 for all UK graduates.

Firm: *see* Attachment.

Formative assessments/exams: Exams or assessments that will not officially contribute to your year mark. They are, however, compulsory and are an excellent indicator of your progress.

General Medical Council (GMC): All medical degree courses must be approved by the GMC. It is the medical profession's self-regulatory body, which ensures professional standards are maintained and patients are protected. Doctors must be registered with the GMC to practise in the UK.

Honours year: *see* Intercalated degrees.

Integrated courses: Integration is the merging of several disciplines into one (hopefully more meaningful) course. Integration may be partial, within a single year or phase (for example combining anatomy, physiology and biochemistry to teach body systems – respiratory, cardiovascular, reproduction, etc.), or it may be full, across all years, starting clinical teaching with basic medical sciences from the outset.

Intercalated degrees: Most schools offer students the opportunity to take an extra year (or two) in the middle of the course to study a subject of interest, leading to a BSc (Hons) or equivalent at the end. Some schools only offer this to high achievers, while others have an intercalated BSc (Hons) built into the course for everyone.

MBBS: The degree awarded to Medical School graduates. (This varies slightly between schools, for example MBChB, MBBChir, but all are equivalent.)

Medical Students Committee (BMA): UK committee of elected representatives that looks after the interests of all UK medical students.

Medical microbiology: The study of micro-organisms and the diseases they cause.

MedLine: A widely used and comprehensive computer database of articles published in medical journals.

Objective structured clinical examination (OSCE): A relatively new form of assessment where the students are set several tasks: taking histories; examining patients; or performing tests/procedures to complete in front of the examiner within a set time. The student is marked according to a standardised marking scheme. Every student is thus assessed identically, ensuring fairness and comparability of results between individuals.

Pathology: The study of disease processes and their effect on the structure and function of the body.

Peripheral attachments: Placements in hospitals/general practices outside the university area and normally outside the university town.

Pharmacology: The study of the action of drugs and their application.

Physiology: The study of the functioning of body systems and tissues.

Postgraduate Medical Education and Training Board: government board responsible for continuing education once you have received full registration with the GMC. Oversees all the exams and diplomas offered through the Royal Colleges.

Premedical year: Students without the necessary science entrance qualifications can apply to do a premedical year, which takes them to a sufficient level of scientific knowledge to join the medical course the following academic year (not offered at all schools).

Preregistration house officer (PRHO): A newly qualified doctor working in the first year after graduation. House officers, while able to call themselves doctors and prescribe drugs, are provisionally registered by the GMC until they have completed this year satisfactorily. After this they achieve full registration.

Problem-based learning (PBL): Students learn from researching and solving a relevant (usually clinical) scenario, rather than being given all the information passively. Small group problem-solving tutorials, facilitated by members of staff, take the place of lectures.

Prosections: Predissected cadaver specimens of the human body used to teach anatomy. These have replaced actual dissection by students themselves in many schools.

Provisional registration: Conditional registration with the GMC after graduation from medical school. Full registration is granted at the end of the first year of working once competencies have been achieved.

Registrar: A doctor who is undergoing specialist training (usually for between 3 and 9 years) before becoming a consultant or general practitioner. This is the next step up the ladder after SHO.

Self-directed learning: Learning under the student's own initiative from lists of objectives rather than didactic teaching (such as lectures).

Senior house officer (SHO): A junior hospital doctor who has completed his/her year as house officer.

Special study modules (SSMs): Periods of the course when students study areas of interest outside the core curriculum (see above). These may be taught, or may be independent research projects.

Tuition fee: Student contribution to the cost of undertaking a university degree which is payable for each year of study.

Top-up tuition fees: Differential fee charged by the university for courses within their institution, payable from 2006 entry. The amount of fee levied may depend on the type of degree studied.

Teaching hospitals: Normally the main hospital(s) in the university town or city. Services provided are part of the NHS, but the senior clinical staff will often be employed by the university and hold medical academic posts. Teaching hospitals usually handle specialist cases, which can be referred to them from DGHs across the region. Many such hospitals will have regional centres for particular specialties or centres of excellence, such as cardiology, plastic surgery, neonatal intensive care, etc.

Viva: An oral examination (sometimes referred to as a viva voce).

Abbreviations

BMA:	British Medical Association
BMAT:	Biomedical Admissions Test
CAL:	Computer-assisted learning
CSYS:	Certificate of sixth-year study (Scottish students)
DGH:	District general hospital
GAMSAT:	Graduate Australian Medical Schools Admissions Test
GMC:	General Medical Council
MCQs:	Multiple choice questionnaires
MSC	BMA's UK Medical Students' Committee
OSCE:	Objective structured clinical examination
PBL:	Problem-based learning
PRHO:	Preregistration house officer
SHO:	Senior house officer
SSM:	Special study module
UCAS:	Universities and Colleges Admissions Service

Further information

British Medical Association

The British Medical Association (BMA) is both the doctors' professional organisation and their trade union, protecting the professional and personal interests of its members. It is the voice of the medical profession in the UK and represents the profession internationally. Members and staff are in constant touch with ministers, government departments, Members of Parliament, and other influential bodies, conveying to them the profession's views on health care and health policy. Most medical students and practising doctors are members.

The BMA's head office is in London, and there are national offices in Scotland, Northern Ireland, and Wales. There are an additional 15 regional offices throughout the UK. The BMA is a medical publisher in its own right, but also includes the BMJ Publishing Group. The BMJ Publishing Group is a major medical and scientific publisher and publishes the weekly *British Medical Journal* and the monthly *Student BMJ*.

Student BMJ The *Student BMJ* is an international journal specifically for medical students. It is published monthly and includes articles on education, medical careers, student life, science, and news. Many of the articles and papers are written by medical students. Individuals or schools and libraries can subscribe to the journal.

For more information or a sample copy contact:

Student BMJ
BMJ Publishing Group   Tel: 020 7383 6402
BMA House   Fax: 020 7383 6270
Tavistock Square   Email: bmjsubs@dial.pipex.com
London WC1H 9JR   Web: http://www.studentbmj.com

BMA Medical Students Committee (MSC)

The Medical Students Committee (MSC) represents students within the Association and also to important outside bodies, such as the Departments of Education and Health and the General Medical Council. Through the committee the BMA campaigns on many issues, such as student finances and debt, reforms of the medical degree syllabus, and health and safety. Following devolution the BMA has established MSCs in Northern Ireland, Scotland, and Wales. There are student representatives and BMA committees in every medical school, and the BMA runs many local events and talks for students. The vast majority of medical students join the BMA.

Medical students who are members of the BMA receive a variety of benefits, including a free sub-scription to *Student BMJ*, free guidance notes, a free copy of *Clinical Evidence*, library and informa-tion services, and book discounts to name but a few. General information, guidance, and student chat board can be found on the BMA's Medical Students Committee website.

British Medical Association
BMA House
Tavistock Square
London WC1H 9JP

Tel: 020 7387 4499
Fax: 020 7383 6494
Email: students@bma.org.uk
Web: http://www.bma.org.uk/students

The remainder of this chapter is divided into sections relating to education, finance and welfare cor-responding to the different subcommittees within the MSC. Information in the other organisations section relates to other medical student organisations that have a member that sits on the MSC.

Education

Universities and Colleges Admissions Service (UCAS)

Universities and Colleges
Admissions Service
Rose Hill
New Barn Lane
Cheltenham
Gloucestershire GL52 3LZ

Tel: 01242 222 444
Web: http://www.ucas.com

- *UCAS Handbook and Application Pack*: essential reading and material for applicants to university courses.

Department for Education and Skills

England

Tel: 0870 000 2288
Web: http://www.dfes.gov.uk
Email: info@dfes.gsi.gov.uk

Castle View House, Runcorn
Castle View House
East Lane
Runcorn WA7 2GJ

Moorfoot, Sheffield
Moorfoot
Sheffield S1 4PQ

Caxton House, London
Caxton House
Tothill Street
London SW1H 9FN

Mowden Hall, Darlington
Mowden Hall
Staindrop Road
Darlington DL3 9BG

Sanctuary Buildings, London
Sanctuary Buildings
Great Smith Street
London SW1P 3BT

Scotland

There are many publications about higher education and funding for Scottish students available on the web or from:

The Stationery Office
Lothian Road
Edinburgh EH3 9AZ

Tel: 0131 228 4181 71
Fax: 0131 622 7017
Web: http://www.scotland.gov.uk

Scottish Executive Education Department
Victoria Quay
Edinburgh EH6 6QQ

Tel: 0131 556 8400
Fax: 0131 244 8240

Wales

Tel: 0800 731 9133
Web: http://www.dfes.gov.uk
Email: info@dfes.gsi.gov.uk

Northern Ireland

Department of Education
Northern Ireland
Rathgael House
43 Balloo Road
Bangor Co Down BT19 7PR

Tel: 028 9127 9279
Fax: 028 9127 9100

Finance

Financial information

Financial arrangements and support vary depending on which country you intend studying in. Some support is provided by Departments of Education and Skills, and some from Departments of Health.

The Educational Grants Advisory Service provides information about student support systems in the UK and can help identify additional sources of funding.

Family Welfare Association

501–505 Kingsland Road
London E8 4AU

Tel: 0207 254 6251 (opening hours: Mondays, Wednesdays, and Fridays 10 AM–12 PM, and 2 PM–4 PM)
Email: egas.enquiry@fwa.org.uk
Web: http://www.egas-online.org.uk

Relevant contact information for each nation is below.

England

For information and guides on student support ring the Department for Education and Skills (DFES).

Helpline: 0800 731 9133
Web: http://www.dfes.gov.uk

Financial Help for Health Care Students, a booklet by the Department of Health, explains NHS funding in more detail. Order one or download from the website:

Department of Health
PO Box 777
London SE1 6XH

Tel: 0845 60 60 655
Email: doh@prologistics.co.uk
Web: http://www.doh.gov.uk/hcsmain.htm

You can obtain bursary information from:

NHS Student Grants Unit
22 Plymouth Road
Blackpool FY3 7JS

Tel: 01253 655655
Fax: 01253 206 1499
Email: nhs-sgu@ukonline.co.uk

Scotland

Student Awards Agency for Scotland
3 Redheughs Rigg
South Gyle
Edinburgh EH12 9YT

Tel: 0131 476 8227
Web: http://www.student-support-saas.gov.uk/

Wales

Further and Higher Education Division of the National Assembly for Wales
Tel: 02920 825 831
Web: http://www.learning.wales.gov.uk
You can obtain bursary information from:

NHS Wales Student Awards Unit
2nd Floor Golate House
101 St Mary's Street
Cardiff CF10 1DX

Tel: 02920 261 495

Northern Ireland

Information for students from Northern Ireland can be obtained from the Department for Employment and Learning. Web: http://www.delni.gov.uk

Also try:

The Department of Health,
Social Services and Public Safety
Human Resources Directorate

Tel: 02890 524746
Web: http://www.dhsspsni.gov.uk

Charities

Copies of the following books should be available in the reference section of most public libraries:

- *The Charities Digest* – published by the Family Welfare Association
- *Money to Study* – published by UKOSA/NUS/EGAS
- *The Educational Grants Directory* – published by the Directory of Social Change
- *Directory of Grant-Making Trusts* – published by Charities Aid Foundation/Biblios.

The British Medical Association Charities Office (see BMA address) has information about awards and grants for mature and second degree medical students.

Welfare

National Union of Students (NUS)

For general information on issues relating to students:

National Union of Students
Nelson Mandela House
Holloway Road
London N7 6LJ

Tel: 020 7272 8900
Fax: 020 7263 5713
Email: nusuk@nus.org.uk
Web: http://www.nusonline.co.uk

Gay and Lesbian Association of Doctors and Dentists (GLADD)

GLADD was formed in 1995. It has an active student section and provides professional support, educational and social meetings, both locally and nationally. **GLADD** campaigns vigorously within the health service and in the country at large on issues of equality relating to the lesbian, gay, and bisexual community.

Email: gladd@dircon.co.uk
Web: http://www.gladd.dircon.co.uk

Skill

National Bureau for Students with Disabilities is a registered, national charity, which promotes opportunities for disabled people in further and higher education, training and employment. Skill operates a freephone information service that provides expert information on studying and training – from applying to university or college through to obtaining a Disabled Students Allowance and getting adjustments in exams. Skill also works with policy makers, tutors and disabled student advisers to ensure that disabled students are empowered to achieve their potential.

Information Service   Tel: 0800 328 5050 (voice) 0800 068 2422 (text)
Email: info@skill.org.uk
Web: http://www.skill.org.uk

Other organisations

Junior Association for the Study of Medical Education

JASME is the Junior Association for the Study of Medical Education. JASME grew out of and is still a subgroup of **ASME** (the Association for the Study of Medical Education). JASME is a group run by 'juniors' (medical students and doctors in training grades) primarily for juniors interested in medical education. Membership to JASME is not restricted to juniors only though – anyone who is interested in medical education can be a member.

JASME   Telephone: 0131 225 9111
c/o ASME   Fax: 0131 225 9444
12 Queen Street   Email: info@jasme.org.uk
Edinburgh EH2 1JE   Web: http://www.jasme.org.uk

Medical Students International Network (MedSIN)

Founded in 1997, MedSIN is an independent, student-run organisation that aims to facilitate medical students' involvement in humanitarian and educational activities at local, national, and international level. MedSIN groups in medical schools carry out sex education projects, international exchanges, bone marrow registration drives, seminars on topical issues, and much more. Through its membership of the International Federation of Medical Students' Associations (IFMSA), MedSIN also provides opportunities to go on projects all over the world, from Angola to Zimbabwe. The IFMSA was founded in 1951 and promotes international co-operation on professional training and the achievement of humanitarian ideals. To get in touch or find out more, visit the MedSIN website: http://www.medsin.org

Other useful information

Armed forces: cadet recruitment

Army
Royal Army Medical Corps
Recruiting Office
Regimental Headquarters
Army Medical Services

Slim Road
Camberley
Surrey GU14 4NP

Tel: 01276 412 730
Fax: 01276 412 731
Email: ramc.recruiting@army.mod.uk.net

RAF
Medical and Dental Liaison Officer
Directorate of Recruiting and
Selection (Royal Air Force)
PO Box 100
Cranwell
Sleaford
Lincolnshire NG34 8GZ

Tel: 01400 261201 ext 6811
Fax: 01400 262220
Email: mdlo@royalairforce.net

Royal Navy
Med Pers (N)2
Room 133
Victory Building
HM Naval Base
Portsmouth PO1 3LS

Tel: 02392 727818
Fax: 02392 727805

Further reading

The Essential Guide to Becoming a Doctor by Adrian Blundell, Richard Harrison and Benjamin Turnkey, published by BMJ Books, ISBN 0727917390.